PRAISE FOR
FINDING NEW LIFE AFTER THE DEATH OF MY SON

This heart-wrenching memoir begins just hours into a bereaved father's journey as he mourns the tragic death of his teenage son. Bodnarczuk shares the intimate details of his grief, inviting us into his moments of anguish, confusion, forgiveness, hope, and transformation. This deeply honest account illustrates that the more personally a story is told, the more universally it resonates. Mark provides wisdom and resources to help all of us navigate the complexities of our unique journey. His profound insights about faith and doubt, psychology and theology, mystery and paradox challenge all of us to be more curious and alert to ourselves, God, and the people around us. Be prepared to have your heart softened, your mind stretched, and your soul awakened.
—*Reverend Jane Filkin, director of Leadership Development & Spiritual Formation, the Campolo Center for Ministry of Eastern University*

'Life can only be understood backwards; but it must be lived forwards.' Bodnarczuk reflects Kierkegaard's wisdom, inviting the reader into his labyrinthine memoir. This book will break your heart wide open, and it reveals a much-needed battle against fentanyl poisoning. It is a love story, it is a tragedy, it is raw, brutal at times, and honest. Bodnarczuk reflects on decades of recorded dreams and opens his soul, reflecting on every parent's worst nightmare. Readers will feel the author's anger, despair, love, and hope—all at the same time—in this very human and exceedingly holy reflection. It is filled with "thin places" where heaven and earth are pinched closely together. It is at once another teenage tragedy and a clarion call for mindfulness and relationship. Be cautious, reader; this memoir will change your life.
—*Reverend Garrett Struessel, senior pastor, First Evangelical Lutheran Church, Longmont, Colorado*

As a parent who lost my son to fentanyl, Mark Bodnarczuk's new book, *Finding New Life After the Death of My Son*, is directly relevant to me on many levels. Anyone looking to explore the experience of rebuilding one's life after a devastating event—which is everyone, ultimately—will benefit from reading this book. *Finding New Life* is both deeply intellectual and readily accessible, as Mark presents his innermost reflections in the context

of the events surrounding Thomas's sudden and tragic death. The takeaway is simple and applies to us all: life is a series of obstacles, and some of them have the potential to destroy us. We must embrace life's challenges and help each other carry the crosses we are destined to bear.
—*Ed Ternan, president, Song for Charlie*

It has been said that there is no loss more painful than the loss of one's child. As a grieving father, Mark Bodnarczuk invites us to follow his psychologically profound journey down to the depths of despair and then back up to a new sense of life's return and transformation. Following his son, Thomas's, death from fentanyl poisoning, Mark has been challenged in every way—emotionally, relationally, and at his deepest core, psychologically and spiritually. We are privileged to experience a Dante-like journey down to the deepest levels of the psyche, through Mark's eyes. He beautifully blends the world of dream interpretation and Jungian individuation with his deep Christian faith, and we see the mystery of his son's life and death unfold on the path he walks. Mark's commitment to face his grief fearlessly, his commitment to his son, and his faith carry him on what at times seems like an impossible journey of doubt and sorrow. This is a book that challenges its reader, and if we take up the challenge, our reward is the message of an enduring truth, which we, like Mark, may carry into the world. Thank you for this gem, Mark Bodnarczuk.
—*Lara Newton, Jungian analyst; president, C. G. Jung Institute of Colorado; founding director of training, C. G. Jung Institute of Colorado; and author,* Brothers and Sisters: Discovering the Psychology of Companionship

Joan Didion once wrote, "Grief turns out to be a place none of us know until we reach it." With indelible sincerity and penetrating detail, *Finding New Life after the Death of My Son* explores the traumatic crevices and sacred peaks of this mountainous terrain of bereavement, giving readers an unvarnished glimpse into the excruciating experience of losing one's child. Exploring both the pedestrian events of everyday life and the beatific moments of enlightenment, Mark Bodnarczuk paints a vibrant portrait showing that hope, healing, and self-growth can be found even in a world marred by death, destruction, and the devastating carnage generated by the age of counterfeit pills and fentanyl poisoning. At the same time, this memoir also dares readers to rethink their own perspectives regarding not only the universal experience

of loss but also the radical power of forgiveness and the immense meaning of their dreams. Some books you page through, and others you read; this memoir is one you'll wrestle with in the best way possible.
—*Blake A. Jurgens, PhD, MDiv; chief editor, Great Lakes Editing Services*

Mark Bodnarczuk has written a deeply personal memoir that has universal importance. What we hear in the news of cartels pushing lethal doses of fentanyl hidden in counterfeit pills seems far away from our daily lives. Yet it came crushingly close to Mark and his wife, Elin, on May 2, 2021. Their eighteen-year-old son fell prey to such a counterfeit pill. The bright light, a sensitive and loving person, gone. What do we do when the unthinkable happens? This book does not deny the horror of such a death. With love, intelligence, and faith, it holds open true hope for NEW LIFE.
—*Reverend Gary Stratman, chaplin, The Manor at Elfindale*

There are hundreds of books written by bereaved parents who describe the unspeakable horror that strikes the heart of a parent when they discover their child has died. This book is different—it stands alone. After forty years of walking with God and documenting and studying his dreams, Mark Bodnarczuk, much like the biblical dreamer "Joseph," takes us into his private world as he shares his faith and his grief about the death of his son, Thomas. Bereaved parents around the world will find this volume helpful as they search for meaning and a path forward while mourning the death of their child.
—*Reverend Dennis Apple, connection and care pastor, Church of the Resurrection, and author,* Life after the Death of My Son

I took this book very personally. I knew Thomas and loved him. I shared holidays, dinners, and regular gatherings as a part of the Bodnarczuk family, talking with Thomas about school, church, and things that were important in his life. A sudden shock came over me when I heard about Thomas's death. I was one of the first people Mark talked to, just days after he found Thomas dead in his room. Now, as I read this memoir, I'm amazed at how Mark describes the journey of grief, pain, and suffering he's been on. It's a story of how one survives the unthinkable and finds new life and hope in the wake of a tragedy that would have destroyed others.
—*Marshall Yancey, Philip Yancey's brother*

FOREWORD BY PHILIP YANCEY

FINDING NEW LIFE AFTER THE DEATH OF MY SON

Grace and Forgiveness in the Age of Counterfeit Pills and Fentanyl Poisoning

MARK BODNARCZUK
with Elin I. Larson

BRECKENRIDGE PRESS

Copyright © 2024 by Mark Bodnarczuk
All rights reserved.

FIRST EDITION – October 2024

No part of this book may be reproduced or utilized in any form or by any means, electronic or mechanical, including photocopying and recording, or by any information storage and retrieval system, without permission in writing from the author.

Edited by Blake A. Jurgens

Book design by GKS Creative

Front and back cover photograph © Mark Bodnarczuk

This is a nonfiction memoir. The names, descriptions, and identifying characteristics of the individuals and places who are included in the narrative have been changed to protect their privacy. Any resemblance to real people or places is purely coincidental.

Unless otherwise noted, all quotations of Scripture derived from the New American Standard Bible® (NASB). Copyright © 1960, 1962, 1963, 1968, 1971, 1972, 1973, 1975, 1977, 1995, 2020 by the Lockman Foundation. Used by permission. www.Lockman.org

Hardcover ISBN: 978-1-963461-20-6
Paperback ISBN: 978-1-963461-21-3
eBook ISBN: 978-1-963461-22-0

Library of Congress Control Number: 2024905582
Subjects: LCSH: 1. Parental grief. 2. God (Christianity). 3. Jung, C. G. (Carl Gustav).

Published by
Breckenridge Press

BRECKENRIDGE
PRESS

This book is dedicated to
THOMAS LARSON BODNARCZUK
MAY 16, 2002–MAY 2, 2021

*In death, as in life, you continue
to have an enormous impact on us.*

Also by Mark Bodnarczuk

Diving In: Discovering Who You Are in the Second Half of Life

Island of Excellence: 3 Powerful Strategies for Building a Culture of Creativity

The Breckenridge Enneagram: A Guide to Personal and Professional Growth

Making Invisible Bureaucracy Visible: A Guide to Assessing and Changing Organizational Culture

CONTENTS

Foreword xiii

Preface xvii

PART ONE: SURVIVING THOMAS'S DEATH

Chapter 1	My Son Thomas 3
Chapter 2	First Mother's Day without Thomas 7
Chapter 3	Thomas's Nineteenth Birthday without Him 11
Chapter 4	First Father's Day in Carmel without Thomas 15
Chapter 5	The Funerals 21
Chapter 6	What Should We Do for Christmas without Thomas? 31
Chapter 7	First Christmas 35
Chapter 8	First New Year: I'm Marked for Life 41
Chapter 9	The Arraignment and Forgiveness 49
Chapter 10	The Plea and Forgiveness 59
Chapter 11	The Journey Home to Colorado without Thomas, but He Keeps Showing Up 71
Chapter 12	Reflections on the First Year 75
Chapter 13	I Survived the Death of My Son 87

PART TWO: FINDING NEW LIFE

Chapter 14	Thomas's Tree House and the Emergence of a New Normal	95
Chapter 15	It Will Be a Milestone When We Can Say "We're Here in Aspen. It's Beautiful."	107
Chapter 16	Why Don't You Just Get Over It?	117
Chapter 17	Navigating a Perfect Storm	123
Chapter 18	Three Strikes and You're Out	135
Chapter 19	The Reality of Thomas's Death Permeates to Deeper Levels	145
Chapter 20	The Preliminary Hearing	153
Chapter 21	I'm Okay (Just Okay) Living Life without Thomas	165
Chapter 22	Almost There	173
Chapter 23	A Judge, a Defendant, and a Tiny Bit of Justice for Thomas	179
Chapter 24	The Sentencing	181
Chapter 25	More on Forgiveness and Grace	195
Chapter 26	A Tale of Two Little Boys	207
Chapter 27	I Found New Life after the Death of My Son	223
Chapter 28	But the Pain Doesn't Go Away	235

PART THREE: THE JOURNEY HOME

Chapter 29	Assuming Everything Would Work Out	249
Chapter 30	The Proxy War	263
Chapter 31	The Orange Hippie Van	273
Chapter 32	Digging Deeper	287
Chapter 33	Lingering Questions	305
Chapter 34	The Journey Home	323
Chapter 35	What Others Have Said about Thomas	329
	Friends	330
	Pastors, Youth Group Leaders, and Other Adults	334

Notes 343

About the Author 387

FOREWORD

IT'S THE WORST NIGHTMARE of every parent. Hearing no sounds from your child's bedroom, you presume your son or daughter must be oversleeping. You knock on the door, get no response, knock louder, and then open the door to find your child unresponsive, their body cold. The awful truth hits you like a heart attack: your child is dead.

Precisely that happened to Mark Bodnarczuk and his wife, Elin. Their son, Thomas had bought a single dose of an antianxiety pill from an acquaintance on Snapchat, unaware it was laced with three times the lethal dose of fentanyl. He ordered a meal from DoorDash, but he did not live long enough to eat it. Thomas fell victim to a tragic and underreported epidemic in the US of being deceived and poisoned by counterfeit pills. Annually, more Americans die as a result of drug overdoses than die from auto accidents and gun deaths combined. The majority of these overdoses involve synthetic opioids such as fentanyl.

The Bodnarczuks have joined the campaign to raise awareness of this health crisis, primarily through the cautionary tale of their son, an Eagle Scout and recent high school graduate. I have known Mark for four decades, both in Illinois and in Colorado. I held Thomas as a baby, and over the years listened to many stories from two proud parents who lovingly crowed about the accomplishments of their sole child. "The pain of waiting for a lifetime for my son—the very first person that I ever loved, and who loved me—only to lose him at such a young age is a pain that I can hardly bear," Mark says. To this day, Mark signs letters with this identifier: Mark Bodnarczuk, Thomas's dad.

This book tells a family love story, a tribute from parents who lost their son before he had a chance to go to college, find a career, get married, or have children of his own. The parents took seriously their job as stewards of Thomas's life, and they present him as a whole person, someone whose memory they will not let fade away. Through a website dedicated to Thomas, and through this book, they hope to honor their son while helping others cope with tragedy and grief.

After Thomas's death in 2021, I sent Mark this quote from Dietrich Bonhoeffer, who wrote about grief in a letter from a Nazi prison:

> There is nothing that can replace the absence of someone dear to us, and one should not even attempt to do so. One must simply hold out and endure it. At first that sounds very hard, but at the same time it is also a great comfort. For to the extent the emptiness truly remains unfilled one remains connected to the other person through it. It is wrong to say that God fills the emptiness. God in no way fills it but much more leaves it precisely unfilled and thus helps us preserve—even in pain—the authentic relationship.

Mark could have titled this book *An Anatomy of Grief*, for it sets out the agony of grief in all its stages. The anesthetic shock of discovering the body. Carrying on family traditions of Christmas, Easter, and birthdays without Thomas. Packing his belongings and moving to another state. Sudden bursts of tears at the oddest times. A search for counselors and a support group. The trauma of reading the autopsy report. Guilt over having a good time at a nephew's wedding. Rabbi Earl Grollman puts it this way: "Grief is not a disorder, a disease or a sign of weakness. It is an emotional, physical, and spiritual necessity, the price you pay for love. The only cure for grief is to grieve."

Besides grief, the book interweaves such subthemes as Jungian psychology and the meaning of dreams. Mark describes his life as a journey of faith along an Inner and Outer Labyrinth that has been shaped and defined by two books. The first book is the Bible, which reveals the nature and character of God and the nature and character of human beings. The second book contains more than twenty-five hundred dreams he has recorded and analyzed over a forty-year period. From the trauma of finding Thomas's lifeless body through the writing of this book, Mark's faith sustained him.

Mark's account also gives a front-row view of the American "justice" system, which often seems tilted in favor of the perpetrator. Seven times, Mark rearranged his schedule to appear in court, only to have bureaucratic

FINDING NEW LIFE AFTER THE DEATH OF MY SON

roadblocks delay any sentencing. In one of the most moving passages, he confronts the man who sold Thomas the counterfeit pill that killed him. Thus ensues a drama of forgiveness that is put to the test over the months of delays.

It took three years and a move to another state for Mark to begin to accept the new reality of life without Thomas. That in itself he describes as a "hollow victory, seasoned with a deep, dull sense of pain and grief." He admits he's a much better person now because of Thomas's death, "but that's come at a price that I would never have agreed to pay if I'd been asked."

Bonhoeffer added this advice to his friend: "Furthermore, the more beautiful and full the remembrances, the more difficult the separation. But gratitude transforms the torment of memory into silent joy. One bears what was lovely in the past not as a thorn but as a precious gift deep within, a hidden treasure of which one can always be certain."

This remembrance of a young man who died two weeks short of his nineteenth birthday is a gift from two loving parents to all of us who will experience loss—in other words, to all of us.

Philip Yancey

Mark Bodnarczuk dressed in his Easter best with his favorite stuffed animal

PREFACE

TWELVE YEARS BEFORE I realized God was preparing me to survive the death of my son, I was sitting at a circular table with my wife, Elin, and our pastor, along with twelve other people in a church membership class. Each of us was taking a turn sharing our faith journey for a few minutes. Sounds easy, right? Well, it's not. For weeks, I had been boiling my forty-six-year journey down to the three-hundred-and-three words below:

> I attended services and Sunday school at the Hungarian Reformed Church and was confirmed using the Heidelberg Catechism when I was about twelve years old. During this time, I became deeply introspective about what I actually believed about God, and I experienced an inner sense of having a calling or destiny, but I didn't understand the what (or the how) of this experience. Following my confirmation, my family's attendance at the Hungarian Reformed Church became sporadic, and I began attending a youth group at our neighborhood Presbyterian church in Clifton, New Jersey. In junior high school, I went to a Thurlow Spurr and the Spurrlows concert and went forward to an altar of prayer after the concert. I once again experienced the cleansing power of God's grace and forgiveness, now at the age of fifteen. For more than forty years now, my journey of faith has been like an Inner and an Outer Labyrinth that have both happened together at the same time.[1] This path has been powerfully shaped and defined by two books. The first book is the Bible, which reveals the nature and character of God, the nature and character of human beings, and the scarlet thread of God's plan of salvation throughout history that culminated in the life, death, and resurrection of Jesus. The second book contains more than 1,400 dreams that I've recorded and analyzed

over a thirty-year period that reveal the unfolding patterns of my calling and destiny through what Carl Jung called the individuation process.[2] My testimony today is that Jesus is the Lord of my life and that God has been faithful to me and to His promises over all these years. I am committed to following Him and to experiencing all that He has for me as my life continues to unfold according to His design, purposes, and plan.

After the person next to me finished, it was my turn. I started to read the first few words but began to sob uncontrollably. I tried to restrain myself, taking a deep breath to calm down before starting again. I got a few words further this time only to have inconsolable grief, pain, and loss mixed with grace and forgiveness flow over me. Once again, I was silenced by the artesian flow from within. I lowered my head to the table. People gawked as I desperately attempted to regain my composure. I tried a third time, but halfway through the first sentence, I was bludgeoned to silence by the numinosity of God's presence. Finally yielding to this invisible power, I handed the sheet to Elin and signaled for her to read it for me as the others gazed in bewildered silence.

While sitting through the Sunday church service that followed the membership class, I shook my head as I typed on my phone, trying to capture the essence of what had just happened in an email to myself. As I struggled to put a face on this extraordinary experience and translate it into a cohesive linguistic representation, I kept asking myself, "What does it mean?"[3] I wrestled with each word as I tapped on my phone's keyboard. What I had experienced went beyond what I could describe through writing.

Trauma leads to deeper, inner trauma that is buried alive and needs to be unearthed, bandaged, and healed. Maybe, I thought in my pew, I was puking up the lingering pain and anguish from growing up in a clinically dysfunctional family, including a father who was mentally ill, heavily medicated, and physically and emotionally abusive for most of his life. I reflected on those emotion-packed memories of the physical beatings and emotional abuse I received as a young child, images of a thick leather belt and a cat-o'-nine-tails—two of my father's implements of choice used to punish me for being a curious, high-energy, precocious little boy with a mind of his own.[4]

FINDING NEW LIFE AFTER THE DEATH OF MY SON

But *this* sacred, sanctified experience of God's presence was nothing like I'd ever felt before. The words that finally emerged along the fringe of my consciousness echoed those of the prophet Jeremiah: "A voice is heard in Ramah, lamenting *and* bitter weeping. Rachel is weeping for her children; she refuses to be comforted for her children, because they are no more" (Jeremiah 31:15).

The day before the membership class, Saturday, May 1, 2010, my seven-year-old son, Thomas, and I were having dinner after a movie. "Papa, how do you know if you're going to heaven?" he suddenly asked. I was both pleased and taken aback by his question.

"Why do you ask, son?" I replied, curious what triggered his inquiry.

"We've been talking about it in school, and I am wondering if I'm worthy to go to heaven," he responded, his voice registering concern.

In that moment, I was on holy ground. My son's open, searching heart was channeling his namesake: the biblical Thomas, who also wanted to know God deeply and personally by firsthand experience. I tried to assuage his honest doubts by reminding him about what he had learned from his homeschool Bible studies with Elin and his Bible classes at the Boulder Christian Academy. "Thomas," I began, "no one is worthy to go to heaven because of the things they've done or fail to do. It's only by faith in Jesus's sacrificial death and resurrection that we experience eternal life." I continued by quoting Thomas's favorite Bible verse: "For God so loved the world, that He gave His only Son, so that everyone who believes in Him will not perish but have eternal life" (John 3:16).

"Do you believe this, son?" I queried.

"Yes, Papa," he responded, his face showing some visible relief.

Eleven years later to the day, Thomas would end up taking a Xanax pill he bought on Snapchat for fifteen dollars. He wanted to calm his fear and anxiety about the COVID-19 pandemic that quarantined him in our home, along with some of the other things that eighteen-year-olds care too much about in a world gone mad. That counterfeit pill was filled with three times the lethal dose of fentanyl. He died in his bed at about 10:00 p.m. that night. I found his cold, lifeless body on Sunday, May 2, 2021, when I went to wake him for our online church service, exactly eleven years after I sobbed through the first line of my faith journey.

Carl Jung calls such meaningful coincidences synchronistic events, that is, circumstances connected to one another by an "acausal connecting principle."[5] Events like these don't have a cause-and-effect relationship along what I refer to as the Outer Labyrinth, that is, the destiny we create with our day-to-day choices. But they do have a deeper and more profound connection that emerges from the destiny we have in God from the beginning of time, what I call the Inner Labyrinth, as revealed in our dreams. The empirical reality of synchronicity is how God accomplishes His sovereign will through the conscious and unconscious (intended and unintended) beliefs, mindsets, and actions of people in all times, places, and sociocultural settings. But most people don't recognize that God uses their lives, their decisions, and their stories to achieve His ends, purpose, and will.

I now realize God used my tear-filled experience on May 2, 2010—along with symbols in both my dreams and Thomas's that we recorded together from the time he was two years old—to prepare me to survive the loss of my son. Through those experiences, God was strengthening me to tell this story. At the time of Thomas's death, these things were a profound and disturbing mystery. But looking back now, I see these experiences as acts of mercy and love from an all-knowing God who foresaw from the foundations of the world that Thomas's life would be challenging and short.

If you allow me to be the docent, I'll lead you on a journey down into the depths of grief and pain that plagued my soul, and then back up through my process of finding new life and a deeper sense of meaning after the death of my son.

PART ONE
SURVIVING THOMAS'S DEATH

Thomas and Mark on Father's Day 2020 at Palermo's

CHAPTER 1

MY SON THOMAS

May 12, 2021 (10 Days After)

My wife, Elin, and I had a deal when she became pregnant. If we had a girl, then she would name her, but if we had a boy, then I would name him. When our son was born, I chose the name Thomas based on the story of Jesus's disciple in John 20:19–29. I've long felt the biblical Thomas got a bad rap being labeled a "doubter." I always saw him as someone who just wanted to know God deeply and personally. So, I was amazed when the lectionary Gospel reading for Sunday, April 27, 2003—the day my Thomas was baptized—just happened to be the passage about the biblical Thomas. I took that as a sign God would be with my son over the course of his life. But I had no idea then just how short his life would actually be.

Elin and I were committed to raising Thomas in a Christian home, one where faith, prayer, regular church attendance, and Bible reading were the foundation of our routine life. We created a Christian family culture built on the principles of trust, transparency, teamwork, forgiveness, and mercy. From the age of three until the Sunday before Thomas died, we always had a family meeting after dinner, where each of us would give praise or feedback to one another. Even at a young age, we wanted Thomas to feel like a person whose opinion mattered and whose presence was valued. For years, I would pray an evening prayer with my son every night when I put him to bed.

> Thank you God for Thomas.
> Thank you for his spirit, his keen mind, and his curiosity, dear Lord.
> I pray you bless him and keep him safe tonight and show him his calling and destiny in life. In Jesus's name. Amen.

When I was on the road doing consulting work, Elin would also perform this nightly prayer with Thomas. I've been saying that prayer to myself ever since Thomas died to keep my mind and heart close to the son I love, to the boy I lost at such a young age.

We lived in the high country of Colorado near Breckenridge until Thomas was five years old, after which we moved just outside of Boulder. Elin homeschooled Thomas all the way through first grade. When Thomas was ready to start second grade, we enrolled him at the Boulder Christian Academy, a private Christian school whose curriculum included the rigorous study of the Bible, much like we practiced at home. Having a higher education background in theological studies, I was always amazed at how much of the Bible's content Thomas knew, and how deeply he yearned to know what it meant. While at Boulder Christian Academy, Thomas began his long journey through the scouting ranks, eventually becoming an Eagle Scout in 2019 when he was sixteen. I even went to Cub Scout camp with him and was Thomas's instructor for his "God and Me" and "God and Family" merit badges.

We were members at Faith Presbyterian Church while living in Boulder, where Thomas was active in Sunday school and the young people's program. When he was eleven years old, Thomas announced he wanted to make a public reaffirmation of his faith. I was pleased, sensing the Spirit of God was moving in my son. Speaking before the congregation, he described how Elin and I baptized him as a baby and promised to raise him in the faith, and how now, being old enough to understand these things, he wanted to profess Jesus as his savoir. He even recited John 3:16, his favorite Scripture verse.

From the time he was a little boy, I used to tell Thomas he taught me what it was like to be a child again. I loved watching his reactions to things, how he made decisions, and the way he reasoned about life and his friends at his young age. I wanted him to be his own person, develop his own opinions, and voice them within the boundaries of our family culture. He would say, "Papa, ya know what I think?" and I would always respond, "What do you think, son?" before he would go on to share an observation or opinion about a situation, person, or issue he was reflecting on. We would discuss whatever was on his mind for as long as he wanted. Sometimes, Elin was amazed at how patiently I would listen to what he had to say, no matter how many questions he asked.

FINDING NEW LIFE AFTER THE DEATH OF MY SON

At his best, Thomas was perceptive and analytic, respectful and thoughtful, sensitive, and kind. He was also someone who could be incredibly passionate about life, even if he kept such feelings to himself. Under pressure, he was an unreachable loner who had a difficult time interacting with people and managing the daily demands of life. It was difficult for him to spontaneously express strong emotions without having time to think through his response. Like a kid looking through the window of a candy store, Thomas was an observer of life, a stranger in a strange land who had to study and figure out how to act and respond in social interactions. He operated in the background of many situations, guarded against outside demands on his precious space, time, and energy.

Even before Thomas was born, Elin and I understood the importance healthy boundaries and personal space played in families and relationships. This fit well with Thomas's personality and his need for space and time alone. When we got married, we agreed our house would be divided up into "personal space" and "common space." Personal space belonged to an individual family member, and, other than concerns about environment, safety, or health issues, they could use that space and maintain it any way they wanted. It was off-limits to other family members. Thomas's room was his room, and we respected that boundary. On the other hand, common space belonged to us as a family, and no one-person's presence or "stuff" could dominate it.

As a self-professing Christian, Thomas wrestled with intellectual questions related to the scientific worldview of a universe composed entirely of quarks, leptons, dark matter, dark energy, and the forces by which they interact. Like most people, he had no firsthand experience of supernatural phenomena and struggled to see how they could happen without violating conservation laws. He also struggled with doubts about how a loving God could allow suffering and sin to exist in the world. As someone who sometimes struggled with similar doubts, Thomas and I would discuss these difficult questions together over coffee or dinner. He died a self-professing Christian, with these doubts living side by side with his faith in God.

Thomas had a desire for things to be fair and equitable in life and in his relationships. He also had a deep sense of integrity. For Thomas, true integrity was not perfection. Rather, it was a commitment to course correction—to coming back to his principles, values, and inner truths after making a wrong decision. Thomas made some wrong decisions in his life, but over time, he would have found his way, as he always did. He would have found his calling and destiny in life had it not been stolen from him so soon.

◇ ◇ ◇

On May 2, 2021, Elin and I would discover our son, Thomas, dead in his bedroom. Four days later, the police sergeant in charge of the investigation into Thomas's death called and told me they arrested the person who sold Thomas what was advertised as Xanax but was really a counterfeit pill made with fentanyl. That one pill killed him. They booked the suspect into the Santa Clara County Main Jail on several narcotics sales charges. So, my son, Thomas, did not overdose (i.e., take too much)—he was deceptively *poisoned* with fentanyl.

Upon hearing this news, my longtime friend Philip Yancey, who knew and loved Thomas, wrote to me saying, "There is no 'good news' in such a tragedy. But at least you know that Thomas did not die of despair of life, or some deeply buried wound. That's so important for you and Elin to recognize."

Elin and I keep asking ourselves why Thomas had to leave us at such a young age. But we both know there is no answer to this question on this side of the grave. As Carl Jung said, "All the greatest and most important problems of life are fundamentally insoluble. They can never be solved, but only outgrown."[6] Whether he knew it or not, from the moment he was born, Thomas was on a lifelong journey to discover his calling and destiny in life, like the prayer I prayed for him each night as a child. Along the Outer Labyrinth of his day-to-day life, he was creating his destiny with the choices he made. Along the Inner Labyrinth of the unconscious, he was living out the destiny he had in God from the foundations of the world.

Despite Thomas's death, I have continued to trust fully in God and have faith in Him and His sovereign plan for Thomas, for Elin, and for myself. In the words of Job 13:15: "Though He slay me, yet will I trust in Him." I also believe God understands our pain as grieving parents because He gave His only begotten son for the whole world.

CHAPTER 2

FIRST MOTHER'S DAY WITHOUT THOMAS

May 15, 2021 (13 Days After)

Carmel has long been a holy and sacred place to Elin and me. Thomas loved Carmel, too, but for different reasons. The day he left his beloved Colorado to move to California, he wore a T-shirt with the words "Ocean Avenue" spread across it. This was the name of a song recorded by Yellowcard, one of Thomas's favorite bands, whose members grew up in Carmel. That T-shirt still hung on the wall of Thomas's room thirteen days after his death.

I'll never forget the first time I took him to Point Lobos State Nature Reserve just a few miles south of Carmel. As we drove by the exit for Ocean Avenue on Highway 1, with Carmel High School to our left, he told me the story of how the guys in Yellowcard wrote some of their best songs about this sleepy little town on the California Coast while they were in high school. I promised him that we'd stop there on our way back home and have dinner.

◊ ◊ ◊

Thomas had a deep love for all different kinds of music from all different eras, ranging from pop punk and alternative to Christian rock, the Beatles, and even jazz and classical music. Thomas went to many concerts during his adolescence, memorizing the lyrics to all his favorite songs by heart. He even played several instruments, including the trumpet, acoustic and electric guitar (a Les Paul), the bass, and the ukulele. I often heard him playing and singing songs quietly in his room into the wee hours of the night.

Thomas was a complex person. On the one hand, he had a very sensitive heart. He was empathic, perceptive, and attuned to both his own emotions and those of others. He could sense when things were not right

Thomas and Elin in Carmel on Mother's Day, 2020

in a relationship and needed to be talked out. But he kept much of his emotional life hidden inside. He was a deeply private person who valued his psychological and intellectual space, his autonomy, and his freedom. He was most himself when he was alone in his room surrounded by walls covered with signed posters of his favorite bands, paper tickets from concerts he had been to, and pictures of his family and friends. This sacred, cluttered, dissonant theater was a window into the mystery of who my son was.

On the other hand, Thomas was "edgy" and stood apart from many societal expectations, exhibiting an unconventional type of wisdom that exceeded his years. He was imaginative, audacious, and nimble within the world of his mind. Thomas wielded exceptional intellectual firepower. He was an unconventional thinker who had the natural ability to solve very complex and vexing problems. He could digest enormous amounts of information very quickly, and in discussions with peers and well-educated adults, there was rarely a topic or issue that Thomas didn't already know about and have a perspective on. He stood outside the sociocultural context of "the crowd," which gave him a unique vantage point for insights and commentary on the world around him and the nagging existential questions of life.

◊ ◊ ◊

That first trip to Carmel together was such a peaceful experience. We hiked, talked, and took pictures of the natural beauty surrounding us as we forgot about life for a little while. After exploring most of Point Lobos's magnificent Pacific shoreline, Thomas and I headed back north to Ocean Avenue, just as I promised him. We walked the beach, breathed in the fresh ocean air, and just enjoyed each other as we continued talking. We made it all the way to the Pebble Beach Golf Course and back, traveling the entire length of Carmel's pristine white beach. Afterward, I took Thomas to Tommy's Wok for dinner, a little hole-in-the-wall Chinese restaurant. Thomas thoroughly enjoyed the food; we even ordered enough to take home to Elin.

Thomas loved Point Lobos. It was a place where both of us, father and son, could get away from the fast-paced, pulse-pressing life of Silicon Valley. My son and I would make that trip to Carmel and Point Lobos (and to Tommy's Wok) many more times over the years. Elin also loved Point Lobos for many of the same reasons that Thomas and I did (including the food at Tommy's Wok). During the pandemic when Santa Clara County shut down tighter than a cow's ass in fly season, Carmel had fewer restrictions because they had very few hospitalized COVID cases. So, after months of being sequestered in our house in Campbell, we decided it was time to escape. The three of us drove to Carmel, sat along the ocean shore, and watched the waves roll in. We walked the beach and then went to Tommy's Wok, ordering food to go. We sat on the curb in the parking lot outside the restaurant and chattered on and on as we ate, embracing our tiny moment of freedom in a world that was sheltered in place. Even prior to this renegade outing, we had a family tradition where we would take Elin to Tommy's Wok every Mother's Day for dinner. In the weeks prior to Thomas's death, I asked Elin what she wanted to do for Mother's Day dinner. Without hesitation, she said, "Tommy's in Carmel."

Seven days after Thomas died on May 2, 2021, Elin and I kept our tradition and went to Carmel for Mother's Day. But this time, we went without our son. Elin and I did what our family always did in Carmel—we sat on a bench, watching the ocean waves roll in, and then walked along the Pacific coast. As we strolled, Elin said, "The last time we did this, Thomas was with us." We both felt the sting and reality of his loss more intensely in that moment. Elin and I went to Tommy's Wok for Mother's Day lunch, eating our food in the muted silence of the loss of our son. We still trusted the words of Romans 8:28 that all things work together for good for them who love God and are called according to His purpose. But we could not even begin to imagine what "good" might come from our son's death.

On that first Mother's Day in Carmel without Thomas, the lyrics of the song "Ocean Avenue" by Yellowcard—one of Thomas's favorite bands—echoed how I was feeling that day about the loss of our son.

> If I could find you now, things would get better . . .
> There's a piece of you that's here with me.
> It's everywhere I go. It's everything I see.

That first Mother's Day without Thomas left an inexplicable, gut-wrenching pain and sense of loss and confusion sitting in my soul, like bad food that needed to be puked up. I sense those feelings even now as I reflect on that day or look at the pictures of Elin that we took. The shock that accompanied the trauma of Thomas's death was a gift from God, like an anesthesia that kept me from feeling the enormous suffering and pain of this loss. I trudged my way through the mundane realities of work and life at home, placing one foot in front of the other. It was all my grieving soul could manage as I was swept along by the relentless flow of time. There were no words to describe what I was experiencing then. I'm struggling to explain it now.

CHAPTER 3

THOMAS'S NINETEENTH BIRTHDAY WITHOUT HIM

May 16, 2021 (14 Days After)

Before he died, Thomas told us wanted a new iPhone for his nineteenth birthday. He also told Elin he wanted his favorite chocolate cake with white rather than dark icing this time. Last year for his eighteenth birthday, a special milestone, we placed a two-pound rock that we brought with us from Colorado along with a large picture of a thousand-dollar bill in a gift-wrapped box. You should have seen the perplexed look on Thomas's face when he saw the rock, then the quizzical stare when he saw the picture of the bill, and then the smile on his face when he realized he was getting the money as a present. His girlfriend, Villy, was with us, and she also smiled as she saw Thomas's reaction to the same kind of respectful humor that Thomas was famous for.

On what would have been Thomas's nineteenth birthday, our home was filled with the fading scent of the sweet-smelling flowers from his funeral just eight days prior. His blanket was still sitting in the empty place on the couch where he always sat when the three of us would watch our online church service during the pandemic. What does somebody do to "celebrate" their son or daughter's birthday a couple weeks after they've died? Do you bake a cake? Do you walk out into the dining room with the candles lit, singing "Happy Birthday"? Do you invite anyone? How do you bear the pain of this loss so soon after their death? Elin and I had no answers to these and a myriad of other questions in those early days.

That Friday, our doorbell rang. I opened the door, and a tall, long-haired young man with glasses and a face mask stood there nervously holding a beautiful bouquet of brightly colored flowers. I asked him who he was, and he said his name was Alan and he was a good friend of Thomas. He had come to pay his respects to Elin and me. As I glanced

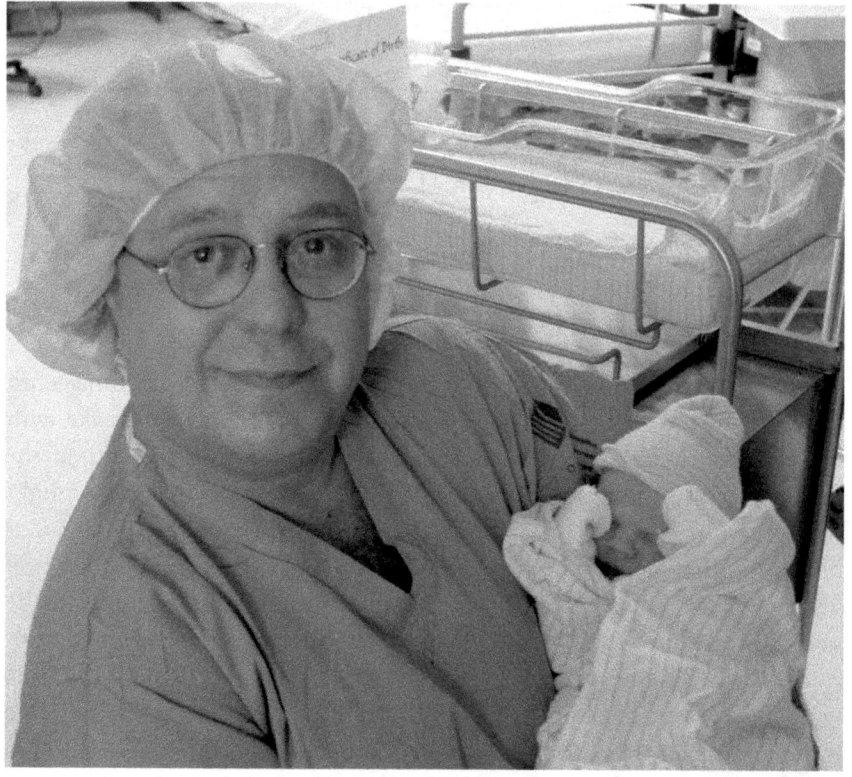

Mark holding Thomas when he was only ninety minutes old

out into the street, I saw his mom watching from their car. It took a lot of courage and integrity for Alan to do this. The little card that came with the flowers said:

> With deepest sympathy. I'm so sorry to hear about Thomas.
> I loved him like a brother, and he was my closest friend.
> If you ever need anything, please contact me.

Alan included his mobile phone number as well. My heart was comforted by his courage and the message on the card, so I decided to text him a few minutes after he left. In his text response, Alan said that he'd just found out about Thomas's passing the day before, and he was devastated by the news. He went on to say, "I know he was too young, and I was always so proud of him. I plan on getting a few people together on his birthday just to remember him. I will never forget him and always remember him dearly."

I asked Elin if she would consider baking two identical cakes, one for the celebration of life that Elin, Villy, and I were going to have on Sunday, and another one for Alan and Thomas's other friends. She eagerly agreed to bake the cake and was comforted that Thomas's friends thought so much of him that they were going to remember his special day and celebrate their friendship. I texted Alan again and told him about our plan. He was absolutely thrilled.

Elin baked the two birthday cakes, and we dropped off the second cake at Alan's house, complete with candles, so he and Thomas's friends would have it for the next day. Elin also texted Alan, thanking him for bringing the flowers and asking him to let Thomas's friends know how much he valued their friendship over the years. Alan quickly responded, thanking Elin for the cake and telling her how much he appreciated how we welcomed him into our home as Thomas's friend. He mentioned how he didn't have any friends at the beginning of high school until Thomas came along and how he couldn't have asked for a better friend.

So, despite our grief and the lingering existential questions about why Thomas and why us, Elin and I knew exactly how we were going to do to celebrate Thomas's nineteenth birthday. Elin took our cake, and I created a short celebration service by modifying the "Burial of the Dead: Rite Two" from the *Book of Common Prayer* to include the prayer of St. Francis, a beautiful prayer that echoed the impact Thomas had on his family and friends.

> Lord, make us instruments of your peace.
> Where there is hatred, let us sow love;
> where there is injury, pardon;
> where there is discord, union;
> where there is doubt, faith;
> where there is despair, hope;
> where there is darkness, light;
> where there is sadness, joy.

Grant that we may not so much seek to be consoled as to console;
to be understood as to understand;
to be loved as to love.
For it is in giving that we receive;
it is in pardoning that we are pardoned;
and it is in dying that we are born to eternal life. Amen.

So, on what would have been Thomas's nineteenth birthday, we conducted the same private service Elin and I performed at his funeral a couple weeks before, this time with Thomas's girlfriend, Villy, present. We lit the candles, had a word of prayer, blew the candles out, and then shared stories about Thomas as we comforted each other, remembering the person we all loved so much. Elin and I have vowed to conduct this service each year on Thomas's birthday for as long as we have breath in us, trusting in God's love, mercy, and sovereign plan for our lives and for Thomas's short life.

CHAPTER 4

FIRST FATHER'S DAY IN CARMEL WITHOUT THOMAS

June 20, 2021 (49 Days After)

My first Father's Day as a dad was on June 16, 2002, when Thomas was just thirty-one days old. Before beginning my journey to fatherhood, I was living in Alma, Colorado, a small town of about two hundred people. At 10,361 feet above sea level, Alma is the highest town in North America. (It is also home to the South Park Saloon, one of the places that inspired the *South Park* cartoon series.) At the time, I was going to church at St. John the Baptist Episcopal Church about seventeen miles north in Breckenridge. Eventually, I decided to move there in hope of meeting a woman, getting married, and having a family.

Breckenridge is a ski town, and as a skier, I loved living there. But the culture in ski towns tends to be transient, so finding someone who wants to settle down and have a family can be difficult. After a couple of years, I began contemplating another move, this time down to the Boulder area where there were a lot more people. When I told one of the priests at St. John the Baptist that I was planning to relocate to Boulder to find a wife and start a family, he sent me an email telling me about a woman named Elin Larson whom he thought I would like. Then he asked if he could make an introduction.

Our first date was on February 11, 2000, at an Italian restaurant named Ti Amo's in Frisco. Seven months later, Elin and I were married in Aspen on September 16 in an outdoor service held in a stand of aspen trees just below the peaks of the Maroon Bells. I sold my place in Breckenridge and moved into Elin's townhome that backed up onto Lake Dillon with a spectacular view of the fourteen-thousand-foot, snow-covered peaks of the Grays and Torreys.

About a year later, on September 8, 2001, Elin and I were sitting in the snack shop at the Denver Museum of History and Science when she got a

Thomas and Mark in Carmel on Father's Day, 2020

call from her doctor saying she was pregnant with Thomas. We were both thrilled and began preparing for his arrival by childproofing our house and painting and decorating what would become his first bedroom. Thomas was born on a Thursday, and we brought him home three days later on Sunday, May 19, 2002. Because of the high elevation, Thomas was on oxygen following his birth for about a week until his tiny body adjusted to the altitude.

I was raised in a family where my maternal grandmother would say, "Children should be seen but not heard." So, in contradistinction, when Thomas was born, I committed myself to knowing my son deeply, having a good relationship with him, and understanding who he was as a unique person. I saw this as my stewardship from God as Thomas's father. Thomas spoke his first words before he was a year old and could say simple sentences by the time he was two. By his second birthday, it was clear he had a keen mind and was curious about absolutely everything. I was amazed by the childlike depth of his questions, and I shared my observations with him freely as well. From his earliest years, Elin and I affirmed, respected, and loved Thomas as an important member of our family.

Following his afternoon nap on October 6, 2004, when he was a little over two, Thomas insisted on Elin and me accompanying him down to my basement office. He led us into the bathroom and pointed to the scuba diving books that sat on the top of the toilet tank, and then he told us he had had a scary dream that he was in the bathroom and the books were falling from the toilet tank. From that day on, whenever Thomas had a dream that he remembered, he would sit on my lap and recount it as I entered what he described into my laptop. Over the next ten years, we recorded ninety-eight dreams, the last of which was on August 8, 2014, when he was twelve. Thomas and I would discuss the images that appeared in his dreams, how he felt about them, and the broader implications of the messages that his dreams were trying to convey to him. Sometimes, Elin, Thomas, and I would discuss and reflect upon our dreams together.

As Thomas became a young man, I taught him about the work of Carl Jung and the meaning of the labyrinth with a handheld wooden model that I had in my home office. I described how our everyday conscious life was like a journey along an Outer Labyrinth where we create our own destiny with our choices. I likened the world of the dreams he and I were recording to a journey along an Inner Labyrinth of the destiny that we have in God from the beginning of time, with both happening together at the same time.

Many years later during his freshman year in college, Thomas was taking a course on ancient religions. One day he came into my home office with his textbook in hand and said, "Hey, Papa, this guy's talking about Carl Jung and archetypes." This was a topic he and I had discussed together when I would share images and messages from some of the twenty-five hundred dreams I had recorded over my life. Dreams were a way of connecting with my son at a very deep existential level, a place we shared in common with all people across all time periods and cultures.

Thomas had a deep thirst for knowledge and a desire to understand what life was about. One day, Thomas introduced me to Jordan Peterson's work, and we began reading his books together and discussing them. I can't explain my excitement when we read the preface to Peterson's impenetrable first book, *Maps of Meaning*, where Peterson recounts his personal story about his life being lived "on two planes," with one being his day-to-day life and the other being the world of his dreams, both of which were happening simultaneously. This instantly reminded me of the Outer and Inner Labyrinths framework so formative in my own thinking.[7] The fact that Peterson's story and mine were so similar, and that both of us had been illuminated by Jung's work, gave me a sense of credibility with my son—something that is so important in a world where many teenagers think they know everything, and their "old man" is stupid.

Whether he knew it or not, Thomas was already on a lifelong journey to discover his calling and destiny in life, like the prayer that I prayed for him each night as a child. Along the Outer Labyrinth of daily life, he was creating his destiny with the choices. Along the Inner Labyrinth of the unconscious, he was living out the destiny that he had in God from the foundations of the world, as revealed in his dreams, with both happening together at the same time.

<> <> <>

My first Father's Day without Thomas was June 20, 2021, exactly seven weeks after he died. During those weeks prior, I recorded and analyzed six dreams, all of which were about the grief and pain of transforming my experience of Thomas's physical presence into inner memories of our life together—memories supported by the artifacts he left behind. Already, Thomas's physical presence had begun to fade. He no longer studied at the dining room table, washed his clothes in the laundry room, or joined us at Sunday dinner. He no longer asked me for the car keys or sent me YouTube videos to watch. There were no more trips to Carmel together or deep conversations about life.

These actual, physical experiences of Thomas were being transformed into memories of the day-to-day, week-to-week, month-to-month interactions of our life together—things Thomas and I took for granted then, but things I now no longer have. I've tried to hold on to my experience of his actual physical presence to no avail. I slept in his bed some nights after he died to "be where he was." Sometimes I would lay in his bed just to smell the sheets because his scent was still lingering there.

In those weeks after his death, Elin and I left Thomas's possessions and room the exact way he left them. We couldn't even bring ourselves to throw out his long-expired yogurt container from our refrigerator, because he bought it. The yogurt, like all of his other possessions, was an artifact that pointed to Thomas's physical presence with us here on earth. It was painful to even think about what we should do with these testaments, these material pieces of evidence of our life with our son, much less actually begin the difficult process of cleaning out the inner sanctum of his bedroom, his sacred space.

When our family first moved to California in 2015 to start a new phase of our life together, we used a three-step strategy to get our new life in order: shape our new reality, embed it with repetition, and look for the deep emotional connections that would then emerge. We shaped our new reality by deciding where we would live, shop for groceries, and attend church, as well as where Thomas would go to school and what Boy Scout troop he would join. We planned out all the mundane, pedestrian things that we wanted to constitute our new life. Over time and through behavioral repetition, this portfolio of activities, places, traditions, and interactions with people went on autopilot and solidified into a new Bodnarczuk-Larson reality. Eventually, deep emotional connections emerged that solidified "our new life out here in California." But on that first Father's Day in Carmel without Thomas, it hit me that these recurring patterns of our life had been abruptly and tragically reshaped against my will. Elin and I now had to create a new reality, one that did not include Thomas's physical presence but only artifacts. But this new reality would also include the hope that we would see Thomas again in that heavenly kingdom, where tears and death have been abolished.

Entrance to the Ryssby Church and Cemetery where Thomas is buried

CHAPTER 5

THE FUNERALS

August 28, 2021 (16 Weeks and 6 Days After)

We had three funerals for Thomas: two in California and one in Colorado. The first service, attended only by Elin and me with an open casket, was held at the Darling Fisher Funeral Home in Campbell, California, six days after finding him dead in his bedroom. We were in shock at the time; our family and friends were thousands of miles away, and the Santa Clara County medical examiner's office was pressuring us to tell them where to send Thomas's lifeless body after his autopsy. Ten days after this private funeral, Elin and I attended Thomas's cremation on May 18, 2021, at the Darling Fisher Garden Chapel of the Hills in Los Gatos. When we received his remains from the funeral home, we set the hand-carved rosewood urn that contained Thomas's ashes on his bed and forced ourselves to plan what would come next.

Over time, we started planning our son's second funeral, which was to be held at the Ryssby Church back home in Colorado. Elin and I owned two burial plots in the Ryssby Cemetery behind the church, and this would be where we would lay Thomas's remains to rest following the service conducted by one of the Episcopal priests who baptized Thomas in Breckenridge eighteen years prior. Family, friends, and colleagues from all over the country gathered there on August 28, 2021. Prior to the priest's homily, I gave the reflections on Thomas's life and our life together as a family, which are included below.

◊ ◊ ◊

Elin and I appreciate you being here with us today to remember our son, Thomas. This red-and-blue striped tie that I have on belonged to him. It's the tie he was wearing in the picture that's inside your order of service when he made a public profession of his faith on March 3, 2013, at Faith

Presbyterian Church in Boulder, Colorado. I'm wearing it today in memory of that public profession and in memory of Thomas's short but impactful life. So, rather than a typical eulogy, I've decided to share some reflections on the impact that Thomas has had on our lives and the lives of others, on how Elin and I have experienced the loss of Thomas's presence in our lives, and our path forward as we leave this memorial service today.

One of our holiday traditions was for Thomas, Elin, and I to watch the classic Christmas movie *It's a Wonderful Life*. The movie is based on a short story by Philip Van Doren Stern, which he composed based on a set of images that came to him one night in a dream. Unable to find a publisher, Stern originally self-published the story as a small pamphlet and sent it out to about two hundred people as his 1943 Christmas card. One of those cards found its way to Frank Capra, who showed it to Jimmy Stewart, the actor who would go on to play the good-hearted character of George Bailey. The key message of the story is that George never realized the enormous impact that he had in life until he was gone—until his physical presence was subtracted from the calculus of everyday events that shaped and defined the lives of those living in the fictional town of Bedford Falls.

In much the same way, our son, Thomas, had an enormous impact on the lives of others, and this didn't become apparent to Elin and me until he was gone—until hundreds of people posted story after story and tribute after tribute about how his life made a difference in their lives. Currently, there are almost five hundred people who have visited Thomas's memorial site, many of whom have posted stories, memories, and tributes to him.

One of Thomas's friends wrote, "I've never been good with writing endings, so I'll just say this. Thomas was not only my best friend, but he was my first real friend. Even after he moved to California, we'd still talk over email and share goofy stories and internet memes with each other. My one regret is that I never got to tell him how much I actually loved and appreciated him. But at the same time, I think he knew."

Another friend wrote, "One of my last interactions with Thomas was a conversation that he wouldn't let end until I said I loved him, and then he was like 'okay, there; it's ended,' and then he proceeded to send a meme a few minutes later. I'll never forget it. I'll never forget him. I'll never forget the stories, the laughs, the adventures, or his corny sense of humor. Without him, I wouldn't be the person I am today."

Yet another friend wrote, "Thomas taught me many things about compassion, about interpersonal relationships, about myself, and about the world. Thomas cared about the people around him and brought people together. Thomas was the kindest of souls and is a man that I will always aspire to be for the rest of my life."

A colleague of mine at Stanford University who had never met Thomas wrote, "I never had the joy of meeting Thomas and wish I would have. From all the pictures and tributes, he feels like a wonderful young man I would have enjoyed talking with and learning from. I thank you both for sharing Thomas's story and life with us. It has changed my outlook, and a day has not gone by without thinking about you and your family."

Thomas made a difference in the lives of his friends. But what my colleague's post showed us was that these tributes and stories were also making a difference in the lives of people who never knew Thomas personally—those who came to know him only through his memorial site.

For twenty-one years, Thomas was a part of every facet of our lives as his parents—from the planning and pregnancy phase up through the last day of his life. Thomas was a taken-for-granted and tacit part of everyday life, and it wasn't until he was gone that Elin and I realized just how deeply his life was woven into the fabric of our past, present, and future.

The change that his tragic death brought about happened suddenly—Thomas was alive one day and dead the next. But the protracted physical, psychological, and spiritual grieving process of transition, where Elin and I have had to let go of the old reality and the old identity that we had as a family of three before Thomas's death, has been profoundly difficult and painful beyond words.[8] So, I'd like to share some aspects of our transition journey with you, all of which have been centered on the impact of Thomas's presence in our lives.

The first aspect was Thomas's physical presence. It's been sixteen weeks and five days since Thomas died, and Elin and I have gone through an intense, chaotic, and exhausting grieving process around the loss of his physical presence in our lives. He came home from work at 9:10 p.m. on Saturday, May 1, 2021. Elin and I chatted with him about how things went that night and how he was doing in general, and then he went to his room. That was the last time we saw our son alive. We found him dead in his bedroom at 9:55 the next morning when I went to get him for our online church service. In the days that followed, what amazed and deeply troubled us was how quickly the effervescent experience of Thomas's physical presence began to fade. The way he'd come through the back door at night from work, the way he'd ask me for the car keys, the way he and I would go to the movies together or Elin and he would go out for boba tea together, and all the other interactions of our shared daily life. By Father's Day, just forty-nine days after he died, our experience of Thomas's physical presence had faded so significantly that Elin and I were struggling to hold on to the old reality and old identity that we'd had as a family for twenty years to no avail.

What Elin and I discovered was that our daily experience of our son was being transformed into Thomas's memory presence supported by artifacts. His driver's license is an artifact that points to the fact that Thomas once lived, and that Elin taught him to drive. The picture of him making a public profession of his faith in God is an artifact that points to the fact that he once lived, that he knew the Bible well, and that he believed in the God of Abraham, Isaac, and Jacob. His memorial site is an artifact that points to the fact that Thomas once lived and that he had an enormous positive impact on those who knew him when he was alive, and now on those who didn't know him during his life, like my colleague.

The third aspect of our transition has been our experience of Thomas's dream presence. Elin and I have been sharing our dreams and doing dream work together for twenty-one years. I've had fifteen dreams since Thomas has died, and Elin has had fourteen, some of which have included images and interactions with our son. In one of Elin's dreams, Thomas showed up alive. Elin was amazed because in the earlier parts of this dream, she was suffering deeply from the painful sadness and devastating loss of him being dead and cremated. But in the dream, Thomas was back, and she knew he was real, and she felt his presence and a deep joy of having him alive and really with us, like it was a miracle. Elin's dream ended with Thomas going off to see his girlfriend, Villy.

The first time I ever dreamed about Thomas was on September 18, 2002, when he was four months old. I've recorded and analyzed one hundred ninety-eight dreams about him since. As I stand here before you today, I have an inner image of my son in my heart and mind from a dream I had about him on May 29, 2021, just twenty-seven days after he died, where he spoke to me from a heart of serenity and innocence. So, for Elin and me, Thomas's dream presence has been a deeply personal inner experience of our son that goes to the core of our being, and it's something we will always treasure.

What Elin and I have yet to experience with any certainty is Thomas's heavenly presence, that is, a direct experience of Thomas from where he is now with God, something that's different from his physical, memory, or dream presences. Eleven weeks and five days after Thomas died, I was standing in his room talking to him, and I said, "I love you, Thomas," and I sensed a response, "I love you, too, Papa," just like he used to say when he was alive. I asked him if that was really him or my memory of him, or maybe an unconscious memory of him from a dream. There was no response, but this experience had a kind of transcendence about it, and I wondered if it was really my son, if Thomas was reaching out from his heavenly presence. I still feel the remnants of that experience standing here today.

The next day, Elin had the dream I recounted earlier, where Thomas showed up alive. Later that day, Elin met with Thomas's girlfriend, Villy, and she told her about my experience in Thomas's bedroom and her dream. Villy subsequently had a dream where Thomas showed up alive and talked with her. In the dream, Villy said to Thomas, "They really miss you, you know" (meaning Elin and me), and Thomas said, "Yeah, I know." It was a very short but powerful dream. Elin and I believe this is more than just a coincidence or the power of suggestion. Rather, it's what Carl Jung called a synchronicity, a strategically orchestrated and perfectly aligned message of guidance that indicates we're on the right path. But Elin and I also agree that we've yet to experience Thomas's heavenly presence in a *yada* sense.

Yada is the Hebrew verb for the kind of "knowing" that comes from direct, firsthand, personal experience rather than an intellectual or textbook kind of knowledge. It's the Hebrew word that's used to describe a deep knowledge of God and the act of sexual intercourse, because in that intimate act, you gain a knowledge of the other person that you can't obtain in any other way. Genesis 4:1 says, "Now the man (Adam) had relations with (literally "knew," *yada*) his wife Eve, and she conceived and gave birth to Cain, and she said, "I have obtained a male child with the help of the Lord." Again, *yada* is about knowing something by doing it, not just thinking about it in your head. I talk to Thomas a lot as I go through my day, such as when

I'm on my walk or during my prayer times. But other than that one experience in his bedroom, I've had no ongoing experience of Thomas's heavenly presence in the *yada* sense. It was in the *yada* sense of knowing that the biblical Thomas in today's Gospel reading demanded evidence that Christ had risen from the dead. He wanted to see in his hands the imprints of the nails and put his finger into the place of the nails. But Jesus's admonition to the biblical Thomas is exactly what God is calling Elin and me to do: "'Because you have seen Me, have you now believed? Blessed are they who did not see [in the *yada* sense], and *yet* believed'" (John 20:29).

In other words, if Elin and I really believe we are more than just our physical bodies, if we believe Thomas is really alive as a heavenly presence despite our lack of an intimate experience of him, how should that belief shape and define our transition to a new reality and a new identity as a family of two going forward?

Jesus's words in John 20:29 remind me of what Jim Collins called the Stockdale Paradox.[9] Admiral James Stockdale was the highest-ranking US military official captured as a prisoner of war in the "Hanoi Hilton" during the Vietnam War. He was beaten and tortured for seven years but continued to provide leadership for his fellow American prisoners and was never broken. In an interview at Stanford, Jim Collins asked Stockdale how he managed to survive. "I never lost faith in the end of the story," he responded. "I never doubted not only that I would get out, but also that I would prevail in the end and turn the experience into a defining event in life, which in retrospect, I would not trade." But Stockdale went on to say, "You must never confuse faith that you will prevail in the end—which you can never afford to lose—with the discipline to confront the most brutal facts of your current reality, whatever that might be."[10] Over the last several weeks, Elin and I have been prisoners of an intense, chaotic, painful, and exhausting grieving process that we can't escape. Like Stockdale, we have no idea how long this in-between time of transitioning to a new reality and a new identity will last.

We will never, ever forget the enormous impact Thomas had in the nineteen years he lived. At the same time, however, we'll face the brutal fact that his memory presence, dream presence, and hope of his heavenly presence are all we have until we see him again face-to-face in heaven. We will never, ever, ever forget the old reality and the old identity that we had as a family of three before Thomas died, but we will face the brutal fact that we are transitioning to a new reality and a new identity as a family of two without Thomas's physical presence. We will never, ever give up hope that God's sovereign will, love, grace, and promise of eternal life for our son will prevail in the end, but we will face the brutal fact that Thomas is dead, and what's left of his physical presence is in the hand-carved Rosewood urn, here in the front of the sanctuary. We know through our experiences that Thomas is dead, but we also know by faith that he is alive—more alive than anyone in this room, because he's with the Lord of life.

God made Elin and me stewards to love and care for Thomas for the last nineteen years. We have been faithful to this task by raising our son in a Christian home, where we were not afraid to admit we were wrong or made mistakes, and where God's love and forgiveness were woven into the fabric of our day-to-day life, when times were good, and when times were bad. When our days are done and Elin and I are buried here in the cemetery behind Ryssby Church and reunited with Thomas in heaven, we hope to hear God say to us stewards, "Well done, good and faithful servants" (Matthew 25:23).

Finally, in terms of the path forward for Elin and me when we leave here today, what we know for sure is that "closure" is something that you do with mortgages, not the death of a child. We have been fearless in facing the brutal facts of Thomas's death, and we are slowly coming to accept and ultimately embrace the long-term implications of a life without his physical presence within the larger context of our destiny in life. Finding our destiny as individuals and as a family—and then actually living it out—has been the foundation upon which Elin and I built our marriage and the culture in which we raised Thomas.

For me, the existential importance of finding and living out our destiny came from biblical truths echoed in the 1994 movie *Forrest Gump*. In that film, Forrest wondered if he had a destiny like Lieutenant Dan claimed, or whether he had to create his own destiny like his Momma said: "Life is like a box of chocolates. You never know what you are going to get, so you have to make your own destiny, Forrest." By the end of the movie, Forrest figures out that Lieutenant Dan and Momma were both right—we both have a destiny that we're called to live out, and we create our own destiny with our choices, and both are happening together at the same time. That's what Elin and I believe.

From the time Thomas was a tiny baby, we prayed God would show him his calling and his destiny in life. As Thomas grew older, the three of us would watch *Forrest Gump* together, and later, Thomas would watch it multiple times on his own with Netflix. One of the most important and most sacred roles I had as Thomas's father was to make investments of time, love, encouragement, leadership, faith, discipline, empathic listening, and financial support to help him find his calling and his destiny in life.

Based on dozens and dozens of tributes and stories posted on his memorial site, it's clear that Thomas was on the path to finding and living out the destiny he had in life and the destiny he was trying to create. But his life was cut short by a single choice he made within the *Zeitgeist* of a cold, calculating, and evil world that has claimed the lives of thousands and thousands of unsuspecting victims like Thomas—people who were deceived and murdered for the financial gain of two Mexican cartels and for global political-ideological power and control by the Chinese Communist Party.[11]

So, Elin and I find ourselves in Forrest Gump's initial dilemma—we know by faith that we have a destiny that was written from the foundation of the world by God, and being Thomas's parents was (and remains) a key part of that destiny. We also know that we must create our own destiny going forward by our choices. But we're still in a no-man's land, an in-between place that's filled with unanswered questions.[12] Despite these unknowns, we don't feel lost, and we know deep in our hearts, in the *yada* sense, that we're on the right path. So, we'll continue to create a new reality and a new identity as part of this unexpected and previously unimaginable unfolding of the destiny we have, which will be forever shaped and defined by the enormous impact Thomas has had on our lives. And we'll do this in the name of the Father, and of the Son, and of the Holy Spirit, Amen.

◊ ◊ ◊

When I look back now at Thomas's funeral at Ryssby Church, I still wonder how Elin and I got through that service. When the service was over, we processed out of the church, following the Episcopal priest who had baptized Thomas and now was conducting his funeral. I carried the urn containing Thomas's remains. Elin held some of the flowers taken from the altar in front of the church. The 150 people who attended the service walked behind us and gathered around the grave site in the cemetery behind the church. The priest read the final words of "The Burial of the Dead: Rite Two" from the *Book of Common Prayer*—the same prayer Elin and I had prayed during our private funeral weeks before—as I lay on my stomach and reached down into a two-foot-deep hole in the ground where I placed what was left of my son to rest.

What I know now that I didn't know then was how long, protracted, and painful the legal process would be to prosecute the defendant who sold Thomas the pill that killed him. Seeing him in the court room, face-to-face, knowing this was the person who helped to end my son's life, was difficult beyond words. Enduring the dysfunctional and lethargic criminal legal process would drive Elin and me to the limits of our patience and endurance. It would teach us deeper experiential lessons about the Bible's admonitions about grace and forgiveness, its commandments to forgive others' sins, and Jesus's instruction to love our neighbors as we love ourselves.

Thomas's first Christmas at our home in Frisco, Colorado

CHAPTER 6

WHAT SHOULD WE DO FOR CHRISTMAS WITHOUT THOMAS?

November 13, 2021 (27 Weeks and 6 Days After)

In early November, I got an email invitation to the 2021 holiday party of one of the science directorates at Stanford University/SLAC National Accelerator Laboratory where I work. That was the first time I'd thought about spending the upcoming Christmas holiday season without Thomas. Being only twenty-eight weeks past my son's death, I was still struggling with sudden and mercurial emotions. For one moment, I would feel like I was moving through the grieving process; in the next, I'd be regressing back into the black hole of the early days of the grieving process. For one moment, I would feel ready to forge ahead with my life; in the next, I'd refuse to move on without my son. For one moment, I'd feel proud of Thomas and the positive impact he made in many peoples' lives; in the next, I'd feel angry that his life was cut short by a single choice he made in this deceptive age of counterfeit pills and fentanyl poisoning. At that time, these day-by-day and moment-by-moment experiences rested on an emotional foundation of pain, loss, and grief. At times, I would shake my head in disbelief that all this had happened to Elin and me.

So, I decided I wasn't going to go to the holiday party.

◊ ◊ ◊

A week later, I walked by several homes in our neighborhood where people had already begun putting up Christmas lights. Once again, I was struck by a deep sense of sadness at the tangible, long-term impact and reality of Thomas's death. I began wondering what Elin and I would, or should, do for the holidays in our home. Myriad thoughts and feelings of Christmases past began to cascade through my heart and mind as I continued to walk in the cool night air.

Maybe, I thought, we shouldn't go to the Chart House on Pier 39 in San Francisco for dinner on Christmas Eve like we always do or attend the 7:30 p.m. service at Grace Episcopal Cathedral afterward, because Thomas won't be with us. Maybe we shouldn't put up our Christmas tree, because one of Thomas's jobs was to help Elin put the ornaments on the tree. Maybe we shouldn't decorate the house with Christmas lights. Maybe we shouldn't decorate the inside of our home, either, with festive and cheerful ornaments when we feel so pained by our son's death.

What about our annual Advent candle on the dining room table that Thomas liked to light at Sunday dinner, or the dinnertime Christmas music that I always played? And then there's Elin's famous Christmas tree cake that Thomas loved to eat, his stocking that hung on the fireplace for the last nineteen years next to Elin's and mine, and the toy trains around the Christmas tree that Thomas loved to play with when he was a little boy. Should we do any of the things that we typically have done at Christmas time now that Thomas wasn't with us?

When I got home from my walk, Elin and I discussed my experience over a dinner of steak, pasta, and red wine. As it turned out, she had been pondering many of these same questions.

◊ ◊ ◊

While walking the Los Gatos Creek Trail the next day, I reflected on these questions again with an open and searching heart. I had a profound insight that we should face our first Christmas without Thomas in the same way Elin and I had faced almost everything else since Thomas's death—fearlessly, head on, with open hearts and minds that didn't run or hide from the painful reality that our son was dead. His physical presence was no longer with us, but his memory presence was, along with many artifacts like his Christmas stocking, ornaments, and trains, all of which pointed to the fact that Thomas once lived here and still lived on in our hearts and minds.

So, I changed my mind and decided to go to the holiday party. Elin and I decided to put up the Christmas tree, hang up Thomas's stocking, and light the Advent candle. We decided to decorate the house, bake the Christmas tree cake, and celebrate all our other traditions with muted spirits, thankful for the impact his life has had on our lives. We would also try to focus on the hope that the life, death, and resurrection of the child born in Bethlehem promises us—that Thomas is still alive (now with a heavenly body) and we'll see him again when we get to heaven. This courageous and hopeful way of grieving was the shortest path for Elin and me to transition from the old reality and our old identity as a family of three to a new reality and our new identity as a family of two.

Thomas on Christmas Day, 2004, standing next to the reassembled Christmas tree in Fairplay, Colorado

CHAPTER 7

FIRST CHRISTMAS

December 25, 2021 (33 Weeks and 6 Days After)

Christmas Day 2021 occurred nearly thirty-four weeks from the day Thomas died. Although Elin and I decided we would face our grief fearlessly and keep all the Christmas traditions we did when Thomas was alive, at the same time, we also wanted to be sensitive to our sad and painful emotions by finding ways to consciously recognize them in the midst of these holiday activities and express them to one another through new traditions. We wanted to embrace these emotions as part of the destiny we have in God's sovereign will for our lives in the wake of Thomas's death as we continued to wait for inner healing and transformation, trusting that a vision for new life would emerge in its time.

My memories of Christmases past still evoked a poignant sense of sadness and pain as I looked through the pictures and posts on Thomas's memorial site and reflected on the nineteen Christmases that Thomas, Elin, and I celebrated together as a family. There was the time in Fairplay when Thomas was two years old and he pulled on one of the ornaments on our eight-foot-high Christmas tree so hard that the tree suddenly fell, crashing onto the hard slate floor like an explosion as dozens of beautiful glass ornaments shattered into a million pieces. Thomas wasn't hurt, but it really scared him. He cried and cried as Elin tried to comfort him and assure him that everything was okay. After purchasing new ornaments and a much stronger base, we reconstructed the tree, snapping the photo of a happy Thomas to the left.

During Christmas 2021, Thomas's empty chair helped me to recognize that the primary focus of Christmas needed to be on our hope in the life, death, and resurrection of the child born in Bethlehem. I decided to reaffirm more intentionally my deep belief that Jesus was the cosmic Christ, the Word who was in the beginning with God (John 1:1) and who was the image of the invisible God, the firstborn of all creation (Colossians

1:15), the infant Immanuel, God with us, born of a virgin (Isaiah 7:14; Matthew 1:23).

But at the same time, I continued to recognize that a significant part of my reality and identity died along with Thomas. I was struggling to find new life after the death of my son, something that I desperately needed but deeply resisted, as evidenced in multiple dreams I recorded and analyzed in the weeks after Thomas died. One of these dreams came to me on September 20, 2021. When I first recorded it, I had a profound inner resistance to accepting the dream's images—a stubborn spurning that emerged from the depths of my soul that I could no sooner stop than I could choose not to sweat if I was in Houston when it was 105 degrees with 95 percent humidity. That inner recalcitrance was an impasse that could not move as I recounted the dream:

> I was walking through a shopping mall. Thomas had already died, but I had an image of him in my heart and mind, a picture, like the one on his memorial site with him wearing the Hawaiian shirt that I bought him in Kona. Walking with me was a two-year-old boy I didn't recognize. It felt like he was like my son, and he was someone who was new in my life, but he wasn't a "replacement" for Thomas, because no one could ever take his place. As the little boy and I walked through the mall, we passed hundreds of people who seemed like they knew me and the situation I was in about Thomas's death. They were rejoicing with me that I had someone new in my life, although they, too, understood completely (without saying anything) that this new life could never "replace" my one and only son. I was deeply connected to this new little boy. I loved him and was deeply proud of him. I was proud to be with him, to have him in my life, and to be his dad. Yet even these deeply positive emotions still left a bittersweet sense of having actually lost Thomas, my only begotten son.

As far back as October, I knew I wasn't lost. I was still on the right path, and God was with me and was leading me through the process of accepting and ultimately embracing Thomas's death as a reality in my life. I also knew that the deep emotions connected with the collective images of the inner mall of my psyche (i.e., the hundreds of people) who were rejoicing with me along the Inner Labyrinth of the dream conveyed a poignant sense of truth that I could not deny. But at the same time, the thought of the grieving me who was walking along the Outer Labyrinth of waking life actually rejoicing about finding this new life so soon after the death of my son repulsed me to the depth of my soul.

The word rejoice is a strong biblical word that has special meaning at Christmas time. It appears hundreds of times throughout the Old and New Testaments.[13] During the holiday season, we rejoice because Jesus's birth brings hope for humanity and for the world. We rejoice because He is the true light that came into the darkness of our fallen world. We rejoice because God has provided the sacrificial remedy for sin. We rejoice because our rebirth is made possible when He is born within us. We rejoice because the Word, who became flesh and dwelt among us, is the underlying reason and meaning of all human history.

On Christmas Day, 2021, I was utterly amazed that God, working through my unconscious in this dream, used that same word to create an inner image of an unconscious rejoicing me—a symbol of healing, transformation, and the new inner life that I desperately needed—who was diametrically opposed to my conscious mindset and emotions of the grieving me, who resisted this vision for new life out of a sense of loyalty, loss, love, and commitment to my son.

One of Carl Jung's foundational principles about the unconscious and dream interpretation is that our dreams have a compensatory function where they reveal the "other side of the story" of who we really are, how we actually behave, what we really want, and why we actually want it.[14] For more than forty-one years, I have seen a preponderance of empirical evidence indicating that God uses symbols of transformation, and the twists and turns along the Inner Labyrinth of our unconscious world through dreams, as a compensatory perspective for the twists and turns along the Outer Labyrinth of our everyday life, with both happening together at the same time. This is how He keeps His covenant with us and accomplishes His sovereign will as the God of the entire universe, so that no purpose of His can be thwarted (Job 42:2).

We see this compensatory function as a key element of the Christmas story recorded in the Bible, where God accomplishes His sovereign will along the Inner Labyrinth of the unconscious through Joseph's dream about taking Mary as his wife. We can see it in the Outer Labyrinth of the magi coming from the East following a star to see a child born in a stable, and along the Inner Labyrinth of God warning those same magi in a dream to return home without revisiting Herod. We can see it along the Inner Labyrinth of God appearing to Joseph in a dream warning him to take Jesus and Mary to Egypt, and in the Outer Labyrinth of Joseph obeying God. We can see it along the Inner Labyrinth of God speaking to Joseph in a dream to tell him that Herod was dead and he should return to Israel, and along the Outer Labyrinth of Joseph obeying God by returning to take up residence in Nazareth, all of which ensured His plan of salvation would prevail.

I've come to see that the Bible, especially the words of Jesus, also has a compensatory function. As the writer of Hebrews tells us, "The word of God is quick and powerful, sharper than any two-edged sword, piercing even to the dividing asunder of soul and spirit . . . and is a discerner of the thoughts and intents of the heart" (Hebrews 4:12 [KJV]). In addition, God's kingdom can reign in our unconscious, where the Holy Spirit and a deep knowledge of the Bible can sanctify our unconscious dream content. There, the Holy Spirit can serve as an inner messenger leading us to become the people we were destined to be in His sovereign will, a sanctification process that Jung called the individuation process. As the psalmist tells us, hiding God's word in our hearts helps to sanctify and direct the deepest and most unconscious elements of our psyche, something to which the messages and symbols of transformation in our dreams bear witness (Psalm 119:11).

So, on the one hand, the grieving me along the Outer Labyrinth rejected the possibility of rejoicing about having a new inner son, that is, about having a new life after Thomas's death. On the other hand, I could not deny that the compensatory image of the rejoicing me in the dream along the Inner Labyrinth revealed a deep desire of my heart to move past the glacial pace of the grieving process for Thomas. I recognized that the Holy Spirit was prompting, motivating, and leading me to reconcile the two opposing perspectives of the unconscious rejoicing me and the conscious grieving me into a third perspective, a wholistic rejoicing-grieving me who would accept and ultimately embrace the reality of finding new life after the death of my son.

FINDING NEW LIFE AFTER THE DEATH OF MY SON

◇ ◇ ◇

On Christmas Day, 2021, the grieving me sat with Elin looking at our Christmas tree, under which we placed assembled LEGO sets, a guitar, and other gifts we previously gave Thomas, along with some of the gifts Thomas had previously given us. As I looked, I intentionally brought the dream images and emotions of the rejoicing me with my new "inner son" back into my conscious awareness while trying to accept the good work of healing and transformation that God had been doing deep within me. But at the same time, the grieving me was still struggling to accept the tragic death of my son, to see this painful loss as a part of the destiny I've been called to live, and to trust that God would use this tragedy for good in my life and the lives of others.

The last part of the new "little boy" dream presents an emotional image of reconciling the opposing perspectives into third something—a transformed rejoicing-grieving me who felt a deep connection and immense pride in the new little boy while at the same time still suffering from the deep grief and pain of losing Thomas. It was a bittersweet foretaste of the person I would become. On that Christmas Day, I struggled to accept and ultimately embrace the eternal spiritual process of finding the new life that Jesus—the cosmic Christ and infant Immanuel—has promised not only Thomas, Elin, and me but also the entire world.

As I look back at myself on that Christmas Day, just thirty-four weeks after Thomas had died, and the person who is writing this memoir today, I am reminded that we see things differently when we see them from a distance. The experience of seeing a fluffy white cloud painted against the bright blue Colorado sky is markedly different than the perspective from within the cloud. What I knew and believed about Thomas's life and death on Christmas Day 2021, that inner state of mind I was in, is so markedly different than the person I am today. It's almost like it happened to someone else.

Being inside the cloud of yesterday's experience is like watching the first segment of season one of the series *The Chosen*, which recounts the story of the life, death, and resurrection of Jesus. Each segment of *The Chosen* has a narrative arc that takes the viewer from the beginning, through the middle, and to the end of its story. The viewer becomes drawn into an inside-out connection to the action and interaction of the characters within the biblical historical setting—an experience that creates a dialectic cycle of transformation, like the one I experienced where God, working through the unconscious, was reconciling the two perspectives of the unconscious rejoicing me and the conscious grieving me into a third something, a wholistic rejoicing-grieving me as part of the overall individuation process.[15] Now, imagine having watched the final segment of the fourth season of *The Chosen*, thirty-one cycles of transformation later, and then backing up and reflecting on the overall perspective and meaning that emerges from the combinatorial complexity of the individual segments of the series, revealing a richer story of Jesus's life, teachings, death, and resurrection. As the saying goes, the whole is greater than the sum of the parts.

From the perch of today's perspective, I look back to Christmas Day 2021, then further back in space-time to my membership testimony in 2010, and even further back to 1964 when I was eleven years old and being confirmed at the Hungarian Reformed Church where I had my first personal experience with God's presence and calling on my life. And in all these events, I see a lifelong process of transformation. I echo what the nineteenth-century philosopher Soren Kierkegaard taught us about the existential now, the historical then, and the potentiality of my future: "Life can only be understood backwards; but it must be lived forwards."[16]

CHAPTER 8

FIRST NEW YEAR: I'M MARKED FOR LIFE

January 1, 2022 (34 Weeks and 6 Days After)

I don't usually make New Year's resolutions, but 2022 was different. Thomas's death reaffirmed my conviction that life is a currency that we spend one day at a time. Most of us live on autopilot, drifting through the pedestrian realities of life, pulled by the swift currents of time. We look back on the weeks, months, and years that pass and wonder where it all went. Wisely spending our precious life currency requires us to live in the moment and to see others (and ourselves) as people who have a story and are creating a destiny we could become involved in, like the Good Samaritan who helped a man who had been beaten, robbed, and left for dead on the road to Jericho (Luke 10:25–37).

The story of how I got my first tattoo at sixty-eight is an example of how I tried to see my son, Thomas, as a person who had a story and was creating a destiny I became involved in as his father. What I question is how successful I was at staying off autopilot, how well I lived in the moment, how wisely I spent my precious life currency. What I know is how deeply I wish Thomas and I could do it all again, and again, and again. A rearview mirror perspective on life is always twenty-twenty, hence, my New Year's resolution.

◊ ◊ ◊

Since Thomas's last years were lived out in California, and since he had many friends there, we held a third funeral on October 2, 2021, at the Lutheran Church of Los Gatos, where Thomas was an active member of the youth program and participated in some of its ministries. Much like the Ryssby funeral, the service was packed full of family, friends, and colleagues, despite the ongoing pandemic.

Mark's 8123 tattoo with Thomas's name added

Just prior to the funeral, Elin and I decided to put our house in California up for sale with plans to move back home to Colorado. After we signed the necessary papers, I told the real estate agent we didn't want our house listed until October 3, 2021, the day after Thomas's memorial service at the Lutheran Church of Los Gatos. He gladly agreed. Our first step was to have pictures taken for the listing as soon as possible. I knew exactly what that meant. I'd have to go through Thomas's room. It was still untouched, frozen in time, with everything exactly where it was on the day he died.

We started the painful process several days after signing the listing papers. Dozens of colorful posters of his favorite bands covered every wall, and his clothes and college textbooks, guitars, and longboard were scattered all around the room. Elin used a wide-angle lens to take a panoramic photograph of everything exactly where it was, ceiling to floor. I wanted to remember my son's personal space, his private sanctuary, the self-designed theater of his room, exactly the way it was when he was still alive.

I approached sorting through his possessions with a sense of reverence, contemplating Thomas and his short life. I talked to him the whole time.

"Here's the LEGO set that you got for Christmas in 2014, son. You put it together without reading the instructions. You brought it with you from Colorado intact, and I'll make sure it doesn't get damaged when we move to our new house back home."

"Here's your high school diploma, Thomas. I know how much you hated high school, but you made it through and got accepted to all three of the colleges you applied to."

As I picked up each item that once belonged to him, I treated it with the same respect, sensitivity, and thoughtfulness that I treated Thomas with when he was alive. Initially, Elin and I tried to define a set of criteria for what we should keep, but in the end, I kept everything. I boxed up his sheets and pillowcases, clothes, and shoes without washing them, because five months after his death, they still smelled like him.

On the top of Thomas's desk was the business card of a local tattoo artist named Bill who gave Thomas his one and only tattoo. I picked up the card, looked at it, and then set it on my desk in my office. I didn't think much about the story behind the card. As I stood in my son's room, looking more carefully at each band poster, I noticed some had the actual concert tickets attached. I reflected on the fact that each poster and each ticket had a story behind it, stories that, over time, became part of the life Thomas and I created together as father and son.

◊ ◊ ◊

In the summer of 2017, Thomas came into my office and asked me to take him to a concert on November 24. I asked who the band was. My fifteen-year-old son told me the group's name and then added that they were his favorite band. I'd never heard of them, but that was true for most of the concerts I took him to see.

"Okay . . . where is it?" I asked.

"Los Angeles . . ." he responded, looking at me and waiting quietly for what he thought would probably be a negative response. I turned to my computer, looked at my Outlook calendar, and saw that I had that weekend free.

"Well, we could make a road trip out of it."

Thomas was thrilled.

I blocked off the entire weekend on my calendar and began planning the trip.

We left early on the morning of November 24 and drove the 370 miles straight to the House of Blues in Anaheim just outside Disneyland. We got there early and had a snack at a cafe just across the courtyard from the concert hall so we could decide when to get in line. As we sat there, I asked Thomas what the name of the band was again; he said it was the Maine. When we got into the venue, I found a table at which to sit at the very back of the concert hall. Thomas and I chatted for a few more minutes, and then he went up to the mosh pit just in front of the stage. I ended up talking to (i.e., shouting in the ear of) one of the security people named Dennis, who was closer to my age. I didn't understand a single word the band sang, but Thomas knew them all by heart and was having a great time, which made me happy.

I had us booked into the Hotel California on the beach in Santa Monica, so after the concert, we checked in and then went for a late dinner at a restaurant on the Santa Monica Pier. After seeing a few of the sights on the pier, Thomas and I walked on the beach in front of the hotel in the dark before collapsing in our room after a very long day.

The next morning after breakfast, we headed to Malibu Beach with our beach towels and hung out on the sand, enjoying the warm Southern California sun. We walked along the shore and chatted. We were amazed at the size of the mansions that were perched on the surrounding hills, wondering which movie stars or celebrities might live there. After Thomas and I had lunch at Duke's, an upscale restaurant on the water in Malibu, we went to Hollywood's Walk of Fame, gazing at the hundreds of five-pointed terrazzo and brass stars embedded in the sidewalk along Hollywood

Boulevard. Since Thomas was already thinking about which colleges to apply to and had mentioned UCLA as one of them, we went to the UCLA campus, strolled through some of the main outdoor areas, and explored a few open buildings to give him an idea of what it would be like to go to school there.

◊ ◊ ◊

By September 28, 2021, I had finished going through Thomas's room in preparation for the listing photos and packed all his possessions. I was back to work in my home office just down the hall from Thomas's room. The tattoo artist's business card kept floating in and out of my mind over the course of my workday. I glanced at the card, then at my computer terminal, and then back at the card again before I finally picked it up and looked at it more carefully. I saw that the tattoo shop was right in town. When I Googled the shop and clicked on the homepage link, I noticed the lower left-hand side of the page said, "Tattoos for life. Jesus for eternity." There was a story behind that business card, and the foggy, half-forgotten memories associated with it were pressing on me from within, trying to get my attention and remind me about an interaction Thomas and I had about a year before he died.

◊ ◊ ◊

In the summer of 2020, Thomas came into my office and said he wanted to get a tattoo. I asked him to describe the image of the tattoo, and he said it was four numbers in a circle that were related to his favorite band. At the time, I didn't connect the words "favorite band" to the Maine concert I'd taken him to in Los Angeles three years earlier. I asked him what the numbers meant, and he said they were the address of a parking garage where the band members hung out when they were teenagers.

I had always told Thomas not to get a tattoo because they're permanent. "Get an earring," I would say, "that way if you don't like it after a while, you can take it out." But I could tell this tattoo meant a lot to him, so I told him to go for it. A few hours later, Thomas returned home, pulled back the upper left sleeve of his T-shirt, and proudly showed me his new tattoo. It consisted of the number 8123, stacked in the center of a circle.

I congratulated him and asked if getting it was painful. "A little," was his response, and then he went back to his room, totally pleased with himself. I went back to work.

◊ ◊ ◊

Back on September 28, 2021, just twenty-one weeks after finding Thomas dead in his room, I Googled the number 8123. I had one of those aha moments when I realized this numeric symbol was connected to the Maine and our weekend trip. I also learned the story behind his tattoo, a window into why it was so important to my son. According to one of the band's fan sites, 8123 was the name given to the collective of the band's fans, a diverse group of passionate dreamers called to encourage one another in following their artistic dreams and life goals. 8123 was a family, one that intentionally supported one another in success and failure as they personally pursued who they truly were.

It was there that I saw my son. I encountered Thomas's story and the destiny he was trying to create, and I was part of it. I recognized why 8123 was something Thomas deeply identified with—so deeply, in fact, that he tattooed that numeric symbol to his body. The meaning of 8123 was also consistent with the encouragement I frequently gave him about identifying and exploring his passions, talents, and desires, be it music or drawing, poetry, or his growing interest in studying ancient religions.

As I sat in my office, I suddenly remembered that three months earlier we had received a UPS package of "merch" from some band that was addressed to Thomas. When the package arrived, Elin and I were surprised and deeply grieved to receive something Thomas had ordered while he was still alive. It was a poignant reminder of the reality that our son was dead. Elin and I opened the package and found a newly released vinyl album along with a T-shirt, poster, and pair of brightly colored socks, all branded with the album's cover art.

I didn't pay specific attention to the contents of the box back in July; I just shook my head in sorrow and placed the package on Thomas's bed. But now, with the unfolding stories of 8123, Thomas's tattoo, and the Maine concert we attended together, I walked back into his room and reopened the box. Sure enough, there was the newly released album by the Maine entitled *XOXO: From Love and Anxiety in Real Time*, plus other band-related merch that Thomas had preordered and was anxiously waiting for.

In that moment, I realized again just how deeply Thomas had marked me for life and how much I missed him. I felt compelled, even driven, to have an outward sign of my inner experience of the impact that his life had on my life. So, I called Bill the tattoo guy and arranged for him to tattoo the number 8123 on me the day before Thomas's memorial service.

As I stood the next day in the Lutheran Church of Los Gatos, its sanctuary packed full with family, friends, and colleagues despite the ongoing pandemic, delivering a eulogy for my son, I felt a private and unspoken sense of contentment knowing my body was permanently marked with the same symbol Thomas had chosen, slightly modified to include his name across the top, because all sociocultural collectives like the 8123 family are composed of individual people who have names, who have stories, and who are creating a destiny.

The sudden and tragic death of my son, Thomas, has reaffirmed my experience and conviction that life is a currency we spend one day at a time. So, I have resolved to stay present in the moment with the key people in my life, refusing to live on autopilot, and to fight the natural tendency to be carried through the pedestrian realities of life by the swift currents of time. Rather, I want to spend the precious life currency I have left in this world wisely, seeing others as people who have a story and are creating a destiny I can become involved in, like a Good Samaritan.

Mark at the arraignment on January 25, 2022,
holding The Unspeakable Loss

CHAPTER 9

THE ARRAIGNMENT AND FORGIVENESS

January 28, 2022 (38 Weeks and 5 Days After)

The trauma of finding Thomas dead in his room threw Elin and me into a daze—a psychological and emotional fog where all we could manage on a day-to-day basis was to put one foot in front of the other. When the paperwork came from our health insurance company, the diagnosis that Elin's grief psychologist submitted for the claim was post-traumatic stress disorder. During those first few months, I wondered if I would even survive the death of my son. It wasn't until nearly half a year after that tragic day when I finally felt a very faint inkling that *I had made it* to the other side of some inner milestone that I understood tacitly but could not yet articulate. It was my first realization that I really had survived Thomas's death.

In the early days after Thomas's death, I refused to see anyone. I walled everyone out. The first person I agreed to meet with was my pastor. Just three weeks and three days removed from Thomas's death, I was a wreck. I was angry. I was devastated. I was not in my right mind. It took another five weeks for me to agree to meet with anyone else. My friend Marshall invited me to have dinner at a little Mexican restaurant near my house. I cried a lot. I unloaded my deep anguish about this unspeakable loss. He could see my pain and desperation. I recounted how I'd talked to the police sergeant in charge of investigating Thomas's death, who told me that they had arrested the guy who sold Thomas the counterfeit Xanax pill and booked him into the county jail. I told Marshall how thoughtful and compassionate the police sergeant was, but I also lamented how slow, bureaucratic, and dysfunctional the legal process seemed, despite this officer's help. Put good people in bad systems, you get bad performance.

Marshall looked at me, paused, and then asked, "Have you ever thought about taking things into your own hands?"

"No, I haven't," I responded. I was taken aback by his question, a little shocked that he would say such a thing. Until that moment, the thought had never crossed my mind. But his question struck an inner chord that continued to resonate within me long after that night.

◊ ◊ ◊

The district attorney who was assigned to prosecute Thomas's case emailed me three days after my dinner with Marshall to set up a time to discuss the case. We met later that day on Zoom. He described the case, the steps of the legal process, and his strategy for prosecuting the case. He also explained the five felony counts the defendant would be charged with. I told him I wanted this individual prosecuted to the full extent of the law, but I could tell he was managing my expectations when he explained how the person would likely not go to jail for long or maybe even at all, depending on how the case went.

One particular issue that limited the extent to which the defendant could be charged for Thomas's death was a recent ruling from the California Supreme Court. As the district attorney informed me, a case tried by the California Supreme Court the year before Thomas's death ruled that supplying a controlled substance to someone who subsequently suffers injury from its use is not sufficient proof that the person providing the substance intended to inflict great bodily harm. This particular case involved an incident where a young man unknowingly supplied fentanyl-laced cocaine to his sixteen-year-old girlfriend, which killed her mere hours later. The young man was charged with giving drugs to a minor and intent to inflict great bodily harm. However, during the initial jury trial, his defense lawyer successfully argued that because his client did not know the cocaine was laced with fentanyl, and because his girlfriend had voluntarily ingested the drugs, it could not be proven he intentionally sought to hurt her. The results of the case were later appealed to the California Supreme Court, which upheld this ruling that the defendant did not intend great bodily harm by giving her the poisoned cocaine.

According to the district attorney, this precedent explained why the felonies his office could charge the defendant with in Thomas's case were limited to possession and narcotics sales. Because the defendant claimed he did not deliberately try to poison Thomas and did not know the Xanax he sold Thomas contained fentanyl, it would be nearly impossible to charge him with intent to cause great bodily harm. This would be something Elin and I would continue to struggle with, as did many of our friends and family members, who did not understand why the defendant was not being charged for murder or even involuntary manslaughter.

Before he ended our meeting, the district attorney also let me know he was about to be appointed as a judge and would not personally be able to take our case. However, he was handing the case over to James, one of his most competent deputy attorneys.

Both the outgoing district attorney and James, the attorney who would be taking our case, attended Thomas's October memorial service in Los Gatos. After the service, the district attorney informed us the suspect had gotten out of jail on bail within a day of being arrested and they would contact me with more details about his rearrest. I thought, *So, the guy who killed my son had been out and about, free, for the last five months.* Two weeks later, Elin and I were contacted by James, who said the judge signed a warrant for the defendant's rearrest and he would be arraigned on all five felony charges. He also requested to meet with us sometime the following week.

When James met with Elin and me at our home, he told us the next step would be to issue the warrant for the defendant's rearrest and then schedule a court date for an arraignment where the defendant would be formally charged for the crimes. James said Elin and I could attend the arraignment, but we would not be allowed to speak. I told him I wanted to be present at every court appearance to confront this guy and let the judge know Thomas's death was not just a number on a court docket. This case was about the untimely end of a human life, the life of my only son. James said many victims and their families do not attend these court dates, but he wished more did. I told him I wouldn't miss one for the world, and I meant it.

Before he left our house, I asked him why the legal process was moving so slowly and why they hadn't already rearrested this guy. It had been five months since Thomas died. What were they waiting for? He explained there had been some type of mix-up between the sergeant investigating Thomas's case and the lieutenant who he reported to but the confusion had been cleared up. I told him I wanted this person rearrested as soon as possible and, again, insisted James prosecute him to the full extent of the law. He agreed but also said the bar for successfully prosecuting this type of crime had been raised very high by a recent decision, alluding to the recent California Supreme Court ruling. I listened patiently as he spoke, but I sensed in my heart he was also managing my expectations that the consequences the defendant would receive likely would be incommensurate with the enormous loss of Thomas's life.

That night, James emailed me a copy of the charges against the guy who sold Thomas the counterfeit Xanax pill so I could know the person's name, age, and address. I'll call him "Adam" rather than use his real name. I searched his name and address online and learned he lived just a few miles away. As I looked at the street view of his house on Google Maps and reflected on the minimal consequences he would likely receive, Marshall's words that I might need to take things into my own hands floated back into my mind.

On November 3, James sent me an email saying the detective assigned to locate Adam at his address had discovered he was no longer living there, which, he added, was not uncommon. Four weeks later, James finally emailed me with an update—Adam turned himself in on the warrant and immediately bailed out. The arraignment date was set for January 25, 2022, at the Santa Clara County Hall of Justice.

◊ ◊ ◊

I tried to put the arraignment out of my mind, as January seemed a long way off. In the weeks before the arraignment, I checked in with James several times for any updates or new details with the case. Through these correspondences, James confirmed Adam would likely be released after the arraignment, since the court probably would not deem him to be a substantial risk to the community, something which thoroughly grieved me. James also informed me the courthouse was limiting in-person attendance of hearings to only necessary parties due to the pandemic. Noting that the arraignment courtroom was in a windowless basement room with poor air circulation, James continued to play down the advantages of attending in-person, especially since he was going to be out of town for it and his replacement would be attending remotely. In fact, James said even Adam might not be there in person.

FINDING NEW LIFE AFTER THE DEATH OF MY SON

I decided that even if the judge, Elin, and I were the only people in the courtroom, I was going to be there in person for the sake of my son. I told James Elin and I would attend in person, and he asked me to write a few sentences for the judge explaining why we wanted to attend. I sent him the following explanation:

> Thomas Larson Bodnarczuk was our only child, and he died because of a counterfeit Xanax pill that was sold to him on Snapchat by the accused. We are older parents and will never have another child. With Thomas's death, we have no heir and no one to carry on our legacy in life. It is important for us to see firsthand that the judicial process in Santa Clara County will treat this matter appropriately. We need to see for ourselves that there will be consequences for what happened, and that our son's life and death have meaning. So, attending in person is very important to us.

Later that day, James emailed me the court order signed by the judge and told us to show it to the guards, who would screen us through the metal detectors as we entered the building.

I took the day of the arraignment off from work. Elin decided to work until it was time to go. The day before, Elin told me, "When I'm not deeply involved in my work as a distraction, I've got a knot in my stomach and an aching in my heart." She also asked, "Are you going to bring a book with you in case we have to wait a long time?" I brought *The Unspeakable Loss: How Do You Live after a Child Dies* by Nisha Zenoff, the same book seen in the picture at the beginning of this chapter.[17]

We got to the courthouse early not knowing what to expect. There were twenty to twenty-five people in the waiting area, but it was quiet. Most people tried not to make eye contact, and I followed suit. Many of the people in the waiting area outside the courtroom looked like tough characters, and each courtroom had a Santa Clara County deputy sheriff who was heavily armed in case there was trouble. As we sat, Elin whispered to me, "They just let these people walk in here?"

"Well, some of them are probably convicted felons, but they're out on bail." I said, dressed in the same clothes I wore for Thomas's memorial services, including the red-and-blue striped tie that belonged to my son—the one he was wearing when he made his public profession of faith. I wore it in memory of Thomas's short but impactful life. Other than the attorneys present in the waiting area, I was the only person wearing a tie.

Elin and I sat at the ends of two benches that met at a ninety-degree angle, waiting to be called into the courtroom. There was a man sitting to Elin's left at the end of her bench about four feet away. I was directly facing him but tried not to make eye contact. He was about six-foot-two, wearing a white shirt and tight jeans with no belt. He was younger than most of the other people waiting there. He glanced at his phone nervously, looking stressed. He would bury his face in his hands for a few seconds and then look back at his phone. Elin turned toward him slightly, trying to get a better look without being too obvious. As the time drew near, we got up and stood outside the courtroom, waiting for the sheriff's deputy to unlock the door and tell us to enter.

◇ ◇ ◇

We finally sat down in the second row of the courtroom. A large TV to our left displayed a man on the screen. I wondered if he was the attorney who would be handling our case that day. After seeing us enter the courtroom and sit down, he said, "Are Mark and Elin in the courtroom?"

I responded, "Yes, we're Mark and Elin."

He introduced himself and said he would debrief James on today's outcome. He continued, "If you have any questions, just call me," and gave me his phone number.

The people who had been in the waiting area outside were now seated or standing at various places in the courtroom. The guy with the white shirt sat behind us and to our right. A well-dressed public defender standing near the courtroom entrance started loudly calling out various names to come see her. Elin turned toward the back of the room and looked at the guy with the white shirt before whispering to me, "I think that's him . . . I thought that might be him when we were sitting in the waiting area."

Once the judge entered the courtroom, we watched as several other defendants were each called to the stand to have their charges read. Their attorney would then talk back and forth with the judge until a new court date was established. Finally, the public defender turned and looked at the guy in the white shirt as if to say, *Are you ready?* As he walked toward the stand, the court clerk called out his name—Adam. We then knew for sure it was him. Tears began to flow from Elin's eyes. She was visibly yet quietly distressed to the point where the sheriff's deputy standing twenty feet away took note, walked over, and handed Elin a box of tissues.

We heard the charges against Adam read aloud, and after the public defender spoke with the judge, the clerk called out a date, time, and location for the follow-up part of the trial. The judge asked the defendant if that day and time worked for him. He said yes, and then the public defender moved onto the next case as Elin sobbed and held my hand tightly. From the TV screen, our representative from the district attorney's office interrupted loudly and said, "Your Honor, the victim's parents are here in the courtroom, and I want to make sure that the date and time works for them." The courtroom got quiet. You could've heard a pin drop. Then, I spoke up, boldly saying, "Yes, Your Honor. That will work for us."

All eyes were focused on Elin and me. We were sitting fifteen feet away from the guy who killed our son. Adam had his back to us but now knew who we were too. The circle was complete. Elin continued to cry as the judge read the final orders. Then Adam turned and slowly walked toward the door that led out of the courtroom, his head looking straight down at the floor to avoid eye contact with everyone, especially us.

Elin was shaken up. I whispered to her, "Let's wait a few minutes until he leaves the building, and then we'll leave." We sat there in a mental fog, blown away by what was happening. After about five minutes, I said, "Okay, let's go." It was uncomfortable sitting there, and it was uncomfortable leaving. The unspeakable loss of our son had been a relatively private thing, shared only with family and friends in his services and on his memorial site. Now, his death had become a very public thing in a room full of strangers we didn't know, in a public court of law.

We walked out of the courtroom and into the waiting area. We turned to the right only to find Adam standing against the wall, waiting for us. This was not what we expected. He looked up at me. I locked eyes with him and stared directly and intently down into his soul. We began to walk past him slowly. I thought, *You're the guy who killed Thomas*, as I took another step and continued to stare him down.

Just as Elin and I were about to pass him, he stepped toward us and said, "I'm so sorry . . ." as he began to cry. "I had no idea."

I stopped. I turned toward him in silence as he continued to cry and waited for my response. I looked at him and said, "I'm Thomas's father, Mark, and this is Thomas's mother, Elin," as Elin moved closer to my side, still crying.

"I haven't been able to sleep since it happened," he said, crying even harder. "I'd do anything to take it back . . . to do it over. . . . I'm so, so sorry for the heartache I caused you."

That was a divinely appointed moment of truth for me. I had known for some time that hating this young man and seeking revenge would not bring Thomas back. Adam had a lot of courage and integrity to wait for us. I took a step toward him and reached out my right hand to shake his. He took my hand in his and wrapped his left arm around my shoulder and back, clutching the fabric of my sport jacket tightly as he pulled me toward him and sobbed into my neck. By this time, I was crying too. I said to him, "Adam, that was my only son . . . my only child."

"I had no idea that the pills could be fentanyl," Adam sobbed. "That's not what I was told. I haven't touched that stuff since. I know I can never make things right, but I'm so sorry. I'd do anything to make it up to you."

"I forgive you." I felt the words flow from the bottom of my heart as we continued to hug and weep. "I forgive you . . . being angry and vengeful will not bring Thomas back." Then Elin reached out, hugged him, and said, "I forgive you too."

Elin, Adam, and I started walking toward the elevator together and then stopped. As Adam continued to cry, he pulled out his phone and said, "Give me your phone number." After he sent me a text, Adam announced, "If there's ever anything that I can ever do for you, just tell me and I will."

As we parted, Elin said, "God bless you."

"God bless you too," Adam responded.

◊ ◊ ◊

It was a tragedy to lose our son, but it was also a tragedy for this young man to have done something unintentionally that he'll regret for the rest of his life. As Elin and I walked back to our car, we shook our heads in amazement at what had just happened to us. We felt a deep sense of peace, contentment, and God's presence knowing we did the right thing. Later, Elin said to me, "Mark, you took leadership in doing a most difficult and Christian act of forgiving this young man. I hope he can recover and straighten out his life."

I called James that night and told him what had happened. He said he was glad there had been some resolution between us. He added that Adam had been remorseful about what had happened to Thomas from the very beginning, something we already knew from the police sergeant in charge of investigating Thomas's death. James also said he would call Adam's attorney and let her know what happened.

"Don't respond to his text," he advised, "or have any contact with him until the trial and sentencing are complete," something Elin and I had already decided.

It was a life-changing experience for Elin and me. It was something we never in a million years would have expected. Since that time, I've continued to reflect on what happened, and I have asked the Lord to show me what, if anything, He would have me do next. In any case, Adam will remain in my thoughts and prayers.

Mark at the plea hearing on March 15, 2022, holding Forgive For Good

CHAPTER 10

THE PLEA AND FORGIVENESS

April 15, 2022 (49 Weeks and 5 Days After)

In death as in life, Thomas continues to have an enormous impact on my journey along the Outer Labyrinth of day-to-day life and the Inner Labyrinth of my deep unconscious. In the days, weeks, and months since he died, my journey of grief has led me back through many of the weaknesses I've faced over the course of my life. Having grown up in a clinically dysfunctional family with a father who was mentally ill, heavily medicated, and physically and emotionally abusive for most of his life, one of the most difficult issues I've had to face has been learning to forgive people who have hurt me.

Back in 2007 when Thomas, Elin, and I moved back to the front range of Colorado from our home in the mountains, I read about Fred Luskin's work with the Stanford Forgiveness Project. The cover for his book *Forgive for Good* claimed things like, "Holding a grudge is hazardous to your health."[18] Luskin argued that forgiveness was "a proven prescription for health and happiness." I bought six or seven other books on the topic with titles like *The Power of Forgiving*, *Exploring Forgiveness*, and *Forgiveness: Theory, Research, and Practice*, all of which were written by clinical psychologists and researchers from prominent universities. I added them to my library with the goal of delving into this intriguing (and personally troubling) issue, but I never got back to it.

Fast forward to the arraignment on January 25, 2022. Elin and I forgave Adam for being the conduit through which Thomas's life was tragically ended with a counterfeit pill containing fentanyl. Never would I have predicted that experience of grace and forgiveness. In the days following the arraignment, I was working in my home office when I happened to glance to my left and saw the books on forgiveness gathering dust on my shelf. As I thumbed through Luskin's book, I was confronted with a deep and troubling paradox—how could I forgive Adam for killing my son, Thomas, and yet struggle to forgive others who have hurt me? I started reading *Forgive for Good*, and because I was now working at Stanford University, I decided to contact Fred Luskin through his university email address. I sent a quick email and then moved on to other things.[19]

<> <> <>

As I continued reading *Forgive for Good*, I tried to put the upcoming court date out of my mind. I was captivated by what I read, but I also experienced a deep sense of psychological resistance to the first few pages.

First, Luskin claims that people tend to take real or perceived offenses against them too personally.[20] They see the hurt or offense subjectively as something unique that happened to them. But they fail to factor in the objective perspective that many of the hurts and offenses that we suffer are common and happen to millions of other people. Moreover, people also tend to assume that those who caused the hurt did so intentionally, dismissing the unintended consequences that result from miscommunication, blind spots, personality types, or being under stress.

Second, Luskin states that people tend to blame others for how they feel and expect others to "do" something to right the wrong that was done, like an apology.[21] Blaming others for how we feel breeds either a sense of dependency on them doing something for us or a sense of vengeance where we take things into our own hands and try to right the wrong. Both options have serious consequences that anchor us to our past hurt, and this in turn prevents us from moving on in life.

Third, Luskin observes that people create a grievance story that they tell others and themselves repeatedly.[22] Over time, the grievance story becomes a self-fulfilling prophecy that shapes and defines their lives. This is because people are what they do; we become our choices.

Finally, Luskin argues that when we obsess over an offense that happened in the past, we rent too much "psychological space" to that grievance. To put it in my words, we experience an inappropriate level of "psychological energy" around the person or situation. We don't just have thoughts or emotions about what happened; those energy-packed thoughts and emotions have us and derail our normal decision-making process. As described in Romans 7:14–25, we "know" we shouldn't be angry, resentful, or vengeful toward the person or situation, but powerful emotions shape or define our choices, against our conscious desires and will. So, too, forgiveness doesn't mean we shouldn't have anger about the person or situation, but rather the anger shouldn't have us. Forgiveness does not mean that what the other person did wasn't wrong, cruel, or even unthinkable. Rather, forgiveness means it's not our job to punish them. Nor does forgiveness require us to reconcile with the person. Rather, as the apostle Paul tells us, "If it is possible, as far as it depends on you, live at peace with everyone. Do not take revenge, my dear friends, but leave room for God's wrath, for it is written: 'It is mine to avenge; I will repay,' says the Lord" (Romans 12:18–19 [NIV]).

By this point in reading, my initial resistance to Luskin gave way to an enormous, paradigm-shifting sense of inner healing and transformation. It was as if the psychological truths Luskin described, like a precise diagnostic arrow, hit some intuitively obvious inner mark that I couldn't articulate but knew was true. I found myself mapping what he said to the principles of personal growth I'd been using for the last forty-two years. Not only was his view consistent with mine, but it also helped me to see the issues and challenges I faced with forgiving others from a very different and eye-opening perspective. The principles, practices, and examples he gave had the quiet ping of truth about them. They described my own experiences along the Outer Labyrinth of everyday life in hurtful interactions with others and the grievance stories I'd crafted and maintained over the years.

There was also something very fundamental about what I read that connected deep down into the unconscious world of the Inner Labyrinth—profound images, emotions, and stories I'd recorded and analyzed in my dreams over the years but had remained a mystery. As John Sanford argues, dreams are God's forgotten language.[23] We see, experience, and can later describe the images, emotions, and stories in our dreams, but it's difficult to understand what they really mean. In many ways, dreams are like parables that test our openness to and desire for the truth about ourselves, others, and God. As Jesus said, "This is why I speak to them in parables: Though seeing, they do not see; though hearing, they do not hear or understand" (Matthew 13:13). There was something about Luskin's work on forgiveness that began to pull back an inner veil that had obscured these inner mysteries.[24]

◊ ◊ ◊

As the next court date drew near, Luskin's book provided enormous insights into the way forgiveness flowed so naturally and spontaneously from the depths of my heart in my encounter with Adam at the arraignment. These insights prepared me for what would come next in the protracted legal process that Elin and I were drawn into.

During this next court date, Adam had to give a formal answer to the charges against him. Known as a plea hearing, a defendant at this point in the legal process can admit to the charges by pleading guilty, deny the charges by pleading not guilty, or plead no contest and accept the conviction but not admit guilt. A plea of guilty or no contest would be followed by a subsequent court date where the defendant would be sentenced. A defendant can also be offered a plea bargain, that is, a deal where they enter a guilty plea in exchange for lowered or dropped charges or a shorter sentence.

Elin and I developed a plan before the March 15 plea hearing so we'd have no contact with the defendant—not even eye contact. A couple days before the hearing, Elin asked me, "What if he comes up to us?"

I responded, "I'll handle it. I'll simply tell him, 'Adam, we meant what we said about forgiving you, but it's not in your best interest to have contact with us until the case is over.'" I was hoping that would send the right signal and, at the same time, get Elin and me out of another very difficult and uncomfortable situation.

When March 15 finally arrived, we got to the courthouse and were ushered into a small private consultation room by James from the district attorney's office. It contained a square, government-gray table with four black chairs. James closed the door, looked at Elin and me, and empathetically asked how we were holding up before proceeding. James began by giving us an overall context of the charges he was bringing against Adam and the spectrum of possible sentences that could be imposed. By and large, he reiterated what he'd told us at our house. He was charging Adam with five felonies related to the possession, transportation, and sale of fentanyl and Xanax. He told us that the maximum sentence could be eight years and four months in prison, with the minimum being probation with no jail time.

"I believe strongly that the defendant should serve some jail time because what he did resulted in Thomas's death," James told us. "So, I'm going to present him with a plea deal that I want you to weigh in on. I'm going to propose three years in custody, with one year served in a county jail and two years served on parole while remaining in custody. But if this guy does one thing wrong during probation—drugs, a DUI, getting into a fight—I'm going to insist that he serve the entire three years in the county jail! Regardless of whether the defendant is remorseful, or whether he intended to kill Thomas, the end result is that your son is dead, and there must be a significant consequence for that."

"There also needs to be a strong admonishment that's read to him as part of the court record," I quickly added. "Now that he knows that there are counterfeit prescription pills out there like the one he sold Thomas, if he does this again, he should be tried for murder." James agreed wholeheartedly and assured Elin and me that this would be an essential part of the deal and the sentencing statement. Elin then asked if there would be any programs available to help rehabilitate Adam so he could get his life back on the right track.

"The jail will evaluate him once he arrives," James responded, "and they'll offer him a variety of treatment and counseling programs, but they can't be mandated as part of the sentence. The defendant will have to decide if he wants to participate."

Elin and I looked at each other, and then she responded, "Okay, then it's up to him."

Next, James warned us that Adam's defense attorney would push back on this proposal and argue for the minimum consequences with no jail time. "So, in the end," James predicted, "we'll probably end up in the right place."

At that moment, James arose and left the room to see where our case was on the court docket. Elin and I waited in silence for his return. I was overwhelmed by what was happening and deeply pained about the death of our son. I stared at the wall and drifted into inner emotional space. I found myself reflecting on Fred Luskin's work on forgiveness, what was happening around me today, and what had happened with Adam at the arraignment.

First, I knew Adam did not intend to kill Thomas and had been remorseful for having done so ever since he was arrested. Adam believed he was selling Thomas a prescription Xanax pill; he had no idea it contained a lethal dose of fentanyl. Although subjectively I was in enormous pain about Thomas's death, I also knew objectively that fentanyl poisoning with counterfeit prescription pills (known as fentapills) was not only common but had become an epidemic. Elin and I knew many other parents who'd lost their sons and daughters to this dark crime. So, as traumatic and painful as Thomas's death was, we knew this type of tragedy was not unique to us.

Second, I could blame Adam for the enormous sense of loss and pain I felt, and I could expect him to "do" something to right the wrong, but there was nothing he could do to bring Thomas back. Blaming Adam for how I was feeling would anchor me to the past trauma of finding Thomas dead in his room and the current reality of being forced to live life without my son. This wouldn't bring Thomas back. Blaming Adam for my feelings would also prevent me from processing my grief in an emotionally healthy way, experiencing inner healing and transformation, and finding new life after the death of my son. At the arraignment, Adam offered to do anything he could to make things right, but my forgiveness was not based on him doing anything to fix something that was unfixable. Rather, my forgiveness was given freely and unconditionally.

Third, I knew the grievance story I was currently constructing about Thomas's death and Adam's role in it would powerfully shape and define my life going forward. The story had to be a truthful reflection of what really happened, one that didn't minimize Thomas's role in causing his own death. On the one hand, Adam was deceived about the counterfeit Xanax, but he made the bad decision to illegally sell Xanax. On the other hand, Thomas made a bad choice to calm his anxiety with a Xanax pill bought illegally off Snapchat. Based on the dozens of tributes posted on his memorial site, it was clear Thomas was on the path to finding and living out the destiny he had in life and the destiny he was trying to create. But his life was cut short by a single choice to take things into his own hands and accept the risk of self-medicating in this age of counterfeit pills and fentanyl poisoning.

Luskin's writing yielded enormous insights into my forgiveness paradox. It helped me unpack my spontaneous experience of forgiveness at the arraignment and see it in a more measured, process-oriented way. As I sat there in the small private consultation room, I knew in my heart that this approach to forgiveness would become a model I could use to deal with the equally robust task of forgiving others who had hurt me previously in my life—people who did so repeatedly and were not remorseful about the pain they'd caused me.

Suddenly, James opened the door, poked his head in, and said, "Okay. I think we're set. Let's head out into the courtroom. When we get inside, find a seat near the front. I'll go talk to the defendant's attorney about the deal, and we'll see what he says. He'll probably tell me that he needs to talk to his client, so it's likely that things won't be settled today." James swung the courtroom door open and motioned for Elin and me to follow him.

◊ ◊ ◊

There were people everywhere in the courtroom. I quickly scanned the seating area, and out of the corner of my eye, I saw Adam sitting in an aisle seat about halfway toward the front of the room. There was a severely handicapped man propped up in a wheelchair in the middle of the aisle. I guided Elin around the wheelchair to the third row on the left side. Adam was four or five rows behind us and across the aisle. At the other end of the courtroom, seated high above the rest of us and wearing a black robe, was the judge.

We watched as the cases before ours appeared before the judge. Suddenly, the courtroom was filled with the pulsating, guttural sound of someone snoring! Elin leaned over and whispered to me, "That's the guy in the wheelchair." I looked over my left shoulder toward the back of the room to avoid making eye contact with Adam. Sure enough, the guy in the wheelchair was sound asleep. People in the room tacitly understood what was happening and ignored these episodic outbursts. I looked at Elin, smiled, and thought, *You just can't make this stuff up.*

When Elin and I first entered the courtroom, James approached Adam's attorney and explained he had a deal to discuss with him. They walked to the back of the courtroom, and a few minutes later, James returned and sat in the row in front of us that was reserved for attorneys. He leaned back toward Elin and me and whispered, "He wants some time to think about my deal, but what he really wants is a program. I'll explain what that means when we talk later." James continued, "When they call our case, I want you to come and stand with me at the left of the podium."

Eventually the court clerk called Adam's name, and Elin, James, and I rose and walked toward the podium. Adam's attorney also stood at the podium with his client on his right side just a few feet away from me. We all looked straight ahead at the judge.

The public defender began, "Your Honor, I call your attention to line twelve on the docket."

The judge recognized James as the prosecutor and greeted him by name, identifying him as the legal representative of the people of Santa Clara County. James thanked him and quickly added, "Your Honor, I'd like the court record to note that I'm standing here with the victim's parents."

At this point, it felt like all eyes in the courtroom turned toward Elin and me. Of all the cases that had been called since we entered the courtroom, ours was the only one where both parties were present. Everyone in the room knew what was happening and stared at us with curiosity. James informed the judge that he presented a plea bargain to the defendant, who wanted time to think about it. He requested that a follow-up plea hearing be set for May 24. The judge agreed to defer the plea, and as the court clerk entered the follow-up date into the court record, James turned to Elin and me and said, "Have a seat, and I'll be there in a minute."

I turned to my right to leave with Elin behind me. Adam, who was standing only a few feet from me, looked away so there was no chance of making eye contact. Elin and I walked back to our seats, trying to take in what had just happened as James discussed some final details with Adam's attorney.

"Let's go back to the private consultation room again," James whispered when he joined us a few minutes later.

"His attorney says he's got a new job, he's back in college, and he's trying to get his life together," James said once we'd gathered around the gray table again. "The defendant wants what's called supervised electronic confinement or home confinement." James looked at me and then at Elin to gauge our initial reaction to the proposal.

James went on to explain that home confinement was a sentencing option where a judge confines an offender to their residence for the period of the sentence as an alternative to a traditional jail sentence. This type of sentence was available only to low-risk, nonviolent offenders. For this type of sentence, the offender must abide by well-defined rules, such as curfew restrictions, random drug testing and alcohol monitoring, movement-tracking anklets, and community service with regular meetings with the offender's parole officer. Adam would be required to wear an electronic ankle bracelet and would also be responsible for paying the costs associated with a home confinement sentence, which is typically twelve to fifteen dollars a day.

Under this sentencing option, James said, Adam would be allowed to leave his residence only to go to work or attend school, travel to medical appointments, participate in counseling or psychotherapy, or any other court-approved activities. He could also be visited by family and friends, but the names of these people had to be included in the written rules governing the home confinement sentence. If the monitoring agency tracking the ankle bracelet got an alert that Adam had violated the rules of his home confinement, it would notify his parole officer. Under California law, the parole officer had the right to rearrest Adam without a warrant if that happened.

When James finished explaining these details, Elin and I just looked at each other in silence. This was James's case, not ours. We had no legal say about how Adam was prosecuted or sentenced. But James had visited Thomas's memorial website, attended his October memorial service in Los Gatos, and even came to our home so we could get to know him as a person. Now, he was looking into the eyes of two grieving parents who had lost their only son, people who did not want Thomas's death to be meaningless and without consequence. Elin and I were faced with another difficult choice, much like when we forgave Adam at the arraignment.

Elin spoke first. "We already forgave him for Thomas's death. Now, I want him to recover. I want him to learn a lesson. I want him to turn his life around and become a productive person. I don't think putting him jail will teach him a lesson or help him become a better person." Elin looked at me as if to say, *What do you think?*

I looked back at her and said to James, "What comes to mind, James, is an experience that I had forty-seven years ago when I was a student at Nazarene Bible College. One of the last requirements for graduation was that we do some type of field experience. I went to the medium security prison in Buena Vista, Colorado, to preach a sermon about God's grace and forgiveness in both the men's and women's portion of the penitentiary. When they slammed that door behind me, I was in another world. I felt a deep and profound sense of fear and vulnerability, even though I knew that in just a few hours, the guards would open that same door and I would return to my life on the outside."

I continued, now looking directly at James. "I agree with Elin that Adam needs to learn his lesson. I know this might sound silly, but I've watched the 1994 movie *Shawshank Redemption* many times. In fact, I've watched it a few times with Thomas. I can't help but wonder what kind of lessons Adam will learn in jail. I can't imagine that the lessons that those inmates will teach him will make him a better person or help him get his life back on track. They will probably ruin him rather than help him."

Seeing that Elin and I were supportive of the home confinement program, James said, "Okay. I'll follow up and verify that the defendant has a job and is going to school, and I'll get back to you with what I find. But if he violates any of the rules, I'll insist that he serve the remainder of his sentence in the county jail." James's response was empathic toward what Elin and I wanted, but it was also tempered by a deep conviction that he had a job to do. He had to keep criminals off the streets of Santa Clara County.

"I agree entirely," I quickly said, "and don't forget to include the strong admonishment in the deal. If he does this again, he should be charged with murder." James nodded his head in full agreement.

I had hardly finished speaking when Adam's attorney opened the door. He stuck his head in, looked at Elin and me, and said, "I just want to say that I'm sorry for your loss." Before we had time to respond, he quickly closed the door.

"As you know," James said following the interruption as he looked at Elin and then at me, "I've been promoted to a new assignment, but I've requested that I keep this case until it's finished. I want you to know that I've been deeply and personally affected by your case and by the death of your son, Thomas."

James continued, "I was raised as a Catholic and only nominally practice the faith, you know, mass on Christmas and Easter." He began to tear up as he spoke. "I've also been deeply impacted by you and your wife—by your faith, by the way you've handled yourself, the decisions you've made, and the people you are. Thank you for that." This big burly hulk of a man wiped a tear from his eye.

James walked us out of the building to make sure that Adam wasn't waiting for us like last time. We chatted about how Elin and I would be living in Colorado by the next court date. But we also affirmed our commitment to fly back and be present at all future court dates. As Elin and I walked back to our car along the same route we took after the arraignment, we again shook our heads in amazement at what had just happened. We felt a deep sense of peace, contentment, and God's presence knowing that we did the right thing again. Now, it would be up to Adam to straighten out his life. If he didn't, that would be between him and the Lord.

Picture of Long's Peak from the back deck of our new house

CHAPTER 11

THE JOURNEY HOME TO COLORADO WITHOUT THOMAS, BUT HE KEEPS SHOWING UP

March 12, 2022 (44 Weeks and 6 Days After)

Elin and I had been through so many ups and downs since Thomas died. Moving back to Colorado presented even more of these experiences. Colorado has always been our home, the place we love and the place Thomas loved so much. But going home without him felt like an enormous defeat that drove home the long-term reality that he was never coming back, that life must go on. At the same time, there was a sense of loss that Elin and I felt as we dismantled both the space the three of us lived in for the previous six years in California and the overall context of our life together there.

Over time, the spaces we create and live in along the Outer Labyrinth of day-to-day life become woven into the fabric of our conscious memories, identity, and reality. They become a key element of the destiny we create with our choices. But the spaces we shape and define also become integrated into our inner unconscious memories, identity, and reality along the Inner Labyrinth of our dream world—that is, the destiny we have in God from the foundation of the world. That's why dreams people have about their current house, or a house they used to live in, are so important. They are composite inner images that symbolize their outer identity and reality because their houses are where they keep their stuff, where they live their lives. But dream images of houses also symbolize our inner identity and reality in the deepest parts of our hearts and minds. As Sir Winston Churchill said, "We shape our buildings, and afterwards our buildings shape us."[25]

◊ ◊ ◊

The move to Colorado would be the second time I went through Thomas's things. Six months earlier, I took down his colorful band posters and sorted through Thomas's personal possessions as Elin and I prepared for the listing photos to be taken of our house. During that first time, I placed his things in carefully labeled moving boxes, reflecting on his short but impactful life as I stored them in his closet, hidden from the many people who would tour our house when it went on the market.

Time can be your best friend or your worst enemy. Having moved further through the grieving process in the passing months, the task of preparing for the moving van to arrive seemed easier in some ways. Thomas's physical presence seemed so much more distant. But at the same time, it felt like the dull, throbbing inner pain of facing the reality that he was gone, lost to this temporal world forever, would never go away.

When we moved to California, we consciously shaped the larger context of our new life there, and then we embedded that new reality with day-to-day, week-to-week, and month-to-month repetition. Over time, the three of us recognized deep emotional connections that emerged and what seemed like a clear path to our future. Our conscious life-shaping choices solidified into a Bodnarczuk-Larson identity and reality. Moving back to Colorado meant deconstructing the empirical remnants of our life in California as we journeyed back home without Thomas.

Over our last few weeks in California, the process of deconstructing that reality and identity was like dismembering the life that we had together with Thomas, one box at a time. One March afternoon as Elin and I were closing on our house, I went to Home Depot to buy more boxes to pack up our stuff. As I pushed the cart full of boxes, packing tape, and Bubble Wrap to the checkout counter, I found myself talking to Thomas, almost like he was walking with me.

"We're packing our stuff and leaving California, son. I'm taking your stuff too. I can't tell you how much I wish you were going with us, Thomas." I wasn't paralyzed with bone-rattling pain as I chatted with Thomas in almost a matter-of-fact way. But a few minutes later as I waited for the traffic light at the end of the parking lot, I looked across the street to the Kohl's department store where Thomas once worked. Suddenly, the inner pain and sorrow of this unspeakable loss stabbed me in the heart and penetrated down into the depths of my soul. I began to sob as the light turned green. I cried all the way home.

FINDING NEW LIFE AFTER THE DEATH OF MY SON

Elin had been having the same type of intermittent experiences, as evidenced by a dream that she had a few days previously. I've included her dream below:

> Mark and I were in my sewing room office here in Campbell, and the room looked like it did before I started packing—nice and "show ready." I was sitting at my work desk with my back to the door, and Mark was sitting facing me. I think the door was closed or mostly closed. We were talking about the move back home to Colorado and the house there. Thomas walked in from behind me without knocking, like he came in to get something. He looked as he did when he died. He was the same age with long hair. The dream ended there.

Elin had this dream in the early morning just before she woke up. As she walked into the kitchen where I was sitting, she was sobbing. So, we sat as she shared her dream with me. We realized that although we were going home to Colorado without Thomas, he kept showing up when we least expected it. We recognized his presence both along the Outer Labyrinth of day-to-day tasks like buying moving boxes and packing supplies at Home Depot and along the Inner Labyrinth of our dream world. As deeply painful as it has been when Thomas shows up like this, we are thankful and even long for these experiences, because they're empirical evidence that Thomas once lived in this world, that he continues to live in our hearts and minds, and that by faith we believe we will see him again in heaven.

As Elin and I prepared to go home to Colorado without our son to begin the next phase of our life together as a family of two, we had already begun to define the personal space and common space of our new house in Longmont, Colorado. This included a personal space belonging to Thomas, a space where some of his earthly possessions could concretize and help us remember the enormous impact that his short life has had on our lives. We also used the same three-step strategy to shape and define the larger context of our future lives together. We decided we would shape our reality, embed it with repetition, and recognize deep emotional connections as they emerged.

The picture at the beginning of this chapter is the view of the Rocky Mountain range from the back deck of our new home. It's a mountain called Long's Peak that soars to 14,259 feet above sea level. Our Colorado house also looks out upon the same lake where Thomas played in a treehouse with his friends as a little boy. The house is only seven miles from the cemetery behind Ryssby Church where we laid Thomas's remains to rest.

We know from experience that, over the next few years, the daily lives Elin and I live within the personal space and common space of our new home, and the larger context we're intentionally shaping, will continue to slip below the level of conscious awareness, go on autopilot, and solidify into a new Bodnarczuk-Larson reality and identity. We'll once again embed our initial choices through repetition by doing them and living them over and over again.

While we were excited to be going home to Colorado, we were also deeply pained and saddened to be going without Thomas. But we thanked God that Thomas kept showing up in our lives along the Outer and Inner Labyrinths. Elin and I also knew that staying in touch with Thomas's memory presence and dream presence meant staying in touch with the abiding pain and sense of loss we have without his physical presence here on earth. This pain and sense of loss continues to morph and soften over time, but they will never go away. What we fear most is the alternative—the deafening silence of Thomas not showing up in our lives going forward.

CHAPTER 12

REFLECTIONS ON THE FIRST YEAR

May 2, 2022 (52 Weeks and 1 Day After)

Our family headstone in the Ryssby Cemetery sits above the place where Elin and I laid Thomas's remains to rest on August 28, 2021. In the first days after he died, I desperately sought to preserve his memory so his brief but impactful life would not be forgotten in the relentless march of time. My goal was to gather as much information as I could about Thomas's life in a central place with his online memorial site so family, friends, and people who didn't know Thomas could learn about his life and come together as an online community to honor his memory.

    I contacted everyone I could and asked them to go to the memorial site and post something. For people who knew Thomas, I asked that they read the main page, reflect on their interactions with him, and contribute their own stories about Thomas. The email I sent them said, "Your memories of my son are all memories that Elin and I do not have because we weren't there. If you don't write them down, they will die with Thomas and you." For people who did not know Thomas, my email asked them to read about his life and then post a few words as a tribute to Thomas. Since we started the website, hundreds of people have helped to create an historical repository of his life that is priceless to Elin and me.

    I used my posts on the memorial site to express and process my grief about my son's death. These posts have also become a historical record of the details of our grief journey in the form of snapshots in time. But there were times when the grief and pain were so deep, so intense, so overwhelming that I wondered if I would survive the death of my son. I fearlessly sought after and even demanded answers to this nagging question.

    The bad news was that Thomas's sudden and tragic death pulled me down into a personal hell that is difficult, if not impossible, for a person who has never lost a child to understand. The good news is I did not return from that hell empty-handed, as evidenced by the enormous sense

The reality of Thomas's death evidenced on our family tombstone

of inner healing and transformation I've experienced during the first year following his death.

I survived this tragedy because of the myriad experiences, interactions, challenges, insights, and memories that happened in the wake of Thomas's death. These were behind-the-scenes details about the ongoing impact of Thomas's life and death that only Elin and I experienced. Much like my advice to others about the memorial site, unless we write these personal memories down, they will die with us. Many people have told me that our experiences with Thomas's death have resonated with something deep within them. That's because each of us has our own story about difficult times, pain, and grief. Like Carl Rogers said, when we think of something that is so personal, so deep inside that we'd rather die than admit it to others, that very thought or feeling is often most universal.[26]

By writing about my process of transitioning from our old reality and identity as a family of three to our new reality and identity as a family of two, I hope those who read this and who have experienced immense loss may come to realize you are not alone in your grief and pain. There is a way forward, a journey we can travel together. As the character of C. S. Lewis so wisely says in the movie *Shadowlands*, "We read to know we're not alone."[27]

◇ ◇ ◇

I went to get Thomas from his bedroom at about 9:55 a.m. on May 2, 2021, for our online Sunday church service. I knocked on his door. There was no answer. I thought he was still sleeping, so I knocked again. When he didn't respond, I opened the door, saw him lying in bed, and called his name. He didn't respond. I called him a bit louder, but he still didn't respond. I stepped back into the hallway as Elin walked toward me. "El . . . he's not responding," I said, still not comprehending what was happening.

She walked directly into Thomas's room, touched his arm, and said, "Mark, he's cold."

I stepped toward his bed, felt his arm, and with an uncomprehending sense of shock, said, "He's dead, El."

Elin started sobbing, thrashing her arms up and down, and screamed, "No. It can't be. It just can't be. Someone needs to fix this. Someone needs to fix this!"

I was in shock, speechless. After a few seconds of confused silence, I managed to utter, "I'll call 911."

The police came in minutes but stayed for hours. They did what police are supposed to do when they find a dead body and two traumatized parents. Some combed every square inch of the house, while others asked us question after question about what had happened, who Thomas was as a person, and what had been going on in his life recently. After they'd been there for an hour or so, one of the police officers named Paul found Elin and me sitting at our kitchen table in a daze. He approached us and stood there in silence for a moment.

"Ya know, this job takes me into a lot of houses with a wide spectrum of people," he said with a soft, empathic tone. "I've only been here about an hour, but I can tell by just looking around that you're good people and that your son was a good boy. He was an Eagle Scout," Paul said, having seen Thomas's certificate on the desk in his room.

"Yes, he was," I responded as Elin and I began to cry, comforted yet deeply pained by his kind words.

When the flow of uniformed officers and plainclothes detectives abated, a group of six policemen and a woman from the coroner's office gathered around Elin and me at our dining room table. The sergeant in charge summarized what they'd found. "We'll have to wait for the toxicology report," he said, "but I'm more than ninety percent sure that your son died of fentanyl poisoning." I couldn't comprehend what he was saying. I didn't know what fentanyl was.

The woman from the coroner's office standing at the head of our dining room table spoke next. "A truck from the coroner's office will be here in a few minutes, and we'll be taking Thomas to the morgue for an autopsy."

"You can't take Thomas's body out of our home until Elin and I have had a chance to say goodbye to him," I stated, expecting her to understand.

"You'll be able to say goodbye later at the funeral home," she responded, dismissing what I said with a sense of formal authority backed by the six cops standing around us.

"No," I insisted, raising my voice a little, "we're going to say goodbye to him here, in his room, in his personal space where he lived with us."

"No, we can't do that," she responded, now raising her voice to match mine. The tension in the room rose.

I scanned the faces of the police officers and then finally the coroner's face before responding even more forcefully. "This is still my house, and my wife and I are going to say goodbye to our son here, or you're not taking him."

The woman backed down. "Okay. But you can't touch him."

"My wife and I want to kiss him goodbye."

"No . . . you can't do that," she replied as if I had crossed some other line of permissibility.

I was furious. I could feel my anger rising from deep within. I stood up, slapped my hand on our dining room table with all my might, and screamed, "Then we're going to break the law! We're going to kiss our son goodbye or he's not leaving our house!" The emotional tension in the room was now so intense, you could've cut the air with a knife.

One police officer stared at me with an anxious facial expression, wondering where this was going. Another officer's eyes teared up; he knew what I was talking about. They all knew I was right. Elin and I went back to Thomas's room surrounded by police and bitterly sobbed at the sight of our dead son in a black body bag that had been rolled back halfway so we could see him. He looked horrible. His fingernails were dark blue from his coagulated blood. He'd been dead for about ten hours, his body in rigor mortis. We took turns kissing his cold, lifeless, and sweaty forehead as we said goodbye to our precious son.

Once we'd left Thomas's bedroom, they zipped up the body bag and wheeled our son out of our house on a gurney. I stood on the front porch with my iPhone and snapped a picture of this unbelievable moment; two husky men loading a black body bag containing Thomas's corpse into the back of a white truck that had "Coroner's Office" stenciled on the driver's side door. The woman from the coroner's office stopped, turned, and looked at me as I took the picture as if she was going to scold me, but she knew better. It was the last time Thomas would leave our home.

After the police left our house at about 3:00 p.m., I called the Darling Fisher Memorial Chapel to arrange for Thomas's body to be picked up at the morgue when the autopsy was done. I called Rick, the caretaker of the Ryssby Cemetery, and told him we would have to open one of our family grave plots to place Thomas's remains. The rest of the day and night were a blur. I have no memory of what happened. I hardly slept that night.

By the next morning, I knew things were going to get worse, much worse, before they got better. The day-to-day reality of our loss, the matter-of-factness and finality of Thomas's death, began to unfold in ways I never anticipated. Elin walked into my home office that morning and said, "I need to talk to someone." I knew exactly what she meant. I quickly found her a clinical psychologist who specialized in grief therapy. Five months earlier in November 2020, I had resumed my dream work with my longtime Jungian analyst, Lara Newton, who was also a psychotherapist, so I already had professional support to help me deal with the trauma and grief I was feeling.[28]

I also discovered a support group called the Compassionate Friends (TCF), whose focus was on people who had lost a child. Elin and I both contacted TCF through their website, and almost immediately, empathetic, and supportive people who had themselves lost children reached out to both of us with materials and online support. They also provided a directory of local TCF support groups that were meeting online.

I tried to comfort and reassure my wife, saying, "We're going to be all right, but we're never going to be the same." But the nagging question about whether I would survive was never far below the surface.

MARK BODNARCZUK

◇ ◇ ◇

Four days after Thomas died, the police sergeant who was heading up the investigation into Thomas's death called and said they'd arrested the person who sold Thomas the pill that killed him. The preliminary toxicology report indicated Thomas was poisoned by a counterfeit Xanax pill made with fentanyl. This confirmed what the police told us around our dining room table that fateful Sunday morning.

The next day, May 7, 2021, Elin saw a charge on Thomas's debit card for food he ordered around 9:30 p.m. from DoorDash on the night he died. After Thomas came home, he chatted with us, went to his room, and took what he thought was a Xanax while he ordered food, probably to relax and play some video games after work. But he never lived to eat it.

In those first weeks, the demands, responsibilities, and tasks that Elin and I were forced to do dragged us through each day. We struggled to do the right thing for our son and for ourselves, fighting to put one foot in front of the other just to make it through another day. Given our state of mind, I don't know how we did what we did. I wrote Thomas's eulogy and the first post for his memorial site entitled "My Son, Thomas." Elin and I emailed and called family and friends to tell them what happened. We picked out a casket for the private funeral we'd planned for May 8 that only Elin and I would attend. I wrote the memorial liturgy for the funeral, and together we picked out the hymns for the service. These were mind-numbing decisions that had to be made and made quickly.

On the morning of the funeral, I was lying in bed trying to comprehend what was happening. I heard the sweet, sorrowful sound of a mourning dove. Thomas and I had just talked about mourning doves a few weeks before. Two of them were trying to build a nest under our carport and kept setting off the motion detectors of our security system during our online church service. I realized that morning during breakfast that almost every thought I had in life was somehow connected to Thomas. His life had been woven into the fabric of my life for the last nineteen years. Over the course of each day since he died, these emotion-packed connections emerged out of nowhere, unannounced and unasked for. The pain of his loss penetrated my heart over and over again. I also realized that although new connections would form, Thomas would not be a part of them physically. I struggled to comprehend this reality in those early days. I'm still struggling to understand and accept these empirical facts now, all this time later.

We got to the funeral home that afternoon. Thomas was laid out in an open coffin, a beautiful but tragic image. The room was filled with sweet-smelling flowers sent by family members and friends. Given how horrible Thomas looked on the day he died, he looked more like himself now. Between the hymns, all the Scripture readings, and Communion, the private service took almost two hours. After the service, we loaded all the beautiful flowers into our two cars, dropped them off at home, and then went to Palermo's Italian Restaurant in San Jose for dinner as our private repast. While Elin and I were physically there that day, the whole thing seemed like a dream.

Ten days later, we returned to the funeral home for Thomas's cremation. His casket had already been loaded into the hearse when Elin and I arrived. From there, Elin and I would drive to the cremation site in our car, closely following the hearse with our hazard lights flashing. As the hearse pulled out of the funeral home parking lot onto Santa Cruz Avenue, traffic stopped in both directions out of respect for what was happening. When we arrived, Elin and I walked hesitantly to an event that we never envisioned happening in our lives. We were led to a small open courtyard with a large tree towering in the center of the circle. There was a set of large metal swinging doors that led to the crematorium on the left. I was surprised and saddened. I thought the entrance would look more decorative, but it seemed like a service entrance into a shop area.

Elin and I watched in uncomprehending silence as they rolled Thomas's casket out of the back of the hearse, brought it into the cremation room on a gurney, and positioned it in front of the door of the cremation vault. Earlier, I had informed the funeral home that we wanted to perform a brief service before the cremation. Knowing this, the hearse driver looked at me and said, "Let us know when you're done," as she and the cremation manager walked outside to wait. I conducted the service using the words shown below:

> I am Resurrection, and I am Life, says the Lord. Whoever has faith in me shall have life, even though he die. And everyone who has life, and has committed himself to me in faith, shall not die for

ever. As for me, I know that my Redeemer lives and that at the last he will stand upon the earth. After my awaking, he will raise me up; and in my body I shall see God. I myself shall see, and my eyes behold him who is my friend and not a stranger. For none of us has life in himself, and none becomes his own master when he dies. For if we have life, we are alive in the Lord, and if we die, we die in the Lord. So, then, whether we live or die, we are the Lord's possession. We are here to celebrate the life of Thomas Larson Bodnarczuk, to pray for his eternal soul that is now with God, to pray for Elin and me in this time of deep and profound grief, and to hear again the promise of Jesus who said, "For God so loved the world, that He gave His only begotten son, that whoever believes in him should not perish, but have eternal life." O God of grace and glory, we remember before you this day our son, Thomas. We thank you for giving him to us, his parents, to know and to love as a son and a companion on our earthly pilgrimage. In your boundless compassion, console us who mourn. Give us faith to see in death the gate of eternal life, so that in quiet confidence we may continue our course on earth until, by your call, we are reunited with Thomas and with those who have gone before, through Jesus Christ our Lord. Amen

When Elin and I had finished the service, I signaled to the hearse driver. The crematory manager went right to work. He grabbed tools and materials from a large wooden workbench on the back side of the crematory vault. After placing something in a vise that was mounted to the workbench, he picked up a large hammer and began to pound on a thick piece of metal. Elin and I watched, looking at one another periodically, not knowing what to think.

When he had struck the last blow with the hammer, he loosened the vise, retrieved the piece of metal, and walked directly toward us with the item in the palm of his hand. "This is a unique identifying coin that is associated with your son." It had the name of the funeral home and the number 35277 that he had pounded into the metal with the hammer. I took a picture of the coin in the palm of his hand. He walked toward the cremation vault and threw the coin inside as he explained, "The metal will withstand the heat of the fire and will become a permanent record of the cremation." Then the cremation manager positioned three hard cardboard tubes on the floor of the vault and slid the casket into the vault on top of the tubes. He locked the door, sealed it tightly, and, after making a few adjustments, looked at me and asked, "Are you ready to start?"

I looked at Elin, then at him, and answered, "Yes," not knowing what to expect. He pushed a large red button on the right side of the vault. We could instantly hear flames engulfing Thomas's casket.

"It will take about three to four hours at two thousand degrees Fahrenheit for the process to be complete," the cremation manager added. "Then, it will take about two days for the contents, including the identifying coin, to cool down." Thomas's remains would then be taken back to the funeral home and placed in the hand-carved rosewood urn we bought for him. A small portion of his ashes would be placed inside a heart-shaped necklace that Elin picked out, and another small portion of Thomas's ashes would be placed in two circular-shaped orbs we'd purchased—one for Elin and one for me.

Elin and I were both weeping as we left the crematory. I tried to comfort and reassure my wife with the only words I could muster: "We're going to be all right, but we're never going to be the same." But the nagging question about whether I would survive Thomas's death forced its way into my heart and mind. Yet, at the very same time, I had a deep and profound sense that I was not lost, that I was still on the path God called me to walk.

A few days later, we received a voicemail saying Thomas's remains were ready to be picked up. I waited eighteen days before getting them. I just wasn't ready to take the next step of accepting my son's death. Each of these tasks created a deeper and more concretized sense of the reality and finality that Thomas was gone.

◊ ◊ ◊

Everything I just recounted happened behind closed doors. These were experiences only Elin and I were privy to by design. Many people tried to reach out to us those first few days. They offered condolences and support in the currencies they were most comfortable with rather than the one thing I specifically asked for—to post on Thomas's memorial website. Some offered food, others sent cards, still others sent flowers, made phone calls, or sent emails.

I rejected all of these gestures at the time. I was devastated and not in my right mind. I had no psychological bandwidth to deal with people who didn't seem to "get" what we were going through. Some people called my mobile phone anyway, despite what I asked for. They would leave voice messages starting with phrases like "I don't know what to say." I responded to their phone message by email, pleading with them to go to Thomas's website and write a few words about his life or of comfort to Elin and me. Unlike their phone messages, those words would still be there twenty years from now.

Some people never posted on Thomas's website. One person even lectured me on their personal philosophy about not posting anything online. Another longtime friend sent me quotes on death and grieving that struck me as heartless, cold, and overly intellectual. I responded to his email with intolerant and unkind words. These interactions only added to the pain, grief, and frustration Elin and I already felt. It was at that moment that I decided to consciously and intentionally wall out everyone. I didn't want to have to go back and repair a hundred relationships down the road.

When I look back on my journal notes, website posts, and pictures from those early days, I remember feeling called by God to walk the path of inner healing and transformation with Him as my primary support. From a theological perspective, I had a deep knowledge of the Bible, a personal relationship with God, and a Christian discipline that I prayed through daily. I sensed the Lord speaking to me through timeless scriptural principles: "Depend on me. My grace is sufficient. You can't lead people any further than you've been yourself." From a psychological perspective, I had already been on the path of deep personal change and transformation for forty-one years, and my plan was to use the same models, tools, and processes I'd been using for over four decades—the principles and practices I describe in my books on personal and professional growth.[29]

Looking back to that tragic day, I also see that walling people out of my life was the right choice. My entire network of relationships was reshaped by inner and outer forces. Some people on the fringe of my relationship portfolio before Thomas's death were drawn into an inner circle of facilitators and strong supporters of inner healing and transformation. Others who had previously been considered friends or family vanished into thin air or infuriated me with thoughtless words and gestures that revealed their fear of death, especially the death of a child.

An indirect indicator of where a person fit within the reshuffled relationship network was their willingness to walk the path of grief with Elin and me by posting stories and tributes on his memorial site and by periodically logging in to read new posts others made. The hundreds of people who had access to Thomas's memorial site became an online community of support for Elin and me. Another more direct indicator was someone's willingness to allow Elin and me to talk freely about Thomas's life and death.

What I find utterly amazing today is that as traumatized and devastated as I was in my state of shock, anesthetized by the cold, stark reality of my son's death, my faith in God held firm. I lived in an essential tension between the nagging question *Will I survive the death of my son?* and a deep and profound sense that I was not lost, that I was still on the path God called me to walk. It made no rational sense, but I kept walking by faith based on how God had worked in my life over the last forty-one years.

My faith wavered; it was tested, but it held firm. I never blamed God or doubted He was still sovereign over the destiny I created along the Outer Labyrinth of daily life with my choices, and the destiny I had in Him along the Inner Labyrinth from the foundations of the world as revealed through my dreams and the Bible. To be clear, this was not only because of what I did or didn't do. My actions and inactions during this timeframe were necessary but not sufficient to explain how my life unfolded in the wake of Thomas's death.

Mark placing the urn containing Thomas's remains in the ground at the Ryssby Cemetery

CHAPTER 13

I SURVIVED THE DEATH OF MY SON

May 2, 2022 (52 Weeks and 1 Day After)

The circumstances surrounding Thomas's death stirred up my unconscious in unpredictable ways.[30] The deeper our emotions, traumas, and beliefs are, the less conscious and more powerful they tend to be when they finally manifest themselves along the Outer Labyrinth of quotidian life. I only recorded two dreams in the first weeks following Thomas's death, and those dream images indicated my psyche was fragmenting from enormous inner and outer pressure. They revealed a misalignment between the outer reality of my everyday life along the Outer Labyrinth and the inner reality of my deepest self along the Inner Labyrinth. I was at an impasse but saw a path forward in the third dream that I recorded and analyzed on May 27, 2021, just nine days after the cremation service.

> I was away on a trip with Thomas, and during this trip, he died. My sense is that his death was much like his actual death. I held a funeral and had him cremated in a place much like Los Gatos, where my real son was just cremated. These were things I knew in the dream before the images and narrative action of the dream started.
>
> Then, as the dream starts, I'm at some type of church-related gathering or potluck dinner with Elin, who seems like she is "kind of" like my actual wife, Elin Larson, but not quite. The meal was over, and Elin and I were sitting at a table fellowshipping with some people from church. But what is most important about this opening scene is that I had just arrived at the potluck straight from my trip. But she still did not know that Thomas had died during the trip. From the first moment of this dream, I kept wondering in my heart and mind just how and when I was going to tell her Thomas was dead. So, I had to pretend things were all right so she wouldn't catch

on to what had happened. As Elin and the people we were with continued talking and laughing, my heart was *screaming* inside of me because no one in the room knew Thomas was dead except me. Things began to wind down, and we were slowly getting ready to leave. I decided to go to the restroom before we left. On my way there, I had an aha moment about how I would tell Elin that Thomas was dead. I would not say a word the whole trip home, and when Elin would walk into the house and ask me, "Where's Thomas?" I would then tell her. I continued to roll the plan around in my mind over and over again. Somehow, I knew this was how it was meant to happen. Then the dream ended.

There are many layers of symbolic meaning in this dream, but I'll just mention some key points. The description of the opening setting and the image of "me" in the dream symbolizes my inner reaction to the events that were happening along the Outer Labyrinth of my daily life. This outer reality is juxtaposed with the image of "Elin" who symbolizes my soul and very deepest emotions, what Jung called the Anima, along the Inner Labyrinth of my unconscious.[31] A core message of the dream was that the objective reality of Thomas's death that I knew all too well in waking life had not "sunk in" to the deepest, unconscious elements of my psyche, as symbolized by the inner image of Elin who didn't know (i.e., was not yet conscious of) the reality that Thomas was dead. The religious setting of a collective, group meal that happened under the auspices of a church, with Elin and me fellowshipping with other people of faith, symbolized that the reality of Thomas's death had not "sunk in" to my underlying belief and faith that God was sovereign over all that happens along the Outer and Inner Labyrinths.

As I sit here writing this, I still shake my head and say to myself, *I can't believe this happened to me.* The reality that Thomas is gone hasn't sunk in yet. I look back on his funeral, cremation, and the other experiences I've had along the Outer Labyrinth, and it really does seem like a dream. My sense is that the glacial process of Thomas's loss sinking in will go on for the rest of my life.

◊ ◊ ◊

FINDING NEW LIFE AFTER THE DEATH OF MY SON

A month after having this dream, I started preparing for my annual personal planning meeting, my first one since Thomas's death. Each year, I use this time to review my goals from the previous year to see how I did, and then I envision new goals for the upcoming year. It suddenly hit me that Thomas was a major part of my annual plan. At my prior planning meeting, one of my goals was to keep being transparent and truthful in my interactions with Thomas, to be more intentional in spending quality time with him and having deep conversations together. Another goal was to take more trips with Thomas ranging from local road trips to our "rite of passage" trip to Greece and Israel that we'd planned before the pandemic.

Since he was gone, I would have to remove Thomas from next year's goals because his physical presence was no longer with me. Going on in life required me to transition to a new reality, a new identity. I can't explain the deep profound pain that removing Thomas from these goals caused me. I decided that next year's goal should be to provide spiritual, psychological, and practical leadership as Elin and I transitioned to our new life without our son. I also pledged to use Thomas's memorial website to preserve his memory so the positive impact that his life had on others will live on and not be forgotten.

I looked at Thomas's pictures on my desk. I glanced toward the crystal desk piece containing some of his remains. I stared at his picture on the memorial site, and I sobbed as I said to my son aloud, "Thomas, I've got to take you out of my goals, son. I don't want to. I wish I didn't have to. I wish we were in Greece and Israel like we had planned, but you're gone, son . . . you're gone, and I'm not. I'm still here at home, alive, with Mom, down the hall from the room that you died in. I don't want to, but I must go on without you."

Later, I pulled the first edition of my book *Diving In* off the bookshelf. It was the copy I signed and gave to Thomas in 2003 when he was only a year old. I read the note that I wrote on the first page above my signature: Thomas, I waited a lifetime for you! I then pulled down the second edition of my book, which I signed and gave to my son when he was seven years old. The note said: Thomas, you have taught me what it's like to love and be loved; probably for the first time in my life. The pain of waiting for a lifetime for my son—the very first person I ever loved, and who loved me—only to lose him at such a young age is a pain I can hardly bear sometimes. I am still trusting the Lord, but the pain of waiting and trusting Him seems like more than I can take sometimes. So, I'll continue to wait and hope as God encourages me. In words of the prophet Isaiah, "Yet those who wait for the Lord will gain new strength; they will mount up with wings like eagles, they will run and not get tired, they will walk and not become weary" (Isaiah 40:31).

◊ ◊ ◊

During the June following Thomas's death, I was dealing with the bureaucracy of my insurance company regarding his life insurance policy. I'd been back and forth with three or four different people about documents they required me to submit to close out the policy. There were only two things left that I needed to send: the autopsy report and the toxicology report. I was very eager to get this painful task off my plate, so, when I got an email from the Santa Clara County Medical Examiner's Office on July 6, 2021, saying these two items were now available, I drove to their offices immediately to pick them up.

But I made a mistake.

As I walked back to my car, I scanned the first page of the autopsy report. Once I sat in my vehicle, I read it in its entirety. I was traumatized as I read the exacting description of my dead son. It conjured up images of the coroner cutting Thomas open and examining him organ by organ to get the kind of detailed information that was included in the report. Intense, turbulent emotions of pain, sorrow, and desperation that had been trapped and pressurized deep within suddenly erupted and flowed upward with artesian force. I sobbed uncontrollably and inconsolably, unaware of time passing. When I finally settled down, I placed the report on the passenger's seat, started my car, and cried all the way home. I haven't looked at the report since, and I never will again.

I was deeply shaken by the autopsy experience. It disrupted the emotional equilibrium that enabled me to make it through my grief-filled days. It amplified and distorted the nagging question about surviving Thomas's death. My survival instincts took over. I needed anchors and points of reference that were outside the inner waves of chaos that washed over me and threatened to pull me down into the deep waters of the unconscious.

FINDING NEW LIFE AFTER THE DEATH OF MY SON

At the time, I was doing dream work with Lara, my longtime Jungian analyst. She had been a trusted guide and powerful catalyst for transforming my life for over a decade. She had helped me become a better person, a better husband, and a better father. She and I even have the same dominant Jungian function, introverted-intuition, the perfect personality perspective for exploring the deep regions of the unconscious along the Inner Labyrinth. She is the best Jungian analyst I've ever worked with. But the oppositional images I was seeing in my dreams embodied the very opposite of my dominant Jungian function. These images had an extraverted-intuitive orientation that was focused primarily on the Outer Labyrinth of day-to-day life—the world of dead sons, fentanyl poisonings, funeral and cremation services, insurance policies, autopsy reports, and working fifty hours a week in a world of people who are almost entirely out of touch with the inner world of their dreams.

I knew then and there that the next thing that I had to do to survive Thomas's death was the hard work of integrating and aligning these oppositional psychological forces. So, I decided to face this inner opposition fearlessly. On July 15, 2021, I started doing dream work with John Beebe, a psychiatrist and well-known Jungian analyst whose dominant Jungian function was extraverted intuition, the same as the inner forces that were tearing my psyche apart and had led me to a psychological impasse.[32] Over the next three months, I analyzed the same dreams with both analysts without telling them about each other. This provided the kind of perspective and dimensionality I so desperately needed to navigate the deep waters through which I was sailing.

I worked with each analyst for an hour every other week, and the rest of the time, I continued to walk the path with God as my primary support. I maintained my daily practice of Bible reading and prayer. I continued to use the same psychological models, tools, and processes that I'd been using for the past forty-one years. Elin was an enormous support to me from the very beginning. We were on the same platform. We were in the same container. We were equally yoked to plow the demanding fields of life to which God had called us. Elin and I also continued to share and reflect upon our dreams separately and together. Unlike many couples who lose a child, we talked about and openly processed our feelings with a sense of trust, transparency, and teamwork. We respected the fact that we grieved differently, and we valued our different ways of seeing and expressing our grief.

◊ ◊ ◊

Over the following months, the process of inner healing and transformation continued unabated along the Outer Labyrinth and deep within me along the Inner Labyrinth without my conscious participation. In late October, about three weeks after Thomas's memorial service in California, I was on my daily four-mile walk along the Los Gatos Creek Trail when I experienced an emotional turning point, one that rose from deep within me.

All of that day, I had been feeling raw, with deep pain and a dull aching in my stomach. My emotions were very close to the surface as I wept, sometimes uncontrollably, on and off all day long. But, as I told Elin afterward at lunch, I felt this distinct sense that I had made it, that I was going to survive this. I couldn't get those words out of my mind: I made it.

At that moment, I knew my task going forward was to stay in touch with this very deep, aching pain in light of the testimony that *I made it*. I made it with God's grace. I made it with the psychological tools that Elin and I had embraced since Thomas's death. I made it and was moving forward toward a new reality and a new identity that I was still discovering.

This was the beginning of a deep inner realization that I had survived the death of my son, that I'd made it to the other side of something that, at the time, I knew tacitly but could not articulate or explain.

Farmers don't *cause* their crops to grow. Rather, they facilitate a natural process by using tractors and tools to fertilize soil, spread seeds, water crops, and encourage the natural biological and chemical processes that *do* cause the growth. In much the same way, I facilitated a natural process of inner healing and transformation over that first year following my son's death. But it was God who caused the growth. This echoes the biblical truth expressed by the apostle Paul: "I planted, Apollos watered, but God was causing the growth. So then neither the one who plants nor the one who waters are anything, but God who causes the growth" (1 Corinthians 3:6–7).

When my burden became too much for me to bear, when the trauma of Thomas's tragic death forced me into a quasi-conscious autopilot state just to survive, God carried me. Even when I walked through the valley of the shadow of my son's death, God was with me. He supported me. He gave me the strength and resilience to continue down the path.

PART TWO
FINDING NEW LIFE

Thomas's tree house across the street from our new house

CHAPTER 14

THOMAS'S TREE HOUSE AND THE EMERGENCE OF A NEW NORMAL

August 20, 2022 (1 Year, 15 Weeks, and 5 Days After)

Upon arriving back in Colorado, it took several months for Elin and me to finally move into our new home by McIntosh Lake. Some grief counselors advise people not to make any "big decisions" in the first year after a major loss, such as moving into a new home in a different state. But one year after Thomas's death, Elin and I had been living in a constant state of inner and outer change and transition. There were times when I would just shake my head, thoroughly amazed by all that had happened, all we'd been through, all we'd yet to finish with prosecuting the person who killed our son, and how fast time had passed since that fatal day.

Over the summer of 2022, the deep penetrating pain and grief about Thomas's death had begun to soften and morph into a new normal. While I'd come to accept Thomas's death as the destiny that God has called us to walk, I was still struggling to embrace this tragedy as part of the life I'd been called to live, wishing instead that our life together as a family could have unfolded in another way. This new normal in Colorado was emerging within the 120-mile radius of a "mountaintop experience" I had with Thomas eight years previously on the peak of Mount Evans during one of our weekend trips.

◇ ◇ ◇

June 28, 2014, was a bright sunny day. Thomas was twelve years old. We drove the narrow hairpin road up State Highway 103 to Echo Lake at the foot of Mount Evans. After a quick stop at the Echo Lake Lodge Restaurant so Thomas could get a snack and a trinket at the souvenir shop, we hopped back into my Toyota 4X4 and drove fourteen rugged miles to the top of

Mount Evans, the fourteenth tallest mountain in Colorado. This is the highest paved road in North America. It's one of those nail-biters with no guardrails and steep thousand-foot drops. In places, the pavement is only wide enough for one vehicle to travel at a time.

Once we parked the vehicle, Thomas and I huffed and puffed up the steep trail to the very top of Mount Evans. It was an amazing day—sunny, warm, and clear with only a gently blowing wind, a rare event in Colorado's high country. From the summit, we could see over a hundred miles in every direction. We were encircled by the visual presence of Pike's Peak, the Tenmile Range, the Hoosier Pass, and the other mountain peaks that defined my life in Colorado, the place I had lived for nearly forty years. Standing there, I remembered attending the very first Christian Artist's Music Seminar at the YMCA Camp in Estes Park in the summer of 1974 before moving later that fall to Colorado Springs—sixty-nine miles as the crow flies from where we were perched—to attend Nazarene Bible College.

Colorado was Thomas's home too. He was born at 10:18 a.m. on May 16, 2002, at Presbyterian St. Luke's Hospital in Denver, just thirty miles east of Mount Evans. The area within this circumference was also the place that Elin calls home ever since 1978 when she took her first ski trip to Steamboat Springs—about ninety-four miles away from where Thomas and I were standing. It was that trip that led her to move to Colorado and take a job at the Denver-based Petro Lewis Corporation in 1979.

Elin and I met at St. John the Baptist Episcopal Church in Breckenridge on January 30, 2000, just twenty-three miles from Mount Evans, and we were married in Aspen on September 16, 2000, just 113 miles west of where Thomas and I stood.

As a family of three, we set down deep roots in the fertile land that encompassed Thomas and me. At the time, our home in Longmont was just a block off the south shore of McIntosh Lake. From Mount Evans's peak, Thomas and I could just make out the area where the lake was. A year earlier, in 2013, Elin and I had purchased two burial plots at the Ryssby Cemetery in Longmont, barely visible from where we stood. In that moment with Thomas, I would have never imagined that he would be the first one to occupy Elin's plot.

That sunny and clear day on the top of Mount Evans with Thomas was a providential time that we shared together. I realized Thomas and I were standing at the very center of the circumference within which the destiny I had created with my choices along the Outer Labyrinth, and the destiny I had in God from the foundations of the world along the Inner Labyrinth, had happened together at the same time. I tried to explain this to my twelve-year-old son as best I could. The landscape encircling us wove Thomas's story, Elin's story, and my story together into a single space-time tapestry, a shared story anchored to mountains and valleys stretched out as far as we could see.

As Thomas wandered off to explore the rest of Mount Evans. I stood silently as my mind was drawn back eighteen years to another mountaintop experience—my second trip to Israel. I was presenting a paper at the Israeli Society for Quality meeting in Jerusalem on the problems that business process reengineering had caused for organizations and their employees in the United States. But I was also on a spiritual pilgrimage on that trip. I was searching for God. I was claiming the promise of Jeremiah 29:13: "And you will seek Me and find Me when you search for Me with all your heart."

After the conference, I spent two unhurried, reflective weeks visiting numerous holy sites, one of which was the magnificent church perched on top of the Mount of Beatitudes, the place where Jesus gave his famous Sermon on the Mount. As I looked out over the Sea of Galilee facing west toward the setting sun with the moon rising behind me to the east, I made two vows to the Lord, both of which were anchored to Scripture.

First, from the steps leading up to the church, I vowed to meditate periodically on John 3:1–21, the story of Nicodemus and being born from above. I asked God to form these biblical truths in me at the very deepest level of my soul—at the level of dreams in what Jung called the Self.[33] Second, as I stood at the altar in the church, I made another vow to meditate on the Sermon on the Mount in Matthew 5–7 and adopt this as my code of conduct, the criteria for how I lived my life. I asked God to form these biblical truths in me at the level of dreams, to sanctify and transform the Self and the other psychic elements so they would become more faithful guides who would lead me to the destiny that I have in His sovereign will, and the destiny I must create with my choices. I wanted God's kingdom to reign in both my conscious and unconscious life. I wanted to love the Lord my God with all my heart, with all my soul, with all my mind, and with all my strength (Matthew 22:36–40). I was hungry and thirsty for righteousness and integrity in a deep and unquenchable way.[34]

Eighteen years later and 6,848 miles from the Sea of Galilee on the top of Mount Evans with my twelve-year-old son, Thomas, who was now peering curiously down into the valley floor a thousand feet below, I silently reaffirmed those two vows. From that moment on, the seemingly unrelated connections between the historical Jesus, the cosmic Christ (John 1:1–5; Colossians 1:15–17), the infant Immanuel (Isaiah 7:14; Matthew 1:22–23) who came and dwelt among us (John 1:14), the 754-mile geographical area that was centered on the top of Mount Evans, and my day-to-day life with Thomas and Elin in Longmont, Colorado made sense.

I recognized that the twists and turns of my daily life along the Outer Labyrinth for the last forty years had been woven into the complex and elegant pattern of a fabric; it became the life I had lived and the destiny I had created with my choices. I felt an inextricable bond linking Mount Evans in Colorado and the two vows that I made on Mount of Beatitudes in Galilee, the land where Jesus lived, taught, died, and rose again from the dead.

◊ ◊ ◊

On June 19, 2022, a few weeks after Elin and I had first moved back to Colorado, we had lunch at the Echo Lake Lodge Restaurant. This was my second Father's Day without Thomas. After lunch, we drove to the top of Mount Evans, but it was a very different type of day than eight years prior when I was there with Thomas. This time, when we huffed and puffed our way up the steep trail to the very top of Mount Evans, there was zero visibility at the peak, and the wind pounded us mercilessly and relentlessly. As I stood there, I remembered that day when I reaffirmed my two vows to the Lord while Thomas explored the peak. I could not see the circle of mountains that punctuated the 120-mile radius in which I'd lived since 1974, but by faith, I knew they were there. They had become anchors, points of reference to orient me within the swirling events of the year since we'd lost our son. I reaffirmed my two vows yet again, this time with Elin at my side and Thomas buried in Ryssby Cemetery.

◊ ◊ ◊

FINDING NEW LIFE AFTER THE DEATH OF MY SON

An important part of encouraging a new normal has been reflecting on the Inner Labyrinth of the destiny that I've had in God, as revealed in my dreams. This deep inner work has become the fertile ground upon which the seeds of the new normal have taken root and begun to grow in ways beyond my conscious intentions. I saw signs of the inner process of healing and transformation in a dream I had on May 31, 2021, just four weeks after Thomas died.

I was somewhere high up in the mountains in Colorado, and I had a house that was up on a ridge that overlooked an enormous fertile valley that lay far below. I was standing in front of my house, which was undergoing some repairs or remodeling. It was dark, not nighttime but more like dusk or morning just before the sun comes up. There was a large elegantly designed white sign with red script-like letters a couple of hundred feet over on land on the left side of my house. The sign was advertising the development and construction of a new, self-contained community that looked enormous. The community was about 550 homes plus other amenities like shops and places to get coffee and eat. I walked over toward the sign, looked over the ridge to the valley floor below, and saw the great expanse of the valley that was filled with bright Colorado sunshine.

As I walked closer to the edge of the ridge and looked down, I saw giant earth-moving equipment, like Caterpillar D-8 bulldozers, carving a narrow dirt road out of the bright-red Colorado soil of the slope that led down, down, down to the valley below. I was amazed at how steep it was, and I wondered how anyone would be able drive up that hill in the winter when there was snow on the ground. I looked at the sign for the new community again, and then I glanced back to my left and saw a couple standing there who was also watching this scene unfold. They walked a little closer to me, and I said to the woman, "I hope that's really a self-contained community like they say, because I don't know how anyone will be able to drive up that road in the winter with how steep it is." She didn't say anything in response, but her body language and my intuition told me that she agreed and was wondering the same thing too. The dream ends here, as I'm watching the giant earth-movers carve a narrow, steep, bright-red dirt road from the dark ridge I was standing on, down, down, down to the bright, sunny, enormous expanse of the valley floor far below where the new self-contained community was already being prepared and being built, with the couple on my left watching this same thing unfold.

As I recorded and analyzed this dream, I recognized the dream image of an enormous, fertile, sun-filled Colorado valley with bright-red soil was a symbol, a promise, of the fertile psychological and spiritual ground upon which the seeds of a new normal life were already being sown by God, working through what Jung called the Self. This dream was also foreshadowing how the new normal would unfold in Colorado, not in California, within the 120-mile radius of the mountaintop experience I had with Thomas on Mount Evans seven years earlier.

The dream image of "my house" symbolized my current psychological state, with the repairs and remodeling being images of the inner changes and deep grief that resulted from Thomas's death. The fact that my inner psychological reality and identity (i.e., my house) sat in darkness high up on a Colorado ridge was symbolic of my state of mind at the time I had the dream. It wasn't the deep nighttime darkness of depression and despair. Rather, it was the kind of darkness that comes just before dawn—an inner light that was already rising and shining from the valley far below.

In day-to-day life, "signs" are things that point the way to other things. In this dream, the elegantly designed, red-letter sign pointed to a great expanse of undeveloped psychological and spiritual territory in my heart and mind, a self-contained community, within which God had already begun the process of building the inner foundation for the next phase of my life back here in Colorado.

The design and planning aspects of this inner psychological and spiritual work were underway, as imaged by the very basic task of powerful D8 bulldozers carving out the bright-red Colorado soil, creating inner roads that would provide access to this previously undeveloped psychological and spiritual terrain. This was one of the first things that needed to be done, even prior to shaping and defining the new foundations of inner meaning and potential in my heart and mind.

The fact that the road down into the valley was very steep meant the journey down to this inner land of potential and promise would be challenging yet certainly possible. In contradistinction, the steep upward pitch of the road from the fertile valley floor back up to the dark ridge where my house was (i.e., a regression to my psychological state of mind triggered by reading the toxicology report on July 6, 2021) would be a very treacherous and unlikely trip. These symbols from the unconscious were telling me that once the hard, painful, deep work of inner healing and transformation in the valley had been done (and done properly), there would be no need to go back over that part of the painful grieving process again.

When I first reflected on this dream, I knew, at some level, that these symbolic images would be the way my life would unfold. The dream created a spark of hope in me that lived side by side with my agonizing pain and grief. But it was only in retrospect that I recognized the connection between the sun-filled Colorado valley in the dream and the emergence of a new normal from my mountaintop experience with Thomas on Mount Evans seven years earlier.

◇ ◇ ◇

This dialectical reflection between the Outer and Inner Labyrinths is not just an intellectual or philosophical exercise. For me, it has been a very concrete way of broadening my perspective about Thomas's death. It's something I experience every week when I stand in front of our family plot in the Ryssby Cemetery where Thomas is buried. I see Thomas's picture, Elin's picture, and my picture, but only Thomas's has both a birth and death date. The absence of my death date summons me to live each day with my mission before me and God's presence leading the way. As I look at the patch of bright green grass that has grown over the hole into which I placed the hand-carved rosewood urn that held Thomas's earthly remains on August 28, 2021, and then alternately look at my picture on the tombstone, I know this ground will be my last stop on this earthly journey. It will be Elin's last stop too.

In the entire expanse of a universe composed of billions of galaxies that are moving away from an undefined central point from which the eternal God spoke the universe into existence thirteen billion years ago as a Big Bang, the 120-mile radius extending from the peak of Mount Evans is the sacred region of space-time within which I see the first glimmer of new life after Thomas's death. It is the holy circumference within which a new normal, one without our son's physical presence, has been promised for Elin and me. It's the place where I'm starting to experience a new normal as a self-regulated partnership between myself and a purposeful, intentional force of the God who created and sustains both the universe filled with billions of galaxies and the Rocky Mountains—a God who knows Thomas, Elin, and me by name.

The symbolic bridge between Mount Evans and the common space and personal space that we had yet to define in our new home at that time is shown in the picture at the beginning of this chapter. It's the tree house Thomas played in with his friends when he was growing up on McIntosh Drive here in Longmont. The actual wooden steps shown in the picture are visible just across the street from the back patio of our house. I can see them when I sit at our kitchen table, with Elin's normal place at the table to my right and Thomas's empty chair to my left. The visual connection between the empty dinner chair to my left and the stairs leading to Thomas's tree house is a constant reminder of the fragility of life, the impossibility of replacing a person, and the finality of death—something that's become real for me, for the very first time.

◊ ◊ ◊

The story of how Elin and I came to live in our new house across the street from that tree house is another example of how the destiny we have and the destiny we create with everyday choices are happening together at the same time—whether we're aware of it or not. It's another instance of how Elin and I have been discovering links between the rituals, holiday traditions, and places we've gone with Thomas that have always been there, even though we'd never seen them before, and how we're intentionally *creating* new links to rituals, holiday traditions, and places we go now without Thomas.

In the fall of 2018, Elin suggested we buy a house in Colorado so we would have a stake in the frenzied, cost-escalating housing market. Thomas was already thinking about going to Colorado State University in Fort Collins, so it made sense for us to look north of where we'd previously lived in Longmont. We found a house near the university in November 2018 and finalized the sale in January 2019. The house was on a small lake, had incredible views of the mountains, and had a bedroom where Thomas could stay when he came home from school on weekends or hang out during the summer break.

While Elin and I were in Colorado for Thomas's funeral at Ryssby Church, I drove up to the Loveland house a couple of times to show family and friends where we had planned to live when we moved back to Colorado. Each time, I had an unsettled feeling, a growing inner conviction that I just can't live here. The day after we buried Thomas, Elin and I drove up to the Loveland house. It was then I poured my heart to Elin about what I'd been feeling. Now that Thomas was gone, I wanted to live back on McIntosh Lake where the three of us had lived together as a family.

Elin also wanted to live at McIntosh Lake, but houses on or near McIntosh Lake rarely came on the market, and the few that did were gone in a day, selling for well over asking price. Plus, the logistics of flying from California to Colorado at the drop of a hat made our chances of seeing a house in person before making an offer almost impossible. Later, we drove to McIntosh Lake and sat on a bench along the water's edge. It was one of the benches we used to sit on with Thomas when he was alive. We knew deep in our hearts that this was our home.

For months, Elin rigorously searched online for a home at McIntosh Lake to no avail. With March 22 approaching—the day our California house was scheduled to close—we were nervous. Luckily, as a safety net, Elin found a two-bedroom apartment two blocks from McIntosh Lake that we could rent on a month-to-month basis, along with a ten-by-thirty-foot storage locker where we could store our possessions. So at least we knew we'd have a place to land as we continued our frustrating search for a new home. Only now, in retrospect, have we begun to understand the enormous emotional pressure we were under as grieving parents just ten months into one of the most unimaginable experiences in life—the loss of our only child. This was only compounded by the pain and grief created by going through the rest of Thomas's stuff again to get it ready for the move, by the dozens of boxes piled throughout our California house for months on end, by the ongoing legal issues associated with prosecuting the person responsible for Thomas's death, and by various uncertainties surrounding the sale of our house. At times, this was almost more chaos and uncertainty than we could bear.

On March 2, 2022, Elin marched into my home office with a sense of urgency and said, "Come look at this!" It was a beautiful house just across the street from McIntosh Lake. It had been on the market for only a few hours. We called our real estate agent and made an offer that was considerably above the asking price. Our agent, who knew our story and how badly we wanted to move back to McIntosh Lake, actively monitored the sales activity on the house, giving us hour-by-hour updates on the frenetic bidding war that evolved.

Two days later, I was down on the California coast walking on the beach with a longtime friend, and my mobile phone rang. It was Elin. She excitedly announced that our agent was speaking with the woman selling the McIntosh house and told her our story about Thomas. She wanted to sell the house to us, but she needed us to raise our offer another $50,000 to meet one of the counteroffers. There was silence as Elin waited for my response. I looked at my friend, took a deep breath, and said, "Sure. Let's go for it."

We bought the house without seeing it in person. We had to. Over the next few days, Elin and I were looking through the pictures of the house on Zillow, some of which were aerial shots that showed the position of the house relative to McIntosh Lake. At one point, Elin said in passing, "I think that's the lake where Thomas used to hang out." She pointed to a small lake that was right across the street from the house.

"Really? How do you know that?" I responded, pleasantly surprised I didn't know this part of Thomas's history in Longmont.

"He took me there once and showed me," she explained. "He and his friends had a tree house somewhere on that lake that they used to play in. I think someone tore most of the tree house down before we moved to California."

Elin's comment planted a seed in my mind—a symbolic bridge between our new house and Thomas's tree house across the street. But this was news to me. I'd driven by that place a million times when we lived in Longmont and never noticed the lake because it was elevated above the road and hidden behind trees and large banks of dirt. What pleased me most at that time was the incredible view of Long's Peak that we would have from our new home. But the symbolic bridge between the top of Mount Evans and the tree house across the street from our house hadn't occurred to me yet.

We took possession of our new house on what would have been Thomas's twentieth birthday, May 16, 2022. Then we began finishing the sixteen-hundred-square-foot basement. Over the next six weeks, I went to the house every day to check on the status of what turned out to be a complex and drawn-out construction project.

FINDING NEW LIFE AFTER THE DEATH OF MY SON

During the construction that summer, one of Thomas's closest friends, Jillian, texted me and wanted to get together for coffee to catch up. Afterward I took her to see the bench on the shore of McIntosh Lake, as I had recently asked the City of Longmont to designate it as Thomas's memorial bench with a bronze plaque, which was still being fabricated at a foundry. I also took Jillian to our house, where Elin warmly greeted her. We showed her the main floor and the construction chaos that was going on in the basement. Finally, we walked out onto the flagstone patio at the back of our house to show her the spectacular view of Long's Peak.

"And that's the lake where Thomas and his friends used to hang out in a tree house," I said, forgetting that the young woman who was standing with me *was* one of Thomas's closest friends back then. As I spoke those words and pointed across the street with my index finger, my attention was suddenly drawn to a specific tree. For the very first time, I *saw* the horizontal wooden steps that were nailed to the tree and led to Thomas's tree house. It was one of those aha moments when the scales fell from my eyes. I had looked in that direction, at that tree, dozens of times, but only now did I actually *see* those wooden steps and the remnants of Thomas's tree house. I could hardly contain my amazement, almost shouting, "Look! Look there!" I pointed across the street. "I see the steps that lead to Thomas's tree house."

Jillian and Elin took a step to the left to get a better view. "Yes! That's it!" Jillian exclaimed, "Thomas took me up in that tree house one time."

◊ ◊ ◊

Being back in Colorado has been good for Elin and me. The deep penetrating pain and grief about Thomas's death have begun to abate and morph into a new normal that's hard to put into words. Close your eyes and try to imagine having an arm amputated and trying to button a shirt, open a jar of peanut butter, or play a guitar. Beyond the awkward, maddening, and sorrowful frustration at being unable to do simple tasks that came so easily prior to the amputation, imagine how it might start to dawn on you that life will never be the same again. How long would it take for you to reach a new normal, for a new reality and a new identity to emerge? How long would it take for you to begin to see yourself, and be seen by others, as a *whole* person, with one arm? As Viktor Frankl discovered while surviving the unspeakable horrors of Auschwitz, "When we are no longer able to change the situation—we are challenged to change ourselves."[35]

Thomas was *amputated* from our lives, changing us into a family of two. Beyond the awkward, sometimes maddening, and often saddening frustration of being unable to celebrate Thomas's birthday, Mother's Day, Christmas, Sunday dinner, and our family meeting the way we did prior to his death, it continues to dawn on Elin and me that our lives will never be the same. But a new normal is emerging, one where we're starting to see ourselves, and be seen by others, as a whole family, not a couple that has one of its members missing. Echoing Frankl, I can't change the situation of Thomas's death. So, I'm trying to change myself, while recognizing that the process of finding a new normal is a self-regulated partnership between me and a purposeful, intentional God.

The process of "discovering" Thomas's tree house was no accident or random act of fate. The connections between my mountaintop experience in Israel in 1996, my experience with Thomas on Mount Evans back in 2014, my May 2021 dream about the bright Colorado valley where the seeds of a new normal would take root and grow, and my trip to the top of Mount Evans on the second Father's Day after Thomas death were all the result of the destiny I was creating with my choices, and the destiny I've had since the foundation of the world in God, both of which are happening together at the same time.

This destiny can only be understood by looking back in time, but it must be lived moment by moment in the existential now going forward. I tend to recognize God's leadership, sovereign power, and His faithfulness to me in retrospect after He has accomplished His sovereign will through the conscious and unconscious (intended and unintended beliefs) strategies, mindsets, and actions of the people in my life. God does this even though most people don't recognize or suspect He is using their lives, their decisions, and their stories to achieve His ends, purpose, and will. As Job 42:2 reminds us, the sovereign flow of our destiny in Him cannot be thwarted. Recognizing these rearview mirror insights and patterns of transformation while having hope for God's leadership on the path ahead have created the fertile ground upon which the seeds of a new normal have taken root and begun to grow.

CHAPTER 15

IT WILL BE A MILESTONE WHEN WE CAN SAY "WE'RE HERE IN ASPEN. IT'S BEAUTIFUL."

October 10, 2022 (1 Year and 23 Weeks After)

While Elin and I have never related to its billionaire residents and the hoity-toity opulence of its mansions and designer shops, we have always felt a deep connection to Aspen. After all, it was in Aspen, nestled among its magnificent mountains and lakes, its sprawling fields of colorful wildflowers, and its golden aspen leaves that Elin and I got married. Ever since we got married, we dreamed about having a child together. A year later, Elin got the call that she was pregnant. Our whole lives shifted to a more concrete view of our future that included an entirely new person who would be joining us in about nine months, someone whom we would eventually name Thomas Larson Bodnarczuk.

Thomas was born on May 16, 2002. Only five months later, the three of us headed to Aspen and hiked up the steep, rocky trail to Crater Lake that sits just below the majestic Maroon Bells. Thomas had it easy. He was in a backpack. (The picture on the next page shows us when we arrived at our destination.) This started an annual family tradition where the three of us would hike to Crater Lake to celebrate our wedding anniversary. Four years later, Thomas hiked the entire four-mile journey on his own for the first time, something we were all proud of, especially Thomas. Aspen was a beautiful and happy place for our family.

This annual tradition was interrupted when I moved to California in August 2015 to take a job at Stanford University and Elin and Thomas stayed back in Colorado so he could finish middle school. When Elin and Thomas drove to California the next summer, she played John Denver's song "Rocky Mountain High" most of the way. She cried her heart out because

Elin hiking with Thomas in a backpack at Crater Lake under the Maroon Bells in Aspen

she was leaving her home here in Colorado. At the same time, Thomas was trying to prepare himself for what lay ahead. On that trip, he wore his *Ocean Avenue* T-shirt. *Ocean Avenue* was the name of an album by one of his favorite bands, Yellowcard, who grew up in Carmel, California, which was just a ninety-minute drive south of our new home in Campbell. During the year I lived alone in California, I was also trying to prepare myself and adjust to this new life out west. I was also looking for connections between Colorado and California, between the destiny I was creating with our choice to move west, and the destiny I had, the path I'd been on till then.

In addition to our family traditions and the connections Thomas, Elin, and I had to Aspen, I had a deep personal connection to the town because it was one of the first places that I had ever experienced the alignment (i.e., the coming together) of the Outer Labyrinth of day-to-day life and the Inner Labyrinth of the unconscious world of my dreams.

◊ ◊ ◊

On April 29, 2013, one of those soul-shaking dreams emerged from the Inner Labyrinth of my unconscious. In this dream, I saw a condominium complex I recognized. When I awoke, I recorded the dream. In the real-life context of the Outer Labyrinth, this complex consisted of a small group of buildings along the Roaring Fork River on the east end of Aspen, where Highway 91 begins its steep and winding narrow path up and over Independence Pass. Thomas, Elin, and I drove there a few months later while on a camping trip to Redstone, a small Western town just a few miles up the valley from Aspen. Elin pulled over and let me out of the car, and I walked to a narrow bridge that spanned the swiftly flowing river. She parked, and then she and Thomas joined me on the bridge.

It was there that the dream images and narrative from the Inner Labyrinth seemed to merge with the concrete reality of standing in that place along the Outer Labyrinth. I recounted how, in the dream, I was suspended about six feet in the air near the middle of the bridge, with the river flowing beneath me and the condo complex on my left. As Elin and I stood there fully awake, I alternately glanced at the raging flow of the Forking Fork River flowing beneath us and the small complex of upscale condos on my left, and I sensed the silent and spontaneous ping of truth from within, confirming that the Inner and Outer Labyrinths were aligned and happening together in that place at that very moment.

From that day on, I held my annual personal retreat in one of the condos on the riverbank just below that bridge, knowing, in the *yada* sense, that this was holy ground. This was a place where the destiny I was creating with my choices, and the destiny I had in God from the foundation of the world, came together within the 120-mile radius of Mount Evans that I discussed in the previous chapter.

◊ ◊ ◊

The choice to move to California had many significant consequences. But an important one was that I needed a new place to hold my annual personal planning meeting, another place where the Outer and Inner Labyrinths could connect and align, like they did in Aspen.

After I moved to California, it hit me that my November annual personal planning meeting was approaching quickly and I had nowhere to hold it. I could just "decide" on a new place to meet, but I needed some guidance and directionality from within, a sign or indicator that linked the Inner and Outer Labyrinths. I had the following dream on October 20, 2015, just a month before I normally held the retreat:

I was standing by the ocean in what looked like an old fishing town. Hanging over the water on the pylons of a pier was an eighteenth-century, Aspen-style wooden building. Suddenly, the water offshore erupted as a huge, dark, almost black sperm whale blasted up out of the water like the whale in the story of *Moby-Dick*. Its body was about halfway out of the water, and it just stood there suspended between heaven and earth. There were a few older people standing there next to me, and I said something like, "That's a sperm whale." It was about one hundred feet long, and its head seemed huge, maybe thirty or forty feet wide. He was hanging right there in front of us.

Then the whale turned toward us, moved to its left, and tapped the wooden building lightly with its huge head. The whole building shook and trembled like a toy. Then the whale turned back toward the sea, went back to its place under the water, and we stood there utterly amazed by the sheer size and power of this enormous and powerful yet gentle giant from the deep.

If the whale had been angry, it could have utterly destroyed the building with a single blow. Yet, he just nudged it, almost for fun. The dream ends as I'm standing there watching all of this, simply amazed and astounded.

As I awoke from the dream, I had a deep emotional connection between the old Western building in this dream and old Western towns like Aspen in the Colorado mountains. I also sensed that the ocean spot from which the whale arose was the Monterey Bay area and the sleepy ocean village of Carmel.

There were other deeper, stratified layers of meaning in this dream, but what I knew was that the sperm whale was a symbol of the Self, of fertility and undiscovered possibilities rising from the depths of the unconscious. This gentle giant meant me no harm. He was calling me, leading me down to the deep waters of the unconscious where my decades-long journey of transformation and individuation would continue in California. My conscious waking self along the Outer Labyrinth, symbolized by me in the dream, had a deep connection to the image of the whale-Self, but it was not a relationship between equals. The numinosity and presence of the Self was unthinkably more powerful and all-knowing than I was. It was a relationship, a kind of partnership, but it was not an alliance between equals.

It was in the wake of this dream that Carmel—a place that would later foster so many profound memories—first became a "sister city" to Aspen for my family and me. Set on the shores of the Monterey Bay—the same place where John Denver died in a plane crash—Carmel is an affluent city like Aspen, with many upscale houses and designer shops. Like Aspen, Carmel is also full of natural beauty and tranquility, such as the Point Lobos State Natural Reserve just a few miles south of town. I eventually even found a quaint, early twentieth-century hotel just a few blocks from the ocean where I could hold my annual planning meeting. I had shaped my reality upon arriving in California, embedded it with repetition, and now the unconscious was revealing deep connections between Aspen and my new home in California in this dream.

◇ ◇ ◇

In September 2022, Elin and I returned to Aspen for our twenty-second anniversary. We made the bittersweet journey as a family of two, not three.

It was the first time we would hike the Crater Lake trail without Thomas since he was born twenty years prior.

When we arrived in the afternoon, we checked into the quaint Aspen Lodge right on Main Street. As we walked to our room, I happened to glance to my left and saw an eight-by-twelve framed picture screwed to the wall. I stopped dead in my tracks.

"Elin, look! It's John Denver."

Sure enough, it was a picture of Denver and the sculptor who built the Aspen Lodge in the 1970s. Denver's handwritten inscription on the picture read, "Far out." This artifact gave Elin an emotional connection to the lodge. "Yeah," she said, "he used to say 'far out' a lot."

Over the next few days, Elin and I would travel to a number of places that she and I once visited with Thomas. We drove up the meandering road to Ashcroft, a historical ghost town that was once a bustling, late-nineteenth-century silver mining camp. As Elin and I browsed the historical artifacts and old pictures of this once booming town, it was difficult to envision what this valley looked like back then. In much the same way, it was becoming increasingly difficult to remember our life together with Thomas, the everyday experience of his physical presence fading to the point where it was getting increasingly difficult to remember our life together in space-time.

Our real-life experiences were being transformed, against my will, into memories of our life together, memories supported by historical artifacts, much like the ones we saw that day in Ashcroft. I still have my son's artifacts—his guitar and band posters, his toothbrush and shaving cream—but I don't have him. This brutal reality has troubled me deeply. Like someone struggling to hold on to a rock with all their might so the slow, powerful, and continuous pull of the river of time doesn't carry them away, I have tried to cling to my experience of Thomas's physical presence, but to no avail.

As I stood there that day in Ashcroft with Elin, an inner, voiceless insight emerged on the fringe of my consciousness, an aha experience with the hushed din of truth about it. *It'll be a milestone when you can say "We're here in Aspen. It's beautiful," without adding "but we're here without Thomas."*

◊ ◊ ◊

That day in Ashcroft, the voiceless message that came from the deep regions within me was from the Self, the *Imago Dei*. The words *Imago Dei* are a Latin translation of the Hebrew words *tselem 'elohim*, which means the "image of God." We find the *tselem 'elohim* first mentioned in Genesis 1:27: "So, God created mankind in His own image, in the image of God [*tselem 'elohim*] He created him; male and female He created them." This fundamental belief about the true essence of human nature—that we are made in God's image—is central to both Jewish and Christian teaching.[36]

The Self, the *Imago Dei*, is the innermost center of the human heart. It's where the Spirit of God takes up residence in those who seek and believe in Him. It's the place from which God speaks to us inwardly, from the Spirit of the Depths, within the outer context of the Spirit of the Times.[37] It's from this inner place that Elijah heard the "still small voice of God" (1 Kings 19:11–13). It's where I episodically experience the "peace that passes understanding" (Philippians 4:7) for no apparent reason. I've also experienced the silent inner voice of God speaking through the Self as something like my conscience urging, leading, and even demanding me to do the right thing when I was tempted to do otherwise. That image of the dark, fertile sperm whale rising out of the Pacific Ocean near Carmel and tapping the old western building with its tail was yet another image of the Spirit of God speaking through the Self, rising from the depths of the unconscious that was imaged as the ocean.

The Self orchestrates and integrates our journey along the Outer and Inner Labyrinths. It stands outside of our advances in knowledge, science, and technology, and plays the same compensatory role that it has for more than four thousand years. It's the mechanism through which the Spirit of God spoke to the prophets and biblical writers to carry our God's sovereign will. It's the same deep, inner source of healing and transformation that spoke to me about leaving Thomas's name out when I tried to imagine what everyday life was like in the thriving mining town of Ashcroft back in 1883.

◊ ◊ ◊

As Elin and I drove from Ashcroft back to downtown Aspen, we scanned the forested valleys surrounding us for stands of golden aspen trees. We traded memories about a Colorado Symphony Orchestra concert we'd been to the week before, a show honoring John Denver and the fifty-year anniversary of his iconic song "Rocky Mountain High." The band that fronted the orchestra had three guitarists who had played with Denver prior to his untimely death when his plane crashed in Monterey Bay.

When we got back to the lodge, I had an idea. I got onto Google and found the address of John Denver's nearby house: 570 Johnson Drive. "Hey, El," I exclaimed. "Do you want to go see John Denver's house in Starwood?" She was thrilled. She'd never thought of just going there.

John Denver called Aspen his home. His massive mansion was built in 1972, a year after his single, "Take Me Home, Country Roads," sold over thirty-three million copies worldwide. After we couldn't get past the gate guard, no matter how hard we tried, we decided to go to the John Denver Sanctuary back in downtown Aspen, a place we had gone previously with Thomas. The sanctuary is a public park that serves as a tribute to the man and his music. Elin and I walked among the enormous boulders engraved with his song lyrics before wandering out onto an old, black iron bridge that spans the Roaring Fork River. This was just a stone's throw from the condominium complex where I previously held my annual retreat before moving to California.

As we stood midway across the bridge in silence, watching the crystal-clear Rocky Mountain water flow beneath us, Elin bent down, picked up an aspen leaf that had fallen from a nearby tree, and cast it away from the bridge. We watched it slowly drift down toward the rushing water.

"That was for Thomas," I said, knowing my wife.

"Yes," she replied pensively, "he used to like to throw leaves and rocks into the river." Elin bent down and threw another leaf.

As the leaves floated away on the surface of the water, the inner, voiceless insight floated back into consciousness, this time with a more powerful and deeper sense of urgency and truth. *It'll be a milestone when you can say "We're here in Aspen. It's beautiful," without adding "but we're here without Thomas."* This time, I shared the insight with Elin.

She looked at me intently with sorrowful eyes but did not respond. After a moment of sensing her grief and pain, I offered, "It's a sign of inner healing and transformation. It's a sign that we're moving on in life. But at the same time, we should remember moments like this, and the enormous impact that Thomas has had, and continues to have, on our lives." She turned to face the river and the floating leaves again. No response.

I got the message.

Elin picked up a third leaf, threw it off the bridge. It landed on the water flowing under bridge, so we couldn't see it. We moved to the other side of the narrow structure and waited until it finally appeared, floating on the ripples.

After another moment of quiet tranquility, I broke the silence. "Come on, let's go get a sandwich."

We walked a few blocks to the Butcher's Block, a high-end deli near the center of town where the main Aspen ski lifts climb over some of the steepest, double black diamond runs on Aspen Mountain. We grabbed our hot soup and sandwiches and sat outside at a table in the warm Colorado sunshine. We were just across the street from the Aspen Square Hotel where Thomas, Elin, and I used to stay when we came to town. As we chatted, Elin reminisced about homeschooling Thomas in the hotel lobby next to the blazing fireplace on one of our annual trips. I chimed in with memories about how much Thomas and I enjoyed hanging out in the warm water of the hotel's outdoor hot tub in the crisp mountain air after a hike.

After a pause, Elin looked at me and said, "I hear what you're saying about not adding 'but we wish Thomas was here' to everything we say. I agree it's a sign of inner healing and transformation. I see how it's a sign of moving on in life." She hesitated for a moment, looked me directly in the eye, and said, "But I don't think I'm there yet."

Her words rang true for me too. I reflected on the fact that the "me" who experienced the insight along the Outer Labyrinth earlier that day in Ashcroft and again on the bridge, and the inner Self from which the insight emerged along the Inner Labyrinth of my unconscious, were not aligned. I got the message from within, articulated it with words, but I also struggled to accept the path that this silent inner voice from the deep was urging me to take.

"Neither am I yet," I replied pensively. "But it's a window into how the inner healing and transformation process works, and the journey that we're on. It reveals the flow of the grieving process in time from where we were the day we found Thomas dead in his room, to where we are today here in Aspen, and it points to where we need to be, given the reality that Thomas is dead and is never coming back."

I experienced this same feeling of inner resistance after the dream about the new little boy in the mall I had twenty weeks after Thomas's death. While the grieving me was utterly repulsed by these images, I also knew the meaning and import of these images and the poignant truth they conveyed that something was happening deep within that I could not deny. The rejoicing me in the dream and the grieving me in waking life were being transformed into a third something—a rejoicing-grieving me.

Having lunch with Elin in Aspen that day, I felt that same inner resistance, but I was not repulsed. Rather, I was open to accepting this inner communication from the Spirit of God through the Self, the *Imago Dei*, though I was not quite ready to embrace it. This experience was an important indicator, a milestone of my progress in moving through the inner healing and transformation process. It revealed that I was stepping up to the challenge of fearlessly and tirelessly doing the hard work of processing my grief rather than compartmentalizing it.

I'll continue using my principles, practices, and tools to create scaffolding that allows me to journey down into the unknown regions of the unconscious, and not return to my everyday life empty-handed. But for now, I told myself, I'll keep adding "But I'm here without Thomas" every time I feel a connection, a memory, or a spontaneous urge to do so going forward. I'll continue saying it, until I no longer feel the need to utter it anymore.

CHAPTER 16

WHY DON'T YOU JUST GET OVER IT?

December 27, 2022 (1 Year, 33 Weeks, and 1 Day After)

As Elin and I moved through the second year after Thomas's death, we were struggling to comprehend the fact that all we would ever have of our son was what we once had. Thomas is frozen in time, forever eighteen, and we have been forced to go on living without him. Elin and I continued doing the hard, restorative work of processing our grief rather than kicking that can of loss down the road of denial, a retrospective focus that would anchor us to the past.

Like a powerful solvent, grief had dissolved the veneer of my self-sufficiency. I used to think I knew what life was about and how to live it. Now I wasn't so sure about that. That year had been a regressive tour back through my neurotic moments, personality fixations and weaknesses, and challenging relationships.

Throughout the nineteen months since Thomas died, I had been guided by the Spirit of God's presence in my heart and mind, a deep knowledge of the Bible, my relationship with Elin, my previous work with three Jungian analysts, and a firsthand experiential knowledge of Jung's writings. The picture on the next page shows me holding a copy of June Singer's book *Boundaries of the Soul: The Practice of Jung's Psychology*, at one of the many court hearings Elin and I attended. Singer's book is a clinician's description of walking the path of individuation—the process of becoming the person we were meant to be.[38]

The *Encyclopedia Britannica* defines plagiarism as "the act of taking the writings of another person and passing them off as one's own. The fraudulence is closely related to forgery and piracy—practices generally in violation of copyright laws."[39] I would be a plagiarist if I failed to acknowledge my partnership with the Spirit of God, who sanctified and directed the Self, as the reason I've been able to walk this path. Jung's work has been necessary, but not sufficient, to lead me to where I am today as I am in the

*Mark at another plea hearing on November 7, 2022,
holding* Boundaries of the Soul

process of accepting and trying to embrace a new reality, one where the world has a sense of meaning and purpose without Thomas's physical presence, one where life is worth living. For many years, my Christian faith and my exploration of the unconscious through dream work ran on two parallel but interdependent tracks, but over time, they merged into my biblical understanding of Jung's psychology.

FINDING NEW LIFE AFTER THE DEATH OF MY SON

◊ ◊ ◊

Long before Thomas's death, I recognized how God's inner and outer guidance were shaping the direction of my life. I began to identify synchronistic, symbolic patterns in dreams that emerged from the Inner Labyrinth that mapped to events along the Outer Labyrinth of day-to-day life. I recorded hundreds and hundreds of these synchronistic instances on the timeline in my Christian discipline. Each experience was a deposit in my emotional bank account, building trust in the leadership of the Spirit of God and making it less and less likely that alignment between the complex patterns of inner images, symbols, and historical events happened purely by chance.

Finding Thomas dead in his room wounded me like a razor-sharp dagger thrust into my heart that penetrated to the depths of my soul. That was then. Now, I was starting to realize God was preparing me to become what Henri Nouwen calls a wounded healer—someone who can help others who suffer with grief. As Paul tells us in 2 Corinthians 3:1–5:

> Blessed be the God and Father of our Lord Jesus Christ, the Father of mercies and God of all comfort, who comforts us in all our affliction so that we will be able to comfort those who are in any affliction with the comfort with which we ourselves are comforted by God. For just as the sufferings of Christ are ours in abundance, so also our comfort is abundant through Christ.

A year made a big difference. Previously, I had viewed all of life through eyes filled with mourning and tears. But now, I had begun planning into the future, trying to have fun and reaching out to others in ways I never could have before. A vision of hope and new meaning in life was emerging slowly out of the ashes and tragedy of Thomas's death. Time does not heal all wounds, but it does give perspective.

◊ ◊ ◊

Studies have shown that one of the main reasons many couples divorce after losing a child is because people grieve in different ways and at different rates. Dennis Apple, author of *Life after the Death of My Son*, puts it this way: "Grief is a feeling you carry on the inside, a heaviness of spirit. Mourning, on the other hand, is best described as putting grief on the outside. Mourning is the public expression of grief." Apple follows with a stereotypical statement that generalizes yet informs: "Women mourn, but men replace."[40]

Apple argues that once the initial trauma of losing a child is over for a couple, many husbands (but not all) intentionally dry up their tears, set their emotions aside, and try to replace their deepest pain and grief with "work" and the other obligations and distractions of routine life. A husband may want to go to the movies, but his wife has been crying all day and wants to stay home. She's pensive and withdrawn over dinner, and he wants to lighten up. He gets frustrated when she can't (or won't) go out and have some fun. She's trapped in the deep, dark emotions of overwhelming grief, struggling to make it through the day. Over time, she wonders if their marriage will survive. He gets frustrated, angry, and sends her the message *Why don't you just get over it?*

Over the previous year and a half since Thomas's death, our friends, family, and others around us had also made progress in processing the loss of Thomas's physical presence. The calls, emails, and texts to see "how we're doing" had slowed down, since those people had their own fast-paced, problem-filled lives to worry about. The stark reality was that there was nothing left to say. Thomas is dead. We're not. They're not. That's what's supposed to happen as others process their grief about Thomas's loss. Like Elin and me, their goal was to move on in life. These long-term effects of Thomas's daily absence had the silent and subtle yet brutal ping of truth about them; they couldn't be denied yet remained undiscussable.

These days, it's typical for Elin and me to get together with friends and family who keep Thomas and his life an open part of the conversation, either because we mention him or because they bring it up. The impact his life had, and continues to have, on us and other people are seamlessly woven into the fabric of past, present, and future subjects as easily as if Thomas were sitting in the next room playing video games.

But with other folks, no one mentions Thomas's name. If Elin or I talk about events in his life, or refer to his death in passing, the conversation continues without them acknowledging him or his memory. If Elin or I circle back and make follow-up comments about the impact his loss is still having on us, some people say nothing. Others just move on and tell us how busy they've been with kids or grandkids, a recent bike trip to Europe, or weekend getaways to their mountain cabin. We've tried to understand the fact that friends, family, and others tend to grieve in different ways and at different rates than Elin and me. But it still hurts deeply when the unspoken message that we get is Why don't you just get over it?

What we've found is that the portfolio of friends, family, and others we still actively engage with has been winnowed with the winds of time, tested and refined by the searing fire of deep loss. The persona of some relationships has been dissolved by the same grief-based solvent that's reshaped and redefined our lives. Other than losing Thomas, the overt and covert reshaping of our relationship portfolio has been the most difficult and painful thing we've had to deal with.

When this first started coming into focus, I decided then and there to take this unarticulated question about "getting over it" at face value. I began to view it from the perspective of time. Given all the grief work Elin and I had done, I started asking *Why aren't we further along in the grieving process? Why do we still hurt so much?* The stock answer that "You never get over the death of a child" is utterly true, but it's not the whole truth.

I began using the events and insights that I logged in my journal entries along the Outer Labyrinth of everyday life, and the compensatory guidance and direction from dreams along the Inner Labyrinth, to reconstruct the events constituting the last year and a half. In the next chapter, I will describe what I discovered in this process.

The beach where Thomas and Mark hung out in Carmel

CHAPTER 17

NAVIGATING A PERFECT STORM

December 27, 2022 (1 Year, 33 Weeks, and 1 Day After)

Once the police arrived at our house in Campbell a little after 10:00 a.m. on May 2, 2021, I had to start navigating a perfect storm of four interdependent processes that unfolded at different times, moved in different directions, and proceeded at different rates. The first process was an emotionally exhausting grieving process about Thomas's death that made me a lifetime member in the small, sad club no one wants to join. The second process was continuing the lifelong task of maintaining alignment between the destiny I have along the Inner Labyrinth as revealed in my dreams and the destiny I create along Outer Labyrinth with my day-to-day choices. The third was the enormous pressure and stress of moving back to Colorado and dealing with the mundane realities of life. The final process was enduring the glacially paced and dysfunctional criminal justice process of prosecuting the person who killed my son.

◇ ◇ ◇

While Elin and I were in the throes of navigating the difficult situations that emerged from the emotional weight of these four processes, there were times when our sanity was threatened by psychological and spiritual chaos. But we sensed these experiences were not serendipitous accidents. We knew that we were not lost, that we were on the path we were called to walk by God. We'd memorized, internalized, and tried to model Kierkegaard's wisdom: "Life can only be understood backwards; but it must be lived forwards." We reminded ourselves of this truth over and over again.

I learned that work could be my best friend or my worst enemy. On the one hand, it was a stabilizing factor. When everything else in life had changed with Thomas's death, my job was something I knew how to do well that didn't change. Working in a basic science laboratory where we explore the fundamental constituents of the universe and the forces by which they interact also helped. The SLAC National Accelerator Laboratory at Stanford is an energized, creative context in which important scientific discoveries are made. My role continued to give me a sense of meaning and contribution in life. It also gave me the comfort of knowing that I "had a paycheck," that my financial future was secure.

But on the other hand, it required an enormous amount of psychological energy for me to just "show up" because I had to intentionally put my overwhelming sense of grief and pain aside. Stanford/SLAC is a sixteen-hundred person, $700 million dollar a year research laboratory with over four billion dollars of scientific projects in the pipeline. It's also a tight-knit, science-based community where nearly everyone from the laboratory director down to frontline workers knew what happened to Thomas.

In the early days after May 2, 2021, it was difficult for me to lead meetings that were populated with hard-hitting, intellectually savvy physicists and mission-support staff without breaking down when I least expected it. In fact, one of the objective indicators of my progress toward inner healing and transformation has been my ability to function at my job without bringing up Thomas's name or having my voice unintentionally crack and weep in front of a room full of people or on a screen full of faces during a Zoom meeting.

Many of my Stanford/SLAC colleagues attended Thomas's October memorial service at the Lutheran Church of Los Gatos. Others rallied around Elin and me by posting words of comfort and support on his memorial site. By a strange and unfortunate twist of fate, my manager in the director's office lost his twenty-one-year-old son a few years earlier. We are both members of that small, sad little club of parents who had lost a child. He was further along in the grieving process, so he had a wider perspective on what lay ahead for me. But the similarity of his tragic loss to mine was (and remains) a constant reminder of Thomas's death. I still keep the remembrance card handed out at his son's funeral on my home office desk, and he keeps Thomas's remembrance card on his office desk. It's a sign of an unbreakable bond between us, an outer sign of inner solidarity.

◊ ◊ ◊

The second process that helped accelerate the perfect storm was the need to integrate the ongoing, artesian flow of powerful and exhausting emotions from multiple dreams into my conscious waking life. Some of these dreams I've already mentioned in this book; others I'll explore in the chapters to follow. All of these dreams related to our experience of losing Thomas. When properly interpreted, dreams provide deep insight and direction; they help facilitate the grieving process in forms that cannot be accomplished in any other way.

By including these dreams in this book, I do not want to create the mistaken impression that gaining access to the unconscious has been easy. Nothing could be further from the truth. Although anyone can do it, recording and analyzing dreams is part of the difficult and demanding work of inner healing and transformation that Elin and I have pushed to accomplish. It takes time and requires psychological energy, the courage to face our shadow-side, and a willingness to live by faith in God's sovereign will acting the world. As Jesus commands in Matthew 7:1–5, we must become more skilled at hunting the unconscious logs in our own eyes *first* rather than seeing or projecting our dark shadow-side as being out there in the specks of others' eyes.

Dreams creatively and symbolically describe the misalignment between what we say about ourselves and what we actually do in real life. Much like the Spirit of God working through the Bible, dreams have a compensatory function that reveals the unknown and often darker side of who we are with brutal honesty. As Jeremiah 17:19–20 reminds us, "The heart is more deceitful than all else and is desperately sick; who can understand it? I, the Lord, search the heart, I test the mind, to give to each person according to his ways, according to the results of his deeds." Walking the path of inner healing and transformation guided by my dreams took me to the depths of the deceitful heart that Jeremiah describes. But over time, inner guidance from the Spirit of God took me to an even deeper place of inner healing and transformation that Jeremiah also promises: "And you will seek Me and find Me when you search for Me with all your heart" (29:13).

Through this dream work, I recognize that I've moved down the road of processing my grief. My gut tells me I'm becoming the person I want to be and was meant to be in God. I suddenly notice I'm accepting and ultimately embracing the reality of Thomas's death more deeply. I even sometimes "catch myself in the act" of having fun or joking with Elin about something Thomas said or did. As Jesus says in John 8:31–32, "If you continue in My word, then you are truly My disciples; and you will know the truth, and the truth will set you free." In that moment of inner self-revelation, I am reassured once again that I am not lost. I am on the path I've been called to walk.

◊ ◊ ◊

As I already noted, Elin and I ignored the advice not to make any big decisions in the first year after a loss, as evidenced by the third process that exacerbated the perfect storm—the stress of selling our house in California, moving back home to Colorado, and dealing with the day-to-day problems that these logistics created. We didn't originally want to leave Colorado. I was a successful organizational consultant with the Breckenridge Institute making good money. But I was on the road two weeks a month and wanted to spend more quality time with Thomas during his formative teenager years. Taking the job at Stanford/SLAC would allow me to spend more time with my son. Moving to California was a great opportunity for all three of us. But with Thomas gone, our desire to go home to Colorado intensified. We felt compelled to leave California as soon as possible.

It was at that moment that I had the dream of the sun-filled Colorado valley with its rich red soil I mentioned earlier. The unconscious built the dream symbols and narrative around me observing the image of an enormous, fertile, sun-filled Colorado valley that was covered with bright-red Colorado soil. Along the Outer Labyrinth, the dream confirmed our deep desire to go home, and having already worked remotely for two years because of the COVID pandemic demonstrated we could move to Colorado and keep our jobs. Along the Inner Labyrinth, the valley was a symbol, a promise, of the fertile psychological and spiritual ground upon which the seeds of a new life and a new normal were already being sown by the Spirit of God working through the Self. After this dream, the deep stirring in our souls continued to morph and became an overwhelming inner force that was more and more difficult to contain with each passing day. We had to go home to Colorado, regardless of the price we'd have to pay.

FINDING NEW LIFE AFTER THE DEATH OF MY SON

◊ ◊ ◊

The fourth and final process that fed this perfect storm was the glacially paced and dysfunctional criminal justice process over which we had little or no control—a series of six court dates that led to the November 7, 2022, preliminary hearing for the person who killed our son. As I describe the details below, it's important to remember that the other three processes continued to run in the background of our hearts and minds, eating up the psychological energy and the emotional bandwidth we needed to face the daily challenges of life without Thomas, much like how running multiple apps on a mobile phone eats up battery life and bandwidth and denigrates performance.

When a person is first charged with a crime, he or she must respond to those charges in court at an arraignment. This was the first court date Elin and I attended on January 25, 2022, almost nine months after Thomas died, which I described in chapter 9. At the arraignment, the defendant, Adam, announced his intention to plead not guilty. The judge scheduled a follow-up court date called a plea hearing, at which the defendant would formally plead not guilty, guilty, or no contest to the charges against him. The first plea hearing happened about two months after the arraignment, an episode I recounted in chapter 10. But there are important parts of the story that must be added to those stories to explain the difficulty Elin and I had being dragged through multiple frustrating and, at times, maddening court appearances as part of the perfect storm.

The evidence against Adam was strong. The Campbell Police set up a second Xanax purchase on Snapchat using Thomas's phone, which they'd confiscated as evidence on the day Thomas died. When the defendant showed up to deliver the pill, they surrounded him with rifles and arrested him. The police sergeant told me that when the detectives told Adam his counterfeit pill had killed my son, he began to sob, his body convulsing violently. He almost threw up. He claimed he didn't know it was fentanyl and he never would have sold it to Thomas if he had known. His confession was captured on the body cams of the police and detectives who were in the room.

Originally, based on the strength of the evidence, James predicted we could expect to have three court dates: an arraignment, a plea hearing, and a sentencing. But that's not what happened. Elin and I were unprepared for the protracted legal process that turned into *seven* court dates, spread over the next year.

James had a fiduciary responsibility to the taxpayers of Santa Clara County to get criminals off the street. Adam's public defender was trying to get the best "deal" and minimum consequences for Adam. Like a merchant bartering with a customer in a bazaar, James and the public defender argued back and forth within the bounds of legal precedents. Court records indicated that the maximum sentence imposed for this type of felony in the State of California was eight years and four months in a state prison, whereas the minimum sentence was probation. As I briefly described earlier, at the first plea hearing, James offered Adam a plea deal squarely in the middle of the legal precedent range—three years in custody with one year in a local county prison and two years of probation. Adam's public defender argued that it was likely he would be able to get less severe consequences than this if the case went to trial. She said the defendant was turning his life around. He had a job. He was back in college. He had already learned his lesson and was striving to be a law-abiding citizen. Her counteroffer was Supervised Electronic Confinement (SEC) where Adam could serve his sentence in the privacy of his own home and continue working and going to school. Elin and I had forgiven Adam and supported this option, so long as the sentencing statement contained a strongly worded admonishment.

James told the public defender he'd accept her counteroffer with one condition. He wanted objective evidence to support Adam's claims. He wanted a letter from his boss stating Adam was a good worker and got along with people. He also asked for a letter from at least one of his college instructors and a transcript of the courses Adam had finished to date. Back in the courtroom, James informed the judge about the plea deal. But Adam's public defender responded that he wanted some time to think about it and needed to gather the objective evidence James had demanded. The judge scheduled a follow-up plea hearing for May 24, 2022.

However, with the other three elements of the perfect storm running in the background of the trial, the pressures and stress of moving to Colorado and dealing with the mundane realities of life pushed their way back onto center stage in our lives.

FINDING NEW LIFE AFTER THE DEATH OF MY SON

◇ ◇ ◇

Signing the contract to sell our California house was bittersweet. On the one hand, selling the house gave us hope that we were really going home to Colorado. On the other hand, we absolutely dreaded the fact that we were going home alone.

Just after New Year's Day, 2022, with a signed offer in hand, we called a moving company and found a realtor in Colorado who began looking for houses that met our requirements on or near McIntosh Lake, the neighborhood where Thomas grew up, which was only seven miles from Ryssby Cemetery where he was buried. Our realtor in Colorado sent us a constant stream of Zillow notifications and emails about houses that were on the market in the area. But almost none of them were near McIntosh Lake. The McIntosh Lake area was a stable community. Houses like the one we wanted rarely came on the market.

Unfortunately, the California house deal fell through five days after we signed the contract with the movers. This was also only two weeks before the January arraignment hearing. We put the Campbell house back on the market. We also ran the numbers to determine if we could carry two mortgages in case the California house didn't sell and we happened to find a house to buy in Longmont. Elin notified the movers and pushed our move date back to March 23. Elin rescheduled the move eight days after the first plea hearing so we could attend the court date while we were still living in California. Our plan was that after we moved to Colorado, we'd make one more trip back to California for the sentencing. We'd spend a week so Elin could work onsite at her company in the East Bay while I'd work in my on-campus office at Stanford. We'd both take a few hours off to attend the court case and then head back to work.

We finally got a cash offer on the California house on February 3. However, this brought only more headaches. The deal was contingent on the buyer getting approval from the homeowner's association, but he kept avoiding the required meetings with the HOA. A week later, our California realtor, Gary, repeatedly attempted to contact the buyer and his agent but never got a response—it was almost as if the buyer disappeared into thin air. While I wasn't upset with Gary, I was beyond frustrated with the situation. If the deal didn't go through, we had to face the prospect of floating two mortgages. Moreover, even if the deal did happen to go through, we still had nowhere to land in Colorado. Compounding the pain, we had just buried our son, Thomas, nine months earlier and were still overwhelmed with grief and loss.

Gary was the same realtor who sold us our house back in 2015, so he had also met Thomas. When we first started listing the house after Thomas died, Gary said we'd have to take photos for the MLS listing. He was the first person to see Thomas's room since the day we found him dead. I can still remember leading Gary down the hallway to Thomas's room, watching him stand among Thomas's band posters in deathly silence as he imagined what had happened there. Clothing, records, and books were still scattered across the floor. The desk was piled with half-eaten snacks, Thomas's house keys and wallet, and other personal items. It was the typical teenager's room. It was a wreck.

Gary slowly scanned the room before looking at me. I finally broke the silence. "We haven't touched a thing since he died," as my voice cracked. Both Elin and I began to cry as Gary put a supportive hand on my shoulder. Elin and I were still trying to comprehend what had happened to our son in that place, and what we were going to do in life without him. As Gary began gently going over the details of having the MLS photographs taken, it hit me how difficult it was going to be for me to go through Thomas's belongings. I decided to do the most difficult job first. I started with his room.

A few days later, Gary stopped by the house to help me fill out a disclosure statement, a legal document that requires sellers to provide previously undisclosed details about the property's condition for the prospective buyer. As I was completing page after page, answering dozens and dozens of mind-numbing, yes-or-no questions, suddenly Gary stopped me. "I think you want to answer yes to that question," he said without making eye contact. I read the question again: Has anyone ever died in this house? It felt like someone had kicked me in the chest as the reality of Thomas's death struck me once again. I looked at Gary, then back at the sheet. I checked the "Yes" box in the allotted space and printed the words *My son died in his bedroom*.

◇ ◇ ◇

By the third week of February, we still had no updates from the buyer, and we didn't have a place to live in Colorado either. The Colorado real estate market was on fire. There was nothing on or near McIntosh Lake, so Elin suggested we extend our area of interest about fifteen miles north. This was not what I really wanted, but Elin was feeling desperate. Discouraged by the dearth of properties, we decided to make an offer on a house in Loveland at the end of February. It wasn't McIntosh Lake, but at least it was back in Colorado. With the possibility of our contract falling through before the March 22 closing becoming more imminent, Elin and I also decided we would load up the truck and move to Colorado on March 23, regardless of whether we sold the Campbell house. Unfortunately, our Colorado realtor called us a couple days later saying that before he was able to get our offer on the Loveland house in writing, the sellers accepted another offer.

Looking back, it is hard to explain how stressed, grieved, angry, and discouraged we both were in that moment. Elin was especially devastated, as her connections to the archetype of "home" go much deeper than mine. The emotional weight of all four elements of the perfect storm had dragged her down into a deep, dark, and hopeless place. After our realtor's phone call, I held her as she cried intermittently between bursts of anger about why life had to be so hard, why it was bearing down on us so brutally, why it was so unfair. She went back to her home office and went back to work, hoping her job might be a respite from the unrelenting series of failures we encountered. I did the same.

About two hours later, Elin burst into my home office. "Come look at this!" As we walked across the hallway, she shook her head in amazement, saying, "You won't believe it!" I looked at her computer screen and saw a beautiful house in Longmont located diagonally across the street from McIntosh Lake. She had just gotten an email saying this house was on the market. Elin called our agent, who hadn't noticed it yet. Within an hour, we made an offer that was considerably above the asking price. We also agreed to let the seller have six to eight weeks to pack and leave—something she made a requirement of the sale.

We tried to motivate the seller to accept our offer quickly by saying the offer expired at 10:00 p.m. that night. That didn't work. The seller's agent took the offer but advised the seller not to accept it, since they hadn't even had one showing. Two days later, after outbidding another buyer, the house was ours with a closing date of March 31, 2022. We were thrilled, full of deep positive emotions with thankful hearts and a sense of hope that we had a concrete path forward back in Colorado.

A few hours after sealing the deal on the McIntosh house, Elin got an email from the company that was creating Thomas's gravestone. The email said, "Your gravestone has been placed," with a picture of the stone attached. Elin opened it immediately. It was a beautiful yet deeply sorrowful sight that reinforced the reality of Thomas's death. Elin wept as she gazed at the stone, marveling at the synchronicity of it being placed in Ryssby Cemetery at the exact time we were finalizing the deal on the house. Feelings of gratitude and hope again welled up from within her, sentiments almost more than she could bear. Like Elin, I also sensed that the hand of a sovereign God was behind this extraordinarily unlikely sequence of events.

We were still in California, so Elin and I drove to the first plea hearing on March 15, 2022, in San José, with our house closing looming over our heads and still no word from the buyer on his HOA approval. Luckily, Gary finally texted me three days later at 5:00 p.m. on March 18 saying simply, "buyer approved by HOA." Four days after Gary's text, we signed the closing papers on the Campbell house without the buyer present. The moving van and five large guys arrived and loaded our stuff on the truck the next day. We left California at 7:00 a.m. the next morning, trusting that the buyer would sign the closing papers later that day. I texted Gary at 10:09 p.m. that night from a Denny's restaurant in Arizona to confirm the house had closed. He responded, "Yes. We're at the finish line."

We drove straight through to Colorado—twenty-eight hours with one pause at a rest stop to catnap in our cars. We got to the two-bedroom apartment that we had rented at about 1:00 p.m. on March 25. It was a block off McIntosh Lake and about ten blocks from our new house. We were exhausted but glad to be back home. We picked up the keys to the apartment and checked it out, but we stayed at the Springhill Suites Hotel about six miles south because our furniture was still sitting in a semitruck in a warehouse somewhere in California, waiting for the moving company to find a driver to take it to Colorado.

Finishing the basement was supposed to take a month. It took four months, so we extended the lease on our apartment and storage locker—twice. We continued our structureless, Bedouin-like existence of going back and forth between the apartment and the house multiple times a day for three of the four months. On July 14, we moved about 2 percent of our belongings from the apartment to the house and started sleeping there, while contractors continued to wander in and out trying to complete unfinished work in the basement. We moved the remaining 98 percent of our stuff from the ten-foot-by-thirty-foot storage locker to the house on August 18, 2022, and the contractor doing the hardwood floors finally finished in mid-September 2022, six months after we arrived in Colorado.

Given all that Elin and I faced over those eighteen months, I'm still surprised we came as far as we did. But little did we know when we finally moved into our Colorado house that this journey was just beginning, that a tedious legal process, combined with the other three elements of the perfect storm, would continue to run rampant in the background of our hearts and minds in the months ahead.

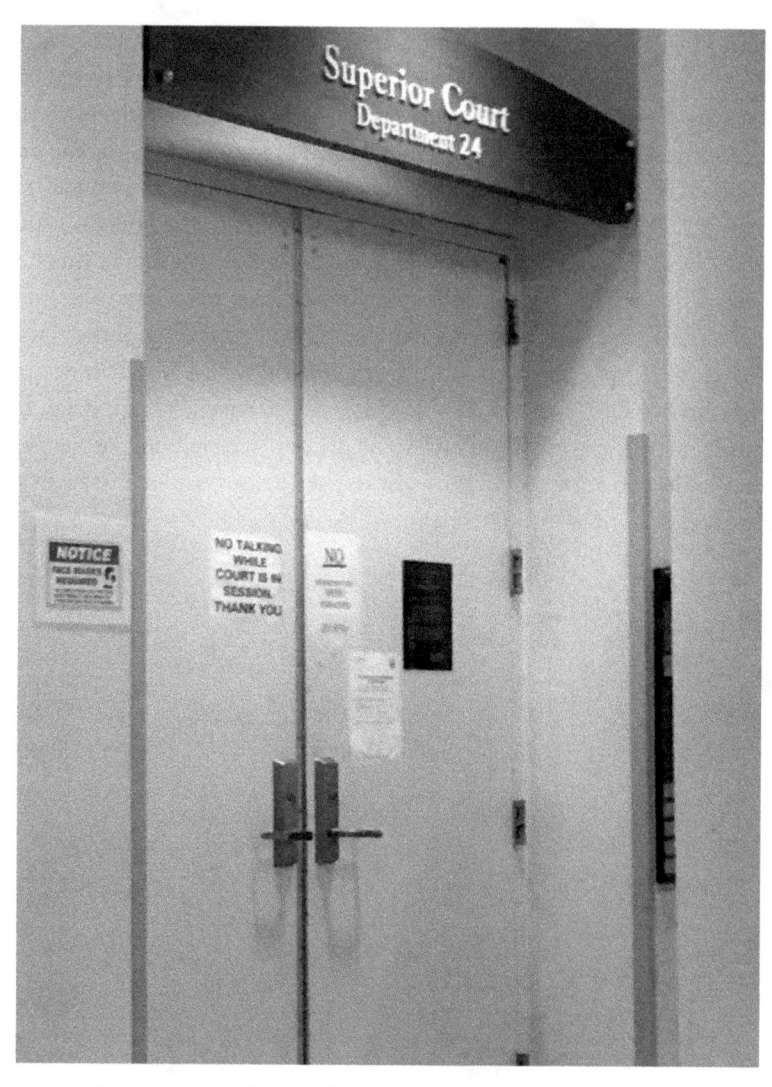

Courtroom 24 where the May 24, 2022, plea hearing was held

CHAPTER 18

THREE STRIKES AND YOU'RE OUT

December 29, 2022 (1 Year, 34 Weeks and 3 Days After)

With the other three elements of the perfect storm running episodically in the background, the up-and-down chaos of the criminal justice process continued to creep back onto the center stage of our lives before, during, and long after our move to Colorado. Ever since the January arraignment, something about Adam's visceral response to learning Thomas had died continued to haunt me. It didn't make sense. After seeing him for the second time at the first plea hearing, I came home and searched for him online. Eventually, I found multiple links to his college football recruiting websites. These recruiting profiles said he was six foot, one inch tall, weighed 174 pounds, wore jersey number 14, and played wide receiver for the Bellview High School football team from 2016 through 2019, the same high school Thomas had attended. He was only a year older than Thomas.

Thomas played the trumpet in the Bellview marching band that performed at all the football games. When Elin and I would go to a football game to watch Thomas play, the defendant was probably on the field playing wide receiver too. As we cheered for the Bellview football team, we were unknowingly cheering on the defendant.

One of the recruiting websites that Adam showed up on said he had 130 followers, some of whom were college recruiters. There were dozens of clips of successful plays, showcasing Adam's abilities as a football player. Thomas, Elin, and I were probably in the background of some of the videos I was now viewing. Whoever this guy was, it's clear he may have had visions of playing college football.

This new information about Adam further stoked my curiosity about his reaction to Thomas dying. It was unlikely Adam would have reacted so strongly to hearing about Thomas's death if he was a total stranger or just some random Snapchat user. The only way his reaction at the police station made sense was if he actually knew my son. This would also explain

Adam's interaction with Elin and me at the arraignment, where he waited for us outside the courtroom. It made the situation much more personal. It explained why Thomas trusted Adam to sell him a genuine Xanax in a world where counterfeit pills were poisoning thousands upon thousands of other unsuspecting young people.

◊ ◊ ◊

Sitting in our Colorado apartment, Elin and I discussed dozens of scenarios as the May 24 date of the second plea hearing drew near. What if Adam didn't have a job yet or wasn't going to school? What should our position be about the drug sale felonies, given that we'd already forgiven him for being the channel through which Thomas was killed? Should our decision to support the home confinement deal be based on his continued remorse and active efforts to straighten himself out, or should it be unconditional?

In the end, it wasn't our call. But we also knew James would factor our perspective into his final decision. So, Elin and I headed toward May 24 in a state of limbo, not knowing how the day or the court case would unfold. We did, however, agree wholeheartedly that we had to let Adam and God sort it out. In doing so, I felt a deep sense of peace, trusting we would ultimately do the right thing, for the right reason, at the right time. I knew we had to focus inwardly in order to seek and find God's will in this situation—not my will, Elin's will, or even what we believed Thomas would have wanted. In the words of the prophet Jeremiah:

> "For I know the plans that I have for you," declares the Lord, "plans for prosperity and not for disaster, to give you a future and a hope. Then you will call upon Me and come and pray to Me, and I will listen to you. And you will seek Me and find Me when you search for Me with all your heart. I will let Myself be found by you," declares the Lord. (Jeremiah 29:11–14)

Since she wasn't able to travel back to California with me for the second plea hearing, Elin said I should make any necessary decisions. She trusted me to represent Thomas, her, and our family. As I prepared to leave for the airport that Sunday, Elin held me tight and kissed me, saying, "I really wish I could go with you, so you wouldn't have to be in court alone, and I also don't want to be here by myself." What Elin really wanted was to have Thomas back. But that was impossible, and we both knew it.

My plan for my time in California was to work in my office at Stanford/SLAC all week, take a few hours off to attend the court date, and then fly home to Colorado on Friday afternoon. Early that morning before the plea hearing, a friend sent me a text about one of the posts I uploaded on Thomas's memorial site. Her words resonated in my heart and mind as I logged onto my Stanford computer account and sipped my Starbucks coffee. She wrote, "I continue to read Thomas's memorial stories knowing how difficult it must be resurrecting painful memories. Perhaps that is part of the horrible process you must go through to find bits and pieces of peace."

There was something about the word resurrecting that struck me very deeply. Was this something I was doing consciously when I wrote the story I had posted? Was this something that happened to me, like an artesian flow of sorrow and grief that rose from within when I least expected it without my conscious assent? Was it both? Her comment helped me explore the essential tension I was experiencing but had not yet concretized into words.

Sometimes, I consciously resurrect painful memories about Thomas when I write posts for his memorial site or record my experiences in my journal. Other times, they are resurrected as I drive past a restaurant Thomas and I used to frequent or see a field where Thomas played soccer. Still other times, painful memories get resurrected when someone like my new Colorado barber tries to make light conversation and innocently asks, "Do you have kids?"

There in my office, in the hours before the second plea hearing, the insights kept flowing. I realized the absence of Thomas's physical presence and the existential sense of loss that was being resurrected episodically were part of my ongoing connection to my son. Colin Murray Parkes argues that "Grief is the price we pay for love." Rabbi Earl Grollman puts it this way: "Grief is not a disorder, a disease or a sign of weakness. It is an emotional, physical, and spiritual necessity, the price you pay for love. The only cure for grief is to grieve."[41]

◊ ◊ ◊

I got to the courthouse twenty minutes early for the 9:00 a.m. proceeding. Much like the arraignment and first plea hearing, I dressed in the same clothes I wore for Thomas's funeral and memorial services, including the red-and-blue striped tie he wore when he made a public profession of faith. I wore it in memory of Thomas's short but impactful life. And again, other than the defense attorneys and prosecutors, I was the only person wearing a tie.

Adam arrived a few minutes later. He was with his public defender and a young woman I later learned was his girlfriend. They sat to my right about ten feet away. I heard a loud click as a guard unlocked the courtroom door from the inside. "The courtroom is open," he said, as people got up and walked toward the doors. As I sat, I could hear the gist of the conversation Adam was having with his public defender. "No. That's not it," Adam said, looking frustrated and scared at the same time. I heard him spell his name and then give her his email address. I also overheard them talking about the letters of reference James wanted, but I couldn't make out the specifics. Just then, James walked down the stairs, and I waved at him. As he walked past Adam and the public defender, James glanced at them and then nodded at me, indicating he already had a plan on how to deal with the situation.

"I haven't heard a word from the defendant about the letters," he said once he came closer. "How are you doing?" he asked, looking me in the eye. I could tell he really wanted to know. I told him it was weird being here without Elin. James looked again at Adam and his attorney as he waited for them to finish talking. Once they finally arose and walked toward the courtroom, James quickly called out the public defender's name. She stopped and listened to James for a few seconds before walking directly toward me, knowing I was interested in what was going on. "I had the wrong email address for the defendant," she quickly stated. "He has a pay stub and a letter with him today. They're on his cell phone, but he doesn't have any phone service down here in the basement. His girlfriend is headed outside to email them to me now." Before I could respond, she turned and headed into the courtroom through the door seen in the picture at the start of this chapter.

"It's what I expected," James said to me after she left. "I'll look at what she sends me, and if it's not what I'm looking for, I'll pull the thread and ask for more." I shook my head, acknowledging what he said. James continued, "So, here's what's going to happen now when we go into the courtroom. The clerk will call our case, you stay seated, I'll explain the situation to the judge, and ask to schedule another plea hearing about two months out."

James and I walked into the courtroom. The defendant was sitting on the right side with his girlfriend about halfway toward the front of the room. I walked past them and took a seat in the third row on the left side. James walked up into the area directly in front of the judge where the public defenders and prosecutors discussed their cases prior to them being heard by the judge.

I sat through six or seven cases before Thomas's case was called. Every one of them was finished in less than five minutes with another court date being assigned. The emotionless transaction of it all was an indicator of how lethargic, bureaucratic, and impersonal the lengthy legal process is. The net result is a judicial system where the actual committing of the crime is so far removed from its imposed repercussions that the gravity of the offense and its relationship to the severity of the consequences get disconnected. As MIT professor Peter Senge puts it, local causation has a nonlocal effect in space-time.[42] In other words, when the cause of a situation is so far removed from its consequences, we have trouble connecting the two. That's why we don't learn from such experiences; it's a natural psychological tendency of the human mind.

On the one hand, this prolonged judicial process ensures criminals get a fair and impartial trial that's not fueled by the raw, unprocessed emotions of the victim's loss. But on the other hand, this places an enormous burden on the victim to maintain the connection between crime and consequence, between loss and justice. Our presence at each court date ensured Thomas's death did not migrate into obscurity, becoming just another number or faceless name on a court docket.

James did his part to maintain the connection between the crime and the consequences. His initial remarks to the judge always began with, "Your Honor, I'd like to call the court's attention to the fact that the victim's parents are here in the courtroom." The judge would then turn to Elin and me and acknowledge our presence and our loss, and the clerk would note it in the court record. But this was emotionally and psychologically exhausting work for Elin and me. It was an active part of the grieving process that intentionally resurrected the painful memories of Thomas's death. But it was also our duty as his parents. This kept Thomas's memory alive and helped to ensure the enormous impact of his short life was not forgotten. But it also felt like we were being rope-a-doped to the point of exhaustion. This ongoing, unproductive series of court appearances almost seemed designed to wear us out, to discourage us from showing up.

Sometimes I wonder whether Adam thought he'd never see Elin or me again after we forgave him at the arraignment. I sensed that each time Elin and I showed up for a court date, Adam may have thought, *It's them again. I thought they forgave me. Maybe they didn't mean it.* In our own minds, Elin and I were always trying to maintain the connection between the grace of forgiving Adam for being the conduit through which Thomas was killed and the five felony counts filed against him. When you pick up one end of a stick, you pick up the other end. You can choose your actions, but you can't always choose the consequences of your actions.

Once Thomas's case was called, Adam and his attorney stood at the podium directly in front of the judge. James stood on the right side of the courtroom. I remained seated. Adam's public defender described the email address mix-up, and James asked the judge to reschedule another plea date for July 19. Strike one.

◊ ◊ ◊

As I drove back to Stanford, I felt discouraged, really discouraged. But I was also committed to seeing the process through and doing the right thing for Thomas, for my wife, and for me. I called Elin to fill her in on what happened at the courthouse. When I finished recounting the confusion and the utter waste of time, she, too, was discouraged by the lack of progress. After commiserating for a few minutes, she asked, "Can I change the subject? I have something I need to share with you." I was all ears.

"I woke up around 2:00 a.m. and couldn't get back to sleep," Elin said. "As I was lying there in bed, I had this strange feeling like Thomas was right there with me. It felt like he was in a different dimension of sorts. I don't know how else to describe it. It was disconcerting and comforting at the same time. I questioned whether it was a real experience of his presence. But I don't think I was making it up. I kept trying to go back to sleep and calm myself down by reading my Kindle. Then I would put the Kindle away and not be able to get back to sleep. Then I would feel the disconcerting yet comforting feeling of Thomas's presence again. I was still feeling it when I finally got out of bed, although I was also feeling so very sad. The feeling of Thomas's presence remained with me as I brushed my teeth and went through my morning routine. But once I logged on to my computer and started working, his presence disappeared."

Elin was deeply shaken by this experience. As we talked, she cried and said how much she regretted reading her book as a distraction from the eerie yet longed for experience. "I should have just laid there and experienced Thomas's presence, but it was so weird. I felt so uncomfortable that I couldn't help but distracting myself."

I just listened, trying to imagine what it must have been like and wishing Thomas would come to visit me.

Elin went on, feeling terribly guilty about what she had done. "I talked to Thomas about this later in the day. I told him I was sorry, and I promised that if he would come back to me again, I wouldn't read, I'd just take in, and try to be comforted by, his presence."

It began to hit me as Elin was talking that at the very same time I was summarizing my insights about my friend's text in my journal, Elin was in the midst of her own deeply transformative experience with Thomas's presence. It was as if Thomas went to be with Elin, because his mom couldn't be in California with me for the court date.

◇ ◇ ◇

When Elin and I arrived at the July plea hearing, I was wearing the same clothes and red-and-blue striped tie as I had the prior hearings. I was prepared for another uneventful waste of time. I was not disappointed. Adam arrived with his girlfriend, and his public defender looked just as disorganized and detached from the case as she did on the previous court dates. As they huddled up outside the courtroom, James walked past them and sat next to Elin and me.

After chatting about how hot it was outside, James looked at Elin and me and asked how we were doing. I replied, "Well, quite frankly, we're tired of getting the run around from these guys. Have you heard anything?"

James answered with an equal amount of frustration. "She sent me the one pay stub this morning, but that's it." He continued, "Come on, let's head into the courtroom."

Like church folks who sit in the same pews week after week, Adam was perched on the right side of the room with his girlfriend about halfway toward the front of the courtroom. We walked past them without making eye contact and sat in our usual seats in the third row on the left side. James walked up into the area directly in front of the judge, ensuring Thomas's case would be called quickly.

Once our case was called, Adam and his attorney stood at the podium directly in front of the judge as she described how the defendant was having trouble getting the character letters from various people. James explained to the judge his frustration in not getting the objective evidence that he asked for as mitigation for the plea deal he was proposing. The public defender assured the judge Adam would get the letters to her as soon as possible and then asked for another month to make good on his promise. James agreed to the extension but told the judge that if he did not receive the letters by the next deadline, he'd ask to schedule a preliminary hearing as the first step toward a jury trial. So, a fourth plea hearing was scheduled for August 30, two months down the road. Strike two.

James walked Elin and me out of the courthouse to the parking garage. Elin and I expressed our feelings of frustration and annoyance at what seemed like delay tactics manipulating the natural entropy of the slow-moving legal system to wear us down and get us to give up our pursuit of some measure of justice for the five felonies Adam was charged with. James said he couldn't agree more, but he reminded us again that going to a preliminary hearing would at least get the case moving toward resolution, and hopefully, a more competent public defender would be assigned to the case by that point.

As I drove back to my office at Stanford, I reflected on this latest development. I began to realize it was *Adam* who had been dragging his feet on getting the letters to support his claim that he was turning his life around. Images from Adam's football recruiting profiles began to float back into my mind as I drove north, along with all the possible reasons that led us to this impasse. *Maybe the defendant is trying to do damage control,* I wondered to myself. *Maybe he's trying to keep the number of people who know what's going on as small as possible. Maybe he's never asked for the letters because he's ashamed.* And then more cynically, my curiosity was piqued. *Maybe he doesn't have a job. Maybe he's not back in school.* These various "maybes" soon became an infinite regress that led nowhere.

◊ ◊ ◊

As the fourth plea hearing approached, Elin and I continued to navigate the perfect storm as all four interdependent processes continued to unfold at different times, moving in different directions, and proceeding at different rates. It was often difficult to tell which of the four processes was at center stage. They all clamored for our time and attention along the Outer Labyrinth. As Elin's experience of Thomas's dreamlike visitation showed, they were also trying to get our attention from the Inner Labyrinth of the destiny that we had as revealed in our dreams.

On the morning of August 30, Elin and I once again arrived at the courthouse. Once again, I was wearing the exact same blue jacket along with Thomas's red-and-blue striped tie. Once again, Adam was there with his girlfriend when Elin and I entered the hall outside the courtroom. And once again, we walked past them without making eye contact and sat at the other end of the hallway. A few minutes later, James approached us in our usual spot.

"How are you doing?" he asked with an empathic tone that signaled he really wanted to know.

"We're okay," I responded. "We're just glad that we're going to be moving beyond this roadblock."

He shook his head in agreement. "So am I," he said. "The defense attorney finally sent me a character letter early this morning." He paused for a moment with a dumbfounded look on his face. "It's from his girlfriend."

"What?" Elin and I cried out almost in unison.

Before we could say more, James arose and signaled for us to get up too. "Well, let's not waste any more time," he stated as he led us to the courtroom door.

"Your Honor," James began when our case was called, "I'd like to call the court's attention to the fact that this is the fourth plea hearing for this case. The defendant has failed to produce the mitigations that I have requested multiple times. I would also like to point out that the victim's parents are present here in the courtroom again today, as they have been for every court date. These ongoing hearings have placed a burden on them, over and beyond the fact that they have lost their eighteen-year-old son, Thomas. Your Honor, I'd like to schedule a preliminary hearing for this case at the court's earliest convenience."

The judge agreed, and the court clerk called out some possible dates about two months out. James looked at Elin and me and asked, "Does November 7, 2022, work for you?"

I quickly responded, "Yes, that works for us," as Adam also indicated that he could make that date.

Just as he did after the previous hearing, James walked Elin and me out of the courthouse to the parking garage. "A preliminary hearing is like a mini trial," James explained. "It's what's done prior to an actual trial."

Elin and I were already tired and worn out from the legal process, so I asked, "What's involved in a trial and how long does it take?"

"If we go to trial, it will take about three weeks," James explained. "One week to select the witnesses, one week to select the jurors, and a week to hear testimony. The only part of the trial that you and Elin can attend is the part where the court hears testimony from witnesses. In terms of witnesses, I'd probably call officers and detectives from the Campbell Police Department, the coroner, a toxicologist, and others to testify." James saw the looks on our faces and quickly followed up with, "Don't worry about it. I'll explain everything in detail as we move further down the road. Until then, try to relax and let me take care of things."

Strike three. You're out.

CHAPTER 19

THE REALITY OF THOMAS'S DEATH PERMEATES TO DEEPER LEVELS

January 3, 2023 (1 Year, 35 Weeks, and 1 Day After)

By September 2022, the stress and pressure of moving to Colorado had subsided, and the long-term task of unpacking, both physically and psychologically, was well underway. With the preliminary hearing scheduled for November 7, a tiny flame of hope for some closure on the legal process began to flicker for Elin and me. But without any warning, one of the other interdependent processes of the perfect storm started demanding my attention.

Thomas and Mark visiting the 9/11 Memorial in New York City

The long-term reality of Thomas's death continued to slowly "sink in" and yield positive yet utterly painful results. A window into this inner unconscious process appeared in the dream below on September 8, 2022, just nine days after the fourth and final plea hearing.

As the dream opens, I'm walking into the lobby of an old brownstone building somewhere in New York City. I'm carrying a child, who is maybe two years old, in my left arm. The dream seems like it's set in a different time, maybe back in the early 1950s—a *Leave It to Beaver* timeframe when life seemed easier, slower, and more well-known in terms of knowing "what life is about and how to live it." The entire lobby looked like it was made of white marble, and the setting was pristine, simple, and elegant yet not rich or opulent—just elegant and middle-class, or maybe upper-middle-class. The setting of the old brownstone building was a place where people "lived"—a community or micro-neighborhood within a larger neighborhood outside this place.

The larger neighborhood outside the setting of the dream consisted of many other brownstones, each of which had its own subculture and group of families and friends that were part of the larger place in the inner dimension of New York City. My sense from the old brownstone building that I walked into was that it was a place where life was simpler than it is now, more knowable, predictable, and somehow "the way it should be." All of this I somehow knew as the dream opened. I walked into this place carrying a child as if these tacit, unquestioned, taken-for-granted assumptions were shared by all who were in the dream, and they were a reflection of the "reality" along both the destiny we have along the Inner Labyrinth and the destiny we create along the Outer Labyrinth with our day-to-day choices. As I walked into the dream setting, the lobby was filled with the positive, familiar, comforting hustle and bustle of people who were composed predominantly of children playing, as if this first room was an indoor neighborhood playground.

When I entered the lobby-like area of this old brownstone house, I had the distinct sense that I was "home" in a place where I belonged—where I was known, welcomed, and wanted. A little boy who was about eight years old walked up to me as he was playing with the other children, and he asked me almost in passing, "Is Thomas coming home?" as if he had no idea that Thomas was dead. He didn't really "say" this to me with actual words. Rather he just communicated it to me directly, so I got the message in the depths of my soul. In some ways, this little boy seemed like he really was Thomas in a previous dream where Thomas was about eight years old, carrying a microwave, and was with a two-year-old boy, like the toddler I was carrying in this dream. I thought, and felt, an answer to his question deep within my soul, "No. Thomas is not coming back." I sensed, knew, thought, felt this answer emerge with a deep and profound sense of sadness, pain, grief, and loss that *I* understood inwardly in the dream, but these emotions were not communicated to the little boy, as he continued playing with the other kids. It was as if life had gone on in real life along the Outer Labyrinth since Thomas died, one year, eighteen weeks, and three days ago, but the reality of Thomas dying and being buried in Ryssby Cemetery had not been communicated to this little boy, or to the others in the dream's context-setting along the Inner Labyrinth—it had not "sunk in" yet.

I realized I needed to tell him and all the other little children that Thomas was dead and would never be coming back. So, I began gathering them together to come sit at a small, rectangular white marble table that was at the very center of the room. There were dozens and dozens of kids gathered in little groups of twos, threes, and fours, with each playing their own little game and playing with, and competing with, other groups of children. There may have been some children also playing alone because they didn't fit in anywhere or hadn't been chosen to play with the other groups of children.

As I gathered the children toward the marble table, I was trying to communicate a sense of urgency for them to come and sit because I had to tell them something important. But I was communicating this to them directly without using words. As I gathered them, I wondered to myself, *How am I going to tell them this sad story in a way where they understand the importance and reality of what I'm saying?*

Many of the children were already seated at the marble table, but some were still playing, and I was trying to get their attention and gather them. I wanted to make sure I had all of them gathered and seated before I began. In the dream, I sensed it was supremely important that they all knew, and that they all knew then and there. The dream ends here, as I continued gathering the last few kids.

I recorded this dream upon waking but didn't log any reflections on it until a month later in a hotel room in Harper's Ferry, West Virginia, the day after my nephew's wedding. The dream narrative consists of the silent dialogue between the dream-ego—the image of "me" in the dream—and the eight-year-old boy, all of this set within the time-stamped context of a collective image of my childhood in the 1950s and 60s back in New Jersey, just twelve miles west of Midtown Manhattan.

Along the Outer Labyrinth of day-to-day life in those days, the TV show *Leave It to Beaver* was built around the narrative of young Theodore "Beaver" Cleaver getting himself into trouble as he navigated his way through an often incomprehensible, sometimes irrational world. The show ran from 1957, when I was four years old, until 1963. Watching the show helped to shape my conscious perceptions about life and channel the impulses and forces emerging from the unconscious, psychological forces that I was almost entirely unconscious of at the time. The show also symbolized the sociocultural context in which I grew up. It was the time when I was beginning to assert my individuality—the time when the bedrock of my tacit, unquestioned, taken-for-granted assumptions about my life, and life in general, were being formed.

The inner healing and transformation that were happening now at this archetypal level went deep. The dream images embodied and were pointing to a time when I was attending the Hungarian Reformed Church prior to my first personal experience of God's presence in 1964 when I was confirmed. The collective image of the little boy playing with all the other children in small groups of twos, threes, and fours was an image of the collective nature of my psyche. The white marble lobby, within which this childlike energy and potentiality was happening in the dream, was made of Greek- and Roman-style white marble that connected the stage upon which the dream was acted out back to the collective archetypal origins of

Western civilization. The four-sided marble table at the center of this room was an image of the Self—the *Imago Dei*.

The dream gave me a front row seat to the ways in which the Spirit of God was processing my grief about Thomas's death in the unconscious and the destiny I had in Him from the beginning of time without my active, conscious, and intentional involvement. It gave me insight into how the archetypal activity of the Inner Labyrinth revealed in this dream was happening together with, and linked up to, the Outer Labyrinth of daily life in Harper's Ferry.

The church potluck dream that I had a year and a half earlier in May 2021, where I knew Thomas was dead but Elin didn't (see chapter 13), revealed the process by which the initial reality of Thomas's death was "sinking in" to the deeper parts of my heart and mind just twenty-five days after finding Thomas dead in his room. In contrast, the New York City brownstone dream above revealed how the reality of Thomas's death in September 2022 had penetrated further down into the unconscious, to the tacit and unquestioned assumptions that were formed in my childhood, at a time when I had my first childlike inkling of "what life is about and how to live it" and "the way it should be." The images of an elegant, white marble setting within the dream narrative connected my personal experience in the 1950s and '60s to the collective, archetypal foundation of Western civilization, the sociocultural context of Greek and Roman society—what Jung called the collective unconscious.[43]

Our experience of the destiny we have in God along the Inner Labyrinth of dreams, like the New York City brownstone dream, often seems far away from the mundane and pedestrian realities of the destiny we create with our daily choices along the Outer Labyrinth. But as I finally logged my reflections on the brownstone dream in Harper's Ferry, I saw experiential evidence that this deep inner healing and transformation process was really happening by the way Elin and I "caught ourselves in the act" of having a good time at our nephew's wedding the previous day.

◊ ◊ ◊

Elin and I arrived in West Virginia on the Wednesday before the ceremony. Much of the trip consisted of lengthy dinners and conversations with family and friends. As introverts, Elin and I knew we were going to be psychologically exhausted from being with people nearly nonstop, but we planned sufficient downtime between the back-to-back social events to recharge our emotional batteries.

The rehearsal dinner was on Friday night at a Peruvian restaurant in northern Maryland. It was the first time the bride and groom's extended families met. So, we were introduced to and circulated among about fifty people, learning their names, who they were related to, and where they were from. During the meal, Elin and I sat with our niece and her husband. As we chatted, they were curious about what was going on in our lives and how we were handling the longer-term challenges of processing our grief. Thomas was a part of the conversation, but we spoke about him and his memory in ways that were positive and didn't allow our deeper grief and pain to color or dominate our time of sharing.

The next day, the wedding was held at a guesthouse farm in Harper's Ferry. The ceremony was officiated under a white wedding arch in a field that sat on a cliff about a thousand feet above the Potomac River, with spectacular views of the autumn colors carpeting the mountains that surrounded the resort. It was a perfect day—warm and sunny, no wind and without a cloud in the sky. As a hundred people watched the ceremony, the bride was radiant, and the groom looked happy and deeply satisfied. The setting was idyllic.

At the wedding reception, we sat with Elin's family—people we knew well and with whom we felt comfortable mentioning Thomas as part of our conversation. About three hours into the reception, Elin and I decided to get some psychological space. We walked back to the field where the wedding took place. As we looked down onto the quiet flow of the wide but shallow Potomac River and the spectacular rolling hills, Elin said quietly, "You know, I'm having a good time," almost like she was making a confession.

I just listened, sensing that this was holy ground as she continued. "I'm dancing, talking to people, listening to stories about how well other folks' children are doing, without the shadow of Thomas's death hanging over me." We sat on one of the benches as she went on. "I don't even feel guilty about enjoying myself, although I do feel a little guilty for not feeling guilty, but then I move back into the mindset of just enjoying the day, my friends, and my family."

I was feeling much the same way. Thoughts of *I wish Thomas were here* were not clouding my heart and mind. I wasn't going down the inner path of what-ifs like had happened so many times before. *I wonder what Thomas's wedding day would have been like. I wonder what he'd be doing for a living after college and graduate school. I wonder how many kids he'd have and what it would be like to be a grandparent.*

I, too, felt somewhat guilty for having a good time, but I was also tired of carrying the burden of grief about Thomas's loss. Even after the wedding, Elin and I enjoyed the afterglow of a really nice day, a brief respite from the painful process of dealing with our grief. It was as if something deep inside of me knew about, had accepted, and was trying to embrace the fact that Thomas was not coming back.

In the month since having the New York City brownstone dream, it was as if the "me" in the dream had finished gathering all the children together and told them Thomas was not coming home, and they all "got it." In that month between the brownstone dream and the wedding, I'd moved a little further down the road of aligning the destiny I have in God along the Inner Labyrinth of my dreams with the destiny I was creating with my choices as I openly embraced the good time I had with Elin at the wedding, rather than resisting and fighting the fact that deep positive changes were happening to me.

The wedding was about three weeks before the preliminary hearing was scheduled to happen. After logging my reflections on the brownstone dream in my hotel room, I decided to ping James with an email about whether there had been any changes regarding the status of the case. James responded early Monday morning that he had not heard from Adam's defense, which was not surprising since he was being assigned a new public defender, but the hearing was still scheduled for November 7.

◊ ◊ ◊

When Elin and I moved back to Colorado, one of the first decisions we faced in shaping and defining the next chapter of our lives was where to go to church. For the first few weeks, we watched online services from our apartment. Then, we decided to go back to Faith Presbyterian Church in Boulder, the same church where Thomas made his public profession of faith.

We were nervous about how this would go, fearing the question "How's your son, Thomas?" from people who didn't know he was dead. That's exactly what happened. Sitting through the service was fine because we were sequestered in a pew by ourselves. What we feared most was standing around during the coffee hour and making our way through the crowd and out of the church building. It felt like an obstacle course as we tried to avoid running into people we knew who did not know Thomas had died.

One Sunday as we walked up the aisle after the service, a person who Elin knew spotted her, waved excitedly from her seat, and then quickly caught up to us in the coffee hour. "It's so good to see you," she began. "How long will you be in town?"

Elin responded anxiously, "Well, we actually moved back here to Colorado on March 25 and just closed on a house in Longmont."

"Oh, that's great!" Elin's acquaintance exclaimed. "We'll have to get together. How's Thomas?"

We decided right then that going to Faith Presbyterian was going to be too hard for us. It wasn't fair to us or our well-intentioned friends, who were genuinely glad to see us and wanted to reconnect. It was awkward and put us and the other people in an extremely difficult position. We didn't know what to say, so rather than trying to explain everything that had happened for the first time, we emailed people an invitation to Thomas's memorial site. After sending the link, some people didn't know what to say, so they struggled clumsily to respond or post something on the site. Elin sent the church friend who asked about Thomas a link to his memorial site. She replied to Elin in an email and expressed her formal condolences, shock, and words of support. But Elin never heard from her again. We decided to find another church.

CHAPTER 20

THE PRELIMINARY HEARING

January 3, 2023 (1 Year, 35 Weeks, and 1 Day After)

Since Thomas's death, I've reflected on the ways in which the Outer Labyrinth of the destiny we create with our choices was analogous to Wesleyan-Arminian theology's focus on free will, and how the destiny we have in God from the foundation of the world is reflected in the Calvinist notion of God's sovereignty. I realized both theological perspectives are right and both are happening together at the same time. As Norman Geisler put it, we are chosen but free.[44]

I've come to recognize more fully that God is accomplishing His sovereign will through my conscious and unconscious (intended and unintended) beliefs, mindsets, and actions, regardless of whether I realize in the moment that He is using my life and story to achieve His ends, purpose, and will, which cannot be thwarted (Job 42:2).[45] In Jesus's day, the hand-hewn wooden yokes that were fitted to the backs of the oxen that plowed in the fields were like a "partnership" between the yoke and the animal. In much the same way, my relationship with God is like a partnership, where I've taken His yoke upon me. As Jesus tells us in Matthew 11:28–30 (NIV):

> Come to Me, all who are weary and burdened, and I will give you rest. Take My yoke upon you and learn from Me, for I am gentle and humble in heart, and you will find rest for your souls. For My yoke is comfortable, and My burden is light.

Since making my two vows to the Lord on the Mount of Beatitudes in 1996, I have committed to allowing God's kingdom to reign in both my conscious and unconscious life, where the Spirit of God sanctifies and transforms the Self (*Imago Dei*) and other psychic elements. The July 2018 dream below provides a window into the inner experience of this yoked

Courtroom 36 where the November 7, 2022, preliminary hearing was held

partnership, as the Spirit of God works through the Self and the dream-ego (the image of my conscious waking self in the dream) to create integrity in depth:

> I was facilitating some kind of church retreat with dozens of people. The meeting was being held in the sanctuary of an old-style white wooden church, the kind with a steeple on top. The meeting was going well. I was doing a good job facilitating, and I was especially watching the interaction of the people, the experience they were having, and the extent to which they were connecting to each other in meaningful ways. As the meeting went on, I was having a harder and harder time staying focused on the facilitation process and the people, because it was demanding so much psychological energy from me—I was getting psychologically tired. My attention began to drift, and I even stepped out of the meeting a couple of times while the group was busy doing an interactive exercise just to be by myself and let the meeting run at its own pace.
> At one point, I had stepped out of the meeting, and when I came back, it was like the entire group (i.e., dozens and dozens of people) were doing an exercise. They were up interacting and connecting with each other and doing things as part of the exercise. The exercise was going at a very fast pace, with lots of action and a high level of energy that was positive and collective to the group. I walked through the group of people looking for my microphone to try to move back into control of the retreat. As I walked through the crowded room full of people, I saw they were interacting and connecting with an even higher level of collective energy, and I could not find my microphone. I began to wonder who was leading and facilitating the meeting and this exercise, and I stopped being concerned about finding the microphone and getting back in control of the retreat. I began to sense I had to let this thing happen, to let this process unfold. I looked at the people as I walked through the crowd, still searching for my microphone and feeling a little out of control of what was going on around me. I was wondering who it was that had designed and was facilitating this exercise, because it seemed to be going really, really, well.

It was clear there was someone (or a presence) who had begun to lead and facilitate the retreat and this exercise while I stepped out of the meeting, but I couldn't figure out who it was. It was as if the exercise was getting more and more complex, and the number of people who were participating in it had increased dramatically. There was an order and pattern to the exercise and what they were doing, but I had no idea who had taken the lead. As I wandered through the sanctuary, I found some stairs that led down to another room in the basement. I walked downstairs, and there was a multitude of people all around me who were all participating in the exercise that was being led by this presence I couldn't identify. In the basement, there were people everywhere, and they all were participating in the same exercise as the people upstairs. To my left, I saw two lines of people that led into a separate room that was all white and was a place where marriage ceremonies were being performed. The two lines of people were moving into this room and doing some other element of the exercise when they got there. To my right, the room spread out enormously and was filled with hundreds and hundreds of people who were all participating in the same exercise. Straight ahead of where I was standing was yet another area that seemed like a lake or body of water that stretched out as far as the eye could see. I thought I should try to go over there to get a better perspective about what was happening all around me.

As the dream ends, I wasn't afraid or overly concerned about what was happening around me, and I had decided to just let this thing happen since it was unfolding so well. I was simply amazed at the enormous scope and complexity of the exercise that was unfolding around me; the myriad of people involved; their level of energy, connection, and intensity, which continued to increase; the orchestration of an exercise of this scale and complexity that was going so well; and the fact that I didn't know who it was that was facilitating and leading this exercise. I realized I had become a part of the exercise. I was no longer the one who was facilitating the exercise. Rather, my role was to observe and explore it and learn how the presence was causing things to unfold in this beautiful and elegant way.[46]

FINDING NEW LIFE AFTER THE DEATH OF MY SON

The dream is set in the collective religious setting of an old, white wooden church with a steeple on top—a time stamp that links the overall context and message of the dream back to the Hungarian Reformed Church in Passaic, New Jersey, where I had my first personal experience of God's presence when I was eleven years old. I attended confirmation classes there using the Heidelberg Catechism that was taught by the pastor. This was the beginning of my personal walk with God.

One day along the Outer Labyrinth of waking life in 1964, in a moment of transparency and innocence, I told my mom, "I don't know if I really want to be confirmed. I don't know if I believe all this stuff." This set off alarm bells in my family. My father and mother, who were not professing Christians at the time, said, "You better talk to the pastor about this."

So I did. The next time the confirmation class met, I waited until all the other kids had left the classroom, then reticently I said to the pastor, "I need to ask you something." I stood there, not knowing exactly what to say or how this would go.

"Come sit down," he responded kindly, sensing that I was nervous and my initiative in talking with him needed to be affirmed.

I went straight to the bottom line. "I'm not sure I want to be confirmed. I don't really understand or believe all the stuff we're talking about here."

"Mark, don't worry about that," the pastor replied with a fatherly and emphatic tone, being pleasantly surprised at my openness and honesty. "Just believe as much as you can now. God understands and loves us still."

It was at that moment when I first experienced an overwhelming sense of the Spirit of God's presence filling my heart and soul. I was saved by grace, through faith, not of my own doing. I was saved through the gift of God.

In conscious waking life, the Hungarian Reformed Church was an old, white wooden church with a steeple on top. The unconscious chose this religious setting as the context within which the images, symbols, narrative, and lessons learned about my partnership with God unfolded in the dream. The Sunday school room where I had that conversation with the pastor became a sacred space for me. I took Thomas there in 2018 and told him the story. I even took a photo of him standing outside the door to that room. In September 2021, just four months after Thomas died, I took Elin to that church, to that exact room, and told her the story again.

◊ ◊ ◊

As the other three elements of the perfect storm ran in the background, the criminal justice process and the November 7 preliminary hearing drifted back to center stage. A week before the hearing, James emailed me and asked whether we could have a phone call prior to the court date. Curious about what he wanted, I finished eating lunch quickly and headed out on my daily walk around McIntosh Lake, calling his mobile phone once I was out the door.

"This court date is going to be different than the other ones," he began, "and I want you and Elin to be prepared."

"Okay," I replied, "what do you mean?"

"I'll meet you at 8:30 a.m., but it's unlikely that we'll get started before 9:30 or 10:00."

"How long do you think it might take," I queried, "so Elin and I can plan our work schedules?"

"You might be there all day, so be prepared," was his quick reply. "The courtroom is going to be functioning like a central holding area, where the judge is going to be hearing multiple cases." He briefly paused. "Unlike previous hearings, you and Elin will sit outside the courtroom, and I'll be inside discussing the case with the defense attorney to come to agreement on what to present to the judge. I already met with my supervising district attorney, and we'll be going for a sentence of three years in custody, with Adam serving the first year in a county jail and the second and third year on probation. If the defense tries to ask the judge for the home confinement program, I'll object because the defendant did not produce the mitigation I asked for."

"There's nothing that these witnesses will say that I don't already know, James," I replied as I picked up the pace of my walk. It was then that I started to see the purpose of his call. Being dragged through the grisly details of Thomas's death again in a public court of law, this time with a hundred people present, might have an unexpected emotional impact on Elin and me. A light began to dawn in my heart and mind. "Now that you mention it, I'm more concerned about Elin. She's not been privy to the details," I continued. "She hasn't seen the toxicology report and the autopsy report like I have, both of which were traumatic experiences for me."

James was silent, tacitly thankful I was led to the same conclusion that he had already come to so easily.

"James," I whispered with a knowing voice, "thanks for being so thoughtful, for preparing us for what's to come."

"You're welcome, Mark," he replied. "I'm glad you understand."

As I finished the last two miles of my walk, I reflected on all James had shared, and I tried to envision what that day in court would be like as I gazed at the magnificent splendor of the lake and Long's Peak.

◊ ◊ ◊

Our flight to California was scheduled for the Sunday before the Monday morning hearing, so Elin suggested we drive to Carmel after we landed. After we arrived at the airport, we hopped into the rental car and headed to Carmel. We talked about Thomas most of the way down to the coast, remembering the things the three of us did while living in California. At times, we laughed as we reminisced about fun times and experiences. But we also shook our heads in disbelief that Thomas was dead. We cried about the things we missed or regretted, and we commiserated about what was to come in the hearing.

On the way to Carmel, we passed our old house in Campbell before starting up through the Santa Cruz Mountains on our way back down to the Pacific coast. "I remember the first time I took Thomas on this road when I was teaching him to drive back in October of 2020," Elin recalled.

"Yeah, I told him to stay in the right lane the whole way so he had more room to maneuver, and so the wacko drivers could just pass him on the left," I reminisced.

"We had a great time that day," Elin replied with a bittersweet tone in her voice. "Thomas drove all the way down the coast past the Bixby Bridge to Big Sur, and he did just fine. I was so proud of him. Then he drove all the way back to Carmel, and we went to the Aaron Chang Art Gallery, and he bought you that picture of Cypress Cove at Point Lobos for Christmas—the last Christmas we had with him."

"Yeah," I said quietly, "never, in a million years, would I have imagined that *that* would be the last Christmas he was alive." A stinging wave of grief washed over me. There was a lull in the conversation as I glanced intermittently at the vast expanse of the Pacific Ocean on my right and then back to the highway.

Elin broke the silence. "How are you doing?" I could tell by the soft, probing tone of her voice that she was checking in to see how I was feeling after that last exchange.

"I miss him, El. I really miss my son. But I can also say that I'm not angry this time." She looked at me curiously, wondering what I meant as I continued. "Well, the first few times I came back to California, I can't explain how angry I was. From the moment I got off the plane, and especially when I got in my rental car and headed out onto the freeway, I felt a deep anger, a rage, welling up inside of me about losing my son out here. But I can honestly say I'm not angry this time, and I know that's good, that's progress."

Once we arrived, we parked along the beach on Scenic Road and spent the next few hours strolling south along the coast to Mara Beach at the Carmel River State Park before heading north all the way to Ocean Avenue to watch the sunset. We were retracing the steps we'd taken with Thomas many times, trying to reconnect to him and the life we once had. We capped off the day with dinner at Tommy's Wok, just as we used to do with Thomas.

◊ ◊ ◊

On the morning of the preliminary hearing, I once again donned my dark-blue jacket and Thomas's red-and-blue striped tie. It was a big day. It was going to be like no other day that I've experienced in life.

As with the previous court dates, Elin and I walked from the parking garage to the courthouse at 8:30 a.m. As we filed through the metal detectors and toward the courtroom together, we wondered how the day would unfold. When we got near the courtroom, we saw the defendant and his girlfriend talking with a man dressed in a suit and tie, who appeared to be his new public defender.

James was already there as well. He was in the middle of an animated discussion with a guy who had a large law enforcement badge clipped to his belt. James nodded and waved at us as we approached, but he kept talking, so Elin and I continued walking, not wanting to interrupt.

After a few minutes, James joined us on our bench. "Good morning. How are you doing today?"

"We're okay," I responded, as Elin nodded in agreement. "How are *you* doing?" I asked him, wondering what the status was.

"I'm good," James replied. "Let me fill you in on what's gone on already this morning. Remember how I said that I still hadn't heard back from Adam's public defender and that he was in the process of getting a new one? Well, I got an email today telling me that a new public defender has just been assigned to the case this morning."

"Wow," I responded, utterly amazed at this last-minute change.

"Well, this new attorney I've worked with before," James replied. "He's a very good guy with lots of experience. I've already briefed him on the case, read Adam's confession to him, summarized the police report, and explained the home detention program that we offered him and how he's never produced the mitigations I asked for. I also told him that the prosecution wants three years in custody, one year in the county jail and two years on probation. I explained that if the defendant objects, I'll bring more charges against him."

"What do you mean?" I asked, curious about how James could do that.

"Currently," James explained, "I'm only charging him with the three fentanyl charges. If he objects to going to jail, I'll also charge him with the two Xanax felonies." With this little bit of good news, Elin and I were relieved and felt hopeful seeing how James's new prosecution strategy was already moving the case forward. When he saw how positively we reacted, James was pleased too.

"Do you think we'll be out of here by noon?" I asked, checking the time on my mobile phone.

"We'll see," James responded. "The guy over there who I was talking to is the Campbell detective who'll present the evidence to the judge. His name is Dale."

"Really," I replied, my curiosity piqued. "Can we meet him?"

"Of course," James affirmed as he signaled for Dale to come closer. As Dale approached, James introduced us, "These are the victim's parents, Mark and Elin."

I reached out to shake the detective's hand and felt deeply powerful and painful emotions rise within me. "Dale, were you one of the people who came to our home the morning we found Thomas dead in his room?" I asked, choking back tears and deep emotions from that fatal day.

Dale was surprised by the depth and emotional impact of my question. "No, I wasn't."

I continued, hardly able to speak as tears began to flow. "I almost sent an email to the mayor of Campbell about how helpful and supportive the officers and detectives were that day when Elin and I were in a total state of shock."

Dale looked at James briefly, not knowing what to say, and replied, "Thank you. I'm so sorry for your loss."

I went on to specifically mention how helpful the police sergeant who was in charge of investigating Thomas's death was. Dale nodded in agreement before James jumped back into the conversation. "I've asked Dale to do a whole lot more work on this case to make sure we have all our ducks in a row, and he's done a great job."

Elin and I both thanked Dale again for his support and diligence in ensuring the evidence for the case was as airtight as possible. He responded again, "I'm sorry for your loss," not knowing what else to say.

An hour later, Elin and I were still sitting on the bench outside the courtroom. James, Adam's new attorney, and Dale were inside discussing the details, evidence, and the nuances of the case. I tried to imagine what was happening behind those closed doors. James had amassed a preponderance of evidence against the defendant, including his unresponsiveness to repeated requests for mitigation. In my mind, this hearing was about as black-and-white as it could be—an open-and-shut case. But the public defender's job was to muddy these otherwise clear waters as much as possible. He was going to argue for the home detention program, since the defendant had no prior felonies on record and claimed that he was turning his life around. James's job would be to push back, citing the defendant's lack of responsiveness about the character letters. As Elin and I sat outside the courtroom, I imagined the back-and-forth dialogue, the hammering out of all the semantic differences until the defense attorney could see no path forward.

It was almost 10:00 in the morning when James emerged and approached Elin and me. "The defense wants to discuss the case with the judge first because they think they'll get a better deal from her," James explained. "You folks wait here." As James turned and walked back into the courtroom, Elin and I had no idea what would happen, but we knew James was determined to do the right thing, to make sure the defendant did jail time, given the fact that Thomas had died.

About forty-five minutes later, James, Adam's public defender, and Dale walked out of the courtroom. James approached us with a sense of urgency. "The judge did not give the defendant a better offer, so if he doesn't accept the one year in county and two years of probation, we'll begin the preliminary hearing." James glanced down the hallway to where Adam was talking to his attorney before looking back at Elin and me. "The pressure is on. Let's see what he says."

By 11:00 a.m., James and Adam's attorney started heading toward the courtroom door. After conferring briefly with the public defender, James came toward us. "Adam took the deal. Once he signs the sentencing appeal waiver, we'll go into the courtroom, the judge will read him the charges, and he'll plead no contest."

"What's the difference between pleading no contest and pleading guilty?" I asked, just to be sure I understood what James was saying.

"Pleading no contest is like pleading guilty in that you accept the conviction for the charges and it goes on your record as a conviction. But if you and Elin were to turn around and sue the defendant in a civil case, you couldn't use his no contest plea as an admission of guilt. Does that make sense?"

"Perfect sense," I replied as I reached up to give James a hug. "Good job, James," I said as Elin and I teared up with a sense of relief and closure.

"I'll be right back," James said, stepping back once he saw the defense attorney signaling for him to come. He returned a minute later. "Looks like the judge wants to take a lunch break now, and she'll reconvene the case at 1:30," James explained. "You two can leave if you want. I'll take care of this and text you when everything's finished."

Elin and I walked back to the parking garage, not knowing what to say. We had a strange sense of relief but, at the same time, a profound feeling of sorrow. We were "happy" to have some sense of closure, but it wasn't like any happiness I've ever felt before. It was a hollow victory, seasoned with a deep, dull sense of pain and grief for our son's loss. It left Elin and me wondering how this could have ever happened to us. I thought about texting friends about the outcome but didn't feel like telling anyone. As with so many other aspects of our life since Thomas died, it was a very private moment that only Elin and I shared.

At three in the afternoon, my mobile phone dinged. It was James. "He'll plead as outlined. The sentencing is scheduled for January 18, 2023, at 9:00 a.m."

I quickly texted back. "Great. Thank you again for all your hard work and commitment to the case and to my wife, myself, and the memory of our son."

"It's been my pleasure," he messaged me right back. "As always, if you have any questions, do not hesitate to ask."

That night, Elin and I went to Maggiano's Italian restaurant in Santana Row for dinner, a place we used to go to with Thomas. When I made the reservation the week before, I thought we were going to "celebrate" this milestone. But that wasn't the right word. It wasn't what we felt. Instead, our mood was muted and pensive. Elin and I held hands over dinner. We clung to each other. We were glad this phase of the legal process was finally over. We talked about how desperately we missed Thomas and mulled over the events of the day over a glass of wine.

"The only word I have to describe what I'm feeling is *anticlimactic*," Elin said sorrowfully.

"What it reminds me of," I responded, "is that song 'Is That All There Is?' by Peggy Lee."

> *Is that all there is?*
> *Is that all there is?*
> *If that's all there is my friends, then let's keep dancing . . .*

CHAPTER 21

I'M OKAY (JUST OKAY) LIVING LIFE WITHOUT THOMAS

February 24, 2023 (1 Year, 42 Weeks, and 4 Days After)

November soon gave way to December and the start of the Christmas season, our second without Thomas. Compared to our first holiday season after Thomas's death, Elin and I were doing much better emotionally. However, while we weren't in the gut-wrenching pain and inconsolable grief that consumed us the prior Christmas, we still felt numb and worn out. We were tired of grieving yet knew this would be a lifelong process.

Christmas 2022 in Colorado, three stockings but no Thomas

We participated in a few Christmas festivities in the weeks following. One evening, we went to a candlelight service at Ryssby Church. Another day, we went out and bought a Christmas tree at the nearby Blue Ribbon Farm before attending a performance of Handel's *Messiah* by the City Chamber Orchestra and Choir. In some of these instances, we'd briefly catch ourselves finding enjoyment in what we were doing, much like we did at the wedding in West Virginia two months back. But all too often, we found ourselves feeling disconnected, as if we were just going through the motions. It was as if the cultural glue that held the complex, emotion-laden bundles of holiday rituals and memories together had dissolved in Thomas's absence.

In the weeks that led up to Christmas, a dream I had on May 30 kept pressing its way into my heart and mind. So, in the still darkness one morning, I finally turned to my dream journal to review and reflect on what I had logged six months earlier about this dream.

> I was producing a movie with a guy and his wife, and there was a movie company, like a movie studio, that was shooting and editing the movie, and they also owned all the rights to the movie. We were far along in shooting the movie, and I was supposed to meet with the studio company to shape and define the last portion of the movie and how the remaining scenes were going to be filmed and how the movie would end. We were all staying in a hotel and were going to meet in the hotel's restaurant to discuss the path forward over dinner. The guy I was working with had some nominal role, but it was really his wife and I who were shaping and defining the design, production, and actual creation of the movie. And of the two of us, she was the one with the real insights into creating the movie and the driving force behind all that we were doing—creating the story; shaping the twists and turns of how the plot would unfold; defining the identity, goals, and desires of the characters; giving heart and soul to the movie, including the emotional ups and downs that were generated; and crafting the overall message and takeaway of the movie, as well as the sense of purpose and meaning it conveyed. All of this happened earlier in this dream or in a previous dream.

So, as this dream opened, I walked downstairs to the hotel restaurant to meet the movie company and the guy I was working with. But for reasons I can't explain, I didn't expect his wife to come, despite the enormously important role she was playing, since I could not have done what I was doing without her. I was the first person to arrive. I was standing there waiting for the others, and the guy I was working with came and was walking around, but he didn't interact with me, which was typical. I was standing next to a rectangular table with a white tablecloth and four chairs, and the guy's wife walked up to me. I was thrilled she was there because she was so important to the entire project. She was beautiful and had dark hair and dark eyes, and she was dressed in all black—a black top and black pants. I remember thinking as I wrote the dream down that her all-black clothes reminded me of an Enneagram Type Four. She was beautiful and classy, and I felt deeply connected and attracted to her like a partner in creating this movie.

Within a few seconds of her arriving, I glanced back at the table where we were going to sit for the meeting with the movie company, and I noticed that it was not set for dinner yet. As I looked at the table, the woman moved up close to me, put her arm around my waist, pressed her body against mine, and whispered into my ear, "You need to trust me with the ending of this," meaning I should trust her to take the lead in shaping and defining the last portion of the movie, as well as the ending. I knew she was right to the depth of my soul because of the enormously creative work she had done up until that point. The dream ended, and I woke up with a sense of peace and calm, feeling like things in my life were going to be all right because I had inner guidance and direction in my life from the Anima, symbolized by the woman, and the Self, symbolized by the four-sided quaternity of the table.

I slowly read through the dream several times, reflectively allowing the images from the unconscious and the deep emotions to integrate into my conscious awareness and day-to-day life. I felt a sense of peace and hope fill me within, as if my life were becoming more fully aligned along the Inner and Outer Labyrinth. I began to recognize that although I was still struggling to tread water in a world without my son, the tiptoes of my conscious waking self intermittently sensed something solid emerging from beneath the waters of the unconscious. Like bouncing off the bottom at the deep end of a pool and then pushing back up to the water's surface, this new psychological bedrock was flowing from some type of inner creative flow emerging like a bubbling river of lava.

My continued reflection on the image and message of the woman dressed in all black revealed a deep inner place of assurance—that is, a solid place to stand. Despite the challenges I faced in life and in writing, I knew I was still on the right path. I was not lost. The Anima image of the woman dressed in all black symbolized an inner bridge and mediator between my conscious waking self (small *s*) on the surface waters of daily life, and the Self (big *S*) in the unconscious, through which the Spirit of God was working. Dreams say what they mean, and they mean what they say. So my role going forward was to trust the woman in black with the ending of my life's story. From my partnership with the woman, the destiny that the Spirit of God had foreordained for me from the beginning of time and the destiny I was creating with my day-to-day choices would emerge naturally.

◊ ◊ ◊

Earlier that fall, I started meeting with Clark for coffee. Clark and his wife, Allyson, were the parents of Jillian, one of Thomas's closest friends from Colorado, the same Jillian who was with Elin and me when I first saw the stairs to Thomas's treehouse off the deck of our new house. After meeting in middle school, Jillian and Thomas spent a lot of time together, whether it was having lunch, going to concerts, or just hanging out. She and Thomas would joke about being dizygotic "twins" because they were born on the same day in the same year, just hours apart. Once Thomas died, Jillian posted many cherished stories on his memorial site and appeared in dozens of pictures with Thomas in the site's gallery section.

Allyson and Clark were also very involved following Thomas's death, helping me with the detailed logistics of Thomas's Colorado funeral while Elin and I were still living in California. Allyson interfaced with the caterer and handled a myriad of other tasks that Elin and I were too overwhelmed to deal with, working behind the scenes to help shape and define the outcome of that difficult day. While most of us were still at the funeral at Ryssby Church, Allyson and Clark were hard at work setting up and decorating rows of tables for the repast. And during the entire day, Allyson took a portfolio of beautiful photos for Elin and me, knowing that we would be too in the moment to do so.

What I didn't understand then was that God, working through the Self, would continue to use the quaternity of Allyson, Clark, Elin, and me to bring inner healing and transformation to all four of us by interconnecting our individual destinies along the Outer Labyrinth of daily life and grafting together the destinies we had in God from the beginning of time along the Inner Labyrinth. This would be evidenced by dreams each of us would have and share with complete openness and transparency with one another. But in those raw moments surrounding Thomas's death, their simple acts of support demonstrated the love and compassion that Allyson and Clark had for Elin and me as "their neighbors." They saw Elin and me as wounded people who had a story and were creating a destiny that they became involved in, like the Good Samaritan did in Luke 10:25–37.

On this particular December morning, Clark and I were meeting at the same coffee shop in Longmont that Thomas and I used to visit together on Saturdays. For almost two hours, we laughed, talked about business, and shared some of the deepest concerns and issues that we were facing in life. During our conversation, I ended up sharing my dream about the New York City brownstone and the kind of inner healing and transformation that I was experiencing.

Driving home from the coffee shop following my discussion with Clark, an insight began to well up from deep within me. It came from somewhere in my unconscious, but it was in the first person, a pointed and personal communication. This message came from a deeper, objective part of *me*—from the Self. The unsolicited insight began to materialize in my heart and mind. *I desperately wish that Thomas was here, alive, doing well and at graduate school. But I'm okay (just okay) with living without him for the rest of my life.* This unasked-for conclusion had been reached unilaterally by this inner part of me just one year and thirty-two weeks to the day after finding Thomas dead in his bedroom.[47]

It wasn't a statement about being "okay" that Thomas was dead. No, not at all. Rather, the statement was about *me*. I was beginning to recognize and accept the fact that Thomas was dead and not coming back. It was the same message that my dream-ego had to deliver to the inner images of an eight-year-old boy and a room full of kids in that New York City brownstone. Given this brutal reality, I had to go on with my life without Thomas's physical presence. I found myself wondering, *Well, what choice do I have?* Yet, I knew there were other options. I could let anger and bitterness dominate my life and relationships. I could run away from the reality of his death and live in denial. I could displace or project my grief about Thomas's death out onto the legitimate task of telling others about the dangers of self-medication in the age of counterfeit pills and fentanyl poisonings—that is, I could do the right thing for the wrong reason. I could even drink myself to death in a trailer in the woods. You get the point.

Once I got home, I sobbed as I described my experience to Elin over lunch. I was deeply ashamed for even having this thought of being okay without Thomas. Yet at the same time, I felt liberated, unshackled from the dark cloud of grief and loss that hung over me. The essential tension between shame and liberation reminded me of the dream I had the previous Christmas when I was walking through the shopping mall carrying the two-year-old child. That boy in the dream was like my son, but he was also like Thomas, yet he was someone new in my life. Yet, he was not a "replacement" for Thomas, because no one could ever take Thomas's place. I remembered how the crowd of people in my dream rejoiced with me that I'd found new life after the death of my son. Back then, the grieving me who lived along the Outer Labyrinth of day-to-day life rejected the inner images of rejoicing about this new inner son. The very thought of it repulsed the conscious, grief-stricken me. But I could not deny that the dream image of the *rejoicing me* along the Inner Labyrinth was revealing a deep, heartfelt desire to move past the glacial pace of grieving for Thomas.

When I first had that dream, I recognized that the Spirit of God was prompting and leading me to reconcile the opposing perspectives of the unconscious rejoicing me and the conscious grieving me into a more holistic rejoicing-grieving me who would ultimately embrace the reality of finding new life after the death of my son. Now, those top-down conscious feelings of shame, juxtaposed by the bottom-up emergence of a previously unconscious feeling of liberation at the thought of being okay about going on in life without Thomas, was having the same compensatory healing properties as the dream image of the new little boy, who symbolized new life and the path forward.

I also recognized at that moment that this year's Christmas insights were a deeper, firmer foundation upon which a more holistic rejoicing-grieving me and a being okay (just okay) me could stand. I saw the same divided yet compensatory pattern that I was currently experiencing in the multiple memoirs I was reading that were written by parents who had lost a child. This shouldn't have surprised me. As I mentioned earlier, more than forty years ago, Carl Rogers argued that when we think about or feel something that is so utterly personal, so shameful and embarrassing that we'd rather die than admit it in public, often that very thought or emotion is most universal.[48] In much the same way, Jung taught us that when we use time-tested psychological scaffolding to descend into the deepest, most objective and symbolic levels of the personal and collective unconscious, many of our individual differences dissolve into a symbolic wholeness that echoes Rogers's perspective.

Thomas, Elin, and Mark at Thomas's Eagle Scout awards dinner

CHAPTER 22

ALMOST THERE

April 11, 2023 (1 Year, 49 Weeks, and 1 Day After)

The day before New Year's Eve, I decided to send James an email to check in and ask whether Elin and I could take him out for dinner at Palermo's—a place we frequented with Thomas—following the January 18 sentencing hearing. Later that day, I got a frantic email from him letting me know that the hearing had just been moved back to January 20 due to a schedule conflict with the judge. Over the past several weeks, Elin and I had invited over fifty people who knew and loved Thomas to the sentencing, meaning we would have to let them all know about the change, not to mention schedule new flights to California. But I let James know that, regardless, we would make this new day and time work. He responded right away apologizing for the change and agreeing to have dinner following the hearing, as long as he could pay for his own meal.

◊ ◊ ◊

Ever since the arraignment, I had been navigating the dynamic tension between grace and judgment, forgiveness and accountability. We had forgiven Adam for being the channel through which Thomas was killed, but the fact was that he was guilty of the five felony charges the district attorney was bringing against him.

The whole process had been an emotional whipsaw with an unpredictable frequency and amplitude. Some moments I would go from thinking, *Is that all he gets? Just one year in county jail and three years on probation?* to feeling that we did the right thing by forgiving Adam, much like Elin and I have been forgiven by God. On other days, I'd vacillate between seething anger about how inherently unfair the legal process is and the fact that Adam would probably be released from jail in only six months to wondering if I should contact Adam once he was released and offer to help him get back on his feet.

As we prepared to leave the Sunday before the sentencing, Elin and I packed our suitcases in silence. We tried to reflect on what we were doing. Normally, we'd be going to church at that time, not to the airport. We were scheduled to arrive in California by noon and wanted to drive down the coast to Carmel upon landing, but the beach in Carmel was being pounded by enormous storm, so the massive waves, torrential rain, and flooding made that risky. There were mudslides all through the Santa Cruz Mountains along Highway 17, so even getting down to the coast would be difficult and possibly dangerous.

As we walked through the Denver airport, Elin held the fourteen-by-twenty-four-inch color picture of Thomas—the same one that appears on the main page of his memorial site. She reminisced about the days when he was alive. "I remember taking him on the train out to Concourse B when he was a little boy," she said, savoring this memory with a poignant sense of sorrow and thankfulness for Thomas's life. "I feel like we're going to another funeral for him."

"In many ways," I whispered softly, "we are." As I spoke, grief welled up from a deep place within that I couldn't quite name.

Upon landing in California, there was something we had to do before heading to our hotel. Every year, I would take Thomas shopping for Elin's Christmas present. For Christmas 2018, Thomas and I walked through the Westgate Center Mall near where we used to live in Campbell. Thomas and I brainstormed presents he could get Elin as we browsed through store after store. We finally found our way to Elegant Jewelers, where Thomas found a beautiful set of purple heart-shaped earrings made of amethyst. Purple was Elin's favorite color, and she treasured them. She'd worn them every day since Thomas died.

One morning, Elin woke up and realized that one of the earrings was gone. She eventually found the back piece on the floor next to our bed, but no earring. Elin cried like a little girl, this outer loss of a sentimental artifact resonating a deep sense of the inner loss caused by Thomas's death. The pain of losing something that was so personal, so irreplaceable, was almost more than she could stand. Elin decided to keep the original earring, but she wouldn't wear it. I told her that I would take her to Elegant Jewelers and buy her another pair, much like I did with Thomas.

When we left the store, we drove past our old house in Campbell, the place where Thomas lived out his last days. But now, just one year and thirty-seven weeks after his death, it all seemed like a dream. That day, sitting in front of the house he died in, was difficult. We experienced the soul-rending reality of the destiny that we have along the Inner Labyrinth of the unconscious and the destiny that we create along the Outer Labyrinth with our everyday choices, both of which are happening simultaneously.

Along the Outer Labyrinth, the days before the sentencing flew by. Every day, I would wake up at 4:00 a.m. to head into my office at Stanford/SLAC by 5:15 a.m. with two dark roast coffees in hand and an uncooked breakfast sandwich. Along the Inner Labyrinth, God was leading us through the unconscious with a dream that Elin had just two days before the sentencing, which she recorded in her journal. In her own words:

> In this dream, I had just found out that I was pregnant, which was a surprising thing, probably because of my age. I didn't have any baby clothes or supplies because it had been so long since I had children, so I knew I was going to have to get some from friends or somewhere.

She and I reflected on and discussed the archetypal significance of the images of a baby and pregnancy as symbols of new life emerging from within and deep inner transformation. Despite the difficult circumstances we would face in two days, we knew we were not lost. We were still on the right path. She and I were aligned. On the same platform. In the same container. As Paul tells us in Romans 8:31–39, we were more than conquerors through Christ who loves us.

◊ ◊ ◊

The night before the sentencing, I was back in our hotel room going through my emails. Elin was still at work at the time. Suddenly, my mobile phone rang. It was Dan, one of the leaders from Thomas's Boy Scout troop. He was upset. Really upset. Dan had been on Thomas's memorial site and read that Elin and I had forgiven Adam for unintentionally killing Thomas, and that we supported the plea deal. It was not surprising how upset he was. After all, it's one thing to hear in the news about the growing crisis of innocent young people being deceptively poisoned by counterfeit pills, but it's quite another thing to actually know someone who was a victim of this dark crime.

Dan ended up relaying this information to the boys and girls during a scout meeting the night before. The young people at the meeting were likewise incensed by Dan's report, outraged by how meager the consequences were. They were angered by the lack of symmetry between the heinousness of the crime committed and the consequences thereof. The scout leaders were also concerned about the "message" this sent to others, worried that it would fail to discourage or deter others from selling illegal narcotics.

While Dan knew the enormity of the loss of our only son intellectually, and while he understood conceptually that we were the primary surviving victims of this senseless crime, the intensity and outrage cultivated at the previous night's meeting became focused on me during his call.

"What message does that meager sentence send to others?" he angrily blurted through the phone. "What's to stop others from doing the same thing and getting away with it?"

I tried to remain calm and reason with him. "This is courtesy of the California Supreme Court, who struck down the charge of great bodily injury. The district attorney wants to win this case, which means he can't charge the defendant with that," I explained.

"I've read all of that on the site," Dan retorted quickly, dismissing my explanation out of hand. "I'd like to say something to the judge tomorrow about how ludicrous this is." Dan was trying to insert himself into the legal process. Regardless of his intentions or the actual meaning of his words, the underlying emotional message I got from Dan was, *Why don't you stand up for Thomas? Why don't you push back on this unfair legal system? Since you won't stand up for Thomas as his father, I feel compelled to stand up for him as a scout leader.*

What Dan also didn't know was that under California's incarceration philosophy of keeping people out of jail, the defendant would probably only serve six total months in jail. Given how upset he was, I wasn't about to volunteer this information. As we continued talking, the thought crossed my mind, *Well, Dan, if you don't like the way the legal system works in California, move out or vote to change it.* But I bit my tongue, thankful Elin and I had voted with our feet and had moved back in Colorado.

"Dan," I pleaded, trying to appeal to his hardened, outraged heart, "I'm not sure you understand how difficult all this has been, and continues to be, for Elin and me. Tomorrow is a big day for us, and you're making it more difficult with what you're asking." He still seemed oblivious to the devastating emotional impact that his eleventh-hour call would have on Elin and me as I continued speaking. "This is really going to upset my wife, Elin."

"Well, I don't want to do that," he shot back, unwavering about intervening in the next day's sentencing.

"Remember, this is not our case," I cautioned. "It's the district attorney's case, and I don't know what he'll say about this." I kept trying to end this deeply disturbing conversation by reiterating the facts. "I'll also talk to my wife about it when she gets back from work, but I want to go on record as saying that we've already settled this in our hearts and minds, and Elin will be deeply troubled by you resurrecting this issue. I'll call you tomorrow after I've heard from the DA."

The call ended with an uncomfortable lack of resolution for both of us.

Dan's anger, outrage, and concerns echoed deep sentiments within me about the tiny bit of justice that was being meted out for the felonies that resulted in Thomas's death. I'd had those very same thoughts in the early days after Thomas died. Yet, my heart told me something wasn't right. Dan's anger, indignation, and demand to stand up against the legal system was not without some basis, but it lacked the silent ping of truth. It was an Old Testament, *lex talionis*, eye for an eye and a tooth for a tooth kind of justice rather than the kind of heartfelt grace and forgiveness we extended to Adam at the arraignment.

When she got back to the hotel, Elin and I went out for dinner at a nearby Olive Garden. Once we were settled at our table, I recounted my call with Dan and how I told him James would have to weigh in on his plan to say something to the judge. As I expected, my poor grieving wife cried through much of dinner.

"I'm afraid that if he stands up and challenges what Adam, the public defender, the district attorney, the judge, and you and I have already agreed to, he'll turn an already difficult time into a circus," she said, dreading the thought. "I don't want him to speak. I'm already under enough pressure about what might happen tomorrow."

CHAPTER 23

A JUDGE, A DEFENDANT, AND A TINY BIT OF JUSTICE FOR THOMAS

January 20, 2023 (1 Year, 37 Weeks, and 4 Days After)

I arrived at my Stanford/SLAC office at 2:56 a.m. on the morning of the sentencing. Much like the previous six court dates, I wore the same red-and-blue striped tie Thomas wore when he made his public profession of faith. I wore it in memory of Thomas's short but impactful life.

Mark's office at Stanford University/SLAC National Accelerator Lab

The first task I had to accomplish before my workday started was to upload the final version of the victim impact statement I would read in the courtroom later that day to Thomas's memorial site. This exact statement would be included in the court's sentencing documents; it would be a part of Adam's criminal record for the rest of his life.

For weeks, I had been wrestling with this statement while reflecting on our grueling journey of pain and grief. The criminal justice system had been slow and dysfunctional, to say the least. It had been nearly a year since Adam, the person who sold Thomas the one pill that killed him, was first arraigned on five narcotics-related felony charges. But today, at 1:30 p.m., he would finally be sentenced for those charges. More than fifty people would be at the courthouse to honor Thomas's memory and to support Elin and me in this difficult time. While this was the seventh time Elin and I had been in court, this was going to be the first time that we would be allowed to speak publicly about the enormous negative impact that Thomas's death has had on our lives.

James let us know that when the case was called in the courtroom, he would ask Elin and me to come forward to the podium. There I would read the victim impact statement while Elin stood by my side holding the large color picture of Thomas she brought with us from Colorado. This picture was big enough for the judge, Adam, and everyone else in the courtroom to see it, even from a distance. By showing our son's picture while reading the victim impact statement, Elin and I wanted to remind everyone there that Thomas Larson Bodnarczuk was an actual person. He was not just a name or number on a court docket. A year, thirty-seven weeks, and three days before, Thomas was very much alive. He had his whole life ahead of him. But now, he was no longer on the planet as a living soul. His earthly remains sat buried in the Ryssby Cemetery. Once the sentencing was over, Elin and I would take the picture back home with us to Colorado and have it placed on the wall of our library alongside many of Thomas's other possessions. The picture would be a testimony to the fact that, as Thomas's parents, Elin and I saw our duty through to the very end.

We wanted Thomas to be symbolically present in the courtroom that day. We wanted him to witness the court proceedings. We wanted him to see the tiny bit of justice that was getting meted out for the crime that was committed against him and us. But we also knew Thomas now resided in a heavenly home—one not built with human hands—where he will be alive for all eternity. Elin and I believe we will see him again when we make our final journey home. As Jesus tells us, "In My Father's house are many rooms; if that were not so, I would have told you, because I am going there to prepare a place for you" (John 14:2). But for now, with this chapter of Thomas's life story complete, Elin and I understood that we had to continue walking the path of inner healing and transformation, discovering a new normal going forward.

Amen.

CHAPTER 24

THE SENTENCING

April 11, 2023 (1 Year, 49 Weeks, and 1 Day After)

With the victim impact statement successfully uploaded, I set about the second task I had to accomplish that morning before the sentencing, which was to send James an email about the prior night's phone call with Dan. In the email, I warned James that one of the leaders of Thomas's Boy Scout troop informed me how upset he and the troop were about how light the sentence was for killing Thomas and how he wanted to try to address the judge prior to the sentencing.

James later called me on his way into the office. After I had filled him in on some of the nuances that were too difficult to explain via email, he said, "Don't worry about it. Have him call me after 9:30." It was clear he wanted to take the pressure off Elin and me.

I hung up and called Dan immediately. His tone of voice had softened from the night before. I gave him James's contact information and told him when to call. "Just so you know," I added, "last night when I told Elin about what you want to do, she immediately broke down and cried. You've known about this for two months. Why did you wait until the very last minute to call me about this?" There was no response. "I'll see you later at the courthouse," I said, breaking the silence, eager to get back to work.

◊ ◊ ◊

Elin and I rendezvoused at the parking garage across the street from the courthouse around 12:30 p.m., the seventh and final time we would need to meet here. The sentencing was scheduled for 1:30 p.m. in the same room the preliminary hearing was held six weeks earlier.

Elin and I were early. After securing our COVID-required facemasks and navigating the metal detectors at the courthouse entrance, we exited the elevator on the fifth floor. Turning right, I scanned the hallway outside the courtroom. It was over a hundred feet long with a solid wall of tinted

Mark and Elin at the sentencing, with the defendant seated at the bottom right

glass windows on the left side that overlooked the runways of the San Jose Mineta International Airport. A polished wooden bench was mounted along the windows and spanned the entire length of the hallway.

I saw three or four people I knew at the end of the hallway, friends from the Lutheran Church of Los Gatos. Elin and I walked toward these familiar faces, glad that we were not alone today like we had been for the previous court appearances. These friends had been part of our painful journey from the beginning, experiencing the dialectic between grace and forgiveness, judgment and accountability.

By the time of the hearing, more than seventy people were present to support us in the conclusion of this heartbreaking legal process. As the minutes ticked by up until the sentencing, family, friends, and other people involved in various segments of our life stepped off the elevator and walked down the long hallway toward us. A crowd was gathering. Much like the repasts after Thomas's two funerals, it was good to see, connect with, and be comforted by people who loved and cared for Thomas, Elin, and me. But this waiting time was punctuated by moments when the reality of *why* we were there struck home. Like mixing ketchup, mustard, relish, hot sauce, chocolate, soy sauce, and milk together and then asking, *What does this even taste like?* these mixed emotions were, and remain, difficult to tease apart, hard to put a face on, and exceedingly complex to describe in any straightforward way.

When Dan arrived, I asked him if he had talked to James. "I called," he replied, "but I couldn't get through." Just then, I saw James walk out of the elevator.

"There he is. I can introduce you to him."

Dan looked at James approaching, hesitated, and said, "No. That's okay," as if he had second thoughts.

"Well, I need to talk with him," I replied as I turned and walked toward James.

"I haven't heard from the scout leader," James volunteered immediately as we greeted each other and shook hands.

"That's the guy I was just talking to," I answered. "I think he may have changed his mind about confronting the judge about the weak sentence."

"I got word today that yet another public defender was assigned to the defendant just this morning," James said, getting back to the business at hand. "I've worked with him before. He's good." James glanced back toward the elevators as Adam and his new public defender emerged. "That's him," James said. "Let me go brief him on the case, and I'll get back with you."

By now, those who came to support us had gathered themselves into small groups. I moved from cluster to cluster, greeting them and offering my thanks for their presence. I also pointed out the defendant and his girlfriend, who were sitting at the very end of the hallway trying to be invisible. Some people turned quickly to sneak a peek at Adam. Others refused to look. Still others turned, eyes glued on the person they'd only heard about. "I can't imagine what you're going through," some of them uttered as they stared at Adam, our situation becoming more real to them as they began to step into the shoes Elin and I had worn throughout the yearlong legal process.

Before we entered the courtroom, we gathered outside the door to pray together, eager to commit what was about to happen into the hands of an all-knowing and omnipresent God. People from all the different areas of our life huddled together as our pastor unashamedly articulated the hopes and desires of those who stood there. Bystanders up and down the hallway who were there for other cases just looked on with curiosity as we stood in solidarity to honor and remember Thomas's life.

Minutes later, I heard a loud click as an armed guard unlocked the courtroom door from the inside. "The courtroom is open," he announced. Elin and I walked through the enormous wooden doors, taking seats in the second row on the left-hand side of the courtroom, which was configured just like the others we'd been in over the last year. The space was divided in half by a wall of glass that separated the public seating area from the front of the room where the formal business of the court took place. The judge sat at the other end of the courtroom at an enormous mahogany bench high above the rest of us. She sat behind a glass partition and spoke through a microphone. About twenty-five feet in front of us on the left was a door that led to the county jail. Another muscular, heavily armed guard blocked the doorway controlling access into and out of the courtroom. The glassed-in rectangular area between the judge and where Elin and I were seated was where the public defenders shared a desk and where prosecutors and defense attorneys conferred before presenting their case to the court.

"All rise for the Honorable Judge Natalie H. Nelson," one of the guards announced loudly. Elin and I rose with the others in the room, and the reality of what was about to happen struck a deep, ambivalent resonance in my heart. The judge appeared from a door at the back left side of the courtroom. She walked up the stairs to her elevated seat with an air of confidence. Once seated, she pulled the microphone toward her, adjusted its height, and calmly said, "Good afternoon," with a quiet sense of authority.

Judge Nelson was appointed to the Santa Clara County Superior Court Bench by California Governor Jerry Brown in 2018. At forty-seven years old, Nelson was selected by *Managing Intellectual Property* magazine as one of the field's top 250 women policymakers, academics, lawyers, and intellectual property law experts in the world. A former partner in a well-respected Silicon Valley law firm, she had litigated a variety of complex business cases. How she came to hear criminal cases like ours I'll never know. Her presence radiated a kindhearted, empathic, and humane image that suggested she cared deeply about the cases she heard. When it came to Thomas's case, there wasn't much she could change or impact that had not already been decided by Adam's plea deal. But I was glad she was our judge.

There were several cases scheduled before Thomas's. The opening ones moved so quickly and were so confusing that it was hard to know what was happening, much less when one case ended and another began. Various prosecutors and public defenders would banter back and forth with the judge and each other about legal details, things done, and tasks left undone before setting dates for follow-up court appearances. The latter cases were even more complicated. Once the court clerk would call a defendant's name and case number, their attorney and the prosecution would try to make deals, debate differences, and assert their client's best interest. Whenever the dialogue would start heading down a legal rabbit hole, Judge Nelson would take charge of the discussion. "We have a lot of people waiting here today, so if we can't settle this quickly, I'll defer this case to another day."

Finally, after over an hour, the court clerk called our case. James looked back at me from the front of the room and nodded as if to ask, *Are you ready?* I nodded back affirmatively without hesitation. In the weeks prior, James notified the court clerk and Judge Nelson that over fifty people would be accompanying Elin and me. He also submitted my victim impact statement as part of the formal record of the court's proceedings and informed Judge Nelson that I would be reading the statement prior to her pronouncing the sentence.

Adam had been waiting outside with his girlfriend. They now entered the courtroom and walked down the center aisle straight to the front of the room, where they sat at the rectangular wooden table directly in front of the judge. His girlfriend took a seat in the front row of the right portion of the public seating area and hung her head.

Judge Nelson spoke first. "I know we have a lot of people in the courtroom who are here for this case. I apologize for making you wait so long," she said with a sincere tone in her voice. She then read the charges against Adam. "It looks like a sentence of three years in custody, with the first year served in the county jail, has already been proposed in the plea bargain, and I accept these terms," she announced as she glanced down at the paperwork.

"Your Honor," Adam's public defender said as he rose from his seat and looked directly at the judge, "I request that the court waive the three-hundred-dollar restitution fee for my client. He doesn't have a place to live. He's been couch surfing. He's currently unemployed, looking for a job, and wants to go back to school and get a degree." As the judge concurred with his request, I thought, *Now I know why we never got the character letters, pay stubs, or college transcripts from him over the last year.* This also explained the protracted, painful cat-and-mouse game we'd played with Adam and his previous four public defenders.

"I understand that the victim's parents want to speak on his behalf," Judge Nelson said, pivoting.

"Yes, Your Honor," James said as he rose and walked toward the public seating area where Elin and I sat. James motioned toward Elin and me as the judge requested us to come forward. We rose, walked toward the front of the courtroom, and faced the judge directly. James came and stood by my right side to demonstrate his support for Thomas and for us, as well as his disdain concerning the crime that had been committed against our son. As planned, Elin stood on my left with the color picture of Thomas. Adam, still seated at the large wooden table, appeared sad and remorseful, as can be seen in the photo at the beginning of this chapter. Meanwhile, his public defender looked down at the ground next to him, having no legitimate objections to make, given the clear nature of the case.

I took a deep breath and tried to control the emotions welling up from deep within me. Looking down at my notes, I started reading. "Good morning, Your Honor." As I uttered these simple words, my voice cracked, silencing me as I began to cry. Natalie H. Nelson, the person, not the judge, gently said, "Please take your time, sir."

I had to summon all my strength and might to control the powerful feelings that spilled forth from the depths of my soul. With another breath, I started over, reading our statement.

◊ ◊ ◊

Good morning, Your Honor. The young man shown in the picture here is our son, Thomas Larson Bodnarczuk. We thank you for the opportunity to share our perspective on the impact that Thomas's death has had on his mother and me and to create a word picture of who he was as a person.

Thomas was born at 10:18 a.m. on May 16, 2002, at Presbyterian St. Luke's Medical Center in Denver, Colorado. His first home was on Lake Dillon in Frisco, Colorado, nine thousand feet above sea level in the high country of Summit County. From the time Thomas was a tiny child, he had a deep love for Colorado—fresh air, clear skies, snowcapped peaks, deep-blue mountain lakes, crystal clear streams, and the laid-back, high-country feel of the Rocky Mountains.

Thomas had a sensitive heart. He was a deep-feeling, empathic, and perceptive person who was attuned to his own emotions and the emotions of others. He could sense when things were not right in a relationship, and when people needed to talk together and work things out. Thomas had character, a conscience, a sense of wanting things to be fair and equitable in life and in his relationships. He had a deep sense of integrity. For Thomas, integrity was a commitment to course correction, to coming back to the principles, values, and inner truths that he believed in, after he had said or done something that he later regretted or after making a wrong decision.

Like all of us, Thomas made some wrong decisions in his short but impactful life. But he was finding his way. He was discovering his calling and his destiny when his life was taken from him just two weeks before his nineteenth birthday. Thomas was a light that burned brightly. In the eighteen years that he lived, he had a powerful impact on the lives of countless people, including his family, friends, and neighbors, over fifty of whom are present here today in the courtroom. They're here to honor Thomas's memory and to support my wife and me in our grief.

Here's what happened on that fatal day from our perspective. Thomas came home from work at about 9:10 p.m. on Saturday night, May 1, 2021. Elin and I chatted with him for a few minutes, and then he went to his room. That's the last time we saw our son alive. Thomas took what he thought was a single dose of the prescription medication Xanax that he bought from the defendant on Snapchat. He had no idea that it contained three times the lethal dose of fentanyl. After taking the pill, Thomas ordered some takeout from DoorDash, but he didn't live long enough to eat it.

I went to wake him at about 9:55 a.m. the next morning. I knocked on his door, and there was no answer. I knocked louder. When he didn't respond, I opened the door, saw him lying in bed and called his name. He didn't respond. I called him again, even louder, and he still didn't respond. I stepped back into the hallway as my wife, Elin, walked toward me. "El, he's not responding," I said, still not comprehending what was happening. Elin walked directly into Thomas's room, touched his arm, and said, "Mark, he's cold." I stepped toward his bed, felt his arm, and with an uncomprehending sense of shock said, "He's dead, El." My wife started sobbing and screamed, "No. It can't be. Someone needs to fix this." I was in shock and speechless. After a few seconds of confused silence, I managed to say, "I'll call 911."

The Campbell Police came in minutes, but they stayed for hours. Before the police and the coroner left, they said they were ninety-five percent sure that his death involved fentanyl. But this didn't make sense because Thomas wasn't a drug addict. He was an Eagle Scout who did numerous community projects. He was a self-professing Christian who was active in the youth group at the Lutheran Church of Los Gatos and built houses for needy families in Mexico. Thomas had a heart for the poor, the needy, and the destitute.

Four days later, the Campbell Police sergeant in charge of the investigation into Thomas's death phoned me and said that they had arrested the person who sold my son the pill that killed him. They booked him into the Santa Clara County Main Jail on several narcotics sales charges. The sergeant also told me that the defendant (who is sitting to my left in the courtroom today) was visibly upset and extremely remorseful when he learned that the pill that he sold Thomas had killed him.

I've since learned that my son knew the defendant—they were fellow students at Bellview High School. My son played in the marching band, and the defendant was on the football team. This explains why Thomas trusted that the defendant was selling him a single dose of Xanax in a world where counterfeit fentapills are poisoning thousands and thousands of young people. It also explains why the defendant was so remorseful when he learned that Thomas died from taking that pill, because the defendant did not know that it was a counterfeit pill filled with fentanyl.

Thomas was our only child. We'll never see him graduate from college. We'll never see him find a profession and make an adult contribution to life. We'll never see him get married. We'll never see him have children. Elin and I will never have grandchildren, and we have no heir to carry on our legacy. These are some of the hardest things my wife and I must deal with for the rest of our lives.

As Elin and I faced this sentencing day and a future life without our son, we've been constructing a grievance story about Thomas's death and the defendant's role in it—a prepackaged script that we will tell people for the rest of our lives when someone asks us, "What happened to Thomas?" or when someone innocently asks, "Do you have children?"

What we know beyond a shadow of a doubt is that only the truth will set us free (John 8:32). So, our grievance story must be a truthful reflection of what really happened, one that doesn't minimize the role that the defendant played in Thomas's death, or the role Thomas had in causing his own death.

We believe the defendant did not know that the Xanax pill he sold our son was counterfeit and contained fentanyl. But we also believe that he made a bad decision to illegally sell Xanax, which is why we're here today. Your Honor, we hope the court includes a very strong admonishment statement in the defendant's sentence. Now that he knows that one pill can kill, if the defendant sells them again, my wife and I believe he should be tried for murder.

We also know that Thomas was on the path to finding and living out the destiny that he had in life and the destiny he was creating with his choices. Our son made a bad choice to calm his anxiety about life, his relationships, and being a prisoner of the COVID-19 pandemic with a Xanax pill that he bought illegally on Snapchat. But we also know that Thomas was deceived, and his choice to buy that one pill should not have been a death sentence. His life was cut short by a single choice made within the *Zeitgeist* of a cold, calculating, deceptive, unforgiving, and evil world, where fentanyl poisonings have claimed the lives of thousands and thousands of unsuspecting victims like Thomas.

Your Honor, our language shapes our reality. So, it's important to be perfectly clear about what happened that day. People like Thomas who were deceived by these counterfeit fentapills did not "overdose." They were *poisoned*. As the September 2020 Drug Enforcement Agency Intelligence Report tells us, they were deceived and murdered for financial gain by two criminal drug networks in Mexico (the Sinaloa Cartel and the Jalisco New Generation Cartel) and for global political-ideological power and control by communist China, the main supplier of fentanyl precursors to these cartels.

It is a tragedy that we've lost our son, Thomas, to this growing crisis. And it is a tragedy that the defendant did something unintentionally that he'll regret for the rest of his life.

Your Honor, Thomas is not just a name or number on today's court docket. One year, thirty-seven weeks, and three days ago, he was very much alive. He had his whole life before him. Today, he is no longer on the planet as a living soul. I know this because I lowered my son's earthly remains into a two-foot-deep hole in the ground of the Ryssby Cemetery in Longmont, Colorado on the afternoon of August 28, 2021.

Thomas now resides in a heavenly home—one not built with human hands—where he will be alive for all eternity. My wife and I will see him again when we make that final journey home. As Jesus tells us, "In My Father's house are many rooms; if that were not so, I would have told you, because I am going there to prepare a place for you" (John 14:2). Amen.

◇ ◇ ◇

As I finished saying "Amen," I stared directly at Judge Nelson, purposely making eye contact with her as I punctuated the scriptural promise. Even from thirty feet away, her eyes—the windows of the soul—revealed that my words had hit the mark. I also noticed that Adam and his attorney both had their heads down, their eyes averted from Elin and me, and the picture of Thomas she was rotating for everyone to see. But I did witness Adam reach for a tissue, lower his face mask, and wipe a stream of tears from his eyes.

"In closing, Your Honor, my wife and I would like to thank you for bringing some sense of closure and fair process to this difficult and heartbreaking legal case." I concluded my statement to a deathly silence permeating the entire courtroom, one that lasted for several seconds.

"Thank you, Mr. Bodnarczuk, for taking the time to put together such thoughtful remarks," Judge Nelson began. "As I sit here looking at the picture of Thomas that your wife is holding, he reminds me of my own son. So, my heart goes out to you and your wife in this enormous loss." She paused briefly before speaking again. "Is there anyone else in the courtroom who would like to say something?"

The courtroom went silent again. I sat there wondering if Dan would speak up. When it was clear no one else wanted to speak, James rose and said, "Your Honor, the people of Santa Clara County would like an admonishment to be included in your sentencing."

Adam's attorney stood and played the only card he had in his client's defense. "I object, Your Honor."

"Overruled," was Judge Nelson's immediate response.

James then began reading the admonishment to Adam.

> We are advising you that illegally bought, sold, or obtained drugs, often in pill form, sometimes contain fentanyl. We are warning you that fentanyl is a drug that is extremely dangerous. Even small amounts of fentanyl can kill very quickly. You cannot tell if a drug has fentanyl in it by looking at it. Drugs with small amounts of fentanyl have killed hundreds of people in this county. All drugs and counterfeit pills can themselves be deadly, but they become much deadlier when they are mixed with substances such as fentanyl and analogs of fentanyl. These substances alone, or mixed together, can kill in very small doses very quickly. If you provide a substance containing fentanyl to someone and that person dies as a result, you can be charged with murder."

Once James had sat down, Judge Nelson continued speaking. "In addition to the three years in custody, I'm admonishing you about the following. You cannot do drugs. You must submit to regular drug testing. You must not possess any firearms. When you get out of jail, you are to report directly to your probation officer. If you want to leave the state or the country, you are required to inform your probation officer at least forty-eight hours prior. When you return to the state or reenter the country, you are to report directly to your probation officer within forty-eight hours. Do you understand what I'm telling you?"

"Yes, Your Honor," was Adam's clear but muted response. I watched as the officer guarding the door to the county jail walked toward Adam to take him into custody, taking a firm hold of his left arm. Adam turned toward me and waved goodbye in my direction, as the officer led him into custody.

I wasn't sure what was happening. What message he was trying to send? Why would he wave to me? I looked at him directly but did not respond in any way. I turned toward the back of the courtroom and suddenly realized Adam was waving goodbye to his girlfriend, who was sitting on my right.

◇ ◇ ◇

I walked out of the courtroom quickly, heading directly for the restroom. After I had dried my hands, I pulled the restroom door open to walk back out into the long hallway when I suddenly ran right into Dan as he was walking through the door. He looked at me with teary eyes and a deeply pained face and gave me a big bear hug. No words were spoken, but I knew that he was visibly moved by what I'd said. He approved. There was nothing left to say.

Afterward, everyone chatted in the hallway outside the courtroom, sharing observations and exchanging insights and new perspectives they had gained from actually seeing the person responsible for Thomas's death. All of us who attended the sentencing now shared a new emotional bond. We experienced this together. One person told me, "I read the victim impact statement on Thomas's site early this morning when you posted it. It was one thing to read the words. It was quite another to hear you read them boldly in the courtroom."

Little by little, people said goodbye as they wandered toward the elevators in small groups and left for their homes or offices. Elin and I were some of the last to leave. As scheduled, we drove to Palermo's Italian Restaurant to meet James for dinner.

"I'm a little worried," Elin confessed on the way there. "What are we going to talk about with him?" She paused as she struggled to cross the six lanes of traffic to get to our exit.

"Don't worry about it," I assured her. "He's a genuine, good-hearted guy, and we'll share a special bond with him for the rest of our lives." I knew James more deeply than Elin did, since I was the primary interface with him for the last year and a half. As Thomas's parents, Elin and I saw this protracted legal process through to the very end. We did the right thing for our son. We stood up for Thomas and the importance of his life and his death in seven court proceedings.

At Palermo's, Elin, James, and I talked for almost three hours about everything under the sun. As the conversation came to an end, I finally asked, "James, can you contact the Campbell Police Department and tell them we'd like to get Thomas's phone back?" When we found Thomas dead in his bedroom on that fateful morning, his cold, lifeless fingers were wrapped around his iPhone. The Campbell Police took it as evidence of the crime that was committed and had not yet returned it to us.

"Sure," he responded immediately. "I'll send them an email on Monday."

◊ ◊ ◊

Elin and I sat at the gate in the airport early Saturday morning, eager to get home to Colorado. The week seemed like a blur. I felt a sense of peace about how things turned out. But at the same time, I was emotionally exhausted and on the verge of tears. I needed time to process what had just happened. I needed space.

By Monday morning, I noticed I had an email from James waiting for me.

"Good morning," James began with his usual salutation. "I reached out to Campbell Police Department about Thomas's cell phone. I asked if it can be mailed or if you had to pick it up in person. I will let you know what they tell me."

I quickly responded, "Thank you, James. I appreciate you looking into this for us. If necessary, we can pick it up at the police station the next time we're in town. Thanks again for all that you've done for us, and we really enjoyed having dinner with you last Friday. Take care, Mark."

Thomas on a tube being pulled by our rented boat at Vallecito Reservoir

CHAPTER 25

MORE ON FORGIVENESS AND GRACE

July 2, 2023 (2 Years, 8 Weeks, and 5 Days After)

With the sentencing behind us and the prospect of getting Thomas's cell phone back after two years of being sequestered by the district attorney's office as evidence in the case against Adam, the gale force winds and plunging waves of the perfect storm began to subside and slowly ebb away as Elin and I continued along the path of inner healing and transformation. Looking back, we struggled to understand all that had happened to us, to take it in, to process it. We also sought comfort, guidance, and direction along both the Outer Labyrinth of our day-to-day choices and the Inner Labyrinth as revealed by our dreams.

Now, one year, thirty-eight weeks, and one day after Thomas's death, everyday life was like a walk along the ocean shore. Sometimes the waters of grief and pain gently washed over our feet. Other times, the sea rose up violently, plunged over our heads, knocked us down to the sand, and tried to drag us out into the emotional abyss. The overwhelming emotional experiences by now had become episodic. They came without notice, but they always subsided. We had learned that the pounding waves of pain and grief did eventually roll back out into the ever-shifting collective sea of memories that still connect Elin and me to Thomas and our former life together.

About two weeks after the sentencing, I got curious about where Adam ended up after the guards led him out of the courtroom. So, I went out to the Santa Clara County Jail website and used the online visiting registration option to locate him. When his record appeared on my computer screen, I learned that he'd been taken to the Elmwood Correctional Complex Facility in Milpitas, California and was assigned to a minimum-security section there. I had seen the facility once from the sliding glass doors of my friend Marshall's house in Milpitas. Looking far across the street, I remember marveling at the enormous complex of barbed wire fences and buildings. I even called Thomas over to witness the massive scale of the penal facility designed to "correct" and "rehabilitate" people who had broken the law. That was where Adam was serving his time.

On the computer screen, I also noticed that alongside Adam's booking date was his scheduled day of release: July 20, 2023, just six months to the day from the time he was incarcerated. Adam was sentenced to one year in jail, but James said that he'd probably get out early for good behavior. But this was odd. He'd only been there a couple of weeks. Hardly enough time to establish a record of "good behavior." My sense was that the reduction in detention time was automatic, not based on how well he behaved and integrated into the jail's population. The reality was that Adam would serve the entire one-year sentence only if he misbehaved and caused trouble.

I told Elin what I'd discovered about Adam's release date. "Are you going to contact him when he gets out?" she asked, catching me by surprise.

"That's a great question," I replied. After a moment of silent contemplation, I said, "No," before adding, "But I'm open to whatever the Lord will have me do if he contacts me." The spontaneous nature of my answer surprised and intrigued me.

A few days later, I received another email from James, checking to see whether the Campbell Police Department had contacted me about returning Thomas's cell phone. In addition to letting him know that no one had contacted us yet, I asked about Adam's already reduced sentence and why his sentence was already cut in half. Later that morning, James emailed me back. After giving me the proper phone number to call to get Thomas's phone released, he explained how the release date posted on the website was like a projected date that presumed Adam's good behavior, noting a huge push by the California legislature and governor to keep people out of jails and prison.

After sending a response to James thanking him for his answer, I sat back in my home office chair and began to wonder, *Why am I disappointed that Adam is getting out of jail early if I've truly forgiven him?* I realized then that while I was truly open to whatever the Lord had in store, I was still living in the essential tension between justice and compassion, grace and forgiveness, in the age of counterfeit pills and fentanyl poisonings. I had forgiven Adam for being the channel through which Thomas was killed, but he was still accountable to the Santa Clara County District Attorney's office for the felonies he committed. That's why he was in jail.

FINDING NEW LIFE AFTER THE DEATH OF MY SON

In the wake of Elin's question about reaching out to Adam, I could honestly say I was free of the burden of unforgiveness. The grievance story I'd read to the judge in my victim impact statement during the sentencing court date was true. I forgave Adam from the bottom of my heart after the arraignment. In that moment when I talked with him, hugged him, and sobbed with him about Thomas's death, it was as if God momentarily lifted the veil of sin and darkness from my heart and mind. That experience was a window into the future of all believers when the alienating consequences of sin would be no more. The Spirit of God filled my heart and mind with His presence and gave me an experience of what true forgiveness was like.

In that moment of truth, light, and transformation, the destiny I *had* along the Inner Labyrinth as a forgiven and adopted son of God, and the destiny I was creating with my choices along the Outer Labyrinth of daily life, were aligned. I didn't feel alienated from myself. Nor did I feel alienated from Adam, my son's unknowing killer. I was reconciled with Adam in the sense that the barrier between us about Thomas's death was removed. The basis of a new relationship and an open line of communication emerged. I still have Adam's cell phone number and the text message he sent me on my iPhone. It's a physical and emotional connection between him and me that has the potential capacity to become or develop into something in the future.

In that moment at the arraignment hearing, I also experienced the cleansing, transforming, and sanctified power of the price Jesus paid to redeem us on the cross when He uttered the Greek word *tetelestai*—it is finished (John 19:30). In the Greco-Roman world, the word *tetelestai* was written on business documents or receipts indicating that a bill had been paid in full. Standing there outside the courtroom at the arraignment, I somehow knew in a profound, experiential *yada* sense that Jesus's death truly paid for the debt of my sin, something I could never, in a hundred lifetimes, have paid for myself. In that moment of forgiving Adam, I experienced a sense of eternal life and true light so strongly, so deeply, so to the bone of my being, that I was without words.

◊ ◊ ◊

Fred Luskin argues in his work on forgiveness that if we're still thinking about or obsessing over something that happened in the past—be it last week or fifty years ago—these energy-packed emotions have us rather than us having them. When that happens, we rent too much psychological space to the offense in our minds. He also argues that forgiveness doesn't mean forgetting about what happened or denying that it was, and might remain, painful, damaging, or even traumatic. Forgiveness doesn't mean what the other person did or said wasn't wrong, unkind, and in Adam's case, criminal. But it does mean that it's not my job to punish him, impose consequences, or demand he right the wrong that was done to Thomas, to Elin, and to me. So, while genuine forgiveness removes the barrier to a relationship, and opens a door to possible reconciliation, it doesn't guarantee there will be an ongoing relationship between the person who was harmed and the wrongdoer. In fact, in some cases when there's been criminal activity or physical, psychological, or sexual abuse, an ongoing relationship should be avoided at all costs.

Since Thomas's death, one question that has constantly circulated in my mind is to what extent Luskin's view about forgiveness and reconciliation aligns with a Christian view of forgiveness. I think here of the words of Martin Luther King Jr.:

> Forgiveness does not mean ignoring what has been done or putting a false label on an evil act. It means, rather, that the evil act no longer remains as a barrier to the relationship. Forgiveness is a catalyst creating the atmosphere necessary for a fresh start and a new beginning. It is the lifting of a burden or the canceling of a debt.[49]

On the same subject, the theologian Miroslav Volf explains why forgiveness is not about forgetting the wrongs that have been done.

> Forgiveness names the wrongdoing to let go of it. The thrust of forgiveness is the letting go of it. That's why you need to name the wrongdoing. To name the wrongdoing, we need to remember it.[50]

In the wake of the horrors of apartheid, Archbishop Desmond Tutu echoed this same perspective.

Forgiving is not forgetting; it's actually remembering—remembering and not using your right to hit back. It's a second chance for a new beginning. And the remembering part is particularly important. Especially if you don't want to repeat what happened.[51]

In many ways, I believe Luskin's approach to forgiveness and the process of constructing truthful grievance stories echoes these theological statements as a powerful solvent that dissolves the psychological and emotional defenses that form around painful, traumatic experiences that result from the consequences of sin.

Pastor and theologian Tim Keller's four-part process of forgiveness adds an even deeper spiritual dimension to Luskin's conceptualization of forgiveness and grievance stories. Keller's view is predicated on the story of Jesus's parable of the unmerciful servant in Matthew 18:21–35.[52] First, according to Keller, forgiveness must begin with genuine truth telling about the wrong done without any cover-ups, rationalizations, excuses, or half-truths.

Second, the person who was wronged must do the deep internal work of empathizing with the wrongdoer. Keller says those who have been wronged must step into the offending person's shoes and see them as a fallible human being who is bound in sin rather than as a villain. We need to take pity on them, just like the master in Jesus's parable. "And the master of that slave felt compassion, and he released him and forgave him the debt" (Matthew 18:27). This doesn't come naturally. Our tendency is to see the speck in our brother's eye and look past the enormous log that's in our eye (Matthew 7:1–5). But if we take a more objective view of the offender, and a deeper look at how the Bible defines sin, we can begin to recognize that they are trapped by the same pernicious consequences of sin that we are.

More specifically, in the New Testament, the word for sin is *hamartia*. It literally means to miss the mark. Imagine you're an archer who's trying as hard as you can to hit the bull's-eye, but you're consistently missing the target. Over time, the negative thoughts and feelings, the arguments and judgments, the harmful actions and interactions that we know are wrong emerge from within and eventually solidify into habits and patterns that further alienate us from ourselves and others (Romans 7:14–25). This includes things we've done and things we've left undone. They permeate our lives and relationships. They become our grievance story about life and the world. We tell ourselves, and others, this story over and over again. They become our paradigm and worldview, our self-fulfilling prophecy, and our history. Again, our thoughts become words; our words become actions; our actions become habits; our habits shape our character; and our character becomes our destiny.[53] Or again, Richard Bach says, "Argue for your limitations and, sure enough, they're yours."[54]

So, the bottom line of Keller's second point about doing the deep internal work of empathizing with the wrongdoer is that while the narratives of others' grievance stories may be different than ours, the underlying root causes of sin—alienation from ourselves, others, and God—are still the same. The fact is that sin causes an inward, centripetal focus on self, and the mechanism by which the grievance stories of others are formed is the same as ours.

The third part of Keller's definition of forgiveness argues that we must absorb the loss that results from the offense. We must refuse to take revenge, remembering Paul's direction in Romans 12:19: "Never take your own revenge, beloved, but leave room for the wrath of God, for it is written: 'Vengeance is Mine, I will repay,' says the Lord." Rather than seeking revenge, making the offending person suffer for the wrong they've done, or demanding they do something to make it right, we must write the offense off like a debt on the balance sheet of our hearts and minds. Following Jesus's example, we must crucify ourselves and utter *tetelestai*—it is finished; the debt has been paid in full. This type of self-crucifixion is hard—very hard. But a failure to absorb the loss and the act of taking revenge empowers the inner wound that the wrongdoer has inflicted on us, a wound that's become ours, not theirs. That wound takes on a life of its own in our conscious and unconscious life, apart from the person who inflicted it. Once it takes root in our souls, the wound keeps hurting us inwardly and outwardly. The failure to forgive anchors us to the person, the past offense, and the wound that now lives within us as the "gift" that keeps on giving.

Keller's fourth part of forgiveness leads us back to Elin's question about whether I was going to contact Adam when he got out of jail. We must be open to reconciliation, especially when the wrongdoer responds with genuine repentance, admits they were wrong, and shows the fruit of a changed life. But as Jesus's parable shows us, a changed life and an ongoing relationship does not always happen. The servant did not respond to the king's forgiveness with genuine repentance and a changed life. Rather, he acted in the spirit of Matthew 7:1–5, where he projected his own inner intentions (i.e., his log) onto his fellow slave (i.e., the other's speck), so the relationship between the first servant and the king was not ultimately restored.

Forgiving Adam remains a life-changing experience for me; something I never expected would happen. I'm still asking the Spirit of God to show me what, if anything, He would have me do now. As of this writing, Adam remains in my thoughts and prayers.

◇ ◇ ◇

About two months after Elin and I moved back home to Colorado, I decided to join the local Rotary club. Prior to moving to California, I spent five years as a Rotary member, so I was familiar with the organization. The Rotary motto is "Service above self," a message that deeply resonates with my own drive to be a positive influence in the lives of others. This was one my first steps toward reentering society and accepting the fact that life would go on without Thomas. As an unrepentant introvert in a decidedly extraverted Rotary culture, I knew this would put psychological pressure on me to get out of my comfort zone and get to know some people.

At Rotary meetings, every Rotarian wears a blue badge that displays their name, the current or former positions that they've held in the club, and a "classification" category—a succinct description of the business or profession that a Rotarian provides to society. There is no classification code that exactly fit my work at Stanford/SLAC, so my classification was "Education-University." One of the purposes of these classification codes is to facilitate conversations about what a new member does for a living and how they might get involved in club activities.

At my second Rotary meeting, I was sitting at lunch when the president-elect of the club, Sally, came up and introduced herself. Noticing the classification code on my nametag, she asked what business I was in.

"I work at a very large physics laboratory at Stanford University," I responded, "but my wife and I just moved back home here to Longmont a couple months ago, so I travel back to work in my office on campus about one week per quarter." She looked surprised that I was really telecommuting to California, so I added, "We used to live about twenty miles south of campus, and after March 12, 2020, I had only been to my office six times in two years. So, my wife and I figured why not come back home rather than sit in my house in California and do Zoom meetings there all day."

"Well, that's great," she replied. "I'm so glad that you found your way to our club. Do you have children?"

That was *the* question I feared whenever I was in a new social situation. Elin and I discussed various options for answering this question honestly in the early days after Thomas's death. If I said yes, then I'd have to explain our very long and complex situation for the first time to people I hardly knew. I wanted to avoid that if possible. If I answered no, then I'd be lying and missing an opportunity to keep Thomas's memory alive and warn others about the fentanyl crisis. I didn't want to do that, either, unless I really had to.

I paused for a moment, lowered my head, and then looked Sally right in the eye. "That's a difficult question," I said in a muted tone. My Rotary sponsor, who was right next to me, looked at me, surprised at my response. I paused again and then said to both, "My eighteen-year-old son, Thomas, was poisoned last year by a counterfeit Xanax pill that was made with fentanyl. I don't like to explain all this to people for the first time in public settings like this, so if you're interested, give me your email and I'll send you a link to his memorial site."

You could have heard a pin drop. Sally was horrified at having asked the question. But how could she have known? It's a simple and safe question that people ask to make conversation. It's a way to show interest in others, to find a mutual connection in life when they first meet someone. Taken off guard and not knowing what to say, she broke the uncomfortable silence with, "I'm so sorry, Mark. My father was a successful businessman here in town. He committed suicide, and I've never gotten over it. Tomorrow, May second, is the anniversary of his death."

I quickly responded, "Tomorrow is the first anniversary of Thomas's death day." Sally gave me her email address, and I sent her a link to Thomas's memorial site. We had something very deep and profound in common: a loss, different in nature and cause but nonetheless devastating and life changing.

Not many people at the Rotary club knew about Thomas's death because I hadn't talked about it publicly, so I found what I thought was a safe way to make this common public knowledge and warn others about this mounting crisis of counterfeit pills and fentanyl poisoning. One of my responsibilities at Rotary was to line up the program speakers for the month of February. I invited Ed Ternan from the Song for Charlie (SFC) organization to be one of our speakers in February 2022. The title of Ed's talk was "Drugs in the Age of Fentanyl." As it turned out, Ed's talk was timely because President Biden had just mentioned the fentanyl problem in his State of the Union address the week prior on February 7, 2023.

As Ed waited on Zoom on the large screen in the front of the room, I introduced him. "As some of you know, I have a vested interest in this topic," I began my opening remarks. "I'm currently exploring ways for our Rotary club and other Rotary clubs in Colorado to partner with SFC to get the word out about the escalating danger of thousands and thousands of young people who are being poisoned by buying what's being sold as prescription medications like Xanax or Adderall when these are often counterfeit pills containing a lethal dose of fentanyl.

I've had people ask me, "I don't understand the business model. Why would anyone want to sell something that kills off their customer base?" My initial response is often that you don't understand that because you don't think like a criminal. A September 2020 US Drug Enforcement Agency intelligence report describes how thousands of young people are being deceived and murdered for financial gain by two criminal drug networks in Mexico. I saw one interview with a cartel member who was mixing the ingredients of these counterfeit pills in an enormous, filthy soup vat in the middle of a field somewhere in Mexico. At the end of the interview, the reporter said to him, "You know these pills kill people, right?" Without hesitation, and in an angry defensive tone, he responded, "Well, I gotta feed my family."

I saw an article in the local paper on Friday about a twenty-three-year-old man in Boulder who was sentenced to five years in prison for selling a single counterfeit oxycodone pill to a twenty-one-year-old woman. That one pill killed her because it contained a lethal dose of fentanyl. During the sentencing, the Boulder County judge said there was empirical evidence from the defendant's phone that this guy actually knew he was selling counterfeit pills that might contain a lethal dose of fentanyl for fifteen dollars each. He took a chance with her life without her knowledge and sold them anyway.

To bring things a little closer to home and to our Rotary club, Sally told me about a person she knows whose son finished a local sports game and took what was sold as a muscle relaxant. It was actually a counterfeit pill with a fatal dose of fentanyl, and he died in the locker room. I've also had people in our club tell me that they've been aware of the counterfeit pill fentanyl crisis from the media, but they never actually knew anyone who'd been personally impacted by this problem until they met me."

At this point, I broke down and sobbed in front of a hundred people. I began weeping so profusely that I couldn't go on speaking. It was unnerving for the people in the room. They stared at me and started squirming in their chairs. It was embarrassing for me too. Sally, who was sitting a few feet from me at the front table with Elin, rose, stood next to me, and put her arm around my waist trying to comfort me. Ed's face just stared into the Zoom camera as his face reflected a deep level of empathic pain. After a moment, still visibly shaken, I continued my introduction.

"On May 1, 2021, my eighteen-year-old son, Thomas, was poisoned by a counterfeit Xanax pill that was really fentanyl." I went on to summarize the indescribable loss of our son, our only child. Then I continued, "My wife, Elin, came to me the next day and said, 'I need to talk to somebody,' so I found her a clinical psychologist who specialized in grief. A couple of weeks later, that therapist sent Elin a link to a newspaper article about Song for Charlie. Elin emailed the Song for Charlie website, and someone contacted us. She, too, had recently lost her seventeen-year-old son to a single counterfeit pill. Within a few weeks, I was on a Zoom call with Ed, who supported me in one of the darkest and most painful times of my life. Ed was able to reach me in that time of deep pain and need, because we were both members of that small, sad club that no one wants to belong to but we were forced to join."

Once I finished, Ed thanked me for the introduction, which teed up his talk about Song for Charlie as a national, family-run nonprofit charity dedicated to raising awareness about "fentapills"—fake pills made of fentanyl. He described how Song for Charlie works with experts, educators, parents, and other influencers to reach the most vulnerable group: young people between the ages of thirteen and twenty-four.

I scanned the room as Ed began his talk. People were engaged, listening intently as he told the story about how his own son, Charlie, had died three weeks before graduating from Santa Clara University with a degree in economics. Charlie was experiencing pain from a previous back surgery, and one night he took what was sold as prescription Oxycontin to relieve his back pain and relax before an upcoming job interview. The pill was counterfeit and contained a lethal dose of fentanyl. That one pill killed him. His friends found him dead in his dorm room hours later. Since meeting Ed and having some involvement with Song for Charlie, I've met many parents who have suffered this same loss, each having their own unique story of how they came to the same end of losing a child to fentanyl poisoning.

Elin and Mark at North Pole in Colorado Springs without Thomas

CHAPTER 26

A TALE OF TWO LITTLE BOYS

September 10, 2023 (2 Years, 18 Weeks, and 5 Days After)

The first year after Thomas died, I questioned whether I could survive this unthinkable loss. Another nagging question that taunted me during the second year was *Will I find new life after the death of my son?* Year two forced me to come to terms with the long-term implications of a life without my son and whether I'd find a new sense of meaning and purpose in life.

I felt like some part of me had died with Thomas, but I didn't know what it was. The perspective I gained during the second year has helped me to articulate this loss, but the English word "life" lacks the granularity and nuance needed to describe what I've experienced. So, I'll use the precision of four Greek words (*bios*, *psychē*, *zoē*, and *aiōnios*) to try to tease apart the subtle but profound facets of finding new life after the death of my son.

After Thomas died, Elin and I were still alive biologically (*bios*). We had the type of biological life that animates the rest of the natural world. We were able to sit up and take nourishment. But on some days, it was a Darwinian struggle to put one foot in front of the other just to make it through the day.

We were also alive psychologically (*psychē*). We were forced to deal with the transactional demands and pedestrian realities of everyday life along the Outer Labyrinth. And at the same time, along the Inner Labyrinth, we had to deal with the unconscious revealed images of our grief and pain about our dead son in our dreams. But we'd lost our overall sense of knowing what life was about and how to handle it. We felt psychologically defeated; we'd lost Thomas, our only child. We were forced to go home to Colorado without him. We wondered if we would ever laugh again without the specter of Thomas's tragic death looming over us in the background.

In those times, I no longer experienced life at its best (*zoē*); that is, I struggled to know what the meaning and purpose of life were within God's will. Thomas's death created enormous change in my life along the

Outer Labyrinth and Inner Labyrinth, and that change was revealed in my dreams. It sentenced me to the amorphous behavioral, psychological, and sociocultural process of coming to terms with a new day-to-day reality. It's what William Bridges calls the neutral zone, the metaphorical equivalent of forty years of wandering in the wilderness in the Bible.[55] It was an existential no-man's-land, an inner wilderness of wandering, an in-between time where the person I was no longer existed and the person I was destined to become had not yet appeared. However, I still recognized the empirical evidence of God's existence, His sovereign power and faithfulness to me that were concretized in historical patterns of transformation over the last forty-two years. I believed, by faith, that God was accomplishing His sovereign will in my life along the Inner and Outer Labyrinth.

I still had eternal life (*aiōnios*) through my relationship with the Spirit of God. But I knew this only by faith because the pain and grief of Thomas's death eclipsed my ongoing inner experience of the "peace that passes understanding" that faith in God brings, despite my daily practice of prayer, reflection, and Bible study. Paradoxically, I still had a subtle but profound intuitive sense that I was not lost. I was on the path the Spirit of God had called me to walk. I had begun to realize that the question *Will I find new life after the death of my son?* was a complex conglomeration of emotional, psychological, practical, existential, and religious questions that had to be, and continue to be, teased apart and processed over time.

<> <> <>

As a little boy, Thomas symbolized new life, a new perspective, the creative process, childlike wisdom, curiosity, a hunger to learn, and boundless potential and possibilities—both for his future and for mine. As I tucked him into bed each night, I thanked God for his spirit, his keen mind, and his curiosity, and I would ask the Lord to show Thomas his calling and destiny in life. What I began to recognize during the second year after his death was that the image of Thomas as a little boy had deep symbolic connections to dreams that I'd had back in 1982, over twenty years prior to marrying Elin or becoming Thomas's father. The inner image of a little boy was collective, archetypal, and it existed in the unconscious beyond the boundaries and constraints of space-time.

FINDING NEW LIFE AFTER THE DEATH OF MY SON

One of the key things to remember about dreams is how important historical and personal context are when it comes to interpreting them. Just as the process of descending down through multiple layers of an archeological site tends to go further back in time, dreams, too, have multiple layers of personal meaning that are built upon the ancient collective layers of the human psyche.[56] Like individual aspen trees that are connected to a single root system, the personal aspects of our psyches are connected to a single, collective root system that Carl Jung called the collective unconscious.

We experience empirical evidence for this aspen-like collectivity in a very commonsense way. When I recount my little boy dream from 1982 below, it will create an image of my dream in your mind. The archetypal images and symbols function like the rows and columns of an Excel file. My unconscious fills the rows and columns with personal memories, collective symbols, and content from my life's journey. Your unconscious will fill the rows and columns with personal memories, collective symbols, and content from your life's journey. That's why we learn from, and are transformed by, sharing our dreams with others. But that's also why only the dreamer can determine the true meaning of their dreams with any certainty.[57]

So, understanding the historical context within which I had the dream below, and my associations with the dream images and symbols, is important when it comes to distilling the core message that the Spirit of God, working through and the Self, was trying to communicate to me, the dreamer. Reviewing the historical context and my associations will help to explain the meaning of the little boy dream image and how it became connected to Thomas's life and death. It will also help to describe the ways in which the Spirit of God has led, and continues to lead, me over the course of my life, including the underlying process of answering the question *Will I find new life after the death of my son?*

First, it is important to know a bit more about my history. Between 1974 and 1980, I earned an associate degree, bachelor's degree, and master's degree in biblical and theological studies. I began my schooling with the idea of going into the pastoral ministry, but over time, I realized this was not my calling. In graduate school at Wheaton College, I toyed with the idea of pursuing an academic career in theology, but this also was not where God was leading me. By the summer of 1980, I was at a personal and professional crossroads. I was a Christian who wanted to serve the Lord, but I didn't know how to cash this deep desire out in my day-to-day life as a career.

In the fall of 1980, I took an entry-level job at Fermilab near Wheaton. Fermilab is a high-energy physics laboratory whose mission is to explore the fundamental constitutes of the universe, the forces by which they interact, and the origins of the universe. From the very smallest things in the universe (i.e., quarks and leptons) to the very largest (clusters of galaxies), Fermilab's goal was to map out the actions and interactions of everything seen and unseen in the universe. As a trained theologian, I was intrigued by the laboratory's mission. I was proud, thrilled, to be a small part of this huge endeavor. I read everything I could find on the history, development, theory, and practice of high-energy physics and cosmology. I went back to graduate school and studied the conceptual development of physics from Babylonian astronomy to quantum mechanics in a PhD program at the University of Chicago.

Along the Outer Labyrinth, I lived in an essential tension between a deep understanding of biblical theology, a historical-grammatical view of the Bible, and the history, theory, philosophy, and scientific practice of fundamental physics and cosmology. Over time, I digested, internalized, and resolved the issues and conflicts that many people have between "science" and "religion." In my view, it wasn't modern experimental science that caused the ancient people who personally witnessed the raising of Lazarus from the dead (John 11) to deny the empirical evidence of their own eyes. They knew nothing about modern science two thousand years ago. From a cosmological perspective, the laws of astrobiology and physics have probably been unchanged for a billion years. More importantly, from a Darwinian perspective, the neurophysiological structure and function of the human brain hasn't evolved that much over the last several thousand years. So, the neurophysiological apparatus through which those who witnessed the raising of Lazarus saw the world was much like ours in the twenty-first century.

From an inside-out perspective, the neurophysiological structure of the human brain is also analogous to the rows and columns of an Excel file. In this manner, the biblical authors processed data about the world much like we do in 2024. Regarding Lazarus in particular, it was the everyday

FINDING NEW LIFE AFTER THE DEATH OF MY SON

empirical experience that "dead people don't rise from the dead" that shaped and defined the personal, psychological, and spiritual data that populated those neurological rows and columns and led to the belief that Lazarus did (or didn't) rise from the dead. The eyewitnesses in Bethany had no framework within which to understand how Jesus had the power to violate conservation laws, to temporarily suspend the natural laws of biology and physics at will when he commanded "Lazarus come forth" (John 11:43). Most called it a miracle. Others said it was sorcery.

Accepting the possibility that conservation laws had been, and still can be, violated episodically as evidence of God's sovereign will was the only scientific price I had to pay to maintain a historical-grammatical view of the Bible within the twenty-first century scientific reality and mission of the high-energy physics and cosmological research we were doing at Fermilab.[58] What a bargain!

From an outside-in perspective, the tension between Thomas Kuhn's subjective, deconstructivist view of scientific practice in his book *Structures of Scientific Revolutions* and the objective, realist view of science in Ian Hacking's book *Representing and Intervening* gave me a powerful tool for understanding and deconstructing the underlying assumptions of Jung's work.[59] Much like how Copernicus and Kepler swapped out a Ptolemaic, geocentric view of our solar system for a heliocentric view with elliptical, not circular, orbits, I swapped out Jung's underlying two-part ontology of the Spirit of the Depths and the Spirit of the Times for a three-part ontology that consisted of the Spirit of the Depths and the Spirit of the Times that were created in the beginning by the Spirit of God as described in Genesis 1:1 and by the Word in John 1:1–5. Because the Spirit of the Depths and the Spirit of the Times were created things, the Spirit of God could exercise His sovereign will over them along the Outer and Inner Labyrinths.

It was within this historical context and conceptual framework that the Self presented me with the dream included below on January 7, 1982, twenty years before Thomas was born:

> I was in a Sunday school class with a bunch of little kids. One of the little boys, who was about two years old, was answering a question that had been asked. His answer was in the form of a little saying, almost an equation, yet it wasn't complicated. It was

his own personal wisdom or idea. The equation seemed strange to me at that time, like it didn't really fit into or explain anything.

Then the scene changed, and I was in a room with this little boy and someone else. We were sitting on the floor playing a game. I was stuck. The boy gave me a little book. It was small and funny looking. At first, I remember thinking how ridiculous it would be to find anything of real value in this silly little book. Then I turned to a page and there was an equation that reminded me of $E=mc^2$. Suddenly, that equation made sense. I had this wonderful, exuberant feeling and insight. I felt, how could I have missed this? I wasn't impressed and didn't see the value of the equation when the little boy said it in class. But now, I couldn't believe how amazing it was. I said to the little boy, "This is what you said in class the other day, isn't it?" He answered, "Yes!" I was ecstatic with the deep emotional experience of creative discovery. It was an aha experience when a light went on in my head. It was like when a kid has a stuffed animal that is all torn, raggedy, and dirty, yet it means so much to them. That's the feeling I had about this book. It was silly looking and childlike, filled with all funny colors, but I knew, in the *yada* sense, that it was a book of wisdom that I could learn from. I remember wanting to look at the rest of the pages for more insights.

This dream presents an image-based narrative of the personal religious mindset and the psychological, scientific, and practical issues that I was facing at the time. Notice how the dream began within the context of a more personal religious setting of a Sunday school class that was connected to my first personal experience of God at the Hungarian Reformed Church. This is juxtaposed to what could have been a larger, more collective setting of a church service.

The scene changes to an even more personal (one-on-one) interaction between the image of me (as an adult in 1982) and the little boy with a third, shadow figure looking on and playing no active role in the dream narrative. Like adults tend to do when playing with a child, I took on the perspective of the little boy in the dream—I became like a little child and sat on the floor. My sense is that the game we were playing was a symbol of

FINDING NEW LIFE AFTER THE DEATH OF MY SON

"the game of life." For me, this was a complex, challenging path of knowing where I was going in life from a Christian perspective, as symbolized by the religious setting. I was stuck. I was at an impasse along both the Inner Labyrinth of the images in the dream and along the Outer Labyrinth of deciding what to do in my personal and professional life. More specifically, I was trained in biblical theology but found myself energized by working in a high-energy physics laboratory—a paradox that was not lost on my scientific colleagues at Fermilab.

The small, funny-looking little book that was a central focus in the dream narrative symbolized the journal that I started on August 24, 1980. My actual physical journal in waking life was a scientific logbook in which I had recorded and analyzed more than 2,500 dreams over a forty-two-year period—sometimes drawing colorful pictures and representations of important dream images. The little boy in the dream was a catalyst for deep insight and profound transformation by sharing his book with me, his little book of childlike wisdom.

At first sight, the symbols, images, and interactions in our dreams can seem ridiculous and nonsensical to our conscious waking selves. They don't seem to have any real value to us as adults who struggle to live lives of meaning and contribution in a world focused on material possessions and the mundane challenges of daily life. This was my initial reaction to the book. I arrogantly assumed that there "just couldn't be" any real value in this ratty, silly-looking, and funny-colored book. But the adult "me" in the dream, who had taught many adult Sunday school classes in waking life, needed to learn a lesson from the little boy's funny-looking book of wisdom and the truths he knew and understood.

With the book in hand in the dream, my curiosity was kindled as I flipped through the pages and something like an equation caught my eye. While it looked like an equation, it was also an inner archetypal *symbol* of transformation. It seemed like Einstein's famous equation, $E=mc^2$, that describes how energy is transformed into mass—how this is transformed into that, and then back again, as a recurring cycle and an eternal process of change and transformation.

Along the Outer Labyrinth of Fermilab's research mission, $E=mc^2$ described a transformational equivalence of physical processes that operated everywhere in a universe that contained more galaxies than there are people on the planet. As a Christian who believed, by faith, that God was the creator and sustainer of the universe, Fermilab's mission, especially its research into the origins of the universe, had deep religious significance for me. As Romans 1:20 tells us, God's invisible attributes, eternal power, and divine nature were stamped on the universe when He spoke it into existence through the Big Bang. For me, Fermilab's scientific mission was to explore God's creative and sovereign power in a rigorous and quantitative way. High-energy physics was an outside-in perspective that described the what, the how, and the when of the universe. Biblical theology and my personal faith in God were an inside-out perspective that explained the why and the who of the human experience of living in that physical universe as a biological-spiritual hybrid being.

God also stamped His image (*Imago Dei*) on Thomas, Elin, and me along the Inner Labyrinth, where the Self is the central organizing force within the human psyche that orchestrates, integrates, and directs all conscious and unconscious life along both the Inner and Outer Labyrinth.[60] The Self is where the Spirit of God takes up residence and lives in the unconscious, when we choose to follow Him. It was through the Self that God's Spirit spoke to, and worked through, people in the Bible using dreams and insights—sometimes without their conscious participation and intent.[61] In my own experience, it was through the Self that the Spirit of God within prompted, tested, motivated, guided, and bore witness to the Son, leading me into all truth (John 14:26; 15:26; 16:13).

So, in the little boy dream, the multidimensional meaning of his book and his equation suddenly made sense to me, and all that I just described was crystallized in my heart and mind. This was the moment of transformation in the dream, where the light bulb of new insight turned on in my head. It was an aha experience about the destiny I had in God from the beginning of time. I was ecstatic with the deep emotional experience of discovery. I had a profound, wonderful feeling deep inside, and I wondered why I hadn't seen this before. The truths contained in the little boy's uncomplicated sayings, his personal wisdom in the book and in the equation, seemed so obvious after the paradigm shift in the dream. I was amazed I'd missed it before. What seemed silly and of little value became the deepest wisdom in the universe.

From that day forward in 1982, the image of the little boy, his book, and the equation symbolized a new perspective, a creative process, childlike wisdom, new life, and the enormous potential and possibilities for the future. The idea of becoming like a little child—sitting on the floor, playing the game of life, and appreciating childlike wisdom—are aligned with Jesus's teaching in Matthew 18:2–4, where he tells us that unless we humble ourselves and become like little children, we will not enter the kingdom of heaven. He reiterates that the kingdom of heaven belongs to little boys and girls, and they will be the greatest in the kingdom of heaven.

◊ ◊ ◊

There are dreams, and then there are *big dreams*, the ones that create deep, profound transformation in our lives. The little boy dream was a big dream. God was working through the dream to provide inner guidance that led me beyond the personal and professional impasse I had reached along the Outer Labyrinth back in 1982. The process of integrating the symbols, images, and deeper meaning of my interactions with the little boy, his book, and the equation into conscious awareness provided new direction for my daily life when I needed it most. The Spirit of God provided the inner resources I desperately needed—resources that were independent of my conscious waking life along the Outer Labyrinth. But these dream images also symbolized a collective, archetypal, creative, spiritual-religious process along the Inner Labyrinth that became like a river of living water that sprung up from the depths of my soul, much like Jesus promised the Samaritan woman at the well (John 4).

Two decades later, my little boy, Thomas, was born on May 16, 2002. Within the first two years following his birth, the unconscious began to merge the dream image of the 1982 little boy in the Sunday school class with a dream image of my son, Thomas. On May 24, 2004, just eight days after Thomas's second birthday, I had the following short but powerful dream:

> I was at Fermilab visiting some people and doing some type of work for the laboratory, and Thomas was there as a little boy (two years old) running around. I loved him so much and woke up with a deep, profound love for him in my heart. Upon waking, I realized that this was the very first time in my life that I truly loved anyone with my whole heart. It was powerful. It was amazing. It was transformational.

In the twenty-two years between having the 1982 little boy dream and having the dream about Thomas in 2004, the image of Fermilab remained a symbol of the Self, the *Imago Dei*. This short but deeply moving dream contained a composite set of symbols where the image of my two-year-old son, Thomas, was linked back to the image of the little boy in my 1982 dream within the context of Fermilab, which had deep religious, psychological, and scientific significance for me. The dream symbolized the creative process and the enormous potential from which new perspectives, new direction, and new life could emerge.[62] These were some of the same qualities I thanked God for each night as I tucked Thomas into bed, thanking God for his spirit, keen mind, and curiosity.

My heart was transformed by the dream of Thomas at Fermilab. The catalyst for this dramatic inner shift in perspective, a long overdue self-discovery, was realizing my deep love for Thomas. Like the fictional character Ebenezer Scrooge in Charles Dickens's *A Christmas Carol*, my heart was hardened early in life by growing up in a clinically dysfunctional family with a father who was mentally ill and abusive for most of his life. So, much like the 1982 little boy dream, I was stuck in the 2004 little boy dream. I had reached an impasse about one of the most basic experiences and abilities needed to play the game of life effectively—the ability to love deeply with my whole heart. This was the inner psychological work that I had gone to the archetypal image of Fermilab, the Self, to work on.

The everyday activities and tasks of being Thomas's dad for the first two years of his life, and the experience of loving him like only a father can along the Outer Labyrinth, had been internalized and had activated the Inner Labyrinth potentiality of my buried, latent ability to love deeply, and to experience love deeply, for the first time in my life. The actuality of Thomas in my day-to-day life, and the creative potentiality of the images in the dream, kindled a flame that both warmed and softened my heart.

It's difficult to overstate the power and importance that loving my son, Thomas, had made in my life. It was a deep, heartfelt experience that began to generalize into other relationships. I started experiencing it in other intimate relationships, like with my wife, Elin, and in learning to love myself.[63] The Spirit of God, working through the inner and outer dimensions of the Self, helped me reclaim the ability to love and be loved, something that was squashed from the time when I was a little boy. From that point on, the image of Thomas in my dreams became a conduit through which the Spirit of God channeled inner guidance, inner resources, and direction to help me keep the second-greatest commandment, to love my neighbor as I love myself (Matthew 22:36–40). Like Ezekiel 36:26 promises, "Moreover, I will give you a new heart and put a new spirit within you; and I will remove the heart of stone from your flesh and give you a heart of flesh."

◊ ◊ ◊

Here's what's important to remember about the difficulty I had in processing my grief about Thomas's loss and my struggle to find new life in the second year after Thomas's death. The deep love that I first experienced for Thomas in 2004 and beyond was a blessing while he was alive. But now as I write this chapter, it's this same deep transforming love that makes his loss—the absence of that intimate outer and inner connection—so much more difficult to bear. Losing Thomas went to the depths of my soul, to the Self that was imaged within me in the dream. This, and nothing but this, is what made my initial search for new life in the second year after his death seem so hopeless.

In addition to having helped give Thomas physical life, one of my most important jobs as his father was to lead him to eternal life. Around the age of six or seven, children enter a developmental phase that child psychiatrists Shapiro and Perry call the "age of reason."[64] Children develop an internalized sense of right and wrong. They experience the first spark of self-determination; they want to decide things for themselves. They begin to problem-solve, identify patterns, and apply logic to questions and decisions. At age seven, children start to manifest what adults call common sense. Seven is also the age when children start to realize other people have their own feelings, desires, and needs. They begin to say "I'm sorry" and really mean it.

Shapiro and Perry's article was published in 1976, but the belief that age seven was a pivotal time has a long history. In medieval times, court apprenticeships began at age seven. Children under seven weren't considered responsible for their crimes under British Common Law, and the Catholic Church offers first Communion to children at age seven.[65] An important indicator that a child has reached the age of reason is the emergence of probing questions, where they try to tease apart the difference between their childhood wonder and fantasy about the world and the realities of everyday life.

Thomas started asking questions about all sorts of things. But one of them was the most important question that anyone, at any age, could ask in life. As I mentioned in the introduction, on May 1, 2010—eleven years to the day before he swallowed the counterfeit Xanax pill that killed him—my seven-year-old son and I were having dinner when he asked, "Papa, how do you know if you're going to heaven?" In the discussion that followed, I reminded him that none of us was worthy to go to heaven because of the things we've done or have left undone. It was only by faith in Jesus's sacrificial death and resurrection that we obtain eternal life. A week later, Thomas shared that he was still worried and had doubts about his own worthiness to go to heaven. He understood the message of John 3:16 in his young, inquiring mind, but he wanted to know this in his tender, searching *heart*. I asked him if he really believed what John 3:16 said.

"Yes, Papa, I believe it," was his response. But he was still worried and had doubts.

"Okay. Let's you and I pray right now so you know for sure," I replied. We bowed our heads, and I led him through a prayer where he told God he didn't feel worthy to go to heaven and asked Him to forgive his sins in Jesus's name. Thomas seemed relieved after we'd prayed, and in that moment, I realized the eternal significance of our conversation. Later that night, I logged the experience on the timeline of my Christian discipline journal.

From that day forward, John 3:16 was Thomas's favorite Bible verse. It was the one he chose as part of the public affirmation of faith he made three years later at Faith Presbyterian Church. It's the same verse Elin and I chose for the landing page on his memorial site. As I mentioned earlier, I now realize that his honest questions and doubts reflected his namesake, the disciple Thomas, who wanted to know the risen Christ personally by firsthand experience. I also realize Thomas was made alive by the Spirit of God in the eternal sense that day we prayed together, just seven days before his eighth birthday.

I felt a sense of inner peace about the fact that Thomas had eternal life. But I also knew that being a Christian in a non-Christian world was the road less traveled. It would bring many difficulties and challenges, even at his age. We are all born as citizens of this world. But when you become a Christian like Thomas did, you are born a second time and your citizenship changes. As Vance Havner says, "If you are a Christian you are not a citizen of this world trying to get to heaven; you are a citizen of heaven making your way through this world."[66] So, like the rest of us Christians, the challenge Thomas would continue to face going forward was how to be in the world but not of the world.

As Thomas grew to be a young man, he became an increasingly important part of my reality and identity as his father as well as the reality and identity of our life as a family. Along the Outer Labyrinth, we spent considerable quality time together through baseball games and movies, day trips and longer journeys. Wanting to cultivate and stimulate his mind and his curiosity, we also read books together ranging from *The 7 Habits of Highly Effective People* by Stephen R. Covey to *Mere Christianity* by C. S. Lewis. We read these thoughtful works slowly, sometimes only a few paragraphs at a time. I would "translate" what the author was saying in a way my little boy could understand, and we would discuss what the author was saying from his little-boy perspective—what was happening to him at school, with his friends, and other questions that emerged in his young life.

By the time Thomas reached high school, he became a somewhat reluctant participant on the road less traveled, the journey along the Inner and Outer Labyrinth, the challenge of discovering his calling and destiny in life. Like many of us, the older he got, the more difficult life became. He was forced to contextualize and live out his childlike faith within an adult, scientific world that tends to see no need for God. Like most of us, he had no firsthand experience with supernatural phenomena, nor did he see how they could happen without violating the laws of science. Thomas also struggled with doubts about how a loving God would allow suffering, sin, and evil to exist in the world—why bad things happened to good people.

Despite my 1982 synthesis of science, religion, and Jung's work, I wrestled with some of these same questions and doubts myself—things Thomas and I would discuss over coffee or dinner after a movie. I now recognize that my son's questions and doubts continued to reflect his biblical namesake till the end of his life. I always saw Thomas as being like the one sheep that Jesus left the ninety-nine to find in Luke 15:1–7, like the prodigal son who finally came to his senses and went back home in in Luke 15:11–32.

Thomas was not a citizen of this world trying to get to heaven. He was a citizen of heaven, one who had eternal life, making his way through a world of global pandemics, political polarization, unyielding social problems, and a collective sense of anxiety and stress about the past, present, and future.

In the fall of 2015, I moved from Colorado to California after I took my position at Stanford University/SLAC, which was a sister laboratory to Fermilab. During that time, my personal life was experiencing its fair share of ups and downs, and I was wrestling with questions about whether I had wasted part of my life diving deep into the unconscious doing introspection and dream work. Yet, I knew I had no real alternative because it was my calling and destiny to walk the path of individuation. At the same time, my professional life had gone through its ups and downs, and this was one of the down times. I was struggling to find new ways to use my creative abilities at Stanford. I tried to map my personal calling and destiny to my professional life and the laboratory's mission so I could find new life breathed into the pedestrian profanities of my everyday tasks. I was desperate to find a new, credible, and compelling sense of meaning and contribution in my life and my work.

Two years later on October 8, 2017, when Thomas was a fifteen-year-old sophomore at Bellview High School, I had the following dream:

> I was with Thomas, and he was a little boy, maybe two or three years old, and we were walking through a garden-like place with plants and trees, and streams of water flowing like the atrium of the High-Rise at Fermilab. I was feeling really connected to him, and I deeply loved him as only a father could love his son. As we walked along, I was thinking, *Can you help me, son?* He was a little boy, but somehow, I sensed that he could help me and I should communicate this to him. My need for his help and guidance were directly communicated to Thomas without speaking any words, and then the dream ends.

Once again, this dream happened within the context of the archetypal image of Fermilab. The sixteen-story, open-design atrium looked like a magnificent European cathedral. This garden-like atrium where Thomas and I walked in the dream was filled with plants, trees, and streams of flowing water, which symbolized the creative process and the recurring, endless flow of life in nature. It was a symbolic remnant of the life and innocence in the garden of Eden before the fall. On the one hand, Fermilab's exploration of the outer universe that God created had a deep religious significance for me, far beyond its scientific importance. On the other hand, Fermilab was a symbol of the inner universe God created, where the Self, God's *Imago Dei* within me, was the central organizing force in the human psyche that orchestrates, integrates, and directs all conscious and unconscious life along both the Inner and Outer Labyrinth.

I continued to struggle along the Outer Labyrinth with questions about how to better use my creative abilities at Stanford/SLAC and how to follow my sense of calling and destiny in life. Much like the little boy in the Sunday school dream I'd had twenty-five years prior, I was stuck. I was at an impasse. And once again, I reached out to the inner Thomas with the question *Can you help me, son?* I sensed he could help me, and my question rang out into the silent nighttime of the dream world as I waited expectantly for Thomas's response, and then the dream ended.

◇ ◇ ◇

What is important to note about this 2017 dream of Thomas and me in the Fermilab atrium is that the unconscious had transformed the image of the 1982 little boy, and the image of my son in the 2004 dream, into a third something that I've come to call the Little Boy Thomas image. This 2017 dream shows the Little Boy Thomas image, within the context of the natural garden in the atrium at Fermilab, as a symbol of new life, a new perspective, the creative process, childlike wisdom, curiosity, a hunger to learn, and enormous potential and possibilities for the future. The 2017 dream was a sign that the Spirit of God continued to provide inner guidance, resources, and direction for my life through the Self and the Little Boy Thomas image.

Looking back, I now see this is why Thomas's death, and the loss of this intimate inner and outer connection, was so difficult to bear. His loss went to the depths of my soul, as imaged in the context of Fermilab as a symbol of the Self. Thomas's death had an existential quality about it that went so deep that I couldn't quite put a face on it or verbalize it. Again, it was this, and nothing but this, that made my search for new life during the second year after my son's death seem so hopeless. Part of me wanted to reduce the grief and pain I had been living with to some small thing I could hold in my hand, stare down, and then hold under water until it died. But another part of me sensed that the Spirit of God was providing inner guidance and direction through the Little Boy Thomas image by leading me to reflect on the ninety-eight dreams that Thomas and I had recorded when he was between the ages of five and twelve. I had looked at them over the years and discussed them with Thomas. But now, I realized there were even deeper levels of pain and grief I needed to process—memories, dreams, and reflections that had been eclipsed from conscious awareness by the trauma of Thomas's death and the perfect storm I had survived.

CHAPTER 27

I FOUND NEW LIFE AFTER THE DEATH OF MY SON

September 16, 2023 (2 Years, 19 Weeks, and 4 Days After)

In the later part of his high school years, it became even more apparent that Thomas had enormous intellectual capabilities. As a junior, he scored in the top 1 percent on the California Assessment of Student Performance and Progress. But Thomas also had a deep sense of self-awareness and emotional intelligence about himself and his relationships with others. Studies have shown that people who have both high intellectual capabilities and emotional intelligence are twice as likely to succeed in life than people with high intelligence alone.[67]

The new life of flowers emerging from the frozen winter snow

Thomas was active in the Lutheran Church of Los Gatos youth group all through high school. One adult leader told me that of all the kids he interacted with, Thomas was one of the ones who took his faith most seriously. Another adult youth leader volunteered, "He was quiet and didn't say much, but when he spoke, he always had something of substance to say." One of the highlights of the youth ministry program was the Love of God (L.O.G.) weekend retreat, where the youths spent three days interacting and ministering to one another at a Christian camp in the Santa Cruz Mountains just off the California coast. One of the last things they did at the end of each retreat was to write a letter to their "future selves" from the perspective of the mountaintop experience of focusing on their relationship with God and others over the course of the weekend. Once written, each student sealed their letter and gave it to the youth pastor, who would subsequently mail it to them a few months later. The letters Thomas wrote to himself are important to me because they reveal his private, inner thoughts about his faith in God as a young man.

I found some of these letters as I packed up his belongings after he died. In the letter he sent to his future self in April 2018, he wrote:

What's up Tommy? I hope you had a pretty chill winter, and you had a good amount of time to relax. You better be passing your classes. L.O.G. is one of the best experiences EVER and I hope your relationship with God has grown. Pray more. Read the Bible some. Don't let your faith fade away just because L.O.G. is over. Also prepare yourself to co-lead with Larissa one day. Ya boy, Tommy.

Another letter Thomas sent to his future self that arrived in March 2019, just before his seventeenth birthday, said:

Hello Future Tommy: I'm writing you this letter at L.O.G., which has been sick as heck. This weekend I've felt close to God like usual, but I'm scared to go back. I'm afraid I won't live up to what is expected of a Christian and I'm scared how I feel right now won't last. And it won't. But I hope you've figured out a way to live out your faith effectively. I love you. Stay safe my dude, 2018 Tommy.

Thomas was on the right path when he died; he was on the journey toward his heavenly home. Yet his life manifested some of the conflicts many Christians have. This is what made his sudden and tragic death two years later even more difficult for me to accept and ultimately embrace as the destiny I've been called to live in life.

◇ ◇ ◇

As I write this chapter for the memoir, Elin and I are on our annual trip to Aspen celebrating our twenty-third wedding anniversary—two years, nineteen weeks, and four days after that fatal day. I tried to describe earlier in this book how the deep penetrating pain and grief about Thomas's death had begun to soften and morph into something else—a third something, a new normal. The example I used there to capture the essence of where I was in processing my grief was a person who had just lost their arm and was now struggling to do common tasks like button his shirt, open a jar of peanut butter, or play his guitar. In those first days after the amputation, it would begin to dawn on him that his life would never be the same. There, I asked the question: How long might it take for him to see himself, and to be seen by others, as being a whole person with one arm? Today, my experience of grief along the Outer Labyrinth is more like phantom pain, the sporadic sensation of pain that feels like it's coming from a body part that's no longer there. Over time, phantom pain goes away as the amputee's brain gets used to the loss. My pain and grief about losing Thomas comes and goes, and these days, it comes less frequently, but it will never completely go away.

Along the Inner Labyrinth, the best way to describe the unconscious dimension of this lifelong process of change is with a dream I had almost forty years ago on May 23, 1986.

> I had a dream last night. I was half asleep and half awake, and all I remember was an image. I saw a river that was being diverted from its path for reasons I did not know. They had blocked it off somehow, and the river began to flow in another direction. As it angled out into a new path, it got further and further away from the original riverbed so that the original riverbanks became more and more distinct as dried walls of dirt and rock. I remember thinking or hearing that another small tributary of the river was, or was going to, dry up. I'm not sure why this was all being done; maybe to dredge out the murky bottom—and it was murky. I just remember reflecting

on what a huge job it was to do this, and how utterly long it took to divert and change the forces of nature.

The image of changing the path of the river in the dream is a symbol of how difficult it is to change, to redirect, the natural flow of human nature, our way of being and psychological health. It shows how difficult it was, and is, for the Spirit of God, working through the Self to redirect our lives given the formidable force of the first two consequences of sin—we're alienated from ourselves and from others.

Looking back over the last forty-three years, I now see that Thomas's death was the latest, and certainly the greatest, challenge I've faced over the last four decades. But I've faced other important challenges prior to his birth, and I'll no doubt deal with other soul-wrenching loss between now and when I'm buried next to my son in the Ryssby Cemetery. When I look back to Christmas 2021, to my Faith Presbyterian Church statement of faith in 2010, and to 1964 when I had my first personal experience of God at the Hungarian Reformed Church, and I see the lifelong process of transformation unfolding along the Outer Labyrinth of the myriad choices I've made, I marvel at how the Spirit of God has worked to bring me to where I am today, sitting with my wife in the Aspen Lodge on Main Street in Aspen, Colorado. I'm in the spectator role, fully present to the actuality of the existential now, bound within the context of the historical then, anticipating the potentiality of my future in God with a new sense of clarity.

I now realize the Spirit of God is helping me to create a more truthful grievance story about Thomas's death, one designed to free me from my bondage to the pain and grief I've felt over the last two years. As Ecclesiastes 3:4 tells us, there is a time for everything under heaven. "A time to weep and a time to laugh; a time to mourn and a time to dance." An even more truthful grieving story was the next logical step beyond first acknowledging Thomas's role in causing his own death in the victim impact statement. I needed to use the same three elements that underlie the creation and subsequent maturing of all grievance stories.

First, I've tended to take Thomas's death too personally. I've come to "see" myself as a member of a sad little club rather than someone who has prevailed over this unthinkable loss and become a much better person because of Thomas's death. Second, I've been tempted to blame others, Thomas, and myself, for this tragedy and how I feel about it, with a tacit expectation that someone should do something to right this terrible wrong. I've recounted my grievance story to others, and to myself, over and over again on Thomas's memorial site and in face-to-face discussions, resulting in the third element where the grievance story has become a self-fulfilling prophecy that has shaped and defined my life during the first two years.

But finding new life means deciding to "see" myself differently. I am what I do; I become my choices. It's what Stephen Covey calls the See-Do-Get Process.[68] During the first two years, I "saw" myself as someone who was mortally wounded by Thomas's death, a father who was processing his grief and pain. I saw myself as a parent who managed to survive Thomas's death, by God's grace, but who was still struggling to find a new sense of meaning and purpose in life. Out of that struggle, specific behaviors and emotions flowed naturally from that way of seeing—that is, the "do" element of the See-Do-Get Process.

But now, in the third year after Thomas's death, I've realized I need to continue keeping the promise Elin and I made to each other. We said we would never be afraid to look back and fearlessly face the grief and pain of Thomas's loss. But at the same time, we vowed to turn our faces to the future and look for new life and a sense of meaning and contribution going forward. Along the Inner Labyrinth, I learned that it took time for Thomas's death to sink in to the deepest parts of my soul. This was evidenced by the church potluck dream where I knew Thomas was dead but Elin didn't, as well as the New York City brownstone dream where the little boy asked me if Thomas was coming home. In much the same way along the Outer Labyrinth, it would take time for the reality of finding new life to sink in to my conscious day-to-day life in the *yada* sense.

But now I'm beginning to "see" myself as an incredibly strong person who has prevailed over an unthinkable loss and become a much better person *because* of Thomas's death. As Paul tells us:

> Blessed be the God and Father of our Lord Jesus Christ, the Father of mercies and God of all comfort, who comforts us in all our affliction so that we will be able to comfort those who are in any affliction with the comfort with which we ourselves are comforted by God. For just as the sufferings of Christ are ours in abundance, so also our comfort is abundant through Christ (2 Corinthians 1:3–5).

Going forward, I will reinforce this new way of "seeing" myself by following another one of Paul's admonitions.

> Finally, brothers and sisters, whatever is true, whatever is honorable, whatever is right, whatever is pure, whatever is lovely, whatever is commendable, if there is any excellence and if anything, worthy of praise, think about these things (Philippians 4:8).

◊ ◊ ◊

The alignment between the Outer Labyrinth of the decisions and promises I made and the process of inner healing and transformation along the Inner Labyrinth was confirmed to me by multiple dreams over the first two years after Thomas's death. I now see that the unconscious was teasing apart the conflated elements of the Little Boy Thomas dream image and creating new symbols of transformation that would catalyze the new life I desperately sought in ways I could not have anticipated. I already had a taste of how utterly painful this would be with the new boy shopping mall dream. As I mentioned earlier, when I reflected on that dream, I felt like my soul was being torn apart. On the one hand, the conscious grieving me was repulsed by the possibility of rejoicing about a new inner son out of hand because I felt like I was betraying Thomas and his memory by wanting to move on. But on the other hand, I could not deny that the rejoicing me in the dream revealed deep desires in my heart that wanted to move beyond the grief I felt about Thomas's loss. The unconscious was using the dream to reconcile and transform the opposing perspectives of the rejoicing me and the grieving me into a third something—the rejoicing-grieving me. But God knew I still needed something more.

About seven months after Thomas's death, I was out on my daily walk on the Los Gatos Creek Trail. I was feeling troubled at the time about the actual state of Thomas's eternal soul, whether he was alive in heaven, despite all the evidence that he was. I asked the Lord to give me a sign that Thomas was eternally alive with Him in heaven. That night, I had the following dream:

> I was somewhere with two little boys. One was Thomas when he was about eight years old, and the other was a little boy who was about

two years old, who seemed like the same little boy from my shopping mall dream. We were outside in an area that had a well-manicured green lawn that was contained within a perimeter of very large square of hand-hewn stones that formed a boundary wall like the castle-type stones and surrounding structures at Lambert Castle in Garret Mountain, off Valley Road in Clifton, New Jersey, where I grew up. It may have either been dusk or dawn, because the bright light of daytime was not shining, yet it really wasn't dark like nighttime. We had a small microwave in a box like the one I bought when I first moved to California. Because Thomas was the older boy in the dream, I asked him to be "in charge" of the box because the other boy was too young to handle it.

All this happened in an early part of the dream, and then the scene changed and the three of us were still there in that place, but there was another guy there now who was about my age and who I knew from work or somewhere else. The guy was standing on the other side of the stone perimeter wall (i.e., outside the courtyard area we were standing in where the green grass was). He and I were chatting about something that I knew in the dream but can't remember now. The two boys were about twenty feet away, on my left, back where we were originally standing in the early part of the dream. I had moved closer to the guy to my right so we could talk easier.

At one point in my interaction with the guy, he looked over and noticed the two boys, and the focus of his attention shifted from me to them. He didn't say anything to me, but I saw him look at them with a deep sense of curiosity, and somehow, I knew that what he was pondering in his heart and mind was the question *who were these boys and what was their connection to me?* This was all communicated between him and me silently, directly, without saying anything. He continued to look at them in silence, rather than look at me, so finally I said to the guy, "These are my sons." The boys had also been directly, silently, without spoken words, connected to the interaction between the guy and me, and with my words identifying them, they started to walk toward me. Thomas carried the box with the small microwave in it, because I had put him in charge of taking care of it.

As the two boys reached me and stood there looking alternately at me and then the guy, he said to me with a deep, pondering, questioning, inquisitive, surprised tone in his voice, "Your sons?" The emotion-filled tone of the guy's question communicated a silent but crystal-clear message to me as if to say, *How can these things be?* It reminded me of the curious and confused tone Nicodemus had when he asked Jesus, "How can these things be?" in John 3:9. I repeated what I said to the guy with a deep, satisfied sense of pride that only a father could have about his children: "Yes. These are my sons," to make it crystal clear that this is what I meant the first time. As the boys stood next to me, I went on, "This is Thomas, and this is X." I said the name of the two-year-old little boy in the dream, but I can't remember it now that I'm awake. I communicated all of this to the guy directly and silently in the dream rather than with spoken words.

The guy was surprised that these were really my sons, maybe because of how old I was and how young they were, but he didn't say anything more because he knew it was true, and my sense was that he was reflecting on what that reality meant without questioning its validity or truthfulness. The dream ends here, with the powerful messages that we had just exchanged ringing out into the dusk/dawn, with the guy and myself silently reflecting on the meaning and import of what had just happened.

I awoke with a deep sense of peace, resolution, healing, and transformation about Thomas. The dream transformed the painful, paradoxical images and emotions of the rejoicing-grieving me into a new fourth something. The Spirit of God was working through the Self to heal my deep inner wounds. This was the first inkling of finding new life after Thomas's death. It was happening far below the surface of awareness without my conscious participation or intent. Along the Inner Labyrinth, I had accepted and began to embrace Thomas's death as the path God called me to walk in His sovereign will. It was amazing. I shook my head with astonishment when I awoke.

The setting in the two-boy dream is archetypal. The perimeter of a very large square of hand-hewn stones that formed a boundary wall like the castle-type stones and surrounding structures of Lambert Castle seemed connected to enormous stone castle walls built a thousand years ago in Europe. The well-manicured green lawn that was contained within this perimeter symbolized new life in an open yet confined outdoor space. The two-year-old little boy was the same age as the little boy in the 1982 Sunday school dream and the new little boy in the mall dream. In this current dream, Thomas was about eight years old, the same age he was in May 2010 when we discussed whether he was worthy to go to heaven and he later prayed to accept the promise of eternal life. The dream was an answer to my Los Gatos Creek Trail prayer from the day before when I asked the Spirit of God to give me a sign that Thomas was alive with eternal life and with Him in heaven.

As the dream continues to unfold, its positive emotional tone indicates the painful, psychological, and emotional tension I experienced with the conflated Little Boy Thomas image in the mall dream was being resolved. Now, the image of Thomas and the image of the new little boy in the mall are discrete images once again. These distinct symbols of transformation play different roles in the dream and in my psyche, yet they are still intimately connected to one another and to the "me" imaged in the dream—the two boys are brothers, and they are both my sons. Upon waking and recording the dream, I felt like I could honestly begin to embrace the images in this dream with a willing and rejoicing heart. I was no longer repulsed by the thought of the rejoicing-grieving me image in the shopping mall dream; no longer did that image make me feel unfaithful, disloyal, and unloving toward my only son. Rather, in this two-boy dream, I was truly proud to introduce them, saying, "These are my sons."

In the dream, I put Thomas in charge of the microwave, a powerful symbol of transformation. The process of cooking food on a gas, electric, or wood stove is also a symbol of transformation, where raw food is transformed into cooked food that can be eaten to provide nourishment to the body, which the body transforms again into waste, that can be returned to the earth to fertilize plants, which in turn transform sunlight into food (through photosynthesis, still another transformation process), and subsequently, the plants can be cooked and eaten, and then the cycle begins all over again, endlessly. But the image of the microwave symbolizes a faster form of transformation cooking than a traditional stove or wood fire. I put the inner Thomas in charge of "holding" and "caring for" this accelerated form of transformation. The dream indicates that Thomas's life and death have been an important catalyst for my progress of inner healing and transformation. In addition, microwaves cook from the outside in. When viewed symbolically, the microwave symbolizes my conscious, intentional (outside-in) strategy for processing my grief over the last two years, where I've intentionally integrated the inner emotions and pain of Thomas's loss into conscious awareness.

The man in the dream is standing in a darker, more removed place outside the stone walls and the well-manicured lawn that symbolizes new life. He's a shadow image of the grieving me connected to my conscious, day-to-day experience of a pain that has lessened and become more muted over time but will never go away. The other guy is also connected down into the dark, unknown, unconscious depths of my psyche, where questions about "why" things happen can never be fully answered in this world. These are questions about the meaning of Thomas's life and death, and the existential meaning of my own life and death, within the context of God's sovereign will.

The image of "me" in this dream is a transformed symbol of the rejoicing-grieving me. In the earlier inner mall dream, I was connected to and resonating with the deep emotions of the hundreds of people in the inner mall who were rejoicing with me. The rejoicing emotions of finding new life after Thomas's death had a poignant sense of truth about them that my conscious waking self along the Outer Labyrinth of conscious waking life could not deny. They reflected the deep desire of my heart that would be imaged months later in the two-boy dream. But back then, my conscious waking self was repulsed by the stark day-to-day reality of Thomas's death. The image of "me" in this two-boy dream has accepted and begun to embrace the new life within. That's why I awoke from this dream with a deep sense of peace, resolution, and healing along both the Inner and Outer Labyrinths.

The unconscious was focusing the deep work of transformation on the man who was standing outside and beyond the lawn that symbolized new life. This shadowy figure of myself was honestly seeking the truth, one who was surprised by and trying to comprehend the reality that the two boys were really my sons. Within the dream, and later when I recorded it, the interaction between the man and me had the same curious and confused tone that Nicodemus displayed in his dialogue with Jesus about finding new life as recorded in John 3:1–21.

> Now there was a man of the Pharisees, named Nicodemus, a ruler of the Jews; this man came to Jesus at night and said to Him, "Rabbi, we

know that You have come from God *as* a teacher; for no one can do these signs that You do unless God is with him." Jesus responded and said to him, "Truly, truly, I say to you, unless someone is born again, he cannot see the kingdom of God."[69] Nicodemus said to Him, "How can a person be born when he is old? He cannot enter his mother's womb a second time and be born, can he?" Jesus answered, "Truly, truly, I say to you, unless someone is born of water and *the* Spirit, he cannot enter the kingdom of God. That which has been born of the flesh is flesh, and that which has been born of the Spirit is spirit. Do not be amazed that I said to you, 'You must be born again.' The wind blows where it wishes, and you hear the sound of it, but you do not know where it is coming from and where it is going; so is everyone who has been born of the Spirit." Nicodemus responded and said to Him, "How can these things be?" (John 3:1–9)

The biblical Nicodemus was misaligned along the Inner and Outer Labyrinths. Like disciples on the road to Emmaus, he found that the words and deeds of Jesus caused his heart along the Inner Labyrinth to burn within. This was juxtaposed with the Pharisaic "truth" he consciously espoused along the Outer Labyrinth. Nicodemus was honestly trying to understand what Jesus was telling him in that late night meeting. But much like me sitting on the floor playing the game with the little boy in my 1982 Sunday school dream, Nicodemus was stuck. He was at an impasse.

The two-boy dream was a snapshot in time that revealed how the Spirit of God was healing and transforming me through an essential tension between (1) the pain and suffering of the grieving me who stood outside the well-manicured grassy area that symbolized new life, and (2) the deepest desires of my heart symbolized by the rejoicing me walking in the inner mall dream, with the outcome being (3) a third something beyond the rejoicing-grieving me who was seen here in the two-boy dream. The two-boy dream also revealed how I was accepting and starting to embrace the path God had called me to walk by acknowledging that these are my sons.

Mark's Aspen retreat workspace overlooking Ajax Mountain

CHAPTER 28

BUT THE PAIN DOESN'T GO AWAY

September 16, 2023 (2 Years, 19 Weeks, and 4 Days After)

One day about a month into the third year after Thomas died, I was talking to a friend named Ben, a Stanford/SLAC colleague who had just retired the previous week. In the final minutes of the phone call, he asked me, "How are you doing?" This was code for wanting to know where I was in terms of processing my grief. Before I could respond, he continued, "I go out to Thomas's memorial site every time I get a notification about a new entry. I've spent a lot of time out there, so thought I'd ask."

"I'm curious," I replied. "Do you have any observations about the site and where you think I am in processing my grief?"

At first, he was taken aback by my question. He thought for a minute and then said reticently, "It seems like the pain doesn't go away." His words had the quiet ping of truth about them.

"What do you mean?" I responded searching for deeper insight into his comment.

Ben was silent as he searched his heart and mind, trying to clarify the tacit observation embodied in his words. Finally, he said softly and contemplatively, "I don't know. The pain just doesn't seem to go away."

"That's a good insight, Ben," I responded. "The pain morphs, softens, becomes more sporadic, and a new normal emerges over time. But you're right, it doesn't go away. It's changed my life forever. I'm a much better person now because of Thomas's death." I paused before continuing. "But that's come at a price that I would never have agreed to pay if I'd been asked. It's even more complicated than that."

I decided at that moment to share some deeper insights with Ben that I'd been reflecting on. "Trauma leads to trauma," I began, as if the meaning of my words was self-evident. "After Thomas's death, I've discovered more levels of grief and pain, grievance stories that descend into the depths of my soul. These are grievance stories that preexisted Thomas's death," I paused, hoping he was following me. "The trauma of Thomas's death has resonated deeper levels of grievance stories like a tuning fork resonates a guitar string. So, teasing apart the difference between my grief and pain about losing Thomas and these other emotional layers has been supremely difficult."

I went on to tell Ben about how the trauma of Thomas's death resonated a deeper repository of memories, earlier traumas that I had in childhood—a second layer of grievance stories.

◊ ◊ ◊

In 2021, Elin and I were back in New Jersey for a family wedding and decided to take a couple of extra days to explore our family roots, something we'd not done before, even though we'd been married for over twenty years. On my day, I took Elin to Passaic, New Jersey, to visit the Hungarian Reformed Church where I was baptized as an infant and then later confirmed in 1964. I also took her to the housing project where I lived for the first ten years of my life. We spent the afternoon driving by the junior high and high schools I attended and the two houses I lived in during those years.

During the trip, we reminisced and laughed about the "good ol' days" of black-and-white television sets, when gas was nineteen cents a gallon and seventy-three million people tuned into the *Ed Sullivan Show* to watch the Beatle's first live performance in the United States on February 9, 1964. As we continued sharing memories, I sensed pain and grief rising from within. I recognized, and could then retrieve, emotional memories that belonged to another familiar grievance story, one that was deeper, older, and not at all about Thomas. I knew these feelings well. They recounted the story of violence, abuse, and intimidation I'd suffered at my father's hands, emotional wounds I'd worked through, and had been healed of, long ago. I observed, explored, and reflected on the people and narrative of this grievance story, rolling it over once again in my heart and mind decades after having come to peace about this part of my life.

I realized that day that the pain and grief from these early childhood traumas do not go away either. They change you permanently, for better or for worse, and the outcome depends on how you deal with it. I'm a much better person now because of what I suffered then, but like Thomas's death, my psychological and spiritual growth around this second, deeper grievance story came at a price I would have refused to pay if I'd had a choice.

I said nothing to Elin about my reflections that day.

The next morning, we headed to Katonah, New York, to visit St. Luke's Episcopal Church where Elin was baptized as an infant and then later confirmed. We drove past the schools she attended and went through her old neighborhood, parking our vehicle across the street from the house Elin lived in until she went to college. It had been modified, upgraded, and expanded to the point where it was unrecognizable to her. From there, we walked down to Lorenz's Pond, a favorite place where she played with the neighborhood kids and her best friends. The heavily wooded country neighborhood of Elin's childhood with its upscale houses was a stark contrast to the filthy, crime-ridden, drug-infested housing project in New Jersey where I lived out my early years.

We decided to have lunch at a diner on the quaint, historical main street in Katonah that Elin knew like the back of her hand. After we'd ordered our drinks and were perusing the menu, I opened my heart to her and shared my experience of becoming aware of another, deeper, familial grievance story. Elin listened intently but had no firsthand experience or point of reference because her family story was so supportive and normal compared to mine. Yet, at the same time, the pain and grief of losing Thomas gave Elin empathic insight into the pain I was feeling, because trauma leads to trauma.

◇ ◇ ◇

In the days following the trip to New Jersey, I recognized an even deeper, third repository of pain and grief—a collective, archetypal grievance story that went far beneath the previous layers and was the underlying cause of my family trauma. It stemmed from the first two consequences of sin— the fact that we are alienated from ourselves and alienated from others. As I searched back through the two thousand dreams that I'd recorded and analyzed, I saw images, symbols, and narratives that described hurts, insults, opposing interests, self-interests, relational and sexual conflicts, and egos battling for dominance and control along the Inner Labyrinth. My dreams revealed all manner of intrapsychic offenses between my father, mother, and me, as well as those between other parents and their sons and daughters. There were dreams about pain and grief related to my grandfathers and grandmothers, as well as my great grandfathers and great grandmothers, and even further back to distant people who I'd never met who were fighting a war in Hungary. These dreams were remnants of the fact that these grievance stories still lived in me in the timeless dimension of my unconscious.

I realized that this repository of archetypal grievance stories, this third level of grief and pain, was even older and deeper than my extended family and existed even more broadly. This grief extended to all people, in all cultures, and from all times. I could recognize grievance stories in Hesiod's *Theogony* in the narrative of the birth of the Greek gods and Zeus's triumph as their king.[70] I saw the same elements evidenced in Homer's *Iliad* and *Odyssey* and the psychodramas of the Olympian gods. These myths and stories were created by early Greek writers to tell the story behind the story. Along the Outer Labyrinth, many people viewed these gods as deities whom they worshiped, made sacrifices to, and sought tangible answers to prayers. But along the Inner Labyrinth within that historical context, they reveal the enduring patterns and episodic chaos of Jungian archetypes that were concretized by these Greek writers in myths and stories that were projected onto the Outer Labyrinth to explain what was right and wrong with the world.[71] This man-inspired narrative from what Jung called the collective unconscious stands in stark contrast to the God-inspired causal narrative told by the author of Genesis.

Consequently, the gods were incredibly powerful beings who controlled the outer forces of nature, the destiny that we have along the Inner Labyrinth, and the destiny that we create with our choices along the Outer Labyrinth. They could make or break entire empires, and their capricious whims could decide the destiny of all people. The stories of their battles, bickering, and sexual conquests reveal gods and goddesses who Jung believed were the projected embodiment of the archetypes of the collective unconscious. And from the biblical perspective I'm presenting here, they manifest a centrifugal inward focus on self that is the signature of first two consequences of sin—alienation from self and alienation from others.

FINDING NEW LIFE AFTER THE DEATH OF MY SON

Along the Outer Labyrinth of the day-to-day life of Greek citizens, these third-level archetypal grievance stories resonated the common human experience of the first two consequences of sin, that profound sense that there was *something missing* in life. That *something's really gone wrong* in life. The Greek gods were "real" in the sense that philosopher of science Ian Hacking argues invisible entities like electrons are real. For Hacking, when something is real, it makes a physical difference. If it makes no physical difference, it's not real.[72] On this view, the socially constructed archetypal reality of Mount Olympus made a physical difference in the conscious and unconscious choices of those who believed. Like Richard Dawkins's notion of *memes*, the grievance stories of the Olympian gods reflected brain-based parasites that connected the collective causal theories of the Olympian gods to the individual brains of the ancient Greeks as isomorphic reflections between the inner world of the Spirit of the Depths and the outer world of the Spirit of the Times.[73]

I realized these third-level grievance stories lived on in me, as well, toward the latter half of 2023, a collective psychological reality that Jung experienced and described in his written works. I realized that the individual and collective psychological causation and sociocultural causation in third-level archetypal grievance stories could ultimately be reduced to physical causation and be explained as natural causes. The genius of Hesiod and Homer's depiction of the Greek gods; the cultural structures and systems of the Hellenistic world through which those *memes* spread; and the ways Greek culture acted like a powerful social mirror, shaping and defining how people should or should not act on those beliefs, could all be explained as the social construction of reality and then ultimately as the products of individual and collective configurations of neurons and yet to be identified neurophysiological processes in human brains.[74] To play on Winston Churchill's words quoted earlier, we shape our buildings and our beliefs, and afterward, our buildings and our beliefs shape us. Or as Covey put it, it becomes a self-fulfilling prophecy that emerges from the conscious and unconscious reality of the See-Do-Get Process.

In the days that followed my insights on the New Jersey trip, I also recognized that third-level, archetypal grievance stories were necessary but not sufficient to describe a still deeper root cause of pain and grief, a fourth level of biblical grievance stories of conflicts between characters such as Adam and Eve, Cain and Abel, Noah and Abraham, and all their descendants, as well as animosity between sociocultural groups of people like Jews and Samaritans, Jews and gentiles. So, the underlying root cause of the first two consequences of sin, our alienation from ourselves and from others, was the third consequence—our alienation from God, the cataclysmic fall of humanity described in Genesis 3 that could only be explained using the supernatural spiritual causes of the birth of sin in the depths of the human soul. As we read in Genesis 2:16–17:

> The Lord God commanded the man, saying, "From any tree of the garden you may freely eat; but from the tree of the knowledge of good and evil you shall not eat, for on the day that you eat from it you will certainly die."

It is in the very next chapter of Genesis where humankind fell under a sentence of death due to their disobedience of God.

On the one hand, I saw that the empirically obvious causal factors of the first two consequences of sin could be diagnosed as having natural causes and could effectively be dealt with using the kind of biblical approach to Jung's psychology described in this memoir. But on the other hand, the *root cause* of the third consequence of sin described in Genesis 3 had spiritual causes. As the apostle Paul reminds us in Ephesians 6:10–12: "For our struggle is not against flesh and blood, but against the rulers, against the powers, against the world forces of this darkness, against the spiritual forces of wickedness in the heavenly places."

The Hebrew Bible describes Satan as a celestial being who accuses God and those who believe in Him of things that are not true. We see this in Job 1–2, where God says Job is blameless before him, and Satan accuses God of having bought Job off with a cushy life and the absence of physical pain. Satan also appears in Zechariah 3:1–2 where Joshua the high priest was standing before the angel of the Lord when Satan starts accusing Joshua falsely. Satan also tempted David to sin in 1 Chronicles 21:1 by inciting David to number Israel. This is why Jesus called Satan a murderer, a liar, and the father of lies (John 8:44). Satan was the father of the first grievance story.

Satan was the illegitimate father of the primordial birth of sin that was conceived in the spiritual "womb" of Eve's heart and mind. In the same way that Thomas did not exist as an embryo until my sperm penetrated and impregnated Elin's ovum, the original sin that caused the alienation and hostility at the core of the fourth-level biblical grievance story did not exist until Eve was deceived and spiritually "raped," with her heart and mind impregnated with the seeds of Satan's accusations and lies.

Satan used the second element of Luskin's grievance story formation to accuse God of intentionally meaning to hurt, slight, insult, oppose, repress, and keep Eve from the knowledge of good and evil. I can only imagine how the woman took these untruthful accusations too personally (the first element of grievance story formation) and felt hurt, slighted, and insulted by the fact that God had kept these things from her, that he had deceived her about this "truth." She probably felt cheated, ripped off, and kept down by God, and this gave birth to a struggle for dominance and control over God for the very first time. Satan pit the free will, creativity, tenacity, and pulsing potentiality of virgin human nature that was made in his image against the all-powerful, all-knowing, and all-creative actuality and potentiality of the God who created the universe in a Big Bang over thirteen billion years ago.

This resulted in the fourth-level, primordial trauma of our spiritual parents being cast out of the garden and their loss of innocence, as retold in John Milton's epic *Paradise Lost*. Unbeknownst to Eve, Satan had enlisted her to fight in the same war this adversary had been waging against God from before the beginning of time.[75] This first biblical grievance story had both collective consequences where the *Imago Dei* (Self) was corrupted and subsequently created the archetypal grievance stories that Homer projected into the Olympian gods, and the very personal consequences of sin where Cain killed Abel.

But in today's scientific, technologically sophisticated world, we have jettisoned the reality of the spiritual root cause of the biblical grievance story as being unneeded, focusing exclusively on the first three levels of grievance stories, all of which can be reduced to natural causes. Columbia University literary scholar Andrew Delbanco traces the change in Americans' view of evil in the writing of America's major figures over the nation's history from a clear, religious understanding to a perplexed helplessness. "So, the work of the devil is everywhere, but no one knows where to find him. We live in the most brutal century in human history, but instead of stepping forward to take credit, he has rendered himself invisible."[76]

Delbanco echoes the first of two errors of either underestimating the power of the devil or overestimating it, as found in C. S. Lewis's classic book *Screwtape Letters* and Paul's words in Ephesians 6. The Bible explains how this alienation and hostility between God and humans can only be propitiated by faith in the life, death, and resurrection of Jesus. But trauma still leads to trauma in this life. Things that have been forgiven still have consequences. Wounds that have been inflicted are the prerequisite for becoming a wounded healer.

We have also distanced ourselves from the notion of death itself, the consequence of the fall. In Genesis 1–2, we see that the world was originally created without death. Death was not part of God's original design for the world. As Tim Keller explains:

> That means that ultimately, even a peaceful death at the age of ninety years old is not the way things were meant to be. Those of us who sense the 'wrongness' of death—in any form—are correct. The 'rage at the dying of the light' is our intuition that we were not meant for mortality, for the loss of love, or for the triumph of darkness. In order to help people face death and grief we often tell people that death is a perfectly natural part of life. But that asks them to repress a very right and profound human intuition—that we were not meant to simply go to dust, and that love was meant to last.[77]

The fact is that we will all die someday. We are all under a sentence of death; the only question is when, how, and where it will happen.

◊ ◊ ◊

These post-New Jersey trip reflections taught me how increasingly difficult it is to detect the pain-grief signal from each descending grievance story level, to tease them apart, and to tune into these interrelated pain-grief frequencies. But my reflections also taught me how important it was to actually do so, because the impact and the consequences of each descending level become more profound and pervasive the deeper they go. The multiple levels of pain and grief from my first-level grievance story about Thomas's death, my second-level personal grievance story of my family abuse, the third-level collective archetypal grievance story, and the fourth-level biblical grievance story of being a sinner who was saved by grace all *guarantee* the pain will not go away.

I didn't know how to explain all of this to Ben in the last few minutes of our phone call, but I tried using the only example that came to mind. "It's like the layers of soil in an archeological dig; the deeper you go, the further back in psychological and chronological time you go. We experience the pain and grief of each grievance story level as a deep and profound sense that something's missing in life, that something's really gone wrong in life. Does that make sense?" I queried, wanting to make sure Ben was following me.

"Yes," he replied reflectively as if he'd had an inner aha experience about what I was describing. "It makes perfect sense."

"Pain is the road back to all four levels of grievance stories," I continued, "so, even though the pain from Thomas's death has morphed, softened, and become more sporadic and manageable in this third year, the pain and grief that emanates from the deeper three levels will never, ever go away. And thank God that they won't," I said pausing, trying to pique Ben's curiosity.

"Why's that?" he asked, not sure what I meant by this.

"Pain is the road back to God, to everything that's right and wrong with the world, to the primordial grievance story recorded in Genesis 3," I responded without hesitation. "C. S. Lewis said, 'God whispers to us in our pleasures, speaks to us in our conscience, but shouts in our pains: it is His megaphone to rouse a deaf world.'"[78] I quickly followed with another Lewis quote from the movie *Shadowlands*: "'To put it another way, pain is God's megaphone to rouse a deaf world. Why must it be pain? Why can't he rouse us more gently, with violins or laughter? Because the dream from which we must be wakened, is the dream that all is well.'"[79]

◊ ◊ ◊

I am still on the path of finding new life. In the biological sense (*bios*), I continue to walk four miles a day, monitor my health, and struggle to regain the discipline needed to lose the twenty pounds I gained because of COVID and Thomas's death.

I'm feeling much more alive psychologically (*psychē*), and I have more emotional bandwidth to face the transactional demands of day-to-day life along the Outer Labyrinth. The inner guidance, inner resources, and direction I continue to get along the Inner Labyrinth of my dreams has been a catalyst for inner healing and transformation that's forming a new identity and reality—the new someone I'm becoming, and only partly know now.

I'm regaining a new sense of knowing what life is about, but I sometimes struggle with how to handle it. Along the Outer Labyrinth of daily life, I've begun to experience life at its best (*zoē*), a heartfelt experience of knowing what the meaning and purpose of my life is within God's will. I've continued to internalize and embrace the empirical evidence for God's existence, His sovereign power, and His faithfulness to me through ongoing deposits in my emotional bank account and historical patterns of transformation over the last forty-three years. I know, by faith, that God is accomplishing His sovereign will along the Inner and Outer Labyrinths, and I have an inner gyroscopic sense of orientation that testifies to the fact that I'm not lost; I'm still on the path God has called me to walk.

I'm still alive with the eternal life (*aiōnios*) that comes from my faith in God, and I experience more frequent glimpses of the "peace that passes understanding" that only faith in God can bring. I periodically hear the "still small voice" of God's presence when I'm on my daily walk around McIntosh Lake, or during my daily time of prayer, Bible reading, and reflection. I believe Colorado will be the last place that I live on earth, and our home is only seven miles from our family plot where Elin and I will be buried with Thomas someday. My picture is on the family gravestone (along with Thomas's and Elin's) as a reminder to begin each day with the end of this life in mind—to remember we're all under a sentence of death, an outcome that can't be escaped and, as Christians, should not be feared.

<> <> <>

Yesterday morning, Elin and I left the Aspen Lodge and retraced our steps from last year's anniversary trip. We walked to the John Denver Sanctuary as I reflected on the powerful, inner, voiceless insight I had last year in the ghost town of Ashcroft and then again, with a deeper sense of urgency and truth, standing on the old black iron bridge that spans the Roaring Fork

River in the sanctuary. *It'll be a milestone when you can say, "We're here in Aspen. It's beautiful," without adding, "but we're here without Thomas."* Last year, I shared the insight with Elin on the bridge with no response. Later over lunch, she looked at me and said, "I hear what you're saying about not adding 'but we wish Thomas was here' to everything we say. But I don't think I'm there yet." I replied pensively, "Neither am I."

Over the last year, the hard work of facing my grief and writing this memoir has created deep inner healing and transformation. Yesterday, as we walked to the sanctuary, I knew I was there. I wasn't sure where Elin was in the process of working through her grief, and I wanted to be sensitive to her—to let her lead, and be led in, her own process. When we got to the sanctuary, I let Elin select the paths she wanted to walk. I waited patiently as we walked among the enormous boulders that are engraved with Denver's song lyrics. We walked to the old black iron bridge, and as we approached it, Elin stopped and picked up a single gold aspen leaf. We stood in the middle of the span, the same place we were last year, and Elin threw the golden leaf off the bridge onto the flowing water below without saying a word. We watched in silence as it floated away, and she began to cry. I felt the silent message she was sending with her tears but didn't respond. After a few seconds, I said, "Are you okay?"

"Yes," she responded, as the aspen leaf got farther away, so far that I had to really focus to see it. "I think it got stuck on a rock," Elin said, not seeing it floating down the river.

"No," I replied as the leaf broke loose from the rock and continued its journey.

"That's like my boy," she said a few seconds later, still crying. "He floated away from me," communicating the deep sense of loss in her voice.

I didn't respond. I let her words ring out into the gentle sound of the flowing river below us. When the time seemed right, I said, "Come on, let's go get a sandwich."

As we walked to the restaurant, I replayed what had just happened in my heart and mind. We sat at a table outside the store in a light mist of rain, eating our soup and freshly made deli sandwiches, chatting about the day. When we were mostly done, I asked, "Remember how we sat here last year, and I said I wasn't there yet? Well, I'm there now." I said this with a quiet sense of confidence and finality.

Elin hesitated for a moment and then responded, "Well, I think I am too," and then almost apologetically said, "Not that I still don't miss my boy."

I looked deep into her sorrowful yet liberated eyes and concurred. "I know. The pain will never go away."

There were other, much deeper things I still needed to process about Thomas's life and death, but I thought to myself, *Enough for today. I'm glad I'm alive. I'm on the road forward.*

PART THREE
THE JOURNEY HOME

Thomas, Elin, and Mark at Palermo's Italian Restaurant on Father's Day, 2019

CHAPTER 29

ASSUMING EVERYTHING WOULD WORK OUT

October 14, 2023 (2 Years, 25 Weeks, and 2 Days After)

Because it took so long for me to put together the missing pieces of my life with Thomas, I've had to leave this part of the story until now. It's only now, looking back through my journal entries, the timeline of events in my Christian discipline, and Thomas's dreams that I realize Thomas was fighting a battle no one knew about.

I remember the day when Thomas, Elin, and I sat at our kitchen table in Campbell discussing the progress he was making dealing with his anxiety with his clinical psychologist, Katie. "Papa," he began, "there's a kid in my youth group at church who's taking Xanax for his anxiety. Can you get some for me too?" he asked hesitantly, knowing how I felt about this.

Thomas wanted to calm his anxiety about the COVID-19 pandemic that quarantined him in our home for months on end, forced him to attend his freshman college classes remotely because of the lockdown, and other things that eighteen-year-olds care too much about in a world gone mad. Thomas was an "old soul" in a young man's body. He was in touch with his inner depths. He strove to understand the meaning of life. He felt like an outsider, and this pained me deeply. His natural tendency to catastrophize about the everyday challenges he faced reached harmonic resonance with the pandemic.

At the same time, there was another epidemic going on in our world that I knew nothing about, one that Thomas thought he could navigate with various risk mitigations. It was the age of counterfeit pills and fentanyl poisonings. In 2021 alone, over 106,000 persons in the United States died from drug-involved overdoses, many of whom, like Thomas, were unsuspecting victims of a dark crime, poisoned by a single counterfeit pill that contained a lethal dose of fentanyl.[80]

"Thomas," I pleaded that day at the kitchen table, "using medicine to deal with your anxiety, or to run from it, only masks the symptoms, son. You need to work on the underlying emotional and spiritual causes and issues, not try to medicate them away."

He knew I was right, but it wasn't what he wanted to hear. In utter frustration, he retorted, "Papa, I don't want to go on a twenty-year inner journey like you did. I just want to take a pill and feel better."

"It's been a forty-year journey, son," I said as I lowered my head. "You need skills, not pills, to deal with life's struggles. You can't just run from this. That's like trying to run from yourself." I pushed my chair back from the table, stood so my body faced the warm California sun streaming through our kitchen window, and turned toward Thomas. "Do you see the shadow behind me, son?" He glanced at the dark image my body cast on the floor, just to humor me. "You can't run away from your deeper self, Thomas," I said as I moved so the dark specter would follow me. "It's a part of you. It's where your creativity comes from. The more you run and resist it, the stronger it gets. You've got to stop and do the hard work of integrating the shadow into conscious awareness with your psychologist's help, the transformation tools I've taught you, your knowledge of the Bible, and your faith in God."

What Thomas didn't understand was that he was already on a journey. He already had a destiny in God that was unfolding along the Inner Labyrinth, as revealed in the ninety-eight dreams we had recorded from the time he was two years old. As his father, I believed this trove of inner revelations would give him the kind of head start in life that I never had, having recorded my first dream when I was twenty-seven. But Thomas was also creating his own destiny with his choices along the Outer Labyrinth of everyday life. As a young man trying to find his own way and identity, some of those individual choices diverged from what I would do. As his dad, my parenting goal was to shape and define the biblically based asymptotic boundaries within which his choices were made, to raise awareness of and help connect and align the Inner and Outer Labyrinths of his life. I encouraged him to benchmark his choices and the inner images and forces of the unconscious in his dreams against the admonitions of the Bible and the principles, practices, and tools of transformation I'd taught him over the years.

FINDING NEW LIFE AFTER THE DEATH OF MY SON

◊ ◊ ◊

My study of Carl Jung's work convinced me that children's dreams were not just silly and meaningless. Rather, they are timeless inner revelations that provide priceless insights into the lifelong process of individuation.

When Jung was three or four years old, he had a dream about a stairway down to an underground rectangular chamber containing a rich golden throne that preoccupied him for the rest of his life.[81] Those early powerful images from the unconscious helped to shape and define who he was, what he was called to do, and the overall course of his life and destiny. Jung's dream played a dominant role in shaping his autobiography, *Memories, Dreams, Reflections*, one of his last works, published posthumously after his death.[82] Thomas's dreams would also shape and define who he was, what he was called to do, and the overall course of his life and destiny in ways I did not and could not have understood until now.

I knew the dreams Thomas had starting at age five were cornerstone indicators of his lifelong journey along the Inner and Outer Labyrinths. These dreams appeared within the first of a five-phase model for dream activity that Jung identified:[83]

- childhood: three to six years old,
- puberty: fourteen to sixteen years old,
- young adulthood: twenty to twenty-five years old,
- middle age: thirty-five to forty years old, and
- prior to death.

Back in 2004 when Thomas and I began recording his dreams, I used eight guiding principles to interpret dreams.[84] These were axioms I gleaned from my deep study of the Bible,[85] Jung's writings, the secondary literature on Jung's psychology, the practical experience of having recorded and analyzed over twelve hundred of my own dreams under the mentorship of two Jungian analysts, and the unfolding mystery of walking the path of individuation for twenty-five years. On the one hand, I knew Thomas's dreams would provide deep insight into the development of his personality and the natural unfolding of his psychological processes. On the other hand, I had no idea how the unconscious would disclose itself along the Inner

Labyrinth, or what that would look like when viewed from the perspective of the Outer Labyrinth of daily life.

I saw myself as a life scout standing in the bow of a boat, peering over the side into crystal clear water of Thomas's unconscious dream world and watching for images of coral reef upon which the boat could be damaged or stranded while signaling back to the captain (Thomas) to make course corrections and choices to safely navigate the difficult waters of living in an inner and outer world dominated by the three consequences of sin. I had a God-given stewardship as Thomas's father to use the foundation of our biblical Christian faith and this priceless dream information to help him find his calling and destiny in life. This was the essence of the prayer I prayed for Thomas every night when putting him to bed.

The first guiding principle assumes a biblical worldview,[86] one where dreams must be benchmarked against a historical-grammatical understanding of the word of God in the Bible.[87] This is because even our dreams are affected by the empirical reality of the three consequences of sin.[88] It assumes the Bible is the ultimate divine authority by which every realm of human knowledge and every human endeavor should be judged, including various models of the structure, dynamics, and nature of the psyche, the interpretation of dreams, and Jung's notion of active imagination.

As mentioned in my 2010 church membership class summary, my journey of faith has been shaped and defined by two books: the Bible and my book of dreams. The Bible is the revelation of God and the history of His reconciling of the world to Himself. My book of dreams is about me and my inner reactions to myself (i.e., archetypes and complexes), others, the world around me, and the unfolding of the destiny I have in God along the Inner Labyrinth as the Spirit of God leads me through the Self. Dreams are not a source of salvific revelation apart from, or in addition to, the inspired word of God in the Bible. They contain little or no gospel content, and they play a confirming, preparatory, compensatory, or complementary role that creates a deeper understanding of previously encountered experiences with Christians or the Bible through the authority of human experience. Knowing by experience was a hallmark of Jung's research, his individuation process, and traditional Jungian psychology, and it has been the focus of my decades-long journey to know myself and God in the *yada* sense.[89]

FINDING NEW LIFE AFTER THE DEATH OF MY SON

This first principle is what distinguishes a biblical approach to the individuation process and interpreting dreams, from Jungian and other methods of dream interpretation.[90] While I fully embrace Jung's psychology (i.e., how he described the structure and dynamics of the personal and collective dimensions of the psyche), I firmly reject his ontology (i.e., what exists and the original causes of the universe).

The second guiding principle was that Thomas's dreams didn't have to be understood to be transformative. In other words, Thomas didn't have to know anything about or understand the depth and complexity of the unconscious, Jung's psychology, or the four descending levels of grievance stories to be deeply impacted by them. He would sit on my lap and tell me the dream as I typed it into my laptop as precisely as possible. As he recounted the dream, the unconscious created an image of his dream in my mind. This connected us at some very deep archetypal level and impacted my psyche, too, where my unconscious conflated the dream images of the little boy in the 1982 Sunday school class dream with the dream image of my little boy Thomas, the first person I truly loved in life.

When we finished recording a dream, we would discuss what was happening along the Outer Labyrinth of Thomas's everyday life with friends, school, church, and our family. Back then, Thomas was a very outgoing little boy who always had a lot of things going on. Independent of what Thomas did or did not understand about his dreams, it was important that I try to connect the images, symbols, and unfolding narrative in his dreams along the Inner Labyrinth to the Outer Labyrinth and the historical context in which Thomas had the dream.

The simple act of writing the dreams down and briefly discussing possible meanings, even at this young age, helped to integrate the contents of Thomas's unconscious into conscious waking life. I knew how important this was from my own experience of doing dream work and from working with Elin's dreams. As Jung points out:

> The psychological rule says that when an inner situation is not made conscious, it happens outside, as fate. That is to say, when the individual remains undivided and does not become conscious of his inner opposite, the world must perforce act out the conflict and be torn into opposing halves.[91]

There was no way to escape God working through the Self in His sovereign will. You either integrated this unconscious material willingly as He commanded, or you were taken there despite your choices by a confluence of inner and outer forces and events that were orchestrated by the Spirit of God working through the Self. It was a lesson Jonah had to learn when he tried to escape from God's prophetic calling. You can run, but you cannot hide from the great hound of heaven.

Once I had documented Thomas's dreams, I used two more guiding principles to help me understand and interpret them, but I did not discuss this part of the dream work with him at that time. The third guiding principle was that Thomas's dreams didn't speak English and needed to be interpreted and translated. More specifically, the unconscious (the Self) did not speak with the kind of verbal surface structure and spoken language we use along the Outer Labyrinth of everyday life. Rather, it communicated using an underlying, emotionally infused nonverbal structure—an image-based transformational grammar composed of symbols, metaphors, paradoxes, parables, and stories that represent the aboriginal foundation of all spoken language.[92] The image-based structure of the dream material veils the symbolic meaning of dreams from people until they open their hearts and minds to its meaning by seeking its truth.[93]

Jesus used a similar pedagogic approach to hide the truth of God from people who had no interest in seeing, perceiving, and hearing the truth of His message using symbols, metaphors, paradoxes, and parables in his teachings. Matthew tells us:

> And the disciples came up and said to Him, "Why do You speak to them in parables?" And Jesus answered them, "To you it has been granted to know the mysteries of the kingdom of heaven, but to them it has not been granted . . . Therefore, I speak to them in parables; because while seeing they do not see, and while hearing they do not hear, nor do they understand." (Matthew 13:10–11, 13)

The Word that was in the beginning with God, and who was God in John 1:1–18 (the *Logos*) created mankind is His image in Genesis 1:26–31. What Jung called the Self was the image of God (the *Imago Dei*) in the personal and collective instantiations of mankind—our psychological and spiritual selves that were marred by the inheritance of sin through the fourth-level biblical grievance story. Yet God is still sovereign over the Self He created, and we experience this as something deep within us that knows there's something missing in life, that something's gone really wrong in life, and it's that part of us that seeks the truth. The Self is the psychological channel through which the Spirit of God communicates and tests us with dreams along the Inner Labyrinth, much like the incarnate Jesus and His recorded word in the Bible tests people with parables along the Outer Labyrinth of day-to-day life.

The fourth guiding principle was that the primary focus of Thomas's dreams was intrapsychic and described what was going on in Thomas's head, *not* the heads of others or in the world. They divulged what was happening in Thomas's inner psychological world. Like Matthew 7:1–5 teaches, Thomas's dreams disclosed his inner responses to people and situations in the world and the forces and directionality of his personal and collective unconscious (his log) rather than imparting clairvoyant insight about others and the world around him (their speck). Thomas's dreams revealed his inner unconscious response to what people and situations in his daily life triggered in him, plus the compensatory or complementary perspectives of the unconscious.[94] The essential tension between his waking and dreaming self was designed to facilitate the alignment of the Inner and Outer Labyrinths and to lead him on the path of transformation, even at his young age.[95] This is true of all people of all ages and cultures who have ever been born on the planet, and God in His sovereignty has called me to be a witness to this transformation process through dream work for purposes I understood only after Thomas was gone.

Thomas's dreams also revealed an early, inner portfolio of personal and archetypal beliefs, attitudes, mindsets, perspectives, strategies, and forces that would powerfully shape and define how he saw himself, others, the world around him, the choices he would make, and the risks he would take along his path in life.[96] At the time, the underlying causes, direction, and symbols of transformation in Thomas's dreams remained a mystery to Thomas and to me. Yet I knew by faith that the God of salvation history would accomplish His sovereign will through my son's conscious and unconscious (intended and unintended) beliefs, strategies, mindsets, and actions. It was through this early dream work that I began to recognize how God would use Thomas's life, his decisions, and his stories to achieve God's ends, purpose, and will. I believed working with Thomas's dreams, within the context of our biblically based Christian faith, would help me be a better father, give me insight into who Thomas was as a person, and would help me support him in his lifelong task of finding his calling and destiny in life.

Thomas's dreams were about him and his destiny, but God in his sovereignty also meant them to be for me so I could be the best father I could be, so I could understand him and teach him the biblically and psychologically based principles, practices, and tools that he would need to find his calling and live out his destiny in life in Jesus's name. Thomas's dreams created a special bond between him and me as father and son. They also made him feel like he was part of a dreaming family when Elin and I discussed our dreams over dinner at the kitchen table or in casual conversation.

Becoming a citizen of heaven also brought many psychological and spiritual blessings and challenges, even at his age. John White argues that the new life that entered Thomas when he accepted God's forgiving grace was the spiritual life of God Himself.[97] Jesus became his shepherd, and a bond was established between Thomas and God that nothing in heaven, earth, or hell could break.[98] White continues:

> You have also established a new relationship with the powers of darkness . . . you are now the sworn foe of the legions of hell. Have no delusions about their reality or their hostility. But do not fear them. The God inside you terrifies them. They cannot touch you, let alone hurt you. But they can still seduce, and they will try. They will also oppose you as you obey Christ. If you play it cool and decide not to be a fanatic about Christianity, you will have no trouble from them. But if you are serious about Christ being your Lord and God, you can expect opposition. "Resist the devil," writes James, "and he will flee from you" (James 4:7). The battle never ends.[99]

Thomas was serious about his faith and wanting to follow the Lord from the time he was seven. Like the rest of us Christians, the challenge Thomas would face going forward was how to be in the world but not of the world.

FINDING NEW LIFE AFTER THE DEATH OF MY SON

◊ ◊ ◊

Back when Thomas and I were recording his first few dreams, my experience doing extensive research in Jung's work, secondary Jungian literature, biblical studies, and my thirty-one years of recording and analyzing my own dreams under the long-term mentorship of two Jungian analysts had convinced me that images of death, destruction, and dark figures in dreams were often symbols of transformation. They were part of the natural, lifelong dialectic process of individuation that Jung identified in alchemical literature, where the first of four steps toward wholeness was working through the dark shadow side of ourselves, also known as Negredo.[100]

The Bible described Jesus dying on the cross and being raised to new life in the resurrection from the dead as a model for a life of sacrifice, sanctification, and transformation into His image. Jesus required his disciples to die to their old selves, be buried in the waters of baptism, and then to be raised to new life in Christ, with water being a symbol of the unconscious and sinful depths of the human heart. Paul describes the lifelong dialectical process of crucifying the passions and desires of the flesh as dying to our old selves in Galatians 5:24 and as refusing to be conformed to this world but instead being transformed by the renewing of our minds in Romans 12:2. So, from both Jungian and biblical perspectives, it follows that children sometimes dream about dark destructive transformative figures, like an ogre from the Harry Potter series or a cloaked man imaged as Darth Vader in the Star Wars series because, as Jeremiah 17:9 tells us, "The heart is more deceitful than all else and is desperately sick; who can understand it?" God knew this about Thomas before He formed him in Elin's womb (Jeremiah 1:5).

I saw this type of symbolism in an important dream Thomas had in August 2007 when he was just five years old.

> In the dream, I was sleeping in my bedroom in Superior, Colorado, on the bottom bunk, and when I woke up in the dream, everything in the world was destroyed and in pieces except for my bed and the things in it. Even our house was destroyed, and I saw pieces of paper from Papa's books lying all around. Then I saw a giant ogre-troll

with a huge bat that had spikes on it like the one in Harry Potter. He had not destroyed my bed, but then he stepped on me when I was still in my bed and that destroyed my bed.

While the transformative images in the ogre dream have multiple levels of personal and archetypal meaning, my sense at that time was that their primary focus was Thomas's inner response to outer adult-world situations that happened to him. More specifically, the destructive inner images in the ogre dream emerged just a couple of weeks after we moved from our mountain home in Fairplay, Colorado, to the Front Range city of Superior. Viewed symbolically, the outer reality of taking apart (deconstructing) the personal space of Thomas's bedroom and bed and the common space of our entire house was imaged symbolically in this dream as the existential destruction of the world as Thomas knew it at that time.[101]

The dream image of our house being destroyed symbolized Thomas's identity and reality in life, where he lived and kept his "stuff." His bedroom was an intimate, private place of safety—his world, his reality, a place he could shape and define in his own image even as a little boy. The ogre was an archetypal symbol of the raw, untamed, and tyrannical male energy of a five-year-old little boy facing this challenge. In waking life, my library contained thousands of books about theology, psychology, physics, organization development, and a spectrum of other disciplines, and Thomas knew this in waking life. So, from a personal perspective, the image of "pieces of paper from Papa's books" symbolized the destruction and transformation of his knowledge at the time, and his perceived authority of me his father. From an archetypal perspective, it symbolized the destruction and transformation of all knowledge and all authority. These were normal, everyday challenges of psychological development and lessons that when learned would help my son navigate the frenetic pace of change in a world where he'd be forced to grow up.[102]

◊ ◊ ◊

Thomas and I recorded another important dream in March 2011 when he was eight. Thomas told me that in his dream:

There was a dark figure that came into my room, and he came close to my bed stand and set things on fire, but I was unhurt. I had this dream at least three times, and the final time I had it, he set my entire bed on fire, and everything was burned up including Kitty, but I was not hurt.

In much the same way as the ogre dream, the images of dark, destructive transformative forces emerged just a few weeks after moving from our apartment in Superior to our home near McIntosh Lake, something that Thomas was very eager and happy to do along the Outer Labyrinth of day-to-day life. But at eight years old, Thomas inhabited a constantly changing inner developmental world that happened to him.

Between the ages of five and eight, children go through enormous physiological and psychological changes as they come to the age of reason. These inside-out, natural, and healthy forces of child development can feel like an existential threat to a child's identity and place in the world. But children like Thomas have to learn that the only way to find themselves is to lose themselves in Christ's forgiveness, the cure for the fourth-level biblical grievance story that was set in motion by Satan's lies and accusations about God in the garden (Matthew 16:24–28). Children tend to focus on the world outside themselves, so they have no context into which to put these enormous inner psychological and physiological changes, and they have no way to understand them at a conscious emotional level. So, the unconscious depicts these experiences in the language of dream images and symbols.

Thomas's associations with the cloaked man in this dream centered around the symbols of death, destruction, and an all-pervading force of evil derived from the Star Wars film franchise, where an all-encompassing force seduces and corrupts an energetic, curious, and spiritually connected little boy named Anakin Skywalker. As Anakin grew to be a young man, we witness the evil force, the Emperor, identify the young Jedi knight's weakness in his love for Padmé, something forbidden by the Jedi order. After Anakin has visions of the pregnant Padmé dying in childbirth, the Emperor tempts Anakin to join the dark side of the Force by promising to save Padmé, a choice that ultimately leads to him being transformed into an agent of evil—Darth Vader. It is only decades later that the archetypal core of good that had been long buried in Vader finally enables him to choose to kill the Emperor and to be redeemed by returning to the good side of the force and his Jedi colleagues.

By 2011, my eight-year-old son, Thomas, and I had watched the Star Wars series at the movie theater during our Saturday time together and multiple times at home with the DVD series. Our Christian family culture and his biblically based education helped Thomas to see the Star Wars symbolism in the movie and in his dream within the larger context of the battle between God and evil described in the Bible rather than a dualistic battle between two equal forces like Jung did. He and I would discuss the deeper Christian meaning of the movie and its connection to the battle we all face as Christians living in a world corrupted by sin.

I sensed that Thomas identified strongly with the character of the young Anakin Skywalker. "Papa," he would ask, "I want to watch the movie where Anakin was a little boy," something I would almost always allow because I had framed the story within the larger context of a biblical journey of faith with a sovereign God who ruled the universe and who eventually defeats Satan and the forces of evil who rebelled against Him, as described in the Revelation 20:7–10.[103]

After recording the cloaked man dream, I asked Thomas what his associations were with the images and symbols and what he thought they meant. He saw the connection between his dream and the dark destructive forces in the Anakin-Darth Vader story, but like most people, he saw the images and what happened in the dream in a more literal sense of his conscious reaction to the movie—that is, out there rather than in the symbolic sense of being about changes that were happening deep within him. Without defining the details of the second guiding principle, I tried to get Thomas to view the images and narration of the dream more symbolically.

I suggested that the mechanism of transformation in this dream was the archetypal symbol of fire. Fire destroys to transform. From his Cub Scout experiences, I described the transformative power of fire, where campfire wood became a source of heat, light, and comfort. It enabled his troop to cook food and provided a sense of safety and warmth on cold nights. The symbolism of fire in the Bible was deep and profound. It represented God's presence and divine judgment. Fire was a visual manifestation of God's presence to Moses in the burning bush. It was also a symbol of purification and transformation, like refining gold in a furnace, and Paul describes it as the mechanism by which a person's work for the kingdom of God will be tested (1 Corinthians 3:10–15). These biblical examples were all things Thomas was familiar with given his knowledge of the Bible.

So, the image of his favorite stuffed animal, Kitty, being destroyed by fire in the dream may have symbolized my son moving from childhood to the age of reason and to being a young man who had to give up childish things. Importantly, Thomas was neither burned up nor hurt in the dream, which was a hopeful sign of transformation. Along the Inner Labyrinth, everything Thomas thought he could count on had been changed, destroyed, or transformed by fire. Ten months earlier along the Outer Labyrinth, Thomas was worried about whether he was worthy to go to heaven, and he willingly prayed for God's forgiveness and accepted it in Jesus's name, resulting in eternal life. So, the image of Thomas in the dream survived the utter destruction he experienced in the rest of the life he knew at that time.

When I reflected on this dream back in 2011, I believed my son was growing up. He was another step closer to becoming the person God meant him to be. The images and symbolism of the third-level archetypal grievance stories of the Olympian gods were reflected in modern-day myths and stories like Harry Potter and Star Wars. I also believed that the Spirit of God, working through the Self, was resonating the frequency of the first two consequences of sin deep in Thomas's unconscious. I took solace in the fact that at the very deepest, fourth-level biblical grievance story, Thomas had made his peace with God. Somehow, I sensed Thomas knew this tacitly, but as an eight-year-old boy, he had no way to talk about it with me, no way to put it into words. He knew more than he could say.[104]

But looking back now from the third year after his death, I see with crystal clarity how I assumed everything would work out in the end for Thomas, just like it did in the stories of Harry and Anakin. But neither of them lived in an age of counterfeit pills and fentanyl poisonings. It's only now that I understand that the timeless dream images of the ogre dream and cloaked man dream that appeared in the self-designed theater of his bedroom were unrecognized synchronistic warnings that echoed one of the third-level archetypal grievance stories of Greco-Roman mythology—the myth of Janus. Janus was the two-faced Roman god of doors, gates, and transitions. Janus represented the middle ground between concrete and abstract dualities such as life and death, beginning and end, youth and adulthood, where one of his faces looked backward toward the past while the other looked to the future. These initial dreams were "thin places" where God was connecting the destiny Thomas had in His sovereign will that I experienced while sobbing through the first sentence of my spiritual journey back on May 2, 2010, to the destiny Thomas would create by ignoring my admonition at the kitchen table and taking things into his own hands with his final choice to take the pill that killed him.

Again, Thomas's dreams were about him and his destiny, but God in His sovereignty also meant them to be for me to help prepare me to survive Thomas's death, to face the path I was called to walk, and to make me strong enough to tell this story. It's twenty-twenty hindsight now that Thomas is gone, but I didn't see it then.

CHAPTER 30

THE PROXY WAR

October 15, 2023 (2 Years, 23 Weeks, and 5 Days After)

In the first days after finding Thomas dead in his room, not much about life made sense. But I did have the very clear and distinct feeling I had lost a war. The fighting was over. My son was dead. His death seemed like an irreversible screw-you victory by an unknown enemy that spoke volumes and silenced me. It was Thomas's war. It was my war. It was the war of every soul who'd ever lived. As Elin and I stood in the Darling Fisher Funeral Home looking at our son's lifeless body in an open casket just six days after he died, I somehow knew we had made it through some type of long, confusing, and demoralizing battle that Thomas did not survive. I knew it tacitly in the depths of my soul back then. But it wasn't until the third year after his death that I could begin to describe what happened in words. It all started ten years earlier when Thomas was only eight years old.

◊ ◊ ◊

It was Easter weekend 2011. Elin had already adorned the house with decorations in preparation for our annual egg hunt on Easter morning and baked her famous Easter bunny cake, its nose, mouth, and eyes made of brightly colored jellybeans and an assortment of colorful pipe cleaners for whiskers. That Sunday, the three of us would head to the Episcopal Cathedral in Denver on Easter Sunday to imbibe the high church liturgy of bells and smells before heading back home for a delicious lamb dinner.

At the time, Thomas was thriving as a third grader at the Boulder Christian Academy. He was also active in Cub Scouts, having earned multiple scout badges, and was thoroughly involved in the Sunday school youth group at Faith Presbyterian Church. But one morning, a couple days before Easter, Thomas walked into my office as I was working.

"Hi, son," I said, looking up from my computer. "You're up early."

Thomas on first day of fourth grade when the cloaked man dreams began

He walked up close to me and put his arm around my shoulder. "I had a dream last night, Papa. I've had it at least three times in the last week or so, but I forgot to tell you about it till now."

"Come, sit down, son," I said as I pushed away from my desk, helping him up onto my lap. "Let's type it into the computer." I opened the file on my laptop containing Thomas's dream book, getting ready to type. "Okay, tell me the dream."

He hesitated for second before simply telling me, "I dreamed that I was Judas Iscariot."

I didn't know what to say. So, I just input those seven words into my computer. As I typed, an image of Thomas's dream emerged in my mind accompanied by a deep and profound sense of pain and grief. It was reminiscent of a moment in the past that I just couldn't put my finger on.

When I was finished typing, I looked at Thomas and asked, "What are your associations with Judas, son?"

"We've been studying the Easter story in school," he responded quickly. "He's the disciple who betrayed Jesus. Why would I dream that, Papa?"

"Well, it's Easter time, and like you said, you're studying the Easter story in school," I replied. "Sometimes, things that happen in day-to-day life trigger deep feelings in us that we dream about at night. That could be what happened with this dream, son."

Thomas seemed satisfied with my answer, so he hopped off my lap and headed downstairs to get ready for school.

What I told Thomas was true, but it wasn't the whole truth. The fourth guiding principle that I used to interpret dreams states that dreams tell us the unvarnished truth about who we are. They are impartial statements from the unconscious not produced by our conscious selves. Dreams provide a compensatory perspective on one-sided conscious attitudes we're unaware of—blind spots, and unknown dimensions of our personality, regardless of our age. In his lectures on interpreting children's dreams, Jung put it this way, "As you know, the dream is a natural phenomenon. It does not spring from special intention. One cannot explain it with a psychology taken from consciousness. We are dealing with a particular way of functioning independent of the human ego's will and wishes."[105]

The fifth guiding principle also states that dreams reveal objective archetypal forces within us, powerful psychological and emotional forces that are collective, not personal, and exist deep in the unconscious. They live far below the surface of conscious awareness and have a path and life of their own. So, the images and emotions in Thomas's dream were independent of the fact that he was only eight years old. Rather they came from what Jung called the "storeroom of the human mind," the collective unconscious.[106]

Finally, I knew dreams don't tell us what we already know about ourselves, so I was curious as to why Thomas had the same Judas dream at least three times in the previous week. Recurring dreams come because the message from the unconscious, from the Self, did not penetrate the natural defenses of conscious awareness the first time. So, recurring dreams create a sense of urgency about a credible and compelling case for why the unconscious argues that you can't go on living the way you have.

Thomas didn't have many associations with the dream, and I didn't want to upset him by probing him about dreams images and messages that came from this objective, Inner Labyrinth level of his psyche. It was a place that was as far below his conscious awareness and choices along the Outer Labyrinth as the earth is from the sun. I questioned my own judgment of what the dream might be trying to communicate to Thomas. I didn't want to overreact by linking the Inner and Outer Labyrinths too closely in a strict cause-and-effect relationship, especially in the chronological day-to-day life of an eight-year-old. But I also didn't want to dismiss the images in this Judas dream as meaningless epiphenomena, a by-product of the natural data processing of the human brain.

In the days that followed, the resonance of pain and grief associated with Thomas's Judas dream continued to ring out in my heart and mind. It seemed like some type of warning sign about something yet to come. Back then, I had yet to discover the principle that trauma leads to trauma. My strategy was to have a wait-and-see attitude. I decided to monitor our lives together along the Outer Labyrinth and log relevant things that I noticed in my journal. I also decided to reflect on Thomas's dreams and my own dreams to identify compensatory images, symbols, and messages along the Inner Labyrinth that were trying to shape and define a path forward for my son and for me. I sought the Lord through my daily Bible reading, praying through my Christian discipline and participating in regular worship and fellowship at Faith Presbyterian Church. But I was unprepared for what came next.

Along the Outer Labyrinth, Thomas's life was defined by our Christian family culture. By every measure, Thomas was a normal, happy-go-lucky kid with many hobbies and vibrant interests who loved and trusted his parents and had a close circle of good friends. But that spring, the unconscious launched a *blitzkrieg* of fourteen more cloaked-man dreams like those mentioned in the previous chapter along the Inner Labyrinth. In one of these dreams, Thomas recalled:

> There was a huge green sea monster (like a snake) that should have been in the sea, but he was on the land with a cloaked man riding him. He was chasing me to get me, but he missed me. Then the cloaked man came after me and shot me dead, and I really died.

About two weeks later, Thomas and I recorded another dream.

> I was standing on the beach watching the sun set when suddenly, I heard a really loud roar. I turned around and saw the cloaked man riding a blood eater (instead of a Death Eater, which is a Harry Potter creature) that looks like a dragon and has really hard scales, a lot of horns, and is huge, and when it gets you, it drinks your blood. Then it got me and bit me.

Eleven days later, Thomas and I recorded yet another dream.

> I was driving a car and was going to the Target store in Boulder to buy a brown Puffle. When I walked into the store, I went to the toy section and I went to aisle E1, but when I got there, a cloaked man was hiding and watching me. He had said a curse on the Puffles that whoever touched them would die.

Along the Outer Labyrinth, the cadence of everyday life still went on as normal. Thomas finished third grade and enjoyed another fun summer playing with his friends at the park and in the tree house near McIntosh Lake. He was engaged with youth group activities and Cub Scouts, and he and I spent many hours together that summer reading, seeing movies, camping, and sharing lots of quality time. But along the Inner Labyrinth that July, the *blitzkrieg* became even more intense as it assaulted the psychological boundaries between Thomas's conscious self and the unconscious collective, with archetypal contents and forces over which he had no control and could not stop.

Recording and discussing his dreams allowed me to peer down into the dark, destructive forces that emerged from the unconscious in my son.

On July 7, Thomas had the following dream.

> I was walking at the Colorado Mills Mall, and I was going toward the LEGO store, and when I saw the LEGO store, a big serpent that was like a basilisk in Harry Potter opened its mouth, and the cloaked man came out. The cloaked man walked toward me, and he had a sword and the dream just ended.

Just two days later, Thomas had another dream.

> I was in the airport with Papa, and as I was boarding the plane, I saw the cloaked man walk by. Then, as we were about halfway through the plane ride, I looked out the window and saw the cloaked man outside the window flying alongside of us, and then the plane went down. My feelings associated with the cloaked man in all these dreams is that he is the devil, Satan, evil, cruel, scary.

Five days later, Thomas had yet another dream that he said seemed like a continuation of the previous dream.

> As Papa and I were going down in the plane, I saw the cloaked man walking down the aisle in the plane. Then we hit the water and went down to the bottom, and even though there were no windows open, water was getting in, and the dream ends.

The very next day, still another dream came.

> I was walking around in our neighborhood, and then I saw the cloaked man. He brought out nunchucks, and then he started fighting me. He would hit me, see if I was alive, and then hit me again. As the dream ends, he's still hitting me.

Two days later, we recorded and discussed the following dream.

> The cloaked man walked into my bedroom, and everything went on fire except my bed and everything that was in my bed. Eventually, my bed caught fire and the dream ends.

Then, two days later, Thomas had this dream.

> Me, Papa, and Mom were out at sea on a Disney cruise line, and the sky went black all of a sudden. Then we went inside the boat, and the cloaked man walked in, too, and then the boat sank quickly, and as the boat hit the bottom of the ocean, we were still inside the boat the dream ends.

Three days later, Thomas had yet another dream.

> I was at a skate park skateboarding, and the cloaked man appeared. I tried to skateboard away, but he put a ring of fire around me. He took out a sword, and then the dream ends. During the dream, I felt scared, sad, and I had a feeling that urged me to go over to his side. I normally feel scared and sad during dreams with the cloaked man, but in this dream, I had a feeling that urged me to go over to his side.

Finally, the very next day, Thomas and I recorded and discussed the following dream.

> The cloaked man walked into my room at the beginning, and there was a big python-like snake, and the snake came right up into my face and stared at me. I was freaked out with the snake looking me right in the eye.

Thomas had ten cloaked man dreams during this short period of time. But I saw no evidence of this intense Inner Labyrinth conflict along the Outer Labyrinth of his daily life. I continued to view these dreams symbolically as archetypal symbols of psychological transformation, where the first step toward transformation is evidenced by facing and then working through the dark side elements in the psyche. I specifically watched Thomas's behavior and attitudes along the Outer Labyrinth of everyday life, and at the same time I brought the images in his dreams along the Inner Labyrinth into conscious awareness looking for connections. But I could not detect any way in which the thematic onslaught of cloaked man dreams that we were recording were linked to or associated with the mundane, pedestrian realities of my son's life during that summer. He was still Thomas, my happy son who played with friends, created interesting objects with LEGOs, collected dozens of Marvel comic books, and was already looking forward to seeing his friends when he started fourth grade. He was still my nine-year-old boy.

So, I prayed and committed my son to the Lord's sovereign care, as I focused on the positive things I was seeing along the Outer Labyrinth. I encouraged Thomas in his schoolwork, youth group activities, and other extracurriculars. I sincerely praised him when I noticed something he'd done well. I engaged him in meaningful conversations about what was going on in his life, talked about God and how He was working in my life and the lives of our family. I tried to model my Christian faith in ways that were meaningful to my son, and I invested time and money in whatever gave him the chance to flourish. But I had a deepening sense of inner pain and grief that I kept to myself. I had a sense that something was "missing" from my understanding, that something was going "really wrong" right before my eyes. But I didn't recognize what it was, nor could I even express what I was experiencing. I didn't want to worry Thomas, but secretly I wondered what was happening to my young son. For reasons that I only dimly understood back then, I felt a deep conviction that I needed to fight against whatever it was that was attacking him in his dreams with all my power.

◊ ◊ ◊

That summer, Elin and I signed Thomas up for a YMCA summer camp that met daily at a nearby elementary school. One of the fun activities that the kids participated in during the day was to dance to a medley of Michael Jackson's hit songs. As the camp counselors tried to come up with an end-of-the-summer show that the kids could put on for their parents, Thomas suggested they do a musical choreography of Michael Jackson's hit songs. The counselors and kids agreed, and they worked on crafting this musical production for weeks. Thomas even asked us to buy him a black fedora hat and a glove like the ones Jackson wore in some of his video performances.

I was glad Thomas was so engaged in this summer activity, but there was something that didn't sit right with me for reasons I could not explain.

FINDING NEW LIFE AFTER THE DEATH OF MY SON

The intensity with which Thomas identified with Jackson and his music had all the signs of a blind spot, that is, a projection of unconscious material that had him in a way that his conscious self could not see. I liked Michael Jackson's music, but his infamous lifestyle and the horrible accounts of his predatory behavior resonated with the dark side of the sociocultural context that we purposely avoided in our biblically based family culture. He was not the kind of role model I wanted for my son, and I was deeply disturbed by the way Thomas was obsessed with Jackson as he rehearsed for the summer camp show.

Music is a universal language. It possesses the incredible power to open the gates to the human heart and mind. But like a Trojan horse, it is important to know what is really inside a song before you let it into your heart and mind. Much like a 440-A tuning fork resonates the *A* string on a guitar, music resonates the conscious and unconscious emotions, beliefs, images, tendencies, and predispositions connected to the destiny we have along the Inner Labyrinth and the destiny we create with our choices. So, it's important for us to know what our "heartstrings" are and how they get resonated by the media we encounter.

Another thing to remember is that music and its lyrics can smuggle messages *into* our hearts and minds that indoctrinate us, sometimes without us even knowing it. The lyrics of a song can bypass the core values and beliefs of our conscious waking self. Some songs can inspire us to be the very best self we can be, the person who we are meant to be in God, and echo biblical truth, even though the artist may not be overtly Christian. Other songs can help us express our deepest pain and grief, longing and hope. Still other songs embody dark thoughts, attitudes, and behaviors that can encourage us to be our very worst selves.

As I briefly noted earlier, Richard Dawkins called the mechanism for transmitting these messages through music and other forms of cultural expression *memes*, which was a play on the word *genes*.[107] While genes are replicators that transmit genetic information from person to person, memes are replicators that transmit cultural information held by individuals or groups that are passed from brain to brain. Elsewhere, I have termed this the Individual-Collective Paradox, which states that organizations or groups of people are collective, cultural entities that are led, managed, and changed one person at a time.[108] Memes can be words, ideas, metaphors, stories, songs, images, beliefs, stereotypes, or even entire worldviews. Memes that are wrapped in the Trojan horse container of music are especially powerful because they often evoke strong human emotions. Memes act like cognitive-emotional parasites that shape and define how we "see" ourselves, others, and the world around us. Once transmitted, that person becomes a carrier of that meme, which they can in turn transmit to others.

Dawkins argued that when we die, the only things we leave on earth are genes and memes, and our memes can have much more staying power and longevity than our genes. Our genetic contribution and the visual likeness between us, our children, and their progeny may last for two or three generations before returning to the gene pool, but memes can last for thousands of years. I doubt there is a single intact genetic strand from Alexander the Great left on the earth, but the memes he spread through Greek culture are still with us twenty-four hundred years after his death in the form of Greek architecture, ways of thinking, and language. The same can be said of the inspired, eternal words of God spoken through the Bible.

I discussed my concerns about Michael Jackson's music and lifestyle with Thomas and contrasted him to Stevie Wonder. As I put it to Thomas, like Jackson, Wonder was a childhood star who was enormously talented and successful. But Wonder's lifestyle and values were built on religious faith and true compassion for others. He was still very much alive and making music the day Jackson died. As I spoke to Thomas, I began to wonder if there was a connection between Thomas's intense resonance with Jackson's music along the Outer Labyrinth and the cloaked man dream series we'd been recording and discussing concurrently along the Inner Labyrinth that summer. Thomas got defensive when I expressed my concerns about Jackson's music, his life, and his early death. I took note of that interaction between my son and me, remaining ever determined to continue raising Thomas in our Christian family culture.

CHAPTER 31

THE ORANGE HIPPIE VAN

November 22, 2023 (2 Years, 29 Weeks, and 2 Days After)

Two days after Thomas's end-of-the-year summer camp show, Elin, Thomas, and I attended the fourth annual Heaven Fest, an outdoor Christian music festival in Loveland, Colorado, consisting of eight stages and more than a hundred performing artists. It was a blistering hot summer day, so the three of us did not know what to expect. Once we arrived, I was amazed seeing how the place pulsated with the excitement of thirty thousand people praising God with song and testimony, even despite the oppressive heat.

Thomas was amazed too. He'd never seen anything like this before. It aligned with our Christian family culture, the values of the church youth group he was active in, and his experience at the Boulder Christian Academy. In that moment, Thomas began to more fully realize that Christianity wasn't just some private little thing we did as a family or something that existed just at school or at church. Christianity was an enormous movement, a collective force in the world he belonged to. Heaven Fest had a big impact on Thomas, and I wanted to fan the flames of this new way to experience and express his faith in God.

After we returned home, I asked Thomas to list his favorite Heaven Fest bands, and I bought him multiple albums for each band, especially his favorite, Skillet. He especially liked the Skillet song "Monster," so I also got him a band T-shirt with an artistic representation of a monster on it and the lyrics "I feel like a monster." I bought one of these shirts for myself, too, and wore it in solidarity with my son. Striving to keep this positive direction going, I also discovered a similar Christian music festival called Rock the Range that was scheduled to happen about a month later, so I got tickets for Thomas and me.

But this whole time, I also kept remembering what Freud taught us almost a hundred years earlier that unexpressed feelings don't die—they

Thomas on Christmas Day 2014 with his LEGO hippie van

get buried alive.[109] Thomas's experience with the Michael Jackson summer camp show resonated powerful emotions deep within him, and I knew that if I tried to repress, stifle, or suffocate those feelings, they would struggle for air. My strategy for raising Thomas had always been to allow him to be in the world but not of the world. I viewed a certain level of non-Christian movies, music, and activities properly framed within the context of a biblical worldview as a kind of vaccination, where Thomas would build an immunity to the negative aspects of our culture.

It was like the parable of the wheat and tares where Jesus said:

> The kingdom of heaven is like a man who sowed good seed in his field. But while his men were sleeping, his enemy came and sowed weeds among the wheat, and left. And when the wheat

sprouted and produced grain, then the weeds also became evident. And the slaves of the landowner came and said to him, "Sir, did you not sow good seed in your field? How then does it have weeds?" And he said to them, "An enemy has done this!" The slaves said to him, "Do you want us, then, to go and gather them up?" But he said, "No; while you are gathering up the weeds, you may uproot the wheat with them. Allow both to grow together until the harvest; and at the time of the harvest I will say to the reapers, 'First gather up the weeds and bind them in bundles to burn them; but gather the wheat into my barn.'" (Matthew 13:24–30)

It was tempting with Thomas to follow the instinct to tear out the weeds (i.e., a secular worldview and its music) which would uproot the wheat. But following Jesus's admonition, I allowed both to grow together until the time of harvest. Much like the parable, the dark destructive forces along the Inner Labyrinth in Thomas's dreams were the only signs I had of the conflict that was raging within him.

◊ ◊ ◊

After the incredible affirmation of the Spirit of God moving along the Outer Labyrinth and the thousands of people at Heaven Fest and along the Inner Labyrinth, Thomas had the following dream:

> I was at the park by our house on McIntosh Lake by myself, and on my way back up to our house, there was dead silence except for the sound of my feet on the pavement. When I got to my house, it was all burnt down, and smoke was coming from it. The cloaked man was in front of the house. In one hand, he was holding fire, and in the other hand, he had a pistol. The dream ended with him pointing the gun at me, and he was only three feet away from me. In the dream, I felt like everything was lost and I had nothing, and when I woke up, I felt scared and was so freaked out that I was having a hard time breathing, so I took my asthma medicine before I went up to Papa and Momma's bedroom in the middle of the night.

Three weeks later, Thomas and I also recorded the following dream:

> I was out front of our house playing, and the sky just went black so you could only see about three feet in front of you. Then a spear came and landed right next to me. I tried to run, but there were footsteps coming toward me in every direction. The dream ends, and I'm surrounded by demons and trying to find a space to run right through where there aren't footsteps coming at me so I could get away. When I woke up, I felt freaked out.

The morning after recording this latter dream of Thomas being surrounded by demons, I was driving Thomas to the YMCA camp. At one point he asked me, "Papa, how do the words 'I feel like a monster' from the Skillet song relate to Christianity?" I felt like I was on holy ground. There was a childlike innocence and sincerity in Thomas's question that echoed our discussion a year earlier about whether he was worthy to go to heaven and his subsequent acceptance of Jesus as his savior.

"That's a great question, son," I replied, wanting to affirm him for his openness and transparency. "We all have a dark sinful side that tempts us to do the wrong thing rather than what's right. That dark sinful part of us is the monster within, our sin nature. It operates without us knowing it, and 'gets' us when we least expect it." I went on to summarize an interview with Skillet's founder and lead singer, John Cooper, that I read in *Christianity Today* magazine, where Cooper said:

> In a theological sense, the song is about original sin. You are born into the human race, you're guilty or sinful, no matter what you hope to be. "Monster" is about the fact that there is somebody we know we don't want to be. Some people call it the old man or the old self. That guy wants to creep out when you're driving, and somebody cuts you off. You wonder as a Christian; how do I keep it at bay? I liken it to the idea of a 50s horror film of this beast inside you coming alive.

I went on to say, "Satan can use this dark sinful part of us to lead us away from God. The Bible teaches us that Satan *accuses* Christians of not being worthy to go to heaven, that he's a liar who creates confusion about what God says and wants us to do, and he's a murderer who wants to kill innocent people."

I paused for a moment to let what I was saying sink in. Thomas was listening intently, weighing every word. After a few seconds of silence, I added, "You can also see what the Bible tells us in the cloaked man dreams that you've been having, son." Thomas said nothing, but his facial expression spoke volumes. "Remember what I always tell you," I said, breaking the silence, "we all have a white dog inside of us who wants to do what's right, and a black dog who wants to do what's wrong. The important question is always, which dog is stronger? You know the answer to that, right?" I paused again as Thomas nodded his head in affirmation. "It's the one you feed the most, son."

Thomas listened intently to what I told him. He seemed satisfied with my answer, but he still had no response. I wondered what was going on in his young heart and mind—what inner or outer experiences could lead a nine-year-old boy to such a thoughtful and honest question. But I didn't ask him. I simply recorded the interaction in my journal and kept watching.

A week later, Thomas and I attended Rock the Range festival in Commerce City, Colorado. Over twenty thousand people attended to watch the many bands performing there, including Skillet. The festival was free admission, and Thomas and I brought our own folding chairs. The concert was sponsored by the Billy Graham Evangelistic Organization and Samaritan Purse, and Billy Graham's son, Franklin, was the host. Much like his father, Franklin Graham preached a powerful message of God's salvation toward the end of the festival and gave an altar call. As thousands of people went forward during the hymn "Just as I Am," Thomas and I, moved by the Spirit of God, joined the crowd at the front of the stage to affirm our faith and solidarity with the truth of God's message that had been preached.

◊ ◊ ◊

Between that August and February 2013, Thomas and I recorded forty-two more dreams, all of which, except one, were about the cloaked man or other dark archetypal figures that attacked him from within. Despite this, I was encouraged by one dream that we recorded on November 5, 2012, because the images, symbols, and narrative structure of this dream seemed to tell a different story than the death and destruction imaged in the cloaked man dreams.

> I was on a playdate with Phineas and Ferb at their house, which was in the country, and we went on a long walk. We had to go over a lot of hills for sixty miles. We got to Pastor Evan's house and had lunch there. Then Ferb went home. After a little while, Phineas's mom called and told him to come home. He created a jet pack to fly home, and then he flew home. I had to walk home. I walked over a whole bunch of hills until I came to a very steep hill. I couldn't climb over it, so I saw a little metal bridge that was only an inch wide that went around it, but below it was a seventy-five-foot drop. I didn't want to take the chance of going across it and falling, so I turned around and I saw an old man who was in an orange jumpsuit and was wearing a head bandana with the peace symbol on it. I asked him how to get home. He gave me a bag and told me to go put it on this spot on the ground that was like a big black spot like an oil stain and that would get me home. I put the bag on the spot, and it flew me over the hill. I started walking again, and then I saw these big explosions going on in front of me, so I went a different way into the mountains. I was walking in the mountains, and I heard miners blowing up the insides of mountains. Then I fell off one of the mountains, but a miner who was on his break or something caught me and chucked me into our house on McIntosh Drive in Longmont. I woke up and thought that this was a very weird dream.

I knew Thomas watched this Disney television show called *Phineas and Ferb* all the time, so when we finished recording the dream, I asked him to explain what the show was about. He told me the show was about a boy named Phineas Flynn and his stepbrother, Ferb Fletcher, who were determined to make every day of their summer vacation fun. Some of their hijinks included building a full-scale roller coaster, becoming musicians, building a backyard beach, and traveling back in time to meet dinosaurs.

Thomas was particularly taken with the image of the old man in the orange jumpsuit wearing a head bandana that had a peace symbol on it in the dream. "That guy's a hippie, Papa," Thomas exclaimed excitedly, "like the hippies back in the sixties who lived in Volkswagen hippie vans."

"Yes, son. That was back in my era in the 1960s," I replied. I began telling him about various aspects of the hippie movement, including Woodstock and my own experiences taking the bus to Greenwich Village during that period. After our discussion, I purchased a DVD about Woodstock, which we watched together, as I tried to explain further what it was like to live in those troubled and turbulent times.

"Most of the people who attended Woodstock were lost, Thomas. They were searching for the truth and trying to find themselves. Woodstock was like Heaven Fest and Rock the Range," I said, trying to give my son something to compare it to. "But unlike Woodstock, the people at the festivals we attended were there to hear music about God and faith, because Jesus is the way, the truth, and the life." I paused briefly. "You know, during that same era, a whole movement sprang up in Costa Mesa, California, that caused thousands and thousands of young people to know the Lord. They were called Jesus People or Jesus Freaks."[110] Thomas was still listening intently as I continued. "Those Jesus People were probably like the guy in your dream with the orange jumpsuit and bandana."

Thomas looked at me directly and asked once I finished, "What do you think my dream means, Papa?"

I waited for a moment and then said, "Well, that dream is like a story, Thomas. It's a story about your journey in life, your journey home."

Overall, I felt good about Thomas's dream. I saw symbols about his childhood in *Phineas and Ferb*, and images of his faith in God and engagement with the youth group in the symbol of having lunch at Pastor Evan's house. After lunch with Pastor Evan, Thomas would leave his childhood behind, symbolized by Phineas and Ferb going home, and then start his long journey home. Back then in 2012, I saw the old man in the orange jumpsuit as a symbol of inner guidance—someone who would help Thomas along his life's journey. Thomas would have a long and difficult journey in life, as symbolized by having to walk a long way after leaving Pastor Evan's house. It would be dangerous—he would have to cross mountains, and there would be explosions both above the ground in his conscious waking life and below the ground in the unconscious. It was the type of journey that a person might not survive. But after conquering those challenges, Thomas would make it back home to a new sense of self, symbolized by our house on McIntosh Drive, safe and sound. After all the dark dreams about death and destruction, I felt like God was providing a vision for Thomas's life that gave me some hope and assurance he was on the right path.

The Inner Labyrinth dream image of the hippie with the orange jumpsuit had a big impact along the Outer Labyrinth of Thomas's day-to-day life going forward. Orange became his favorite color. We bought him an orange coat, shirts, and sneakers—he even had an orange shirt on in his fifth-grade school picture. Every time he saw a Volkswagen bus driving down the road, he'd yell, "There's a hippie van!" For Christmas in 2014, Elin and I gave Thomas an orange hippie van LEGO set that had 1,354 pieces. It was meant for kids four years older than him, but he assembled it quickly with little reference to the instructions, proudly displaying it on a shelf in his bedroom. Up until fifth-grade, Thomas always wanted a crew cut, but from that point forward, he kept his hair long like a hippie.

The orange LEGO hippie van was one of the few fully constructed LEGO sets that Thomas took to California with him when he moved there two years later in 2016. Much to our surprise, there was a Volkswagen repair shop just up the street from our new house in Campbell that always had an orange hippie van parked out in front. Thomas pointed it out the first time he drove to our new house, and over the next five years, all three of us mentioned it often when we drove back and forth to our home just a block away. Despite all the fun we had back then pointing out that van when we passed by, now the presence of that orange Volkswagen van seems like a synchronicity.

Thomas died at home in his bed, just a block from where that van was parked.

When Elin and I moved back to Colorado, Elin carefully wrapped Thomas's LEGO van in Bubble Wrap and transported it in her car so it wouldn't be damaged in the move. It still sits on the shelf in her home office today, a symbol of fond but deeply painful memories of our son, and a sign of the sovereign power of God and how He speaks to us along the Inner Labyrinth through the Self and in our dreams and through the Outer Labyrinth of everyday life.

FINDING NEW LIFE AFTER THE DEATH OF MY SON

◊ ◊ ◊

Evil often takes what God meant for good and subverts it for wicked purposes. Paul describes this in Romans relative to the Law.

> I was once alive apart from the Law; but when the commandment came, sin became alive and I died; and this commandment, which was to result in life, proved to result in death for me; for sin, taking an opportunity through the commandment, deceived me and through it killed me. So then, the Law is holy, and the commandment is holy and righteous and good. Therefore, did that which is good become a cause of death for me? May it never be! Rather it was sin, in order that it might be shown to be sin by effecting my death through that which is good, so that through the commandment sin would become utterly sinful. (Romans 7:9–13)

In the wake of the positive message of the Phineas and Ferb dream, the forces of evil continued to assault Thomas with an even more direct message of death and destruction. Being a hippie in the 1960s was one thing. Being a hippie in the age of counterfeit pills and fentanyl poisonings where a single pill can kill was quite another.

One day in February 2013 after I had returned from being on the road doing consulting work, Thomas told me he'd had the following dream while I was gone:

> I was in my bedroom. A red glow came, and I heard a voice say, "I'm coming for you." I think this was Satan. When I went upstairs and told Mom, she said, "That's not real," and I said, "Yeah, you should read a book, and then you'll know he's real." And Mom said, "What book?" And I said, "The Bible."

After Thomas and I recorded this dream, we discussed his associations with Satan and the Bible, which I totally agreed with. At that time, I viewed the dream symbolically as a sign of psychological transformation, despite the fact that the Satan symbol had a spiritual, biblical meaning for Thomas and me, and despite the sixth guiding principle of interpreting dreams, which states *Dreams say what they mean and mean what they say*.

More specifically, when recording a dream, it is important to bring the dream back into consciousness, reconnect to the intense images and emotions, and then cash these out into word pictures that capture their essence as closely as possible. It is important to let the dream speak for itself and to stay as close to the images, symbols, narrative, and emotions as possible because dreams say what they mean and mean what they say. The key is to reconnect to the inner experience in the dream without reading meaning or conscious interpretations back into the dream images or emotions. It is also important to precisely record so-called mistakes as they have been shown in the dream. Paradoxical or anachronistic images of rivers that flow in the wrong direction, a beautifully forested wooded path high in the sky, or a woman crying as part of a religious ritual as saltwater flows from heaven are not errors. Such images are meant to teach and provide perspective to the conscious waking mind.

Other than the Michael Jackson incident, there were no outward signs of conflict within Thomas's soul. In fact, Thomas had the Satan dream at the exact same time when he came to me and said he wanted to make a public reaffirmation of his faith. During those days, he was excelling with the biblically based curriculum at Boulder Christian Academy, memorizing and learning large blocks of Scripture. There were times when I was amazed at the deep grasp that he had on biblical truth. He actively listened to Christian radio day and night, embracing life as a curious, energetic, and creative ten-year-old boy. But Thomas continued to have dreams, eighteen of them to be exact, which involved the cloaked man or other symbols of death and being attacked. Then, in July 2014, Thomas and I recorded the following dream:

> I was sitting somewhere in front of the TV watching the news and this report came on that Martin Luther King was doing drugs and alcohol and stuff. The dream ends with me sitting there shocked.

After we'd recorded the dream, I asked, "What do you think that dream means, son?" eager to hear what he'd say.

"Well, when I woke up at 1:00 a.m. after having it, I thought that it must have something to do with transformation, since that's the role that Martin Luther King played in the Civil Rights Movement."

I was amazed by the depth and insight of his answer. "Yes, that's right," I added, pleased that he was catching on and beginning to see the images symbolically. "The first step toward deep inner transformation often comes from the dark shadow sides of ourselves, from our sinful selves, and that seems to be what the unconscious is showing you in this dream, son." I waited for a moment before continuing. "Even an iconic figure like Martin Luther King had a dark sinful side, and this dream is showing you that you do, too, son. You need to think about the Martin Luther King image in this dream as an inner Martin Luther King that's a still unknown part of you."

He nodded his head affirmatively. He was catching on. He was starting to see the images symbolically against our natural human tendency to see them as being "out there" in the world. I saw the images as symbols of transformation, as objective and unconscious forces and processes that were trying to raise his awareness of what was going deep within him along the Inner Labyrinth of the destiny he had in God from the beginning of time. But little did I know at that time that these images were also foreshadowing choices Thomas would make to create his own destiny with the recreational use of prescription medications like Xanax in an age of counterfeit pills and fentanyl poisonings.

◇ ◇ ◇

What I've recounted in this chapter is a sort of list of conflicting and compensatory events Thomas and I had along the Inner and Outer Labyrinth. Back in 2014, I saw the dark destructive images of death in Thomas's dreams as symbols of transformation and the first two consequences of sin—alienation from ourselves and alienation from others. They were part of the natural process of individuation that could be explained by natural causes—psychological factors like those described by Jung's psychology and my biblically based Christian faith. The only way I could make sense out of the enormous inner turbulence and conflict I saw in Thomas's dreams alongside the empirical reality of my bright, curious, and spiritually oriented eleven-year-old son who seemed unaffected by the weight and sheer volume of the unconscious messages being sent was to maintain a distinction between my son, Thomas, and the objective and impersonal psychological forces within him.

My son, Thomas, was *creating* his own destiny with his ongoing choices to follow God and the path of the Christian life. He was a citizen of heaven working his way through this world. But the dark, destructive forces of death within him, forces he was largely unconscious of and could not control even if he wanted to, revealed a destiny he had in God from the beginning of time along the Inner Labyrinth of his dreams. And both were happening together at the same time. In retrospect, I now realize that insurgent spiritual forces who were opposed to God and all that is good were standing behind the images of the cloaked man and Satan in Thomas's dreams. They were waging a *proxy war* against my son and his childlike faith in God. Thomas's struggle was not against flesh and blood (Ephesians 6:1–4, 10–12). Rather, Satan and the forces of evil were working against him in stealthy ways that went undetected by me along the Outer Labyrinth of everyday life.

These spiritual forces manipulated elements of Thomas's conscious and unconscious mind to accomplish their goal of frustrating and undermining the work of God in him. Like an elite-level proxy server on the internet hides the identity of the sender by concealing their IP address, so Satan and the forces of evil worked through dream images from Thomas's personal and collective unconscious to relentlessly attack him along the Inner Labyrinth. In the process, they twisted and weaponized the horrible consequence of sin—although we were originally created for eternity, in the wake of the fall, we will all die someday. They plagued Thomas with accusations and ongoing doubts about whether he was "worthy" to go to heaven, even though he was a self-professed child of God, a citizen of heaven. These impacts happened just below the surface of conscious awareness; they were so tacit that Thomas did not know how to verbalize or talk about what was happening to him.

M. Scott Peck argues in his book *People of the Lie* that the traditional Christian model of evil is consistent with what I'm calling a proxy war.

> According to this model, humanity (and perhaps the entire universe) is locked in a titanic struggle between the forces of good and evil, between God and the devil. The battle ground of this struggle is the individual human soul. The entire meaning of human life revolves around this battle. The only question of

ultimate significance is whether the individual soul will be won to God or won to the devil.[111]

As I stood at Thomas's casket on May 8, 2021, looking at his young lifeless body, I understood what Peck meant in an experiential sense. *This* was the war I felt I'd lost. I also knew that the only question of ultimate significance to me was whether Thomas's soul had been won for God. I clung to the fact that Thomas was baptized, that he believed in Jesus's name, had confessed his sins, and was saved by the blood of the Lamb.

Thomas on his tricycle with all his equipment in 2004

CHAPTER 32

DIGGING DEEPER

November 22, 2023 (2 Years, 29 Weeks, and 2 Days After)

The causes and circumstances that surround a person's death shape the form, substance, intensity, and longevity of the grief process. Thanatologist David Kessler is instructive on this point.

> If our loved one had what we believe to be a meaningful death, our grief is likely to be less tormented. If we are mourning a more problematic death, we are likely to have a more complicated grief. . . . Of course, some deaths are inevitably going to be more complicated than others, such as a death by suicide, and overdoses, the death of a child, a sudden death, the death of someone we loved but were estranged from, to name a few.[112]

Kessler raises other important questions, including: Did the person have to die? Could the death have been prevented? Could I have prevented it? Could someone else have? How did the dying person experience what was happening? Was there something I should have done to make it easier? Where is the meaning in death and dying?[113]

The causes and circumstances around Thomas's death have shaped the form, substance, intensity, and longevity of my grieving process. My conclusion that there was a complex, interrelated set of causes and circumstances that included a proxy war instigated by the spiritual forces of evil was an unexpected discovery. I was uncomfortable talking about it. I discussed it in detail with Elin. She understood because she'd lived through it with me as Thomas's mom, but she was as confused about what it meant as I was. I mentioned it to a few close friends, and each time I was met with a blank stare before they changed the subject. I kept thinking, *People will think I'm crazy. They'll dismiss me as naive.*

I used to Google old TV episodes of *The Flip Wilson Show* on YouTube where Wilson, acting as his character Geraldine, would say, "The devil made me do it." It was funny then. It wasn't funny now.

I was still haunted by questions about Thomas's life and death. First, how could have I missed the import of what the unconscious was saying through Thomas's cloaked man dreams across those seven years? Second, how can I tell the difference between psychological phenomena described by Jung (complexes and archetypes) and proxy-based spiritual phenomena that stand behind and direct these psychological processes?[114] Third, what was the ongoing impact that Thomas's dreams had along the Inner and Outer Labyrinth of his life?

<> <> <>

To answer the first two questions, I had to reconstruct what was happening along the Outer Labyrinth of our everyday life and take an even deeper look at the Inner Labyrinth of Thomas's dream life. But the seventh guiding principle for interpreting dreams presented some challenges in doing this, because dreams and their primary meaning belong to the dreamer alone. When Thomas told me a dream, it created an image of his dream in my mind, an image-based structure analogous to the rows and columns of a mental Excel file. Subsequently, my unconscious filled the rows and columns with data from my conscious and unconscious mind, not his. Again, only the dreamer can say what a dream means with any certainty. However, group dream work and one-on-one dream analysis with a Jungian analyst allows others to see meaning and associations in dream images and symbols that the dreamer may not see. Others can also glimpse recalcitrant planks in the dreamer's eye that get projected onto others—blind spots that focus onto the speck in others' eyes, as Jesus taught us in Matthew 7:1–5.

I researched the detailed journal entries that I made from 2007 through 2021 when Thomas died. This included records of road trips that Thomas and I made along with pictures, videos, and memories. I had no recorded dreams for him from August 8, 2014, until the day he died on May 2, 2021. But Jung argued that the first few recorded dreams are often most important—they are both diagnostic and prognostic. As he writes, "These early dreams in particular are of the utmost importance because they are dreamed out of the depth of the personality and, therefore, frequently represent an anticipation of the later destiny. Subsequent dreams of children become more and more unimportant, except when the dreamer is destined for a special fate."[115]

I reviewed my notes from multiple discussions I had with Katie, the clinical psychologist who Thomas worked with from 2018 to 2021. I also scoured my own dreams and numerous entries in my journal that documented important situations and conversations I had with my son over the years. Elin researched her detailed, multiyear journal entries, pictures, videos, and memories, along with her recorded dreams. I went through Thomas's laptop and mobile phone, as well as his social media accounts. His devices also gave me access to his journal, emails, text messages, pictures, songs, and poems that he had written between 2011 and 2021. Finally, I did another extensive review of all ninety-eight dreams that Thomas and I recorded together.

I began working with my longtime Jungian analyst, Lara Newton, to review Thomas's dreams, his associations with those dreams, and my associations with them. Lara functioned as an objective, third-party reviewer of how I was interpreting these messages from my son's unconscious, including the series of dreams he had about the cloaked man. Jung argued that the uncertainty in understanding the dreams of children can be significantly reduced if we have a dream series to work with. As Jung writes:

> We can thus make an assumption about the meaning of one dream and then see whether this attribution of a meaning also explains another one, that is, if it is of more general significance. We can also make control tests with the help of dream series. I would actually prefer to deal with children's dreams in dream series because when we investigate dreams in a series, we most often find confirmation or corrections of our original assumptions in the following dreams. In dream series the dreams are connected to one another in a meaningful way, as if they tried to give expression to a central content from ever-varying angles. To touch this central core is to find the key to the explanation of the individual dreams.[116]

I immersed myself in the images and symbols of Thomas's dream series, bringing the dream content back into my conscious awareness. I searched for central themes and symbolic patterns of transformation that connected multiple dreams over time in meaningful ways, and I juxtaposed these Inner Labyrinth revelations with the concrete reality of Thomas's behavior and choices made in the daily reality of the Outer Labyrinth, as described in the previous chapter.

In addition to the eight guiding principles of interpreting dreams, I used a technique developed by Jung called active imagination where the boundary between my conscious and unconscious mind became permeable. This allowed me to "drop down" into my own unconscious or, conversely, for the unconscious to "emerge" into conscious awareness looking for insights about the archetypal nature of Thomas's dreams that he and I shared as part of our common humanity. Active imagination was the psychological process Jung used to confront the objective forces in his own unconscious experiences that he documented in his *Red Book*. As Barbara Hannah puts it, "[Jung] described active imagination as the only way toward a direct encounter with the reality of the unconscious without the intermediary use of tests or dream interpretation."[117] What follows is a summary of my deeper look at these materials and the answers I unearthed to the questions above.

◇ ◇ ◇

Perhaps the most important overall message I got from this closer analysis of Thomas's cloaked man dreams is that these dark inner forces of death and destruction attacked him everywhere. They tried to convince Thomas he was under a sentence of death rather than being a child of God who was saved by grace. They attacked him in the privacy of the self-designed theater of his bedroom on the stage of his bed. They relentlessly pursued Thomas everywhere—when he was at the beach or driving the car, roaming the aisles of a Target superstore or traveling on a plane, hanging out at the skate park or spending time with his friends in his bedroom. In multiple dreams, benign images of friends, childhood toys, and positive movie characters were suddenly transformed into the cloaked man.

As I looked back at these dream images and brought them into my conscious awareness, I could not imagine the terrifying emotional impact this had on my son, especially the middle-of-the-night appearance of a red glow at the door to his bedroom with the voice of Satan saying *I'm coming for you*. Thomas knew the dream image of Satan was a real spiritual attack as described in the Bible. Images of the cloaked man and forces of evil and death would show up and attack Thomas when he least expected. He was hedged in on all sides. Thomas could not escape the destiny he had in God along the Inner Labyrinth, regardless of the destiny he tried to create in these early years with his choices along the Outer Labyrinth. I wondered why God would allow this to happen—why He would allow these dark forces of death and destruction to torture my son. But the words of Job that I posted on Thomas's memorial site just ten days after his death continued to come to mind as an answer to this question: "Though He slay me, I will hope in Him" (Job 13:15).

Ironically, one of Thomas's favorite lyrical lines from James Taylor's song "Shower the People" was "You can run, but you cannot hide." Whenever we heard that song, Thomas and I would stop whatever we were doing and sing that line together, laughing every time we heard it. But as I look back, I wonder if the unconscious was trying to express a deeper synchronistic message by linking the ritual of singing those words to the ubiquitous nature of Thomas's cloaked man dreams. Later in his life, Thomas could run from what was happening within with Xanax, but ultimately, he could not hide from the consequences of doing so. This was especially true in the sociocultural context of 2021, an age of counterfeit pills and fentanyl poisonings where just one pill could kill.

Next, I turned my attention to Thomas's "journey home" and Martin Luther King dreams as important exceptions to, and commentary on, the cloaked man dream series. As I mentioned in the previous chapter, I felt good about Thomas's journey home dream. After dozens of cloaked man dreams that were filled with symbols of death and destruction, it seemed like God was providing a positive vision for Thomas's life that gave me some assurance he was on the right path. I saw the old man in the orange jumpsuit wearing the head bandana with a peace symbol on it as a symbol of inner guidance—someone who would help Thomas along his life's journey. After conquering various challenges in the dream symbolized by the mountains and explosions, Thomas would make it back home, to a new sense of self symbolized by our house on McIntosh Drive.

However, my more recent reflections on the dozens of cloaked man dreams followed by the journey home, Satan, and Martin Luther King dreams revealed meaningful connections I didn't see back in 2014 and now find to be profoundly disturbing. The underlying symbolic message that emerges today is these dreams were foreshadowing Thomas's "journey home" to the Ryssby Cemetery, not to our home on McIntosh Drive. What the dream imaged as a long, difficult path in life guided by the inner 1960s hippie was cut short by a single bad choice. I can't describe the inner resistance I've had to seeing this truth. What father wants to hear the message that God was allowing the forces of evil, death, and destruction to attack his son—that God was preparing me for Thomas's early departure from this world—all the way back to when I tried to weep through my own journey of faith in 2010?

Viewed symbolically, the hippie in the orange jumpsuit and Martin Luther King were both tied to the 1960s. These dreams also both had strong religious symbolism in that Pastor Evan from the journey home dream and Martin Luther King were both ministers. I also saw the connection between the 1960's time stamp of the MLK symbol, and the 1960s time stamp of the old man in the orange jumpsuit, both of whom lived in a *Zeitgeist* where the widespread recreational use of drugs was accepted by young people. This seemed to foreshadow Thomas's life in California, with the obvious difference being that Thomas lived and died in the age where one counterfeit pill mixed with fentanyl could kill.

The image of Pastor Evan emerged at a time in Thomas's life before the inner death and destruction of the cloaked man dream series had taken its toll on Thomas's heart and mind. Thomas was a happy and outgoing young man who shared his thoughts and feeling openly with Elin and me. This was also apparent by numerous teachers' comments on his report cards from the time he was in preschool. But from 2014 on, Elin and I saw a slow but profound shift in Thomas's personality where he became more inwardly focused and introspective. An iconoclastic attitude of an Enneagram Type Five, combined with a Jungian dominant focus on the past as an introverted sensing type, became increasingly evident after 2014, something I confirmed with two psychometrically validated personality assessments in March 2017 when Thomas was fourteen years old and had consciously identified himself as a twenty-first-century hippie.[118]

FINDING NEW LIFE AFTER THE DEATH OF MY SON

The symbol of the inner Pastor Evan stands in sharp contrast with the level of deception, betrayal, and carnality conveyed by the image of the inner Martin Luther King doing drugs and alcohol, a fact that was publicly exposed in the dream on television. Thomas was shocked by this message both in the dream and in his conscious waking life as we recorded it. Again, my sense now is that the Martin Luther King dream was foreshadowing Thomas's recreational use of drugs and his early death, much as Martin Luther King died before his time. In much the same way, seeing the image of the old man in the orange jumpsuit as a positive image of inner resources that would help Thomas navigate his journey home now appears to symbolize the fact that Thomas was living out both the first and last days of his life at the same time.

The image of the old man in the orange jumpsuit was, and remains, an important symbol of transformation and points to the view that Thomas was in an accelerated process of individuation. The compression of what was normally a lifelong process of transformation that appears in the second half of life may have been why Thomas seemed to be wise beyond his years when he died just two weeks short of his nineteenth birthday. Jung comments on how children possess the seeds of adulthood from the time they're born.

> Strangely enough, however, unconsciously the child already has all the psychology of an adult. As it is, from birth onward—one could even say already before birth—the individual is what it will be. In the disposition, the basic blueprint is already there very early. Such early dreams come out of the totality of the personality, and that is why they allow us to see a great deal of what we later miss in it. Later, life forces us to make one-sided differentiations. But that is why we get lost to ourselves and have to learn, again, to find ourselves. When you are whole, you have discovered yourself once again, and you know what you have been all the time.[119]

As a consequence, the inner proxy war and the compressed nature of the individuation process must have created an intense amount of psychological and spiritual suffering and pain that Thomas was only partially aware of and could not express at the time of having these dreams.

Finally, I came to see the image of the orange hippie van as a synchronicity. As noted earlier in this book, Jung defined a synchronicity as an acausal connecting principle whereby internal psychological events are linked to the external world events by meaningful coincidences rather than causal chains. For example, someone might have a dream about a particular place or object, and sometime later, they might find themselves in that exact location and believe they are meant to experience something special there. As I mentioned previously, there was an orange Volkswagen hippie van parked just up the street from our house in Campbell that Elin, Thomas, and I would often point it out when we drove home. I see the presence of the old man in the orange jumpsuit and Thomas's association with the orange hippie van as foreshadowing our move to California, much like my dream about the red Colorado soil in May 2021 foreshadowed Elin and me moving back to Colorado the next year.

From a theological and biblical perspective, I adopted the same strategy that C. S. Lewis did in the *Screwtape Letters* when exploring the work of Satan and evil in Thomas's dreams.

> There are two equal and opposite errors into which our race can fall about the devils. One is to disbelieve in their existence. The other is to believe, and to feel an excessive and unhealthy interest in them. They themselves are equally pleased by both errors and hail a materialist or a magician with the same delight.[120]

So, as I continued to reflect on and understand what went on back then, I affirmed the biblical reality of Satan and the forces of evil working in our current world, and yet I guarded myself against the seduction to embrace an either-or rather than both-and form of thinking.

◇ ◇ ◇

As I continued my review of Thomas's dreams and compared them with what had been going on along the Outer Labyrinth of his daily life, I became increasingly convinced that the cloaked man images that appeared in his dreams could not be explained as the kind of natural psychological transformation children go through. It was highly unlikely they were examples of third-level archetypal grievance stories that emerged from the collective unconscious, dreams that could be described using natural causes and the first two consequences of sin.

Rather, it hit me that these symbolic images of destruction were a soul-killing assault from Satan and the spiritual forces of evil that were waging a proxy war in the depths of my son's soul. Of course, the seventh guiding principle for interpreting dreams states that only the dreamer can know for sure. But the sheer number, ferocity, and long-term intensity of Thomas's dreams seemed to telegraph a message of intended inner destruction and death, not transformation. It symbolized a desire to kill and murder, not the emergence of new life springing from a symbolic death. The cloaked man dreams reeked of the kind of confusion, lies, and accusations that typify the biblical Satan and a fourth-level biblical grievance story rather than the kind of heuristic sorting that Jesus used to identify those who truly wanted to discover the hidden meaning and truth through His parables and stories.

At this point, I felt anger and rage rising from the depths of my soul. The images that emerged from within me were of a pride of hungry lions hunting buffalo on the plains of the Serengeti. I watched YouTube videos of these fierce predators stalking their hapless prey to connect to the deep feelings of anger and rage. Just as a pride of lions would identify a weaker or younger animal in a herd, separate it from the safety of the group, and attack it repeatedly to wear it down before going in for the kill, sealing its untimely fate, so, too, the unconscious psychological and spiritual forces in Thomas's dreams had hunted him down along the Inner Labyrinth, separating him from the safety of our Christian family culture and attacking him ruthlessly in every which way possible. Thomas could try to run, but he couldn't hide. These forces had weakened him inwardly along the Inner Labyrinth and created a constant emotional sense of fear and anxiety along the Outer Labyrinth of his everyday life choices. It was a picture of what 1 Peter 5:8–9 describes.

> Be of sober spirit, be on the alert. Your adversary, the devil, prowls around like a roaring lion, seeking someone to devour. So, resist him, firm in your faith, knowing that the same experiences of suffering are being accomplished by your brothers and sisters who are in the world.

It's difficult to explain how deeply these images of primal destruction, death, and murder impacted me, as my anger, rage, and desire for revenge took control of my ongoing thoughts, emotions, and passions.

One day in November 2023, I was on my daily walk around McIntosh Lake, and I began to sense that something wasn't right within me. The Spirit of God spoke to me through the Self, and I began to realize I was being drawn in and hunted down by the same spiritual forces of evil that attacked my son, Thomas, in his dreams. The temptation to hate Satan and the forces of evil for taking Thomas down was becoming the kind of deep grievance and hurt that would keep me in bondage. If I continued down this path, I would become the next victim. I didn't have feelings of anger, rage, and revenge toward Satan and the forces of evil; those feelings had me. It was a red flag. These hostile and intense emotions were drawing me into a dark inner place with the same type of hand-to-hand combat used in the proxy war of Thomas's dreams—the kind described in Ephesians 6:10–17.

When I got back to my home office, I began to think through the three elements that underlie the creation of a grievance story and my need to forgive Satan and the forces of evil for what they had done to frustrate and undermine Thomas's life, as well as facilitate and hasten his death. It was much like the way I forgave Adam for his role in killing my son. In terms of the first element of creating a grievance story, I thought, *Mark, you're taking what happened too personally.* At first, this insight sounded ridiculous. How could I not take what happened to Thomas personally? This was as personal as it gets. This was my son! All this was true. But I realized that taking the attacks on Thomas too personally was something different. Taking things too personally is at the very core of human sinfulness; it's a centripetal focus on self into which a hook of anger or rage and a desire for revenge is set.

My research into the Inner Labyrinth of Thomas's dream world caused me to see what happened to Thomas too subjectively (inside-out) as something that was unique to him, like he'd been singled out. I needed to factor in the objective (outside-in) perspective, just as the apostle Peter did in warning the early Christians about the nature of spiritual warfare in 1 Peter 5:8. I also reflected on my discussion with Thomas about the meaning of Skillet's song "Monster" and how the power of evil that lives within us resonates at the same frequency as the evil around us. So, the proxy war that Satan and the forces of evil waged against my helpless son was hardly something that was unique to Thomas. The fact is that this type of spiritual warfare is common—it has happened to millions of other people, claiming the psychological, spiritual, and physical lives of countless victims since the beginning of time. What was true was that Satan and the forces of evil had done this intentionally as they waged war against God and his kingdom described in Revelation 12–14 and in C. S. Lewis's classic book *The Screwtape Letters*. Unlike forgiving Adam, who had an unintentional hand in killing Thomas and deeply regretted what he'd done, forgiving an objective spiritual force that attacked Thomas with the sole intention of facilitating his death was much more difficult.

The Spirit of God was calling me to live out Tim Keller's third definition of forgiveness, which required me to absorb the loss that resulted from Satan's attacks on Thomas. As Paul instructs us in Romans 12:19, I had to refuse to take revenge—"Never take your own revenge, beloved, but leave room for the wrath of God, for it is written: 'Vengeance is Mine, I will repay,' says the Lord."

In retrospect, I thought, *How ridiculous it is to think that I could really take revenge on Satan and the forces of evil. Who or what would I go after? Who or what would I attack? How ludicrous it was to think I could make Satan and the forces of evil suffer for the wrong they'd done, or to demand that they do something to make things right.* They were proxies, hidden behind people and situations in life, so there was no way to attack them directly in return. No, I had to follow Jesus's example and write the offense off like a debt on the balance sheet in my heart and mind.

This type of self-crucifixion is hard, very hard. But my failure to absorb the loss of my son and the absurd act of taking revenge would empower the inner wound that Satan and the forces of evil tried to inflict on me. Had I done so, that wound would have become mine, not theirs. This inner wound would take on a life of its own within my conscious and unconscious life apart from the forces of evil that inflicted it. Once it took root in my soul, it would keep punishing me outwardly and inwardly. The failure to forgive Satan and the forces of evil for helping to kill Thomas would anchor me to them, the past offense, and the inner wound, which would become the "gift" that kept on giving. I saw that Satan was tempting me, to see if my quotation of Job 13:15 that I uploaded on Thomas's memorial site just ten days after his death would be cashed out in deeds.

Along these lines, I could also imagine the same God who first spoke to me at the Hungarian Reformed Church when I was eleven years old, the same God to whom I made two vows to on the Mount of Beatitudes in 1996, and the same God who saw me through the lens of Jesus's sacrificial death on the cross saying to Satan in the same way as he spoke of Job, "Have you considered my servant, Mark, that he still holds fast to me, even after he lost the person who was most precious to him?" But even this I knew I could do only because of God's grace and forgiveness, along with the sustaining power of the Spirit of God transforming and sanctifying the Self.

◇ ◇ ◇

Had the third element of creating a grievance story—telling others and myself the Satan-focused grievance story over and over again—started to codify, my life would have begun traveling down the wrong path. Once I sidestepped the trap that was set for me and removed the hook of unforgiveness out of my soul, I began to sober up from the powerful distorting and destructive emotions that afflicted me. I started to see things differently. Much like Jesus taught in Matthew 7:1–5, once I took the log out of my eye, I began to see clearly, and the answers to the questions I posed at the beginning of this chapter began to emerge in my conscious awareness.

This allowed me to ponder the deeper implications of the eighth guiding principle for interpreting dreams—that the Self is the creator and orchestrator of our dreams and the forces that shape and define our life. In Jung's view, the Self orchestrates and constructs the sequencing of dreams into meaningful patterns that unfold over the course of a lifetime. June Singer describes the purposiveness and directionality along the Inner and Outer Labyrinths that is shaped and defined by the Self.[121] Jung claimed the Self was the image of God (*Imago Dei*) in humans and could not be seen directly. Rather, it appears in dreams as various symbols like mandalas (i.e., a circle enclosing a square), labyrinths, circles with a center, four-sided quaternities (i.e., squares and rectangles), the union of opposites (i.e., male-female, light-darkness), and inorganic elements like soil that are paradoxically united with organic ones, such as the roots, trunk, and canopy of an oak tree.

FINDING NEW LIFE AFTER THE DEATH OF MY SON

In my biblical approach to Jung's psychology, the Spirit of God speaks to all people, in all times, in all cultures through the Self, the Bible, the church, and God's creation of the universe. As Romans 1:18–21 tells us:

> For the wrath of God is revealed from heaven against all ungodliness and unrighteousness of people who suppress the truth in unrighteousness, because that which is known about God is evident within them; for God made it evident to them. For since the creation of the world His invisible attributes, that is, His eternal power and divine nature, have been clearly perceived, being understood by what has been made, so that they are without excuse. For even though they knew God, they did not honor Him as God or give thanks, but they became futile in their reasonings, and their senseless hearts were darkened.

What Jung called the Spirit of the Depths and the Spirit of the Times are created things that God is sovereign over, and through which the Spirit of God moves to accomplish His sovereign will. When we become Christians, the Spirit of God takes up residence in the Self and begins the lifelong process of sanctifying and cleansing it from the distortions of the first two consequences of sin. But accepting Jesus's free gift of salvation and taking his faith seriously, as Thomas did, also made Thomas the sworn foe of Satan, and the forces of evil made him a target. While the Self is the creator and orchestrator of our dreams and the psychological forces that shape and define our life, Satan and the forces of evil can, and do, plant seeds in our hearts and minds along both the Inner and Outer Labyrinths. I'll quote C. S. Lewis's admonition from the senior demon, Screwtape, to his nephew, Wormwood, who was a junior tempter as an example of how this happens.

> I once had a patient, a sound atheist, who used to read in the British Museum. One day, as he sat reading, I saw a train of thought in his mind beginning to go the wrong way. The Enemy, of course, was at his elbow in the moment. Before I knew where I was, I saw my twenty years' work beginning to totter. If I had lost my head and begun to attempt a defense by argument I should have been

undone. But I was not such a fool. I struck instantly at the part of the man which I had best under control and suggested that it was just about time he had some lunch. The Enemy presumably made a counter-suggestion (you know how one can never *quite* overhear what He says to them?) that this was more important than lunch. At least I think that must have been His line for when I said, 'Quite. In fact, much too important to tackle at the end of a morning' the patient brightened up considerably; and by that time, I had added 'Much better come back after lunch and go into it with a fresh mind.' He was already halfway to the door. Once he was in the street the battle was won.[122]

I know belief in this type of intervention and manipulation by the spiritual forces of evil and death sounds naive to people who don't hold to a historical-grammatical view of the Bible. That's because, as Paul writes, "a natural person does not accept the things of the Spirit of God, for they are foolishness to him; and he cannot understand them, because they are spiritually discerned" (1 Corinthians 2:14). Even for people who do have a biblical view of the world, making the distinction between purely psychological forces and those that are motivated and directed by proxy-based spiritual forces of evil requires biblical wisdom and a spiritual gift of the discerning spirits (1 Corinthians 12:10). My background in fundamental physics and cosmology, along with my biblical approach to Jung's work, has helped anchor me to other bodies of knowledge that support rather than undermine my understanding of what happened to Thomas.

But while the Bible tells us that suffering and evil in the world are the result of human sin in general, it also teaches that an individual instance of suffering or evil may not be linked to a particular sin with any level of certainty. Tim Keller argues that evil is not distributed in a proportionate, fair, and predictable way. "Bad people do not have worse lives than good people. And of course, the best people often have terrible lives. Job is an example, and Jesus—the ultimate 'Job,' the only truly, fully innocent sufferer—is another."[123] As Ecclesiastes 2:14 tells us, "The wise person's eyes are in his head, but the fool walks in darkness. And yet I know that one and the same fate happens to both of them." So, going forward, I'll refuse to be drawn into the black-hole search for Cartesian certainty, when the Bible commands me to hold the truth that God is both sovereign over the events of history, and that He has suffered in Jesus's death and resurrection, in an essential tension. I will accept this paradox by faith.

◇ ◇ ◇

On December 2, 2023, I was still struggling to find a deeper sense of meaning in Thomas's death within the sovereign will of God, to continue moving from just accepting his death to embracing it as part of the path God had called me to walk. The verse Job 14:5 came to mind, so I opened my Bible to refresh my memory of the exact wording of the passage, which says, "Since his days are determined, the number of his months is with You; and You have set his limits so that he cannot pass." A question arose from deep within—*Had God determined how many days Thomas would live?* So, I Googled that question. A website came up with a question at the top of the page. It read: "My granddaughter died at the age of 20. She took a Xanax she bought from someone. It was laced with fentanyl. Did God always plan for her to die so young?"[124] Numerous verses from Scripture were then referenced to provide an answer that said that God in His sovereign will does in fact determine the length of our lives.

I read through the Bible passages and, in that moment, the Holy Spirit within me bore witness to the fact that it was God who had determined the length of Thomas's life—the number of days, hours, and minutes he would live. And I also knew that the same God promised He would never leave Thomas or forsake him; He would be with Thomas to the very end of his life (Job 14:5; Matthew 6:27; Psalm 139:16). As Christian psychiatrist John White tells us, "Satan cannot hurt you until your task for Christ is completed. Until that time comes you are truly immortal. He may roar. He may threaten. But he is powerless. When your earthy task is completed, it is possible that he may kill you. But you will achieve by your death more than by your life. Satan is powerless to stop the advance of the gospel through your life."[125]

To be clear, Satan didn't somehow move or manipulate Thomas's hand to log onto Snapchat and buy the pill that killed him any more than Satan demanded that Pilate crucify Jesus or use a hammer to drive the nails into His hands on the cross. Rather, Satan works behind the scenes as a proxy, or as we saw in the C. S. Lewis example above, he uses our weaknesses against us to obtain his ends. In Thomas's case, the great liar and accuser of the saints amplified and focused on Thomas's honest feelings about being unworthy to go to heaven, even after becoming a Christian, and the truth that we were not originally meant to die but will because of sin. Both were true, but they were not the whole truth. The intense psychological suffering and pain Thomas experienced over the course of his short but impactful life, and the need to "take a break" from the inner battle of the proxy war as he got older, increased his risk-tolerance in the age of counterfeit pills and fentanyl poisonings. The rest is history.

As I reflected on these biblically based truths, I felt a sense of relief from the self-condemnation and blame I was feeling concerning Thomas's death, from the feelings of wishing I had been a better dad and the worry concerning whether I'd been asleep at the wheel while Thomas was being tortured in the inner proxy war. I began to feel the peace of God that surpasses all understanding guarding my heart and mind in Christ Jesus. I marveled at the invisible power of God's presence that was already preparing me to survive Thomas's death as I tried to weep my way through my journey of faith on May 2, 2010, eleven years before I found Thomas dead in his bed.

Even more recently, I have been amazed at the invisible power of God's sovereignty that led me to read Tim Keller's book *Walking with God through Pain and Suffering* in the final days of writing this memoir. In this book, Keller describes an essential tension where the God of the Bible is both a sovereign God and a suffering God. "These two truths must be held together as they are in the Bible—both true, not contradicting, but rather complementing each other."[126]

So, on the one hand, the book of Job shows that God is sovereign over all events in history, and He demands that we not question the path He calls us to walk in life along the Inner and Outer Labyrinths. God's "answer" to the questions raised by Job and his friends was, "Where were you when I laid the foundation of the earth? Tell Me if you have understanding. Who sets its measurements? Since you know. Or who stretched the measuring line over it? On what were its bases sunk? Or who laid its cornerstone, when the morning stars sang together, and all the sons of God shouted for joy?" (Job 38:4–7).[127]

On the other hand, the same God of Job is also a suffering God, who sent His only begotten son to live, die, and rise again to pay the price for the sins of mankind. As Philippians 2:8 tells us, "And being found in appearance as a man, He humbled Himself by becoming obedient to the point of death: death on a cross." Again, Keller says, "Because God is both sovereign and suffering, we know our suffering always had meaning, even though we cannot see it. We trust him without understanding it all."[128] Contemplating the sovereign-suffering reality of God began to silence my questioning heart, bring my curiosity to rest, and create a sense of trust and hope that in the end, all would be made right through Him. The trauma Elin and I endured when we found Thomas dead in his bed, and the hollow "victory" we had at Adam's sentencing, would all be made right in the end by a sovereign-suffering God. Keller is instructive on this point.

> The Bible does not merely tell us that evil is punished, as important as that is. In our world, sometimes evildoers are caught and brought to justice, but while we can *punish* evil, we cannot *undo* evil. Imprisoning or executing murderers, for example, cannot bring back the dead they killed or repair the lives they have ruined. But the book of Revelation promises much more than Judgment Day. . . . In Revelation 5, John has a vision of God sitting on a throne with a sealed scroll in his hand. Many scholars have agreed that the contents of this scroll contain "the meaning and purpose of history, the great plan of God for all time."[129]

When that scroll is opened, the reasons and purpose of Thomas's short life and unexpected death will be explained by God in terms of its meaning in all of history, and God will "make things right" forever more.

Thomas's cell phone—his connection to the world

CHAPTER 33

LINGERING QUESTIONS

December 2, 2023 (2 Years, 30 Weeks, and 4 Days After)

Once I came to this point in my search for insight about Thomas's death, answers to the three questions I described at the beginning of the last chapter began to emerge as part of the natural process of healing and transformation. My first question was: How could I have missed the import of what the unconscious was saying through Thomas's cloaked man dreams? Why even ask this question if we serve the sovereign-suffering God of Job who demands not to be questioned about matters of life and death? I was not questioning God's sovereign will over my life or Thomas's life. Rather, my questions grew from the fact that I was creating my own destiny in life with my choices as Thomas's father. The Gospel of Luke instructs us that to whom much is given, much is required (Luke 12:48). And again, James 3:1 says, "Let not many of you become teachers, my brethren, knowing that as such we will incur a stricter judgment." This question was directed toward me and the stewardship God gave me as Thomas's father.

Now I see the extent to which my judgment was flawed back when I was recording Thomas's dreams. As Anaïs Nin says, "We see the world as 'we' are, not as 'it' is; because it is the 'I' behind the 'eye' that does the seeing."[130] As Thomas Kuhn puts it, we see the world through our paradigm at a given point in history, where it is composed of our background, family influences, education, personality, and life experiences. In many ways, we see what we expect to see through the lens of our tacit, unquestioned, taken-for-granted beliefs and assumptions. This default, centripetal, self-focused perspective is a result of the first consequence of sin that we experience phenomenologically as the so-called Cartesian Intuition—I'm in here, and the world's out there. This is the lens through which I saw Thomas's life along the Inner Labyrinth of the destiny he had in God from the beginning of time and the destiny he was creating along the Outer Labyrinth of day-to-day life with his choices. In Matthew

7:1–5, Jesus requires me to first remove the log from my eye, then I'll see clearly enough to help others with their speck. I didn't even realize I was blinded by that log.

But my traditional Jungian paradigm of interpreting the dark, destructive symbols of death in Thomas's dreams as third-level archetypal grievance stories prevented me from identifying the fourth-level biblical grievance story and spiritual proxy war in Thomas's soul that stood behind these archetypal images. This happened despite the fact that Thomas's unconscious created dozens of cloaked man dreams. It is only now in retrospect that I see how one of the applications of the fifth guiding principle failed to shed light on this at the time—that is, that dreams don't tell us what we already know. When the images of the cloaked man appeared over and over in Thomas's dreams, I should have recognized that the message the unconscious was trying to send to Thomas was not getting through. So, it sent it again in the form of a slightly different set of dream images.

My deep understanding of the Bible and Jung's work and the experience of recording and analyzing thousands of dreams under the mentorship of two Jungian analysts were indispensable when it came to aligning the destiny I had in God along the Inner Labyrinth with the destiny I was creating along the Outer Labyrinth of my everyday choices. But it was always the silent, wordless, spontaneous ping of truth from within that was the validating criterion that I had integrated the unconscious content presented in the dream into conscious awareness and had understood the meaning of the images and symbols in the dream at that point in time. But this was impossible to do with Thomas's dreams.

When it came to understanding the meaning of the images and symbols in Thomas's dreams, I had no direct experiential access to the inner validating ping of truth. I would occasionally see a change in his facial expression when we discussed a dream, the kind of radiance that signaled that he'd had an aha experience where the light of new consciousness went on in his head. But given his age, many of the deeper insights he did have into the meaning of his dream images were tacit and could not be expressed in words. Trying to understand the meaning of his dreams now, after his death, was an even more difficult task for all the reasons I've already explained, especially the seventh guiding principle for interpreting dreams that dreams and their meaning belong to the dreamer alone.

FINDING NEW LIFE AFTER THE DEATH OF MY SON

Another reason I missed the import of Thomas's cloaked man dreams was because of the human tendency to deny the reality of death, especially the possibility that our children will die before us. Ernest Becker argues that denying the reality of death is a failure to take the lived truth of life "seriously." Lurking under the mundane and pedestrian profanities of life is a subtle but profound terror of death—a rumble of panic beneath everything.[131] Tim Keller explains it this way:

> When we hear of a tragedy, there is a deep-seated psychological defense mechanism that goes to work. We think to ourselves that such things happen to other people, to poor people, or to people who do not take precautions. Or we tell ourselves that if only we get the right people into office and get our social systems right, nothing like this will happen again.[132]

My tendency to deny the reality of my own death and the possibility of Thomas's dying before me created powerful and distorted quasi-conscious assumptions that emerged from the first two consequences of sin described by the fourth-level biblical grievance story in Genesis 3 and the subsequent struggle to align the bifurcated reality of the Outer and Inner Labyrinths.

The first assumption was *It won't happen to me*. God told Adam and Eve that if they ate of the tree of the knowledge of good and evil, they would surely die. But Satan planted a seed of the idea that this would not happen by telling a lie that was partially correct but totally false. It was a play on words. While it was true they would not die physically at that point in time, they would die spiritually, alienating them from eternal life in God, and then eventually they would eventually die physically too. Death was not something that was in God's original design for the world. Nowhere does the Bible and everyday experience teach us that "It won't happen to me." In fact, they teach the exact opposite—bad things can and do happen to good people, yet we continue to play the odds.

Somewhere deep inside me, I had a sense that something was wrong in terms of what I was seeing in Thomas's dreams back then. I somehow knew then what I know now, but only in some quasi-conscious way. My paradigm then rejected from the realm of possibilities what I see clearly now using the assumption it wouldn't happen to me. I thought, *That can't be right.* This was a big mistake. I thought back then, *I managed my struggles with the dark side, and Thomas will too. I made it through the tough times, and Thomas will too.* But I didn't live in the age of counterfeit pills and fentanyl poisonings, and Thomas did.

Another assumption related to denying the reality of death was to believe the myth that I'm in control. I know what I'm doing. I'm managing the risks. My knowledge of the Bible, Jung's work, and my experiential knowledge of having recorded and analyzed thousands of dreams gave me a false sense of security that I was in control, that I understood these dreams and was mentoring Thomas in the practice of interpreting them. I saw this as a skill that I was giving my son as a head start on living an effective life, using a biblical approach to Jung's psychology. In many ways, I did know what I was doing back then, and I was using time-proven competencies to teach Thomas how to manage life effectively.

I also picked Thomas's therapists very carefully when he got older. I evaluated their credentials, their level of Christian faith, and I worked with them and Thomas in a three-way partnership to bring a Jungian and Christian perspective to their work with my son. Thomas only spent fifty minutes a week in therapy sessions, and the rest of the one hundred and sixty-eight hours a week he lived his life in the context of the family Christian culture that Elin and I constructed in obedience to God's word. But the fact is that we are not ultimately in control of our lives or the lives of our children. Life is fragile and priceless. It's a currency we spend one day at a time.

For all these reasons and more, I was not meant to see then what I see now. Had I fully understood the spiritual nature of the proxy war that was waging deep within my son, I'm not sure what I would have done about it. I discussed what was happening with my Jungian analyst, and we both saw everything within the context of the typical types of problems that kids went through at Thomas's age. No spiritual proxy war red flags were raised for either of us.

So, today, as I contemplate the sovereign-suffering reality of God about this first question, my questioning heart has been silenced, my curiosity has been brought to rest, and I find a deep sense of trust and hope that God will make all things right in the end. I believe the trauma that Elin and I endured when we found Thomas dead in his bed, and the hollow "victory" we had at Adam's sentencing, will make sense and have eternal meaning when Jesus unseals and reads the scroll described in chapter 5 of the book of Revelation.

◊ ◊ ◊

My second question from the previous chapter was: How do you tell the difference between psychological phenomena described by Jung (complexes and archetypes) and proxy-based spiritual phenomena that stand behind and direct these psychological processes? I've come to see this as being like the nature-nurture question. With the nature-nurture question, whether we learn something as a child or whether it was hardwired in us genetically is operationally meaningless in terms of how we deal with it in day-to-day life. In much the same way, I've come to see the psychological-spiritual distinction as being operationally meaningless, a trap that leads to recursive third-level archetypal or fourth-level biblical grievance stories that can't be escaped. Whether the images in a dream are driven by purely psychological or natural factors (i.e., complexes, archetypes, and neurons) or whether they have spiritual proxy forces motivating and directing them, the answer for dealing with them is the same. As Paul tells us in Ephesians:

> Finally, be strong in the Lord and in the strength of His might. Put on the full armor of God, so that you will be able to stand firm against the schemes of the devil. For our struggle is not against flesh and blood, but against the rulers, against the powers, against the world forces of this darkness, against the spiritual forces of wickedness in the heavenly places. Therefore, take up the full armor of God, so that you will be able to resist in the evil day, and having done everything, to stand firm. Stand firm therefore, having girded your loins with truth, and having put on the breastplate of righteousness, and having shod your feet with the preparation of the gospel of peace; in addition to all, taking up the shield of faith with which you will be able to extinguish all the flaming arrows of the evil one. And take the helmet of salvation, and the sword of the Spirit, which is the word of God. (Ephesians 6:10–16)

But Thomas was not an adult Christian like the people Paul was writing to in Ephesus. He was an innocent little boy who had put his trust in Jesus and was walking the path of faith in the only way he knew at his age.

Elin and I tried to create a Christian family culture that allowed and encouraged the defenses of Ephesians 6 to take root in Thomas's life. But this strategy for dealing with spiritual warfare was something Thomas had to do. We couldn't do it for him. My sense is that the sheer number, ferocity, and long-term intensity of Thomas's cloaked man dreams were directed toward inner destruction, not positive transformation. They were designed to kill and murder him from the inside out, as opposed to being images from which new life would spring from a symbolic death. They were filled with the kind of confusion, lies, and accusations that typify the biblical Satan and a fourth-level biblical grievance story that brings death, not a third-level archetypal grievance story from where new life emerges from symbols of transformation at a higher level of individuation.

As such, Thomas's cloaked man dreams had an inner cumulative effect over time, far beneath the Outer Labyrinth of day-to-day life, until it was too late—the inner damage had been done. These spiritual forces manipulated elements of Thomas's conscious and unconscious mind to accomplish their goal of frustrating and undermining the work of God in him. They twisted and weaponized the fact that we will all die someday as a result of the fall, even if we are Christians. They plagued Thomas with accusations about whether he was "worthy" to go to heaven, even though he was a self-professed child of God. Again, these impacts happened deep below the surface of conscious awareness. They were tacit, so Thomas did not know how to verbalize or talk about what was happening to him until the damage had been done.

Even then, the stealth nature of the spiritual proxy war that stood behind psychological phenomena, and Thomas's personality trait of wanting to maintain his privacy and personal space at all costs, meant the true nature of what happened within became something Thomas could hardly entertain. It was a blind spot, something others were aware of but Thomas wasn't. Toward the end of his life, there were red flags others could see, like his recreational use of prescription medications, but Thomas couldn't detect these red flags.

FINDING NEW LIFE AFTER THE DEATH OF MY SON

◊ ◊ ◊

To answer the third question about the long-term impact that Thomas's dream portfolio had on him, I need to digress and return to Thomas's story along the Outer Labyrinth of daily life. Thomas started Del Mar Middle School in Longmont, Colorado, in the fall of 2013. The school principal was a retired US Marine who had zero tolerance for bullying. That September, I got a call from the school saying Thomas was being bullied by a guy named Paul and his friends, and the principal wanted to meet with us. I talked to Thomas about this, and he told me Paul and his friends all came from the same elementary school so they knew each other before coming to Del Mar. For reasons that are still unknown, they started picking on Thomas and bullying him. They called him weird and stupid, and they started pushing him around physically and hitting him when the teachers weren't looking. Thomas said other kids didn't like him. He was different and didn't fit in; he felt weird, but he didn't know why. Thomas also told the principal that if the bullying stopped, then things would go much better for him at school.

When I arrived at the principal's office for the meeting, Paul and Thomas were sitting awkwardly at a table in the principal's office waiting for me to join them. The principal led Thomas and Paul through a process that reminded me of Stephan Covey's fifth habit—seek first to understand and then to be understood.[133] Paul agreed to stop bullying Thomas, and Thomas agreed to let the principal know if things didn't get better. Paul and Thomas shook hands, agreed to these terms, and promised to be accountable for doing them. The meeting ended with smiles, and a sense that things had been settled between the two boys and boundaries for going forward had been established. I felt as good as I could about the meeting's outcome, and on the way home in the truck, I asked Thomas to keep me posted on how things were going moving forward. I also followed up periodically by asking Thomas if things had improved with Paul and his friends at school. Thomas assured me things were better and that he and Paul had become "friends" of sorts.

One night that November, Thomas came into my home office and told me that a friend of his showed him a scary picture of someone who looked like Freddie Kruger from the movie series *A Nightmare on Elm Street*. He said he was too afraid to sleep in his room down in the basement. "Papa, I want to sleep on the floor in your office," he said, "so I'm right across the hall from your bedroom." I was determined to help Thomas and support him in any way I could, so I agreed. What I realize now but didn't suspect then was that the bullying didn't stop. It morphed, went underground, and happened when teachers weren't looking, sometimes even off the school campus.

Thomas came to me again a few weeks later, and we recorded the following dream he'd had the night before.

> I was hanging out in my room with my friends from Del Mar, and we were just talking, and all of a sudden, they turned into cloaked men, and they're coming at me to get me like Paul, and it really creeped me out because it always seemed like they had my back, and the dream ends.

Looking back now in the third year after his death, I see the connection between him being bullied by Paul and his friends at school and the cloaked man dream we recorded that day. Prior to going to Del Mar, Thomas was attacked and threatened by the dark forces of evil, death, and destruction along the Inner Labyrinth of his dreams. Now, he was also being attacked and threatened along the Outer Labyrinth of his day-to-day life. The circle was complete between what Jung called the Spirit of the Depths and the Spirit of the Times. For reasons I can't fathom, I failed to see the connection then, but I can't help but see it now.

Thomas slept on the floor of my office for a year. It was not until November 2014 that he told me he was ready to move back downstairs to his bedroom—that he'd gotten over his fear of the picture he was shown. About three weeks later, I was on my annual retreat in Aspen and my own unconscious, in resonance with his, sent me a message in the form the dream below:

> I was in a car with Thomas, and he was driving. I was in the passenger seat, and there may have been another younger child in the back seat. We had left some place I knew in the dream but can't remember now, and we were driving along on a freeway in some

really big city, and all of a sudden, I'm looking around me and realize I don't know where we are. I said something like, "Thomas, I think we're lost," and I'm not sure whether he had noticed that himself and didn't want to say anything, or whether he had not actually noticed it until I said something. He didn't say anything in response, so I said, "Pull over," meaning pull the car over so we can stop and figure out where we are. He pulled over, and once we were stopped, a car pulled up next to us that reminded me of an old red Rambler like we used to have when I was a little boy. Two kids jumped out of the car and walked up to our car and said to Thomas something like, "Dude, you forgot this," and they handed him a black helmet like you'd use for skateboarding. The dream ends, and I'm thankful that these kids cared enough to follow us to return Thomas's black helmet.

After recording this dream, I reflected on the fourth guiding principle, namely that the primary focus of this dream was intrapsychic and described what was going on in my head, not Thomas's head. This dream disclosed my inner responses to people and situations in the world, and the forces and directionality of my personal and collective unconscious, rather than imparting clairvoyant insight about Thomas and the world around me. Although my unconscious life was the primary focus of the dream, my sense was that it might be revealing my inner response to something that was happening to Thomas. As Jung explained, "The dream is the unconscious reaction to a conscious situation. A conscious situation is followed by a reaction of the unconscious in the form of a dream, whose elements point clearly, whether in a complementary or a compensatory way, to the impression received during the day."[134]

There was something that bothered me about the dream, something I could not explain. I returned home from Aspen the day before Thanksgiving Day. I didn't say anything about the dream to Thomas, but the images of him driving, us being lost, him not being aware we were lost, and the two kids following us because Thomas had "forgotten" (i.e., lost consciousness about) a black helmet (i.e., a link to Darth Vader and the cloaked man dreams) in a childhood activity he'd learned at a young age (i.e., skateboarding) bothered me deeply.

On the following Saturday, Thomas and I went to the Pearl Street Mall in Boulder for our annual Christmas shopping day so he could buy presents for Elin. Over snacks, I shared the dream with Thomas and asked him if it might be telling me something about him in real life. "Are you doing okay, son?" I asked, searching for insight. "Are you lost, Thomas? I've noticed how you've stopped listening to Christian music since you've gone to Del Mar, and you've gotten more secular in the other things you do."

"No, Papa," he quickly responded. "I'm doing fine," he concluded.

I searched my heart and mind for something that would resonate with his response and soothe the nagging feeling I had about the dream. I sensed no relief from my inner quandary.

So, I asked him again. "Are you sure you're okay, son? Are you lost?"

Once again, his answer was, "No, Papa. I'm doing fine."

So, I dropped it, not wanting to nag him. We finished our drinks, watched the Christmas parade of lights move through the Pearl Street Mall area of Boulder, went Christmas shopping, and had a great time.

Three days later, I got the following email message from Thomas's counselor at Del Mar Middle School:

> Hi Ms. Larson and Mr. Bodnarczuk—I apologize for the urgency of this message. I need to connect with you as soon as possible to discuss something Thomas is sharing with another student here on campus. He is discussing harming himself and I would like to have a meeting with at least one of you. Please give me a call to let me know when you could be available.

I called him as soon as I got the email, and over the phone, he told me Thomas had been telling his friends he was depressed, he was cutting himself with a knife, and he was threatening to commit suicide by hanging himself with a belt that he hid in his closet. This was the same way one of Thomas's favorite actors and comedians, Robin Williams, had committed suicide just three months prior. Thomas had all the warning signs—he talked about suicide, he had a plan, he had the resources needed to carry out the plan. All of this happened behind the scenes, with Elin and me having no warning signs along the Outer Labyrinth of everyday life other than the dream I had in Aspen two weeks earlier.

I could not wrap my mind around what I was hearing. I thought, *This can't be happening to me.* "Those scratches must be from our dog," I responded to the counselor. "He likes to jump up on people, and he scratches them."

"I can assure you, Mr. Bodnarczuk, that once you see these marks, you'll know that they're not from your dog," he asserted with confidence and finality. When I got to school and saw the deep bloodied cuts on Thomas's wrists, I was shocked. He kept them hidden by wearing numerous wristbands, something many kids his age were doing.

Thomas and I walked from the counselor's office to my truck in silence. When we got into the vehicle, still in shock from what I'd just heard and seen, I said softly, "Thomas, let's talk when we get home, son. But I need you to tell me the whole truth."

Thomas nodded in assent. "Okay, Papa," he replied as we pulled out of the parking lot and headed home.

Once we were back to our house on McIntosh Drive, we walked to the dining room and sat at the table. "Okay, son. Start from the beginning," I said as I got ready to take notes about what he told me.

"I've been depressed since sixth grade when Paul and the other kids started bullying me, calling me names, and making me feel like an outsider," Thomas said. "I woke up one morning in the middle of sixth grade and didn't want to go to school anymore because I was depressed."

"Okay," I responded as I continued taking notes, "tell me more, son."

Thomas poured his heart out to me about how the bullying got better but didn't stop.

"Why didn't you tell me or your counselor, Thomas, like we agreed?" I probed, heartbroken about the devastating impact this had had on him.

"There was nothing you could do to stop it, Papa. I had to work this out myself the best I could."

I didn't like his response, but I knew he was right. It's one of the most difficult things parents go through—watching their kids find their own way, learning to stand up for themselves, trying to fit into what seems like an endless flow of relationships, social situations, and cultural norms that help to shape and define who they become in life.

"When did you start cutting yourself and talking about suicide?" I asked, wanting to understand the things that led to what we discussed that day with his counselor.

"I was playing my video game *Club Penguin* with some kids I met online," he explained, "and we were talking about the game in the chat room for a while, and then one girl said she was depressed. Another girl said that she was depressed, too, and was cutting herself, and then I said I was depressed as well."

I paused to capture what Thomas was saying in my notes and then asked, "But when did you start cutting yourself?"

"About a month ago," he responded looking down, confused about what was happening to him and ashamed of what he had done.

"Is there anything that Mom and I can do to help you, Thomas?" I gave him a hug as I spoke, trying to comfort and reassure him.

"No," he responded, "you're both doing a good job."

I quickly replied, "Is there anything we're doing to make matters worse?"

He shook his head from side to side. "No, Papa."

My sense was that he really meant what he said.

"What you put in your head helps to shape and define who you are, Thomas," I said. "It's the same thing with the music you listen to and the people you hang out with. I don't want you going out onto that *Club Penguin* site anymore, son," I concluded with a tone of finality.

"Okay, Papa."

I gave Thomas a green, spiral-bound notebook and told him I wanted him to start writing out what he was feeling and drawing pictures of anything that was bothering him inside and express himself.

"It'll be your private journal, son, and Mom and I won't look at it."

From that point on, Thomas began meeting regularly with a counselor at school, and I decided to find him a therapist to work with. After he died, I looked through his journal in search of answers for what had happened to him. In the first days after giving him the journal, he drew a picture and labeled it a "black hole," and he drew pictures of himself with cuts on his arms, and another picture of him standing in a group of kids with a downward pointing arrow with a caption that read, "Falling inside a black hole."

Thomas worked with several therapists over the months ahead and seemed to be making good progress in dealing with what troubled him. I gave each therapist a summary of what Thomas had been through, but most of them dismissed the significance of his dreams, focusing instead on more standard approaches to treatment like cognitive behavioral therapy and dialectical behavior therapy because that's what they knew, and because that's what was generally accepted and reimbursed by most healthcare providers.

After moving to California, I found a clinical psychologist named Katie who was a Christian, was familiar with Jung's psychology, and understood the importance of dreams in the therapeutic process. I told her about Thomas's cloaked man dreams and encouraged her multiple times over the course of her work with Thomas to go deeper and challenge Thomas to reflect on the underlying issues that were causing his day-to-day problems in life. On one occasion when I asked her to go deeper with Thomas and work on his underlying issues, Katie looked at me and said, "Mark, Thomas is a very private person. It's taken a long time for me to earn his trust and get him to open up. I can only work on what he brings to me." I knew she was right, and I was thankful for the progress Thomas had made in their work together.

Looking back, I see now that the images of death and destruction in Thomas's cloaked man dream series had a significant long-term impact on his life. They became an inner black hole, a dark destructive force of death that drew Thomas inward. I have no answer as to why Thomas's life turned out like this. But I know that the suffering God who is sovereign over all of history determined the length of Thomas's life—the number of his days, hours, and minutes. That same God promised that He would never leave him or forsake him, that He would be with Thomas to the very end of his life. Contemplating this takes me to the depths of my sorrow and grief about the enormous, irreplaceable loss of my son. But at the same time, this biblically based truth gives me an equally deep sense of relief from self-condemnation and blame for Thomas's death. I also feel the peace of God that surpasses all understanding guarding my heart and mind in Christ Jesus intermittently as I continue to process the grief and pain that will never go away.

◇ ◇ ◇

There was one more thing I needed to know. For a long time, I wondered what was happening with my boy in the final days of his life. Were there any meaningful connections between the powerful shaping forces of death and destruction in his cloaked man dreams and the struggles he was facing at the end of his short life? What I already knew was that Thomas came home at 9:10 p.m. on Saturday, May 1, 2021, and after Elin and I chatted with him for a few minutes, he went to his room. That's the last time I saw my son alive. But I had his cell phone, so I downloaded the data from his text messages, and I was able to reconstruct the last minutes of Thomas's life here on earth.

The data download from his cell phone showed that at about 9:30 p.m., Thomas ordered some food from DoorDash, and then he began texting a friend named David who worked as a chef at a high-end restaurant in Los Gatos. David wanted to get together after he got off work, but Thomas was tired and wanted to relax, surf the web, watch a movie, eat his food, and chill out with the Xanax pill he bought on Snapchat the day before. Thomas took the counterfeit Xanax pill and continued texting David, not knowing it would kill him. Here's a slightly redacted version of the last text exchange he had while he was dying:

David: I hate this f***ing job (9:13 p.m.)
David: Yo you want to meet up (9:15 p.m.)
Thomas: What time (9:25 p.m.)
David: I'm not off till midnight (9:27 p.m.)
Thomas: Sorry dude I'm chillin tonight (9:30 p.m.)
David: I want out of here rn (9:40 p.m.)
David: I'll f***ing die if I don't get out of here (9:41 p.m.)
Thomas: that sentence is my whole life (9:47 p.m.)
David: Rip (9:56 p.m.)

Thomas's autopsy report said that Thomas died in the self-designed theater of his bedroom at about 10:00 p.m. on May 1, 2021.

David: Yo lets meet up (11:37 p.m.)

On May 2, 2021, I found Thomas dead in his bed at 9:58 a.m. Sunday morning, and then David continues.

FINDING NEW LIFE AFTER THE DEATH OF MY SON

David: Il take that as a naw (5:31 p.m.)

On May 3, 2021, David continues.

David: Hommmmme (10:27 a.m.)
David: I'm bored (10:27 a.m.)
David: Pick the f*** up (10:28 a.m.)
David: Hommmmmmmmme (10:29 a.m.)
David: I.wish you were here bruh (10:30 a.m.)
David: I have not heard from you in a while I do hope you are ok. (5:30 p.m.)
David: Just call me and I'm there if you need assistance (5:32 p.m.)
David: I'm always here for you thomas (5:34 p.m.)

I committed myself to knowing my son deeply, having a good relationship with him, and understanding who he was as a unique person. In many ways, Thomas was a twenty-first-century hippie, like the old man in the orange jumpsuit from his dream. He was like one of the young people in the 1960s Jesus People revolution. He was an outsider who befriended other outsiders. He cared about, and had compassion for, those who didn't fit in—he took them into his circle of friends out of true empathy because he'd been there himself. Like his namesake, the biblical Thomas, my son lived in the essential tension between an honest faith in God and honest doubt. Thomas had character, a conscience, and a deep sense of integrity that he evidenced as a commitment to course correction, to coming back to the principles, values, and inner truths that he believed after he'd gotten off track.

Thomas was an edgy iconoclast who stood apart from many societal expectations and exhibited an unconventional type of wisdom. He knew where the bleeding edge of music was, what was new and exciting in many musical genres, and he helped others go there too. Thomas was a truly imaginative and unconventional thinker who stood outside the sociocultural context of the crowd. This gave him a unique vantage point for insights and commentary on people, situations, culture, and the nagging existential questions of life, things we often discussed during our bonding time together. But most importantly, Thomas was a Christian, a citizen of heaven making his way through this world. Like the rest of us Christians, his challenge was how to be in the world but not of the world, how to live within the all-pervading sociocultural force of the Spirit of the Times but not be assimilated into it.

Thomas's clinical psychologist, Katie, was also a Christian who cared deeply about Thomas, and she helped him work through many of the issues that caused his depression. With his depression under control, Katie and Thomas were getting a handle on his anxiety and tendency to catastrophize and see the glass half empty rather than half full and envision the worst-case scenario in challenging situations. Shortly after Thomas's death, I reached out to Katie and asked her to tell me how she saw Thomas in the last days of his life. Here's what she sent me in an email:

> Recently, a lot of our conversations had focused on his task of individuating and creating his own identity and he felt excited because he had always wanted to be in charge of his own life and finally felt that he was having opportunities of empowerment to make his own choices and be his own man. Previously, he had shared that he might want to be an investigative journalist, but never figured out how that might fit into the life he envisioned for himself, living in the mountains away from people. Amidst our conversations about how he was learning to be independent and find his own way in life, he was surprised to find a deep interest in ancient religions. He had started watching some documentaries on their cultures and customs and found himself more inspired by that than journalism. I remember laughing with him about how he wanted to study religion and be a writer, and how surprised he was by this because it was so similar to your life trajectory, Mark. He noticed how, once he started to become more independent and really explore his own identity, he was actually realizing how similar he was to you, his dad. He accepted it and even looked forward to having more to share with you.

As I reflect on Katie's email today three years after losing my son, it takes me back to our kitchen table discussion where Thomas wanted to take a pill to feel better rather than going on a decades-long journey. His life reminds me of the parable of the two sons that Jesus told.

FINDING NEW LIFE AFTER THE DEATH OF MY SON

"A man had two sons, and he came to the first and said, 'Son, go work today in the vineyard.' But he replied, 'I do not want to.' Yet afterward he regretted it and went. And the man came to his second son and said the same thing; and he replied, 'I will, sir'; and yet he did not go. Which of the two did the will of his father?" [The religious teachers] said, "The first." (Matthew 21:28–31)

Thomas said he didn't want to go on the journey to find his destiny in life, to become the person he was meant to be, but in the end he went. I'm so proud of my son. I wish he were here with me, so I could tell him that.

Thomas's memorial bench on the north shore of McIntosh Lake in Longmont, Colorado

CHAPTER 34

THE JOURNEY HOME

December 2, 2023 (2 Years, 30 Weeks, and 4 Days After)

As I've walked this long, arduous, and painful path since Thomas died, I've read dozens of memoirs by people who have lost children. I've reviewed the spectrum of books by grief experts, psychologists, thanatologists, and much of the Christian literature on walking with God through pain, suffering, and grief. I've been in support groups with grieving parents and at conferences sponsored by the Compassionate Friends, an organization with tens of thousands of members, each of whom has lost a child. For me, the process of surviving the death of my son, finding new life in the wake of this unspeakable loss, and now navigating the journey home has come down to the kind of grievance story I create. I see this working in two ways.

First, I've come to see the importance of processing the pain and grief of Thomas's loss as part of the ongoing, lifelong flow of individuation rather than as a separate, stand-alone thing called a grieving process that comes and goes in times of tragedy and loss.[135] Thomas's life and death are part of the journey of discovering our calling and destiny in life, the person we were meant to be in God. The unfolding of his story is part of the destiny I've had in God along the Inner Labyrinth from the beginning of time and the destiny I'm creating along the Outer Labyrinth with my choices. Don't get me wrong. Thomas's death has been the single most traumatic and devastating loss I've ever experienced on my fifty-nine-year journey of individuation and faith. But as I mentioned in chapter 1 about weeping through my journey of faith, God has been preparing me to survive Thomas's death, and making me strong enough to tell this story, for more than forty years.[136]

Second, I've learned how important it is for my grievance story to be as truthful as possible, because our language shapes our reality. I first learned this while writing the victim impact statement to be read at Adam's sentencing hearing. As I told the judge, my grievance story must be a truthful rendering of the circumstances surrounding Thomas's death, since I'll be using it for the rest of my life every time someone asks me "What happened to Thomas?" or when someone innocently asks "Do you have children?" What I knew back then beyond a shadow of a doubt at the sentencing, and still know now, is only the truth will set us free (John 8:32). So, my grievance story must not minimize the role Adam played in causing Thomas's death, the role Thomas had in causing his own death, and the role the Mexican cartels played within a *Zeitgeist* of a cold, calculating, and unforgiving world where thousands of fentanyl poisonings are traceable to counterfeit prescription medications being made widely available for purchase on Snapchat.

After the sentencing, writing this memoir led me to search for an even truer version of the grievance story than the one I espoused at the sentencing hearing. I used research and historical analysis based on a biblical approach to Jung's psychology and the process of active imagination as scaffolding to descend to deeper, unknown levels of my heart and mind. Those results were described above where I explored the role that I, as Thomas's father, played in causing his death, the role that personal and archetypal psychological forces in Thomas's dreams played in causing his death, the role that the spiritual proxy-based forces of evil and sin played as they waged war against him, and the role that a sovereign-suffering God played in the life and death of His child, Thomas Larson Bodnarczuk.

There was one more thing God was leading me to add to the grievance story, but I had a profound inner resistance to doing it. I knew that what He wanted was the single biggest barrier to me moving beyond accepting the reality of Thomas's death, to embracing it as the path that God had called me to walk in life. Yet, I also knew deep within that without this important dimension, the grievance story would not be complete. It would be true, but it would not be the whole truth. God was leading me to include the positive things and blessings that have resulted from Thomas's death. He wanted people to know that He was causing "all things to work together for good to those who love God, to those who are called according to His purpose" (Romans 8:28). Part of me didn't want to do it. It felt that doing so would betray the memory of my son.

For the first three years after Thomas died, I could not bring myself to talk about it publicly. One-on-one and small group discussions with family and friends were fine, but not in front of a group of people. The inner resistance to doing it was enormous. I had friends who had lost one or more children to counterfeit pills and fentanyl poisoning who had started nonprofit organizations to get the word out to other kids and save lives. They asked me if I would be willing to be interviewed for a video about Thomas's death to support the cause. I always said no, but I could never explain why. I just kept looking to the Lord as my primary support and quietly focused on rebuilding my life with Elin back in Colorado as I worked on writing this book, hoping it might become my way of telling others about Thomas's life and death, and the grace, forgiveness, and faithfulness of God throughout my life.

The first time I spoke about Thomas's death publicly was at the sentencing hearing in a courtroom filled with people who were there to remember Thomas's life. The second time I spoke to a crowd about Thomas's death was about a month later, when I introduced the president of Song for Charlie at the Twin Peaks Rotary Club.

Looking back, I realize I could not have told my grievance story back then because it was still taking shape. At the time, it focused solely on loss and being wounded by Thomas's death. It contained no hint of the biblical truth that God was, in fact, causing things to work together for good—for positive ends. I've become a much more empathetic caring, tolerant, and loving person as a direct result of Thomas's death. His loss continues to have an enormous positive impact on me and countless others. The death of my only begotten son has also deepened my understanding of the price God paid, with the sacrifice of His only begotten son.

So, the pain and grief of losing Thomas will always be there—always. But that's not the whole truth. The person I've become because of Thomas's death, and as a direct result of the Spirit of God working through the Self and the Anima to heal and transform my wounded soul, has been woven into the fabric of my grievance story. James 1:2–4 affirms the truth that suffering has great value when he said, "Consider it all joy . . . when you encounter various trials, knowing that the testing of your faith produces endurance. And let endurance have its perfect result, so that you may be perfect and complete, lacking in nothing."

But this is not just a biblical view. In his book entitled *The Importance of Suffering*, research psychologist and anthropologist James Davies refers to this as "productive suffering," affirming the value and meaning of suffering and emotional distress. Davies critiques the clinical view that many Western psychotherapists hold that suffering should be treated by helping the patient learn how to remove or manage the negative emotions that result from adversity. Echoing one of the founders of psychology, William James, Davies argues that suffering "helps us apprehend new portions of reality."[137]

Robert Emmons, a professor in the department of psychology at the University of California, Davis, argues that suffering changes our priorities and philosophies, which positively impacts our goals and direction in life.[138] He sorts goals into four basic categories: (1) personal achievement and happiness, (2) relationships and intimacy, (3) religion and spirituality, and (4) generativity, which is making a meaningful, lasting contribution to the world. Emmons argues that most people invest the most time, energy, and resources into the first two goals, and these are the most vulnerable to adverse circumstances in life. I have invested the most time and energy in the third goal (religion and spirituality), and God is now leading me to focus on the fourth goal of making meaningful and lasting contributions to the world by sharing Thomas's story with others.

New York University social psychologist Jonathan Haidt discusses the "uses of adversity" and the positive value of posttraumatic growth.[139] After raising the question "Must we suffer?" he describes something called the adversity hypothesis that has a weak and strong version. "In the weak version, adversity can lead to growth, strength, joy, and self-improvement, by the three mechanisms of posttraumatic growth described above. . . . The strong version of the hypothesis is more unsettling: It states that people must endure adversity to grow, and that the highest levels of growth and development are *only* open to those who have faced and overcome adversity."[140] One of the most profound examples is captured in Viktor Frankl's book *Man's Search for Meaning*, which recounts how the psychotherapeutic method of logotherapy emerged from the horrors of Auschwitz. There are many, many others.

Dr. Paul Brand and Philip Yancey's 1997 book calls this "the gift of pain."[141] Brand's fifty-year career as a physician working with leprosy patients in India and the United States convinced him that pain was truly one of God's greatest gifts to us. "As an indicator that lets us know something is wrong, pain has a value that becomes clearest in its absence."[142] Pastor and theologian Tim Keller describes how "God uses suffering to remove our weaknesses and build us up."[143]

Including my Romans 8:28 experience in my grievance story added an objective perspective that moved the narrative from being focused solely on loss and acknowledged the victory God has given me over Thomas's death. I was tested and prevailed. I endured the pain and suffering of having the most precious thing in life taken away from me by inner and outer forces of evil and sin, and yet I am a better person for it. Keller provides a vision for the ultimate redemption of pain, suffering, and evil when he asks, "But why could it not be that God allowed evil because it will bring us all to a far greater glory and joy than we would have had otherwise? Isn't it possible that the eventual glory and joy we will know will be infinitely greater than it would have been had there been no evil?"[144] Given these insights and a changed heart and mind, I don't know where God is leading me on the rest of my journey home, but I refuse to squander the gift of pain and grief that Thomas's death has given me.[145]

Thomas's L.O.G. placemat made by a special friend

CHAPTER 35

WHAT OTHERS HAVE SAID ABOUT THOMAS

Elin Larson

December 21, 2023 (2 Years, 33 Weeks, and 2 Days After)

In the days and weeks after Thomas's death, Mark and I longed to know that we were not alone in our memories of our son, that he was a special person whose impact would outlive his far too short life. I identified a memorial website we could use, and we discussed the vision for the site as we drove to Carmel on May 9, 2021, my first Mother's Day without my precious son. Our goal was to gather as much information as we could about Thomas's life in a central place, one where family, friends, and people who didn't know Thomas could learn about his life and come together as an online community to honor his memory.

During those first days after Thomas died, Mark and I desperately sought to preserve his memory so his brief but impactful life would not be forgotten in the relentless march of time. We contacted everyone we could and asked them to go out to the memorial site and post something. For people who knew Thomas, we asked that they read the main page, reflect on their interactions with him, and then write meaningful stories about Thomas. As Mark and I stated in the email we sent out: "Your memories of our son are all memories that we don't have because we weren't there. If you don't write them down, they will die with Thomas and you." For people who did not know Thomas, our email asked them to read about his life and then post a few words about what they read in support for Mark and me.

Many people responded. There are currently about six hundred people who have access to Thomas's site, with three-hundred and ninety tributes and stories on the site. While many of them are words of comfort for Mark and me in the tragic loss of our son, others are stories that describe the impact Thomas had on people's lives that they will carry into their futures. The memorial site has created a historical repository of Thomas's life that is priceless to Mark and me. As C. S. Lewis said in the movie *Shadowlands*, "We read to know we are not alone."

In addition to the posts of others, I used my "life chapter" posts on the memorial site, and numerous logs in my personal journal, to express and process my grief about Thomas's death. These posts and logs have also become a historical record of the details of my grief journey. But there were times when my grief and pain were so deep, so intense, so overwhelming that I wondered, much like Mark, if I would survive the death of my son. I fearlessly sought after and demanded answers to this nagging question, with Mark by my side. We were on the same platform and moved through the last three years of the process of inner healing and transformation as a team. Many couples divorce after losing a child, and the main reason that happens is because they grieve in different ways and at different rates. That was not the case with Mark and me. We were partners in this tragedy, helping one another and being there for each other as we each allowed the other to grieve in their own way.

As Mark mentioned above, Thomas's sudden and tragic death pulled us down into a personal hell that is difficult, if not impossible, for a person who has not lost a child to understand. But Mark and I did not return empty-handed from this harrowing journey, as evidenced by the enormous inner healing and transformation he and I have experienced over the past three years. What I've included below are slightly edited versions of what others have said about Thomas.

FRIENDS

Thomas was a compassionate friend. He had a soft heart, especially for those who were outsiders, who were left out, who didn't fit in, and who didn't have many friends. This was echoed in several stories from his friends. One friend Thomas had known since first grade said:

> I've never been good with writing endings, so I'll just say this. Thomas was not only my best friend, but he was my first real friend, even after he moved, we'd still talk over email and YouTube and share goofy stories and internet memes with each other. My one

regret is that I never got to tell him how much I actually loved and appreciated him. But at the same time, I think he knew.

Another friend dating back to elementary school wrote this on what would have been Thomas's twentieth birthday:

I miss you buddy. Happy birthday. I know you're having the best party up there with all the angels and I look forward to the day when we can celebrate together again. Until then I know I have you watching over me every day and I'll always have a piece of you in the person I've turned out to be. I love you so much and I can't thank you enough for being my best friend.

A middle school friend recalled how Thomas reached out to him when Thomas saw he was alone:

It wasn't until the start of the eighth grade when Thomas and I properly introduced ourselves to one another. I was sitting alone in a far corner of the field, since I didn't have many friends and my home life wasn't the best. Thomas came over to me and sat down. Didn't say a word. He just sat. And looked at me. The next day I sat in the same place, and Thomas came and sat right where he sat the day before. His friends would watch him from a distance, confused why he was sitting next to me, but after a few days of Thomas silently sitting next to me, his friends came over. We spoke for the first time, shared our names, and the group fed me their lunches. It was the most meaningful start to a friendship I have ever had. He barely knew me besides our encounter in the sixth grade, yet he sat next to me, silently, until I said something to him. We quickly hit it off and our friendship blossomed into one of the most beautiful friendships I have ever and will ever experience in time. Thomas taught me many things about compassion, about interpersonal relationships, about myself, and about the world. Thomas cared about the people around him and brought people together. I would not be nearly as close with some of the friends that I have today if not for him. Thomas was like the glue that held the group together.

His loss is like my world and the worlds of his family and friend's slowly caving in on itself until bitter realization sets in. Thomas was the kindest of souls and is a man that I will always aspire to be for the rest of my life. May he finally sleep.

Another close friend Thomas had known since middle school wrote:

There is not a day, not an hour, that I don't think about Thomas. I still half-expect his name to light up my phone, and the ways my life has been affected by his life and death are infinite.

Some of Thomas's high school friends wrote:

One of my last interactions with Thomas was a conversation that he wouldn't let end until I said I loved him, and he was like "okay there it's ended" then proceeded to send a meme a few minutes later. I'll never forget it. I'll never forget him. I'll never forget the stories, the laughs, the adventures, or his corny sense of humor. Without him, I wouldn't be the person I am today. So, I'm thankful for the time I had with him.

Thomas was always such a bright light in any room he entered. His intelligence was admirable, and he was always willing to help his peers. I had many classes with Thomas, and he always found a way to make them enjoyable and fun with his amazing sense of humor that everyone, except the teachers sometimes, loved so much. I never knew much about Thomas's life or what made him the way that he was, but I could tell it was something special. He was unapologetically himself and never judged anyone else for how they were. That was very rare, especially in our generation. The world needs more people like him, and my deepest condolences go out to his family. He truly had a beautiful soul that I wish could have been shared with more people. Rest in peace Thomas, you will be missed dearly.

He was the most genuine and accepting person I had ever met in my life. I wish that I had understood at the time how rare a person like Thomas is. He was a truly wonderful guy in every way. Rest in peace Thomas, we all loved you so much.

Thomas was also very involved in his church high school ministry and participated in many high school retreats and mission trips. One of his friends from this group wrote the following:

> I've read all these lovely stories and memories of Tommy, from Colorado and California, reminding me of many moments I shared with Tommy at youth group. Each Mexico trip was an amazing experience to be a part of and Tommy always had such a positive attitude and ability to help with any and every task. The youth group also has two retreats during the school year called LOG—Love of God. We went away for a weekend together, with no phone service and lots of spiritual growth. On these retreats we had small groups to carry out meaningful discussion throughout the weekend. On Friday night the groups were assigned and stuck together for the entirety of the weekend. My junior year, I had the privilege of being in a small group with Tommy. On the last day of the retreat, we write our future-selves a letter that will be mailed to us before the next retreat about 6 months later. In addition to a letter to yourself, your small group friends write a short message to you as well. Earlier this week I was luckily able to find my letter from three years ago, when Tommy was in my group. He wrote to me: "You care so much about everyone here and everyone here cares so much about you." I cannot explain how these words have impacted me. He was so kind and thoughtful with every word. He knew what to say to make people feel welcomed, happy, loved, and respected. He cared so much about the youth group, and we all care so deeply for him.

Thomas went on numerous camping trips and adventures with his Boy Scout troop. One of the younger members of his troop wrote about the role model that Thomas was to him:

> When I first read this beautiful eulogy, I wrote a short blurb about his impact on my life but in the weeks since I have struggled with what else to write. I have thought about the positive impact that Thomas had on both me and those around me that also knew him. That's what I think is most important in remembering him. His

impact, what he showed others, and how he impacted their lives. The story that always comes to mind first for me when thinking of Thomas was when we were sitting in a cave-like dugout in Castle Rock in Colorado after a long day of rock climbing. This was toward the end of our two-week scout trip, and we had spent lots of time together already. During our conversation, I expressed some concerns of mine about entering high school. He gave well thought out and genuine responses to my questions. Thomas throughout our time together always was a role model to me. He showed me what it meant to be a real man. To be sympathetic, kind, thoughtful and so much more. Thomas was a one-of-a-kind individual. I appreciate the time that we spent together and the impact that he had on me.

PASTORS, YOUTH GROUP LEADERS, AND OTHER ADULTS

It was not only Thomas's peers who wrote of his impact on the memorial site. From the time he was a little boy, Thomas was wise beyond his years. He could converse and interact with adults as easily as he could with his peers. Many adults who knew him posted their life experience with him on his memorial site. Some of them knew Thomas since he was an infant and watched him grow up. Others were his teachers who had him in class for a year, and yet others who wrote tributes never knew him while he was alive and learned about his life only from his memorial site.

A friend of mine whom I have known since long before Thomas was born said:

> Thomas was a guest at our son's wedding in May 2011, and his kind nature was on display there. My mother, then in her 90s and in the first stages of dementia, kept telling me she wanted to dance with Thomas. Thomas was not shy or reluctant about the request, but got on the dance floor, held hands with my mother and danced with a smile on his face. And as is the case with people suffering from dementia, when the dance was over, she again said she wanted to dance with Thomas. And so they danced again. This wedding was the last outing my mother would take, and we are grateful that a little boy made an elderly woman very happy at her last dance.

FINDING NEW LIFE AFTER THE DEATH OF MY SON

Thomas's history classes in middle and high school were among his favorites. A high school history teacher of his wrote:

Thomas was a student in my very first class as a teacher, second period World History 2017–2018. While the class was clearly too easy for him, he enjoyed being there and brought a positive, humorous energy every day. As a tenth grader, Thomas was very much a deep thinker and loved to ask me questions and have conversations either about history or just life in general. He always had a unique perspective about everything. More than anything else, the Thomas I know is 100% a true original. As an eleventh and twelfth grader, he continued to visit my classroom at lunch to deliver very specific, very "Thomas" jokes, observations, and musings. I still have emails from him in my inbox concocting detailed theories to explain mundane things with dry wit, and I was just recently listening to an album he had recommended. At the end of his sophomore year, Thomas gave me an incredibly thoughtful and humorous handwritten letter which hangs next to my classroom desk to this day. He is, of course, a beautiful writer. He will be deeply missed and his positive impact on those around them, including this history teacher, will not be forgotten. Rest in peace, Thomas.

As we shared Thomas's memorial site with friends and colleagues who had never known him, we were grateful to read tributes about the impact that just learning about Thomas's life had on others. One such tribute read:

Mark and Elin, I never had the joy of meeting Thomas and wish I would have. From all the pictures and tributes, he feels like a wonderful young man I would have enjoyed talking with and learning from. I thank you both for sharing Thomas's story and life with us, it has changed my outlook, and a day has not gone by without thinking about you and your family.

Thomas's pastors had deep insights into his faith from their interactions with him in church, youth-group, and on mission trips. Shortly after his death, one of his pastors wrote:

MARK BODNARCZUK

I heard about Tommy Bodnarczuk before I met him. His father Mark was already here in California and was scouting out a new church home. Tommy and Elin moved to join him and started a new season of life in the Bay Area. I heard about Tommy before I met him because his Dad was so proud of him, was so full of hope for him, and wanted to set everything up for Tommy and their family to flourish. I was always proud that our church was a "home away from home" for Tommy, and I loved watching him make friendships within the youth group and beyond. Tommy was part of a group of kids who would attend worship on Sunday mornings every week and would sit up on the balcony of the church. I am sure that this was partially to be away from their parents (embarrassing!) and far from the pastors (boring!), but it was a way that they could be together, express something of their faith as it formed, and be consistent in this area of life. Tommy was a balcony person, not just because he sat up there on Sundays, but because of how he treated people. To me he seemed quiet, creative, and kind. He made friends with people who were different from him. He was part of large groups, but thrived with others, one-on-one, or even on his own. I remember talking with him at coffee hour after worship in the Social Hall of our church—I had seen him up on the balcony and wasn't sure he was really into it. But when I talked to him, he was so mature, beyond his years. He wanted me to know that he was glad to be there, that he had his friends, that he was open to all that was being discussed. Maybe Tommy was a balcony person in life because he had a higher view of what was going on around him. Not aloof, but thoughtful. He noticed people who were alone. He checked in with those who were struggling. He was encouraging to his pastor (me) just because he kept showing up and showing interest and showing love. I love the words of Psalm 121: "I lift my eyes up, up to the mountains, where does my help come from?" And I lift my eyes up in the church sanctuary with that line on my mind, and I see the place where Tommy would sit. Way up high. And I thank God for his life, even as it was cut much too short. I thank God that Tommy had the view of life while he was here from that balcony, but also that when he lifted his eyes up to the mountains, he knew where his help came from. In life and in death, Tommy Bodnarczuk is held in the arms of God. He has a new view now, from an even higher balcony, and I wonder what he sees. I hope he sees all of us here below, living our lives to the fullest, for the one who is not able to be with us. I hope he sees the love we show each other, even as we remember this beloved boy. I hope he sees the things that we will also one day see.

A youth group leader of Thomas's from his middle school years wrote:

Your son has always been amazing at being there for people when they needed him most. He was gifted at listening and always thought about others in a way that most cannot. I will cherish memories of our times hanging out together and driving out to Longmont to pick him up and hang at the park, our long conversations, and talks and memories we shared of our faith. Thanks for the many ways you raised your son to be a valuable part of our lives and in society. He will be missed and dearly loved from myself and those in our church body.

Another middle school youth group leader wrote:

Few kids that I worked with in my time at the church were as thoughtful and compassionate as Thomas. He was a gentle soul who was always willing to engage in deeper conversation (rare for a middle school student!) and was always listening (also rare). These are things to be treasured as we memorialize his life and the impact that he had on everyone in his life. He will be deeply missed.

Thomas was active in his high school youth group, as well, and one of his leaders had the following to say:

Over the too-few years that our paths on this earth crossed, I found Thomas, Tommy as we called him in the youth group most frequently, to be kindhearted, caring, funny, sassy, and supportive of his peers. I enjoyed talking music with him, trading bands back and forth—though he already knew 90% of my recommendations before I recommended them. His own music was beautiful as well, and I always loved hearing him play the guitar. In Mexico one year, we had a talent show, and he played a rendition of Tracy Chapman's Fast Car. I still maintain that his version is better than the original. I told him as much that day, and he laughed at me, but he played and sang that song with real passion and care. I'll never hear that song without thinking of Tommy. Our conversations had occasionally veered into the spiritual, and I know Tommy was a young man with deep faith who cared about his church family. The mark that Tommy left on our church, our Mexico trips, and our youth group is much larger than the lights he helped install in the Redwood Grove as part of his Eagle Scout Project. But those lights are worth mentioning. Tommy gave us the gift of that space during the current pandemic. The youth group especially has had the ability to meet in person more regularly and more impactfully, and every Sunday night, we meet in the glow and warmth under those lights. If ever there is a small flicker, I look around and see more than a few knowing nods and smiles in the group, and we share the knowledge that our friend has supplied us with this space, this glowing, beautiful place to gather together. Tommy, we miss you. Here at church, and in life, you are gone too soon from us. Thank you for your friendship, the band recommendations, and the light you left behind, both literally and figuratively. Until we meet again.

One of Thomas's other pastors from his high school years knew Thomas well from several mission trips to Mexico to build houses for families. She left a very thoughtful, moving tribute of several of her memories of him:

> Words are inadequate to describe the fullness and beauty of Tommy's too-short life and the pain of his tragic death, but they give us a way to curate memories into stories. Stories have the power to transform us, especially those that help us contemplate God's goodness demonstrated in the best of humankind in the world. Tommy

was an exceptional and loving young man who brought out the best in others and shared the best of himself. I'm one of the pastors at the church where Tommy actively participated together with his parents, and I was grateful to participate in Youth Mexico Mission trips which was where most of my memories of Tommy were formed. As any parent knows, some of the best connections are made on road trips driving kids to various destinations, and the same is true in ministry with youth. Here's my "road trip mix" of memories of Tommy:

Following His Own Beat. The week after Tommy's death, I was waiting to pick up a family member in in my car and began organizing loose CDs when I found Tommy's mix CD that he prepared for the road trip down to Mexico. This is a youth group tradition. I played this CD, and the sound brought me back. I remembered how when the other students heard some of his selections, they said "Hey, what's this?" Some songs they liked, and others not so much. I realized that Tommy's favorites weren't the standard hits, and I appreciated his willingness to not conform to everyone's taste. His music was also enjoyable listening for our long drive. Another song list memory is how some of the songs on the students' mix CDs might have had the tiniest subtle mumbled f-bombs. The students poked each other when I noted it and questioned it. I told them that I thought it was important to note that the artist used it in an angsty way and not in an angry or misogynistic way. In my rearview mirror, I saw Tommy nod and I realized that he understood and agreed with this important principle—and I also realized at once that probably not everyone in the car understood the word misogynistic, but of course Tommy understood.

Opening Up the Circle. Tommy was always attentive to the kids around him, always opening the circle a bit wider to let others in or navigating around the parameter of a group. Most young people don't notice others' needs quite like Tommy did. I'm fondly remembering the kind boy who made another student feel less isolated when a group moved to pile into another car on our way home, leaving others out. Tommy always sought to make everyone feel welcome.

Engaging with Adults. Tommy was poised and articulate around adults, and I think that in part that was due to his intelligence and his upbringing with Mark and Elin, but I think it was also part of the fabric of his character, to truly see and pay attention to others. I always found him thoughtful and comfortable and willing to connect with me, a pastor the age of his parents. Sometimes, as leaders and mentors in Bible studies and reflections, we hold back and let the youth take the lead in discussion, but Tommy kindly treated me like someone he needed to draw in.

Vulnerable and Open. In my mind, I'm remembering Tommy in the middle of the large tent in Mexico during our mission trip, as the kids put together a talent show of sorts as we waited out the rain. There were a number of fun and silly offerings, mostly in groups, then Tommy came forward alone to offer a song, vulnerable and brave. I thought to myself, "what a beautiful and brave soul."

Quietly Serving. I'm remembering the boy who kept working when others got distracted. I remember struggling with a load that was too ambitious for me. I stopped in the middle of the path. Tommy came from behind, quietly asked if I was okay, and smoothly took my load and carried it along with his own load. Maybe it is my own bias as a proud Eagle Scout mom, as Tommy probably had an innate bent for service, but I imagined I saw this influence on Tommy's formation.

Freshman Boys Forever. Tommy joined a rising cohort of boys in youth group who we affectionately called the "freshmen boys" throughout their years in youth group as they formed a larger than usual class and had a distinct personality—kind, silly, and prone to rolling around on the ground, like delightful but unruly puppies. In Mexico, they all drank large amounts of Mexican real sugar Coca-Cola, adding to the energy. Tommy would be with them, enjoying them, and adding his own thoughtfulness and a bit more seriousness to the mix. Tommy would be with this crew and would also gravitate to others. These boys have grown up over the years, once again freshmen but now as wonderful young men and college students. I believe that Tommy's legacy of love and kindness will leave a lasting impact on these young men forever.

I'm reminded of Paul's words to the Corinthians about the abiding power of love to help us through these days. "For now, we see in a mirror, dimly, but then we will see face to face. Now I know only in part; then I will know fully, even as I have been fully known. And now faith, hope, and love abide, these three; and the greatest of these is love" (1 Corinthians 13:12–13). We know that Tommy is safe with Jesus, but the world feels dimmer without him. But we trust in our Lord, and we can feel Tommy's love abide in the world. We know that alongside Jesus, one day Tommy will be reunited face to face with those who love him. While we wait, we let stories of resurrection hope from the Gospels and the stories from Tommy's life form us and console us. My love and continued prayers surround Elin, Mark and all those who love Tommy.

And finally, from halfway around the world in Perth, Australia, came the following tribute:

I knew of Thomas as he was growing up, I knew Thomas through the eyes of a loving mother. And today, for one day of my life, I came to know Thomas through all of you on his memorial site and I am better for knowing him and holding him in my heart. Oh, he lives on. I am sending my love to all of you whose hearts are aching—what beautiful memories you must have.

◊ ◊ ◊

Mark and I hold these stories and tributes close to our hearts and will always be thankful for Thomas's life and his perpetual impact on us and others whose lives he touched. And yes, despite our grief in our loss, we will hold on to our beautiful memories of our son and pray that his impact will continue through all our friends, families, and the countless others who may read this book.

NOTES

PREFACE

1   The word *labyrinth* does not appear in the Bible. It's not a Christian symbol per se, even though they were constructed on the floors of Christian churches in North Africa as early as AD 324, with the most well-known being the labyrinth in the Chartres Cathedral in France. In these contexts, labyrinths were used as part of the spiritual ritual of prayer, confession, and reflection. Unlike a maze that's designed to entrap, there's only one way into the center of a labyrinth and one way out. The path twists and turns back on itself many times, so sometimes we seem closer to the center, which is a symbol of wholeness, and other times we seem much farther away from the center. In much the same way, when we walk the winding path of life, we sometimes experience "thin places," that is, moments in time when the veil that separates the pedestrian realities of daily life parts and we see "reality" at the core of life more clearly. These "aha" experiences (i.e., thin places) are like positions on the labyrinth when we feel closer to the center. Then, without any apparent intentionality or decision-making on our part, the path of life shifts directions and the reality and wholeness at the core of life seem far away or totally eclipsed from sight. The labyrinth is what Carl Jung called an archetypal symbol of the collective unconscious—an image of the Self—that exists in all people, in all places, and in all times. See C. G. Jung, *The Archetypes and the Collective Unconscious*, vol. 9.1 of *The Collected Works of C. G. Jung*, trans. R. F. C. Hull, 2nd ed. (Princeton: Princeton University Press, 1977), 275–89 (§§489–524).

From a biblical perspective, the labyrinth is a symbol of our journey along an Inner and an Outer Labyrinth, and a direct consequence of the first two consequences of sin (i.e., we are alienated from ourselves, and we are alienated from others), things I explain in more detail later in this book. My 2010 statement of faith was trying to describe the difference between my lifelong experience of the "me" who exists in waking life (i.e., the me who is typing this note), and the "me" who appears in my dreams (i.e., the "me" who has walked an inner path that's independent of my conscious, waking free will). So the Outer Labyrinth (i.e., the destiny that we *create* with our choices) is the path that my conscious self has walked since my first personal experience of God at the Hungarian Reformed Church in 1964.

I think of the Outer Labyrinth in the sense of chronological history, like the Greek word *chronos* that's used fifty-four times in the New Testament; see James Strong, *Exhaustive Concordance of the Bible* (Grand Rapids, MI: Zondervan, 2001), 1654. It's the linear, sequential, and quantitative sense of time that's measured by physics experiments. The Inner Labyrinth is the path that my unconscious self (the "me" who appears hundreds of times in my dreams) has walked for the last forty-four years. I experience the Inner Labyrinth (i.e., the destiny that we *have* in God from the beginning of time) as related to the Greek word *kairos* that's used eight-six times in the New Testament and means an appointed time in the purpose and sovereign will of God; see Strong, *Exhaustive Concordance of the Bible*, 1618. The Inner and Outer Labyrinths (i.e., *chronos* and *kairos*) are both happening together at the same time. In much the same way, Karl Barth uses the German word *Historie* (my view of *chronos* and the Outer Labyrinth) to describe this type of time as opposed to *Geschichte* (what I mean by *kairos* and the Inner Labyrinth) to describe the scarlet thread of salvation history (i.e., the German word *Heilsgeschichte*) and God's sovereign control over all that happens in life; see Karl Barth, *The Epistle to the Romans*, trans. E. C. Hoskyns (Oxford: Oxford University Press, 1968), 77. So, much like our unconscious self is still "with us" when we're wide awake and our conscious life (the "us" who appears in our dreams) is still "with us" in dreams when we're asleep, the characteristics we see manifested along the Inner and Outer Labyrinths define who we are, our identity in the fullest sense of the word. Even if people have no conscious memory of their dreams and the "them" who walks this inner path, they often have a tacit, intuitive sense that the Inner Labyrinth is real and seeks to influence and to provide inner direction in life. Because the first step to embracing this path is often the journey through the dark and least understood parts of our lives (i.e., what Jung calls the Shadow), many people experience a deep inner resistance to embracing this journey, what M. Scott Peck calls the road less traveled; see M. Scott Peck, *The Road Less Traveled: A New Psychology of Love, Traditional Values, and Spiritual Growth*, rev. ed. (New York: Touchstone, 2003). This journey is what Jung calls the lifelong process of individuation; see C. G. Jung, *Psychological Types*, vol. 6 of *The Collected Works of C. G. Jung*, trans. R. F. C. Hull, 2nd ed. (Princeton: Princeton University Press, 1990), 448–50 (§§7657–762).

From a Christian perspective, this includes the three consequences of sin. It's what Jesus called the narrow way. "Enter through the narrow gate; for the gate is wide and the way is broad that leads to destruction, and there are many who enter through it. For the gate is narrow and the way is constricted that leads to life, and there are few who find it" (Matthew 7:13–14).

2   Carl Jung says, "I use the term 'individuation' to denote the process by which a person becomes a psychological 'whole.'" See Jung, *Archetypes and the Collective Unconscious*, 275 (§490). He goes on to explain why our conscious selves who exist along the Outer Labyrinth of everyday life cannot constitute our whole psyche. Rather, in the same way that most of an iceberg's mass exists under the water and is not visible, the contents, structures, and dynamic forces of our unconscious exist beneath the surface of awareness, yet they are an intrinsic part of who we are as a person. For Jung, the lifelong process of individuation is the path of becoming aware of those unconscious aspects of ourselves through dream work and active imagination, and then integrating them into conscious awareness, thus broadening and deepening our definition of who we are as individuals. What I call biblical individuation is defined by the first two consequences

of sin—the fact that we are alienated from ourselves, and we are alienated from others. Biblical individuation is the process through which the Holy Spirit works through inner insights and guidance, and through the Bible as God's inspired word, to sanctify and transform the Self, Anima, Ego, dominant complexes, and other psychic elements, so they become more faithful guides who can lead us to the destiny that we *have* in God's sovereign will and the destiny we *create* with our choices. I've had hundreds of dreams filled with images and symbols that reveal this process of inner healing and transformation. Here's one such dream that I had more than ten years ago. In this dream:

There was an older guy who was "promoting" a younger guy (in the sense of marketing or advocating for him) who was (or was going to be) selling a community or complex of homes that looked like caves that were built into the side of a mountain, and the older guy was more like a *presence* than a concrete person standing there. The younger guy had been the victim of some kind of disability where he was physically, mentally, and even spiritually handicapped in ways that fundamentally undermined his functioning as a human being, but these characteristics had been changed, reversed, healed, reconstructed, transformed, and cured to the point that he was a fully functioning human being, almost like the hands of time had been turned back, and he was healthy, functional, and whole again as a human being. When the young guy began the sales process, it wasn't like there was a crowd of people there that he was selling to—it was just him who was ready to begin talking about these new homes that looked like caves. As he began speaking, it was like the scene changed into a time-lapse display that was being viewed from a distance (i.e., that I was viewing from the observer role) where the process of building the cave homes (i.e., the process of laying and attaching the underlying foundation of layer after layer of stone and rock to the side of the mountain) was shown as a backdrop to the process of being changed, reversed, healed, reconstructed, transformed, and cured that the young man had gone through. The dream ends with this time-lapse display continuing to show the evolution of both the completion of the cave homes and the young man as a person.

The net result of the process of biblical individuation is that God's kingdom reigns at deeper and deeper levels of our conscious and unconscious life as we are sanctified and transformed into Jesus's likeness. As the apostle Paul reminds us: "And do not be conformed to this world, but be transformed by the renewing of your mind, so that you may prove what the will of God is, that which is good and acceptable and perfect" (Romans 12:2).

This deep inner transformation addresses the first two consequences of sin, but it does not give us salvation from our sins and eternal life. Rather, it helps us more effectively keep what Jesus called the two greatest commandments—to love God with all our heart, soul, mind, and strength, and to love our neighbors as ourselves (Matthew 22:36–40). Salvation from our sins and receiving eternal life comes only from faith in the life, death, and resurrection of Jesus (John 3:16). For a variety of views on the spiritual dimensions of psychological work, see John Sanford, *The Kingdom Within: The Inner Meaning of Jesus' Sayings*, rev. ed. (San Francisco:

HarperSanFrancisco, 1970). For a discussion of the spiritual aspects of Jung's process of individuation, see Ann Belford Ulanov, "Spiritual Aspects of Clinical Work" in *Jungian Analysis*, ed. Murray Stein, 2nd ed. (Peru, IL: Open Court, 1995), 50–78; Ann Belford Ulanov and Alvin Dueck, *The Living God and Our Living Psyche: What Christians Can Learn from Carl Jung* (Grand Rapids, MI: Eerdmans, 2008); and Ann Belford Ulanov, *Spiritual Aspects of Clinical Work* (Einsiedeln: Daimon Verlag, 2004).

3   Viktor Frankl's autobiographical account of Nazi concentration camps includes a description of his therapeutic doctrine that he called *logotherapy*—a meaning-centered psychotherapy. See Viktor Frankl, *Man's Search for Meaning* (Boston: Beacon, 2014), 92. The focus of David Kessler's approach to dealing with the grief of loss is also about finding meaning in life's challenges; see David Kessler, *Finding Meaning: The Sixth Stage of Grief* (New York: Scribner, 2019). The question I've pondered is whether *meaning* is something that exists objectively (outside our heads) as something to be discovered in the world, whether meaning is something that is subjective (exists inside our heads) that organizes and integrates life experiences into structured patterns that create meaning, or both. My sense is that it's both. The same is true of the connections and patterns of transformation like the links between Mount Evans, Thomas's tree house as the bridge to our new home, and the replica brass benchmark from the top of Mount Evans that sits on the desk in my home office across the street from McIntosh Lake, all of which exist within the 120-mile radius of the peak of Mount Evans, that are also connected to the Mount of Beatitudes. This 120-mile radius in Colorado is the "holy land" that God has sanctified, and to which He called me from my early life in New Jersey, in which I've lived out my life.

4   The inner images of this early trauma in my childhood first emerged from the unconscious in 1980 when I was twenty-seven years old. It was the very first dream I ever remembered, recorded, and analyzed with the help of my first Jungian analyst:

I was a little boy in a room, and there was furniture in the room (tables, chairs, couches). I was terrified to the core of my being and had to crawl on hands and knees on top of this furniture, jumping from one piece to the other. The floor was made out of glass, and there were glass bumps all over the floor. Some were solid and would hold my weight if I stepped on them, but others I knew that if I stepped on them, I would fall through. Under the floor was a giant fish tank that had a great man-eating shark in it. Upon waking, I knew the shark was my mom and the bumps represented emotional interchanges I had with her. Sometimes she was there for me (i.e., the bump would hold my weight), but sometimes she wasn't (i.e., my foot would go through the thin glass and the shark would bite my leg off), but I never knew when this would happen because all the bumps looked the same. My father was just standing by, passively watching all of this and refusing to help me. The dream ends with me being terrified of being eaten alive. I awoke with a deep sense of existential threat, terrified to the core of my being.

5   Jung experienced and mapped out the dynamic interaction between the conscious and unconscious elements of the psyche (i.e., what I call the Inner and Outer Labyrinths).

FINDING NEW LIFE AFTER THE DEATH OF MY SON

The Inner Labyrinth acted in ways that somehow seemed "synched" with day-to-day life along the Outer Labyrinth, but this interaction could not be reduced to cause-and-effect relationships. Jung struggled to describe this inner and outer experience in a world of physics that was defined by a classical, deterministic, cause-and-effect view of nature known as classical mechanics. At about this same time, physicists were developing a radically different quantum, probabilistic, and statistical view of subatomic phenomena. Victor Weisskopf describes the advent of quantum mechanics like this: "The discoveries of the later nineteenth century had shown that it is impossible to understand the structure of matter, the specific properties of material, using so-called classical mechanics." See Victor Weisskopf, "Neils Bohr, the Quantum, and the World" in *Niels Bohr: A Centenary Volume*, ed. A. P. French and P. J. Kennedy (Cambridge: Harvard University Press, 1985), 19–29.

Although the prevailing psychological model at the time (i.e., the Freudian view of the psyche) was billed as being a "scientific" biological view of the psyche's structure and dynamics, Freud's so called "medical model" was based on imposing conscious model of sexual libido onto unconscious phenomena in what Jung called the personal unconscious, which denied the existence of an objective collective unconscious. Freud's model lacked the rigor and precision of the emerging power of quantum mechanism; see Frank Sulloway, *Freud Biologist of The Mind*, (New York: Basic Books, 1979). More specifically, the development of quantum theory in general, and quantum electrodynamics (QED) in particular, were wildly successful. The mapping between the calculated predictions of QED and actual experimental measurements agree to an accuracy of 10^{-12}—more precise than any other scientific theory. For example, if you were to measure the distance between New York and Los Angeles to that level of precision, you'd have measured it to within the thickness of a human hair. See Richard Feynman, *QED: The Strange Theory of Light and Matter* (Princeton: Princeton University Press, 1986), 15.

The advent of quantum mechanics enabled Jung to map his personal and archetypal experience of the "acausal connecting principle" that operated between the conscious and unconscious elements of the psyche (i.e., the Inner and Outer Labyrinths) to something solid in the world of subatomic physics. For a detailed discussion on synchronicity where Jung describes his understanding of a quantum view of the world, see, C. G. Jung, *The Structure and Dynamics of the Psyche*, vol. 8 of *The Collected Works of C. G. Jung*, trans. R. F. C. Hull, 2nd ed. (Princeton: Princeton University Press, 1977), 421–58 (§§812–71). Jung's ongoing dialogue on synchronicity with some of the greatest scientists of this time is captured in C. A. Meier, ed., *Atom and Archetype: The Pauli/Jung Letters 1932–1958* (Princeton: Princeton University Press, 2001), 211.

I've had dozens of experiences of synchronicity, some of which I describe later in the book. At this point, I'm using the word *synchronicity* to describe my experience of the acausal connection between my son, Thomas, asking me if he was worthy to go to heaven on May 1, 2010, and his fatal decision to take what he thought was a prescription Xanax pill eleven years to the day later on May 1, 2021. Events like this don't have a cause-and-effect relationship along the Outer Labyrinth (*chronos*), but they do have a deeper and more profound connection along the Inner Labyrinth (*kairos*). To reiterate, the empirical reality of synchronicity is how God accomplishes His sovereign will through the conscious and unconscious (intended and unintended) beliefs, mindsets, and actions of people in all times, places, and sociocultural settings. But most people don't recognize, at least not right away, that God uses *their* lives, *their* decisions, and *their* stories to achieve *His* ends, purpose, and will.

CHAPTER 1: MY SON, THOMAS

6   The idea that Jung is trying to get across here is that the "truth" that a given individual comes to through the lifelong process of individuation is not "ultimate truth." Rather, it's where a person's curiosity comes to rest; see C. G. Jung, *Alchemical Studies*, vol. 13 of *The Collected Works of C. G. Jung*, trans. R. F. C. Hull, 2nd ed. (Princeton: Princeton University Press, 1983), 15 (§18).

CHAPTER 4: FIRST FATHER'S DAY IN CARMEL WITHOUT THOMAS

7   The symbol of the Inner and Outer Labyrinths is archetypal, meaning it's universal and has been experienced by people throughout all human history. Archetypes have manifested themselves inwardly in the form of dream symbols and outwardly as physical structures built by civilizations that had no known culture contact. For example, the construction of pyramids in Egypt and South America, both of which were an outer expression of archetypal images (i.e., the three, or triad, as opposed to the four, the quaternity), had very different meanings in those sociocultural contexts. Most people don't recognize these archetypal symbols as such, and those who have experienced them often struggle to find ways to describe it.

   Jordan Peterson stumbled onto the experience in his college years, as he began to have intense apocalyptic dreams two or three times a week for a year or more. The experience of integrating material from what I call the Inner Labyrinth into conscious awareness along the Outer Labyrinth (i.e., Peterson's conscious waking life) was profoundly transforming and echoes the experiences I describe in my 2010 church testimony. Peterson recalls, "I was being affected, simultaneously, by events on two 'planes.' On the first plane were the normal, predictable, everyday occurrences that I shared with everybody else. On the second plane, however (unique to me, or so I thought) existed dreadful images and unbearably intense emotional status. . . . The study of 'comparative mythological material' in fact made my horrible dreams disappear. The cure wrought by this study, however, was purchased at the price of complete and often painful transformation: what I believe about the world now—how I act, in consequence—is so much at variance with what I believed when I was younger that I might as well be a completely different person." See Jordan Peterson, *Maps of Meaning: The Architecture of Belief* (New York: Routledge, 1999), xvii–xxii.

The catalyst for this profound transformation was Peterson's reading of Carl Jung's work, which helped him finally understand what he was experiencing. Jung was able to lead the way because he had already walked the path of discovering and aligning what I call the Inner and Outer Labyrinths; an experience he called the lifelong process of individuation. He describes this in C. G. Jung, *Aion: Researches into the Phenomenology of the Self*, vol. 9.2 of *The Collected Works of C. G. Jung*, trans. R. F. C. Hull, 2nd ed. (Princeton: Princeton University Press, 1975), 23–35 (§§43–67) and 222–65 (§§347–421).

CHAPTER 5: THE FUNERALS

8   This transition from an old reality to a new one echoes the model of managing change and transition developed in the book by William Bridges with Susan Bridges, *Managing Transitions: Making the Most of Change*, 3rd ed. (Philadelphia: Da Capo, 2009), 3–10.

9   See Jim Collins, *Good to Great: Why Some Companies Make the Leap and Others Don't* (New York: Harper, 2001), 83–87.

10 Collins, *Good to Great*, 86.

11 See the Drug Enforcement Agency's Intelligence Report, *Fentanyl Flow to the United States*.

12 The idea of being in a "no-man's-land" echoes William Bridges's notion of transition and the need to manage both change and transition; see Bridges, *Managing Transitions*, 5–6.

CHAPTER 7: FIRST CHRISTMAS

13 It's important to note that the biblical word "rejoice" may be translated multiple ways in various English translations based on the semantic bandwidth of the Greek or Hebrew, the historical and grammatical context in which it is used, and the goal of the translators to create a more literal or "polished" version of the text. So my statement that the Greek verb *agalliaō*, meaning "to exult, rejoice greatly," and the Hebrew verb *śāmach*, meaning "to rejoice, be glad," appear hundreds of times is based on Strong, *Exhaustive Concordance of the Bible*, 951–52; Joesph Thayer, *Thayer's Greek-English Lexicon of the New Testament: Coded with Strong's Concordance Numbers* (Peabody, MA: Hendrickson, 2003); Gerhard Kittle, Gerhard Friedrich, and Ronald Pitkin, eds., *Theological Dictionary of the New Testament*, 10 vols. (Grand Rapids: Eerdmans, 1980). See also Francis Brown, S. R. Driver, and Charles Briggs, *The Brown-Driver-Briggs Hebrew and English Lexicon* (Peabody, MA: Hendrickson, 1994), which is fully searchable using the Strong Numbers.

14 Whitmont describes the compensatory or complementary function of the unconscious and dreams as acting in ways that are objective to, and autonomous from, our conscious waking self in an interactive, dialectic relationship. Compensatory symbols highlight instances where our conscious perspectives and beliefs are diametrically opposed to unconscious perspectives and beliefs. With complementary symbols, the unconscious tries to amplify the conscious perspectives and beliefs as if to say "Yes,

that's the path forward. Carry on." Whitmont describes it this way: "This relationship is one of complementation or compensation, inasmuch as it tends to counterbalance vital deficiencies or critically one-sided tendencies of the conscious standpoint. Such unconscious complementation or compensation implies, however, an inherent direction or goal. Complementation or compensation for something missing or exaggerated presupposes a totality configuration or wholeness pattern, even though this may manifest itself in a distorted or deficient way. This purposive wholeness pattern that Jung postulates and calls the Self (at variance with the general usage of the term as synonymous with ego) is conceived—and here again we use symbolic language—to be a superordinated personality that encompasses and meaningfully directs conscious as well as unconscious functioning." See Edward Whitmont, *The Symbolic Quest: Basic Concepts of Analytical Psychology* (Princeton: Princeton University Press, 1978), 42–43. For a discussion on the compensatory nature of the psyche by Jung, see *Psychological Types*, 418–20 (§§693–95).

The unconscious nature of this compensatory process of inner healing and transformation is imaged in a dream I had on September 16, 2014:

There was a first guy who was young (in his thirties) with long blond hair, and he had come to the self-realization that he had a special anointing from God and was holy and like a prophet or even a son of God in the truest sense of the word. Then there was a second guy, who had come to know and understand this truth about the first guy, and he had become a kind of disciple or follower of the first guy, and he had dark hair with an old dirty cloth wrapped around his head like a band that was two or three inches wide.

All this happened in a former dream, or a previous part of this dream, so as this dream opens, the second guy is standing outside a house that reminds me of my house on Warren Street in Clifton with a number of other people, and a third guy has gone up to the second guy and said that he has come to understand and know the truth about the first guy. It's almost like the second guy thought his knowledge was supposed to be secret and not commonly known by people, so the second guy is upset with (and pushing back on) what the third guy is saying, like he either didn't believe him or was resisting the claim that he really had the same kind of inner experience and understanding as he did. Then the first guy with the blond hair came and began to talk to the second guy and tell him it was all right, that the third guy really had come to this inner realization, and what the third guy had experienced was true and real, much like the inner realization the second guy had. The second guy was still resistant to what the first guy was saying—but what could he say, in that the first guy knew infinitely more than the second guy about the actual truth of the situation. The dream ends as the first guy with the blond hair is walking slowly forward toward the second guy (who is facing him and stepping backward), with the first guy trying to reason with the second guy and convince him of the truth of the situation. As I awoke, I knew the first guy was an image of what Jung calls the Self.

In summary, my private discussions with Lara Newton (Jungian analyst, president, C. G. Jung Institute of Colorado, and founding director of training, C. G. Jung Institute of

Colorado) reveal the difficulty of concretizing the experience and concept of the Self into a cohesive linguistic description. Newton made three attempts to do this in a decreasing order of complexity. With her first attempt, she said: "The Self is both the center and circumference of the individual's psychological being; it has a paradoxical nature, and it communicates with us through sometimes offering a centering image and sometimes an image that seems to shatter our heretofore understood sense of 'who we are.'" Wondering if that definition would be too complicated for those who have not had this experience, Newton offered me a second attempt to define the Self: "The Self is the center of our psychological being, and as such it serves to draw us into a greater awareness of who we are." Her final attempt simplifies the experience and concept of the Self even more: "an experience of the Self centers, deepens, and energizes our psychic life." See Lara Newton, *Brothers and Sisters: Discovering the Psychology of Companionship* (New York: Spring, 2007), 9.

15   The ongoing dialectical nature of this inner healing and transformation process was reflected in Jung's study of the alchemical literature; see Jung, *Alchemical Studies*, 116–17 (§151). This alchemical process was also described by Jungian analyst Lara Newton as the axiom of Maria where "One becomes two, two becomes three, and out of the third comes the one as the fourth," and then the process started all over again, with a new one that becomes a two. See Lara Newton, "Thoughts on the Axiom of Maria," August 1, 2012, https://laranewton.com/axiommaria.html.

16   See Soren Kierkegaard, *Journals NB–NB5*, vol. 4 of *Kierkegaard's Journals and Notebooks*, ed. B. H. Kirmmse and K. B. Soderquist (Princeton: Princeton University Press, 2011), p. 73.

CHAPTER 9: THE ARRAIGNMENT AND FORGIVENESS

17   See Nisha Zenoff, *The Unspeakable Loss: How Do You Live after a Child Dies?* (New York: Hachette, 2017).

CHAPTER 10: THE PLEA AND FORGIVENESS

18   See Fred Luskin, *Forgive for Good: A Proven Prescription for Health and Happiness* (New York: HarperCollins, 2002), and Fred Luskin, *Forgive for Love: The Missing Ingredient for a Healthy and Lasting Relationship* (New York: HarperCollins, 2009).

19   In retrospect, I now see that the lifelong process of biblical individuation was healing and transforming the trauma and wounds that afflicted me in childhood. I saw this evidenced in a series of multiple dreams, a few of which I'll share here. The first dream I had in May 2014 begins by describing the background, self-understanding, and history that the "me" in the dream (i.e., the dream ego) had prior to the active narrative of the dream beginning:

In a previous dream, or an earlier part of this dream, I had been on a large cruise ship trapped in a room with my mother, Mary, and another woman, and we were being tortured by my father, Ralph, and all this was being recorded. I had escaped, and then I had come back to help the women escape by exiting the boat underwater and then swimming five or six hundred feet to the surface of the water. In one of these previous dream segments, I remember exiting the boat five or six hundred feet under water and swimming and swimming with this woman toward the surface. When we hit the surface and took in a deep breath of air, we were ecstatic to be alive.

Then, as the active narrative of *this* dream begins, I've come back to the ship, and I'm walking down the hallway toward the cabin Ralph had kept us prisoner in. As I reach the cabin, the door is cracked open with music softly playing, and there is a paper sign taped to the door that says something like "Be Quiet. Recording in Progress," handwritten in blue letters. I walk through the door and see my father, Ralph, shaving like he's getting ready "to go out" somewhere. When he sees me, he looks like he's "seen a ghost," almost like he thought I was dead. Before he could say anything, I began sobbing and hugged him and started saying, "I survived . . . I survived . . . I survived . . . I went over the side of the boat and swam with the others, and we exited through the torpedo tube and swam five to six hundred feet to the surface. Do you know what the pressure was like at five or six hundred feet?" Then Ralph said something like, "With your girlfriend?" And I was shocked and a little insulted because I was married, so I said, "I don't have a girlfriend—it was your girlfriend," and by this I meant it was his wife, (my mother) Mary. I fell to my knees at his feet with a deep sense of victory, having overcome enormous (almost insurmountable) obstacles, and I continued to sob, saying, "I survived . . . I survived . . . I survived," as Ralph stood there speechless, not knowing what to say because he had meant me harm, tortured me, and left me for dead, and here I was back, better, and stronger than ever, despite his efforts to harm me and the others, and I was able to save the women too.

As I awoke from this dream, my sense about the underlying "meaning" of this dream was that it was like the story of Joseph in the Bible where he said to his brothers who had treated him badly and sold him into slavery, "Do not be afraid, for am I in God's place? As for you, you meant evil against me, but God meant it for good in order to bring about this present result, to keep many people alive" (Genesis 50:19–20). In addition to the fact that Joeseph *forgave* his brothers, the passage from Genesis provides insight into the *sovereignty* of God, His ultimate control over history, and its outcome as promised by Romans 8:28.

Over time, with multiple subsequent dreams, I witnessed the deconstruction of the father complex imaged as "Ralph" in the above dream, and instead the unconscious produced dream images and symbols where Ralph and Mary came to help or support me in various ways, indicating enormous inner healing and transformation from the trauma I experienced in my early childhood. My father died on January 4, 2021, and I had the following dream about six weeks later on February 21, 2021:

I had written and published a book, and it was placed in a university library. This happened in an earlier part of this dream or in a previous dream. When this dream begins, I'm in a house with my mom and dad, and I had come from my room, and I was thinking about the fact that I had written and published this book. They were sitting in the kitchen at a square-shaped kitchen table, and the house that the dream took place in was my house on Warren Street in Clifton, New Jersey, where I lived when I was about twelve years old. But the kitchen was upstairs where I never lived while I was at home. I sat at the table and either they knew about the book or I told them about it, but we were discussing it. It seemed like they were pleased and even proud of me for having done this, and I said something like, "It's one thing to write a book and get it published and placed in a university library, but it's another thing to get people to actually read it." My sense in the dream is that we were having a good, productive discussion about the whole situation, and they were proud of me and even respected me.

As we talked, I started to feel a draft in the house—cool air coming from outside. I believe I got up and walked to the kitchen sink and saw there was a window open over the sink, so I closed it. Then I walked to another room that may have adjoined the kitchen, and I sat by myself and was feeling disconnected and distant from them and wanted to be alone. I started to feel a draft of cool air from outside the house again, and I got up and walked to a staircase that looked down onto (and led to) the first floor of the house. I saw the front door about halfway open, so I walked down the stairs, opened the door, and saw there was a young boy out there who was doing some work on the house (maybe concrete work). The work he was doing was on a step/front porch that seems connected to the concrete porch that Elin and I had at our Longmont house on McIntosh Drive where we lived when Thomas was alive. My sense in the dream was that the young boy had left the door open, so I told him I wanted it closed. He just looked at me, didn't say anything, and did what I asked, although he didn't particularly like having to do it. The dream ends here, and I wake up with a sense of good feelings, closure, and healing, wishing that my relationship with my real parents could have been more like the one that was pictured in this dream.

Once awake, my associations with the cool air that was coming from outside the house (i.e., from the unconscious) were that: (1) it was the thing that got my attention (i.e., raised my conscious awareness); (2) it made me feel disconnected and distant from my parents, wanting to be alone (i.e., images and symbols of introspection and transformation); and (3) it was an indication that there were external collective factors and objective forces operating in my childhood psyche and in my family context that could not be reduced to personal experiences with my parents. My parents and the traumatic beatings and abuse I suffered as a child were necessary but not sufficient to have been the sole cause of my psychological and day-to-day suffering in life. The fact that the door that was open was on the first floor of the house (and not underground or halfway underground in a walk-out style basement) indicates I was consciously aware that this transformation had happened, rather than it being an insight I was still unconscious of.

20 Luskin, *Forgive for Good*, 12–20.
21 Luskin, *Forgive for Good*, 21–32.
22 Luskin, *Forgive for Good*, 33–45.
23 For a Christian perspective on dreams, see John Sanford, *Dreams: God's Forgotten Language*, rev. ed. (New York: HarperOne, 1989), and Morton Kelsey, *God, Dreams, and*

Revelation: A Christian Interpretation of Dreams (Minneapolis: Augsburg, 1991). Erich Fromm approaches dreams from a neo-Freudian, existentialist perspective. See Erich Fromm, *The Forgotten Language: An Introduction to the Understanding of Dreams, Fairy Tales, and Myths* (New York: Grove, 1951). What I found most perplexing about the way I felt Luskin's approach to forgiveness connected down to something deeply fundamental in my unconscious was that his theoretical orientation (i.e., positive psychology) and his model for dealing with grievance story formation and deconstruction focuses solely on developing skills and tools for more effectively managing our emotions, interactions, and the destiny we *create* with our choices along the Outer Labyrinth of everyday life. His views seem to echo principles and practices like those used in cognitive behavior therapy; see Judith Beck, *Cognitive Behavior Therapy: Basics and Beyond*, 2nd ed. (New York: Guilford, 2011).

Luskin makes no mention of the unconscious and the role dreams play in revealing the destiny we have along the Inner Labyrinth from the beginning of time. So, where Luskin does not include the role and causal efficacy of the unconscious in his view of psychological processes, Jung proposes a two-part ontology consisting of the Spirit of the Depths (everything that is unconscious) and the Spirit of the Times (everything that is conscious). See C. G. Jung, *The Red Book*, ed. S. Shamdasani (New York: Norton, 2009), 229. Both views differ from the biblical approach to individuation mentioned here. Biblical individuation requires a three-part ontology that adds the Spirit of God to Jung's Spirit of the Depths and Spirit of the Times, both of which were created by a triune God when He "spoke" the universe into existence in Genesis 1:1–31, and again as the Word, who was in the beginning in John 1:1–5 and 9–10. We see the impact of this distinction most clearly when we reflect on Jung's notion of the Self. Jung's psychological interpretation of the symbolism of medieval alchemy viewed the goal of the alchemical process as the philosopher's stone, which Jung interpreted as being a symbol of the Self; see C. G. Jung, *Psychology and Alchemy*, vol. 12 of *The Collected Works of C. G. Jung*, trans. R. F. C. Hull, 2nd ed. (Princeton: Princeton University Press, 1975), 41 (§§44–45). Jung experienced the reality of the philosopher's stone along the Inner Labyrinth through dreams and active imagination, and he painted an image of the Self along the Outer Labyrinth in the *Red Book* (see 121).

Reading about the Self and trying to imagine its impact in conscious waking life is a very different experience from having the Self emerge in a dream like it did for me on July 6, 1985, when I was thirty-two years old:

I had a dream last night, which I totally forgot till now. It's very faint in my memory, and all I can recall is an image. There was a stone, and it was glittering and shining. Then somehow deep in my deepest of souls, I felt a redefinition. It was as if I were shown or realized that *this* was *that*. It was almost like an energy transformation theorem ($E=mc^2$). It was so deep, this feeling—so heavy—I cannot even form it into a cohesive, linguistic equivalent. It was just so. It was just there. It was not just true, it was truth. It was the very deepest truth I had ever realized, and to describe it desecrates it. It was tremendous power, supreme beauty, but elegant—so elegant. Yet it wasn't just the stone. It was the transformation theorem, the redefinition, that made it this way. I can feel my resistance to accepting this image. It's almost like I felt "It can't be. It just can't be." It was as if in the transformation, the stone became *animate*, but not like a person. It was more like a *Presence*. I have this feeling like, "That's it. That's the answer. That's what I've been looking for. That's what my heart deeply longs for, the only thing that will really and truly satisfy." It goes as deep as my feeling about God. In fact, I want to call this thing "God," but something within stops me. God goes deeper. It's almost like I am the stone, like it's me, like we're one, connectedly one. But for some reason, I resist it. I fight its slow, stubborn, and almost immovable steadiness.

I get tired just thinking about it. It takes a lot of energy to be in its presence (i.e., in its power, its strength). It drains me of everything I have just to be with it. It consumes me, absolutely consumes me, and it frightens me. It's so strong, so steady, so constant, so slow and persistent that I'm afraid it will take me over and consume me, suck me in. I am powerless against it for long periods of time, but when I stay with it as long as I can, as exhausted as I get, I somehow come away stronger, having partaken of it almost through osmosis. It's like a silent teacher, a supreme mentor, an instructor that is so different that it teaches by existing, not talking or conveying linguistically. It is not hostile toward me, but by its very nature it would consume, almost like seeing God face-to-face. But I can't call it God. It is more than God, or maybe more than my understanding of God. Yet at the same time, it's not as much as God. I could feel the struggle I had trying to remember it once awake. I had to fight to keep it in consciousness at all. I caught myself saying, almost aloud, "No! I won't call you God." I believe I've seen an archetype for the first time.

When I look back over the forty years since having this dream, my sense is that I "passed a test." I refused to bow down to the power and numinosity of the Self (the philosopher's stone) as if it were the God of the Bible. This echoes another test that our primordial ancestors failed in Genesis 3, where they ate with the false promise that they would become like God. From an inside-out perspective like the one presented in this dream, Jungian psychology appears to be compatible with Christianity and other world religions because Jung's two-part ontology of the Spirit of the Depths and the Spirit of the Times describes the first two consequences of sin (i.e., alienation from ourselves and alienation from others). But a biblical view of individuation sees the Spirit of the Depths and the Spirit of the Times as created things that the triune spoke into existence, and the root cause of what's right and wrong in the world is the third consequence of sin described in Genesis 3—alienation from God. So bowing down to the archetypal image of the "stone" in this dream as if it *were* the God who has existed before the universe and time were created rather than an inner *image* of that God (*Imago Dei*) is idolatry in the sense defined in Exodus 20:3: "You shall have no other gods before Me."

From my perspective, this issue for Jung is an *ontological* one about what *exists* in the universe; a *hamartiological* issue related to the *three consequences of sin*; and an *epistemological* issue of what could be known about universe—something that emerges in the following example. In answering a question about his belief in the afterlife and eternity, Jung responded as follows: "Whether I believe in personal survival after death or not. I could not say that I believe in it, since I have not the gift of belief. I only can say whether I know something or not. I do know that the psyche possesses certain qualities transcending the confinement in time and space . . . the psyche is capable of functioning unhampered by the categories of time and space. Ergo it is in itself an equally transcendental being and therefore relatively non-spatial and 'eternal.'" See C. G. Jung, "Letter to H. J. Barrett," (October 12, 1956) in *Letters*, ed. Gerhard Adler and Aniela Jaffé (Princeton: Princeton University Press, 1975), 2:333. What's important to note here is the Jung saw "belief" as a *gift* that he did not have, and knowing (i.e., by experience, in the *yada* sense) as his epistemological *criteria* for determining what could be known about God and the universe. Jung's view that belief is a gift that is distinct from knowing is consistent with a historical-grammatical view of the Bible. The above believe-know distinction was a key element of an October 22, 1959, BBC interview, where Jung was interviewed by John Freeman and asked, "Do you now believe in God?" to which Jung answered, "Now? Difficult to answer. I know. I needn't, I don't need to believe. I know." In response to that interview, Jung tried to clarify his position in a letter, where he said, "I did not say in the broadcast, 'There is a God.' I said 'I do not need to believe in God; I know.' Which does not mean: I do know a certain God (Zeus, Jahwe, Allah, the Trinitarian God, etc.) but rather: I do know that I am obviously confronted with a factor unknown in itself, which I call 'God' in *consensu omnium* ('*quod semper, quod ubique, quod ab omnibus creditur*'). I remember Him, I evoke Him, whenever I use His name overcome by anger or by fear, whenever I involuntarily say: 'Oh God.'" See Carl Jung's letter to *The Listener*, January 21, 1960, 133.

The conclusion that I've come to about this issue is as follows. I fully embrace Jung's *psychology* (i.e., the structure and dynamics of the personal and collective dimensions of the psyche), but I firmly reject his *ontology* (i.e., what exists and what was the ultimate causes of the universe). Much like dreams are private communications from the unconscious to our conscious waking selves, where only the dreamer can say with any certainty what a dream means, so only Jung and God know where he resides in eternity. But on the face of it, his stated views about these matters are not consistent with: (1) a historical-grammatical view of the Bible described here, (2) the definition of a biblical worldview described in note 90, or (3) the orthodox doctrine of the Christian church contained in the historic creeds of the one holy and apostolic church. For a discussion on image of God, or *Imago Dei*, see Richard Lints, *Identity and Idolatry: The Image of God and Its Inversion* (Downers Grove, IL: InterVarsity, 2015), and Timothy Keller, *Counterfeit Gods: The Empty Promises of Money, Sex, and Power, and the Only Hope That Matters* (New York: Riverhead, 2009).

My stone dream, and others like it, enabled me to understand the distinction between Jesus as the cornerstone of all creation and people like me and Carl Jung who are "stones" made in His likeness. As 1 Peter 2:4–8 tells us: "And coming to Him as to a living stone which has been rejected by people but is choice and precious in the sight of God, you also, as living stones, are being built up as a spiritual house for a holy priesthood, to offer spiritual sacrifices that are acceptable to God through Jesus Christ. For this is contained in Scripture: 'Behold, I am laying in Zion a choice stone, a precious cornerstone, and the one who believes in Him will not be put to shame.' This precious value, then, is for you who believe; but for unbelievers, 'A stone which the builders rejected, this became the chief cornerstone,' and, 'A stone of stumbling and a rock of offense'; for they stumble because they are disobedient to the word, and to this they were also appointed." The image of the "stone" continued to transform along the next four decades and reemerged as the image of the first guy in the three-guy dream in note 18, and what Jung called the Self, based on the distinction between the conscious self or ego (i.e., small *s*) and the Self (i.e., big *S*) described in note 37.

Over time, the ongoing integration of unconscious material into consciousness results in a major shift in the psyche from the conscious "self" being the center of consciousness to a point midway between the conscious self and the "Self" along the Ego-Self Axis (i.e., the center of the personality). We experience this shift as an inner gyroscopic sense of orientation where the totality of our psyche and our journey along the Inner and Outer Labyrinths have a new virtual center that aligns and unifies them, making them much more difficult to perturb. We sense a deep feeling of inner guidance that provides leadership for our lives. From a biblical perspective, the Holy Spirit works through the *Emergent Self* to guide and direct us to do God's will. I discuss the notion of the Emergent Self in Mark Bodnarczuk, *Diving In: Discovering Who You Are in the Second Half of Life* (Breckenridge, CO: Breckenridge Press, 2009), 222, and following.

24 For a detailed discussion on the structure, function, and purpose of Jesus's parables, see Joachim Jeremias, *The Parables of Jesus*, 3rd rev. ed. (London: SCM, 2003); Simon Kistemaker, *The Parables: Understanding the Stories Jesus Told* (Grand Rapids: Baker, 2006); and Craig Blomberg, *Interpreting the Parables* (Downers Grove, IL: InterVarsity, 1990).

CHAPTER 11: THE JOURNEY HOME TO COLORADO WITHOUT THOMAS, BUT HE KEEPS SHOWING UP

25 Following the destruction of the House of Commons chamber by German bombs in October 1943, the Commons debated the issue of rebuilding the chamber in its original rectangular, adversarial pattern as opposed to a semicircle or horseshoe design. During the debate, Churchill insisted that the oppositional shape of the chamber helped to create the two-party system that was the essence of British parliamentary democracy. This led to his famous statement quoted in the text, "We shape our buildings, and afterwards our buildings shape us." It's in this sense that various aspects of our outer world get internalized and become part of the private language of images and symbols with which the unconscious speaks to us in dreams. For the record of Churchill's speech, see https://api.parliament.uk/historic-hansard/commons/1943/oct/28/house-of-commons-rebuilding.

CHAPTER 12: REFLECTIONS ON THE FIRST YEAR

26 See Carl Rogers, *On Becoming a Person* (Boston: Houghton Mifflin, 1961), 26.

27 The 1993 movie *Shadowlands*, in which the character of C. S. Lewis was played by Anthony Hopkins, was based on the play by William Nicholson. See William Nicholson, *Shadowlands: A Play* (New York: Penguin, 1991).

28 Lara Newton is a psychotherapist and Jungian analyst in practice in the Denver area. She is also president of the C.G. Jung Institute of Colorado and the founding director of training, C. G. Jung Institute of Colorado.

29 See Bodnarczuk, *Diving In*, and Mark Bodnarczuk, *Island of Excellence: Three Powerful Strategies for Building a Culture of Creativity* (Boulder, CO: Breckenridge, 2018).

CHAPTER 13: I SURVIVED THE DEATH OF MY SON

30 Jung's writings on the structure and dynamics of the conscious and unconscious provide a powerful and useful way to understand the human psyche. But it's important to remember that the study of the conscious and unconscious dimensions of the human mind began long before the work of Freud and Jung; see Henri Ellenberger, *The Discovery of the Unconscious: The History and Evolution of Dynamic Psychiatry* (New York: Basic Books, 1970), and Lancelot Law Whyte, *The Unconscious before Freud* (New York: Basic Books, 1960).

31 The archetypes of Anima (i.e., the feminine dimension of man), and Animus (i.e., the male dimension of women) relate to our inner soul life, not soul in the metaphysical sense of something that lives on after death. Rather, the archetype of Anima and Animus are an inner psychological force that animates us. The two archetypes are contrasexual, with the Anima representing the eternal feminine aspect in man (Yin) and the Animus representing the eternal aspect of women (Yang). Anima and Animus are also the archetypes that *link* the conscious ego to the depths of the unconscious—the psychological *bridge* between our conscious experiences of everyday life along the Outer Labyrinth and the structures and dynamics of our unconscious life along the Inner Labyrinth. June Singer describes Jung's notion of the Anima like this: "For Jung, the man's anima is a 'soul-figure.' Anima, the word for soul in Latin, is in the feminine gender. Why must the soul be feminine? She must appear to be feminine for a man because she represents that which is 'other,' which is different, which he can never fathom because she is subject to certain experiences which he can never know. . . . So, the anima-soul in a man, being essentially hidden or unconscious, stands in opposition to his ego, which is the center of his consciousness." See June Singer, *Boundaries of the Soul: The Practice of Jung's Psychology* (New York: Anchor Books, 1994), 183–84. For other descriptions of the Anima, see Edward Edinger, *Ego and Archetype: Individuation and the Religious Function of the Psyche* (Boston: Shambhala, 1992), 15; Edward Whitmont, *The Symbolic Quest: Basic Concepts of Analytical Psychology* (Princeton: Princeton University Press, 1978), 185ff.; C. G. Jung, *Memories, Dreams, Reflections*, ed. Aniela Jaffe (New York: Vintage Books, 1963), 186ff.; and Jung, *Archetypes and the Collective Unconscious*, 26–32 (§§55–66).

32 John Beebe is a psychiatrist and Jungian analyst in practice in San Francisco. He is a past president of the C. G. Jung Institute of San Francisco, where he is currently on the teaching faculty. He is a distinguished life fellow of the American Psychiatric Association.

CHAPTER 14: THOMAS'S TREE HOUSE AND THE EMERGENCE OF A NEW NORMAL

33 June Singer offers a basic definition of the Self as follows: "Jung's use of the word 'self' is different from that of common usage in which the self is synonymous with ego. 'Self' as Jung uses it has a special meaning; it is that center of the being which the ego circumambulates; at the same time, it is the superordinate factor in a system in which the ego is subordinate." See Singer, *Boundaries of the Soul*, 210. Jung defined the distinction between the Self and the ego as follows: "I have defined the self as the totality of the conscious and unconscious psyche, and the ego as the central reference-point of consciousness. It is an essential part of the self and can be used *pars pro toto* when the significance of consciousness is borne in mind. But when we want to lay emphasis on the psychic totality it is better to use the term 'self.' There is no question of a contradictory definition, but merely of a difference of standpoint." See C. G. Jung, *Mysterium Coniunctionis*, vol. 14 of *The Collected Works of C. G. Jung*, trans. R. F. C. Hull, 2nd ed. (Princeton: Princeton University Press, 1990), 110 (§133).

In his early research, Jung observed the empirical reality of *intentionality* and *goal-directedness* in his dreams and the dreams of his patients. He pondered who, or what, that entity was that appeared to be influencing the conscious and unconscious elements of his psyche, and the collective unconscious that all people were rooted in, like a strand of aspen trees that's connected to the same root system. He called this purposive force the Self— an overall unifying factor in the psyche that orchestrated and integrated all other psychic elements. Edward Whitmont describes the objective, archetypal nature of the Self as follows:

This entity is experienced by consciousness *as if* it were a central planning system that is not part of, but includes and affects, the conscious system. . . . If the total personality were to be considered a city of which the ego regards itself as mayor, this city would contain not only inhabitants whom the mayor had never seen or heard of (the personal unconscious), but he would eventually find that there were other authorities which were not under his command, seeming to obey a central authority which he did not know existed and which resided elsewhere—in Central Asia, say, or on Mars. This central authority would give orders and the local militia would obey them, disregarding any conflicting orders the mayor may have given. The question remains: Who or what is this authority? What is the 'other' directive unconscious center of the psyche? Jung called it the Self—the Self in contradistinction to the ego. (Whitmont, *Symbolic Quest*, 216–17).

See also Jung's description of the Self in Jung, *Psychological Types*, 460–61 (§§789–91).

34 The concept of integrity in depth was first described in John Beebe, *Integrity in Depth* (New York: Fromm International, 1995).

35 Viktor Frankl, *Man's Search for Meaning* (Boston: Beacon, 2006), 112.

CHAPTER 15: IT WILL BE A MILESTONE WHEN WE CAN SAY "WE'RE HERE IN ASPEN. IT'S BEAUTIFUL."

36   The fact that humans, both male and female, are made in the image of God is a fundamental belief about the true essence of human nature that is central to both Jewish and Christian teaching. See Anthony Hoekema, *Created in God's Image* (Grand Rapids: Eerdmans, 1986); Dietrich Bonhoeffer, *Creation and Fall Temptation: Two Biblical Studies* (New York: Touchstone, 1997); Glenn Sunshine, *The Image of God* (South Bend, IN: Every Square Inch, 2013); and Richard Lints, *Identity and Idolatry: The Image of God and Its Inversion*, (Downers Grove, IL: InterVarsity, 2015). Another way to understanding the image of God is Dorothy Sayers's approach of viewing God's work in the world as being analogous to the creative process of writing fiction; see Dorothy Sayers, *The Mind of the Maker* (New York: Continuum, 1994).

37   Jung defined the Spirit of the Depths as the totality of the personal and collective unconscious, including complexes and archetypes like the Anima. The Spirit of the Times was the totality of the personal and collective consciousness (i.e., the personal and cultural forces and milieu of daily life). The Self is the psychological force within the personal and collective psyche that orchestrates and integrates the Spirit of the Depths and the Spirit of the Times to provide directionality and intention to all living entities to the ultimate goal of unifying these opposing forces into a cohesive whole.

CHAPTER 16: WHY DON'T YOU JUST GET OVER IT?

38   See Singer, *Boundaries of the Soul*.

39   See https://www.britannica.com/topic/plagiarism.

40   See Dennis Apple, *Life after the Death of My Son: What I'm Learning* (Kansas City, MO: Beacon Hill, 2008).

CHAPTER 18: THREE STRIKES AND YOU'RE OUT

41   See Colin Murray Parkes and Holly Prigerson, *Bereavement*, 2nd ed. (New York: Routledge, 2009); and Earl Grollman, *Living When a Loved One Has Died*, 3rd ed. (Boston: Beacon, 1995).

42   See Peter Senge, *The Fifth Discipline: The Art and Practice of the Learning Organization* (New York: Doubleday, 1990), 63.

CHAPTER 19: THE REALITY OF THOMAS'S DEATH PERMEATES TO DEEPER LEVELS

43   Jung described the relationship between the personal and collective elements of the unconscious using a metaphor of the bloom of a plant and its root system. "Life has always seemed to me like a plant that lives on its rhizome. Its true life is invisible, hidden in the rhizome. The part that appears above ground lasts only a single summer. Then it withers away—an ephemeral apparition. When we think of the unending growth and decay of life and civilizations, we cannot escape the impression of absolute nullity. Yet I

have never lost a sense of something that lives and endures underneath the eternal flux. What we see is the blossom, which passes. The rhizome remains." See Jung, *Memories, Dreams, Reflections*, 4.

CHAPTER 20: THE PRELIMINARY HEARING

44   See Norman Geisler, *Chosen but Free: A Balanced View of God's Sovereignty and Free Will*, 3rd ed. (Minneapolis: Bethany House, 2010). Also see J. I. Packer, *Evangelism and the Sovereignty of God* (Downers Grove, IL: InterVarsity, 2008); Roger Olson, *Against Calvinism* (Grand Rapids: Zondervan, 2011); Michael Horton, *For Calvinism* (Grand Rapids: Zondervan, 2011); Roger Olson, *Arminian Theology: Myths and Realities* (Downers Grove, IL: IVP Academic, 2006); and David Steele, Curtis Thomas, and S. Lance Quinn, *The Five Points of Calvinism: Defined, Defended, and Documented* (Phillipsburg, NJ: P&R, 2004).

45   Eric Metaxas is an example of how God's sovereignty works through a person's life, a path he only recognized retrospectively. "Looking back, it seems that God has surreptitiously established a beachhead in my soul and was now laboring to take the high ground, and in a few nights would do just that." Metaxas goes on to describe a dream that he had about ice fishing and lifting a golden fish out of the water. With a deep sense of wonder and insight, he recalls, "Suddenly in that moment I knew that this golden fish I was holding up was no mere fish but was what my father had told me about when we saw the chrome fish on the backs of cars in the seventies. This was that fish, was IXTHYS—*Iesous Christos Theon Yios Sotir*—Jesus Christ the Son of God Our Savior. I knew in the dream—with a new kind of knowing I knew was from God himself—that the living golden fish I held in my hands and had simply lifted out of the water was Jesus, the Christ who had come into our world to die." See Eric Metaxas, *Fish Out of Water: A Search for the Meaning of Life, A Memoir* (Washington, DC: Salem Books, 2021), 271–72.

46   The images and symbols in the dream below show how the partnership between the "me" and the Self in the church facilitation dream functions in two directions along what Jungians call the Ego-Self Axis, because the Self encompasses the totality of both our conscious and unconscious existence. See Edinger, *Ego and Archetype: Individuation*, 3–7. More specifically, the dream below and the church facilitation dream are two different perspectives on the same creative-transformation process, both of which happen together at the same time:

   I was at a large meeting or conference with hundreds of people. The purpose of this meeting was to map out and define the theme and technical program for a subsequent conference on high-energy physics. So, the people who were at this meeting were like a very large "program committee" for the upcoming conference. I'm not sure what my role was at the meeting, but I was not someone in a leadership position. The entire group had met for a few very long and difficult days, and they were *stuck* and couldn't come to closure on what the conference theme and technical program would be. So, there was a lot of frustration, anxious energy, and psychological exhaustion in the room. I decided to take a shot at coming up with what they were supposed to be doing, and I did this on my own, maybe in a corner of the big room or in a separate room so I was by myself. I wrote my ideas on a long narrow sheet of paper that looked like the frames that made up movie film. I sketched out frame after frame of ideas and concepts that rolled up like it was a roll of movie film.

When I had finished, it somehow became known to the larger group that I had done this and had actually solved the problem they had been trying to solve for days. As this news permeated the group in the room, a deep and powerful feeling of anticipation took over the entire group. They brought me up onto a stage, and I had my paper/film roll with my approach written on it in my hand, and people were focusing on me and looking at the roll of paper/film as the psychological energy of finding out what was written on those frames continued to get stronger and stronger. I began to speak, but the room was so large, and there were so many people there, that I was getting hoarse after only saying a few words, so I said to someone, "Can I have a microphone?" Someone promptly gave me a microphone that looked like a hollow cardboard tube. When I spoke into it, my voice carried clearly and loudly across the entire room. But I was thinking in my heart that, prior to actually sharing the details of what I had come up with, I needed to set the tone or provide a larger context for the approach I had developed. So that's what I did. I said something like, "We are part of the historical search for the fundamental constituents of the universe, a search for the ultimate meaning and purpose of all of life." People began to draw in around me and were captivated by what I was saying, because it connected us to one another and gave all of us a sense of meaning and purpose, within which the theme of the conference and technical program had to be framed.

Without this larger historical context (along the Outer Labyrinth of *chronos*) and a sense of meaning and purpose (along the Inner Labyrinth of *kairos*), the conference would not have the impact everyone wanted it to have. In fact, it was the lack of this historical context connected to the larger framework of meaning and purpose that had prevented them from fleshing out a theme and technical program. The dream ends as I'm ready to begin describing the details of what I had come up with.

The church facilitation dream shows the perspective of the Outer Labyrinth (top-down) with the dream-ego leading at the beginning of the meeting and then "recognizing" and "accepting" the fact that the Self (along the Inner Labyrinth) is actually facilitating the exercise (i.e., I stopped trying to get back in charge of the exercise by finding the microphone). The dream above about the high-energy physics conference begins from the opposite perspective of the Inner Labyrinth (bottom-up) with the collective getting stuck about defining a theme and program for the conference, and then the dream-ego (i.e., from the Outer Labyrinth) solving the problem by providing the larger historical context and the meaning and purpose of the proposed conference. Again, the Self encompasses the totality of both our conscious and unconscious existence. So, in this dream, the dream-ego functions as a "mouthpiece" of the Self, solving the problem and addressing the collective by asking for the microphone.

FINDING NEW LIFE AFTER THE DEATH OF MY SON

Taken together, the two dreams provide a wealth of images and symbols that describe how the Self unifies, aligns, and energizes the totality of consciousness (dream-ego) and the unconscious (collective program committee) through the creative process of transformation. I recorded this on April 18, 2021, just two weeks before finding Thomas dead in his bedroom. As I look back from the third year after Thomas's death, I now realize that God was transforming me and giving me the inner psychological tools needed to survive Thomas's death and to find new life.

CHAPTER 21: I'M OKAY (JUST OKAY) LIVING LIFE WITHOUT THOMAS

47 This new sense of hope and vision for the future was based on an emerging sense that I had a mission in life that was yet to unfold, and that I would see my son, Thomas, again in heaven. On the latter, see N. T. Wright, *Surprised by Hope: Rethinking Heaven, the Resurrection, and the Mission of the Church* (New York: HarperOne, 2008).

48 See Rogers, *On Becoming a Person*, 26.

CHAPTER 25: MORE ON FORGIVENESS AND GRACE

49 See Martin Luther King, *A Gift of Love: Sermons from Strength to Love and Other Preachings* (Boston: Beacon, 2012), 47, where he's commenting on Matthew 5:43–45 where Jesus tells us to love our enemies.

50 See Miroslav Volf, *The End of Memory: Remembering Rightly in a Violent World*, 2nd ed. (Grand Rapids: Eerdmans, 2021), 179.

51 See Desmond Tutu, *No Future without Forgiveness* (New York: Doubleday, 1999), 271.

52 See Timothy Keller, *Forgive: Why Should I, And How Can I?* (New York: Viking, 2022), 8–11.

53 This echoes the words of Frank Outlaw: "Watch your thoughts, they become words; watch your words, they become actions; watch your actions, they become habits; watch your habits, they become character; watch your character, for it becomes your destiny." See Frank Outlaw, "What They're Saying," Quote Page, *San Antonio Light*, May 18, 1977.

54 See Richard Bach, *Illusions: The Adventures of a Reluctant Messiah* (New York: Dell, 1989).

CHAPTER 26: A TALE OF TWO LITTLE BOYS

55 See Bridges, *Managing Transitions*, 3.

56 The idea that the human psyche consisted of multiple descending levels came to Jung in a dream he had while on a lecture tour of the United States with Sigmund Freud in 1909. In the dream, Jung was in a house he did not know, yet it was "his" house. It had two stories, and he was on the upper floor, and it occurred to him that he didn't know what the lower floor looked like. He descended the stairs to the ground floor, and everything looked much older, like it dated from the fifteenth or sixteenth century. As he continued exploring the ground floor, he discovered a stone stairway that led down to a cellar. Once downstairs, the floor was made of stone slabs, and he realized this level was from Roman times. He saw a ring on one of the stone slabs, and when he lifted the

slab, he saw a narrow stone stairway that led down into the depths. He walked down that staircase, which led to a low cave that was cut into the rock. The floor was covered in thick layer of dust, and there were bones and broken pieces of pottery scattered all over, as well as two very old human skulls, as if these artifacts were the remains of a primitive culture. See Jung, *Memories, Dreams, Reflections*, 158–62.

57   This echoes the third of ten basic assumptions that Jeremy Taylor uses to do group dream work. See Jeremy Taylor, *The Wisdom of Your Dreams: Using Dreams to Tap into Your Unconscious and Transform Your Life* (New York: Penguin, 2009), 8.

58   For popularized explanation of the Standard Model of the Universe, see Leon Lederman, *The God Particle: If the Universe Is the Answer, What Is the Question?* (New York: Houghton Mifflin, 1993), 275–76. For a technical-scientific explanation, see Lillian Hoddeson, Laurie Brown, Michael Riordan, and Max Dresden, eds., *The Rise of the Standard Model: Particle Physics in the 1960s and 1970s* (Cambridge: Cambridge University Press, 1997), 3–35.

59   One of the ground-breaking books that helped usher in the postmodernist, deconstructivist perspective was Peter Berger and Thomas Luckman, *The Social Construction of Reality: A Treatise in the Sociology of Knowledge* (New York: Anchor, 1966). A popularized version of the postmodernist, deconstructivist view is presented in Walter Truett Anderson, *Reality Isn't What It Used to Be* (San Francisco: HarperSanFrancisco, 1990). Kuhn applied the postmodernist, deconstructivist perspective to the history of science. See Thomas Kuhn, *The Structure of Scientific Revolutions*, 3rd ed. (Chicago: University of Chicago Press, 1996). For a counterpoint, objective realist view of the history of science, see Ian Hacking, *Representing and Intervening: Introductory Topics in the Philosophy of Natural Science* (Cambridge: Cambridge University Press, 1987); Ian Hacking, ed., *Scientific Revolutions* (New York: Oxford University Press, 1985); and Ian Hacking, *The Social Construction of What?* (Cambridge: Harvard University Press, 1999).

60   I already discussed Jung's notion of the Self in note 37. For more discussion on the Self, see Edinger, *Ego and Archetype*, 3–7; Marie-Louise von Franz, *Archetypal Dimensions of the Psyche* (Boston: Shambhala, 1994), 117–18; and Jung, *Aion*, 23–35 (§§43–67) and 222–65 (§§347–421).

61   For example, see the high priest Caiaphas in John 11:49–53.

62   I discuss the creative process in Bodnarczuk, *Island of Excellence*.

63   In addition to the way my heartfelt experience with Thomas generalized to other intimate relationships along the Outer Labyrinth of everyday life, over time I began to see a deep inner transformation happen along the Inner Labyrinth. For example, in the dream I've included below, the Anima appears as an image of my wife, Elin, but at the same time, the image reflects the archetypal function of the Anima in her role as the facilitator of or bridge between the conscious and unconscious dimensions of my psyche:

  I was living in a house with Elin and Thomas that was like the house I lived in on Warren Street in Clifton, and I think we may have been having Sunday dinner. I was just hanging around in my PJs. I looked outside through the window as we were eating, and I saw some people I'd worked with, and I really didn't think anything of it and kept eating. Then it was like I got a glimpse of people who I had known in childhood, in high school, and throughout my entire life, and it began to dawn on me that something was going on. Suddenly, I experienced a cascade of crystallizing thoughts, deep emotions, and attenuated awareness that swelled as some of these people began to walk through the back door of the house near where the bathroom door was. At that moment, it was like scales fell from my eyes, and I exclaimed out loud, "My wife's giving me a birthday party!" In fact, she had invited people from throughout my entire life to come and celebrate my birthday. People from all eras and parts of my life continued to pour into the house— friends, people I had worked with, colleagues, neighbors, and others I had long lost track of. As they continued to pour into the house, they became like an externalized human collage of my life's experiences and emotional memory. I was talking to a couple of them, and it must have been clear how absolutely and utterly shocked I was as I said something like, "I'm standing here in my PJs with all these people, and I haven't shaved or anything." They assured me that it was just fine and all part of the surprise.

In the dream, the Anima invited the people *outside* the house (i.e., in the deep unconscious) who were from all eras and parts of my life—friends, people I had worked with, colleagues, neighbors, and others I had long lost track of—to a birthday party that was *inside* the house (i.e., an image of my conscious awareness), thus facilitating the process of integrating unconscious content into consciousness and the process of individuation along the Ego-Self Axis. See Edinger, *Ego and Archetype*, 3–7. The integration of this unconscious content into consciousness created a new sense of identity and self that the unconscious imaged as a birthday party that happened within the symbolic context of the house that I lived in with my parents from the time I was about twelve years old until I left home at seventeen. What's important to note about this dream, and the impact Thomas had on opening me up to more intimate relationships, is that the unconscious could have chosen any woman, known or unknown, as the image of the Anima in this dream. But the fact that my wife, Elin, was chosen to be the Anima image is significant both psychologically and relationally, because this had an enormous positive impact on me and our relationship in everyday life.

64   Megan Zander, "A Milestone Developmental Stage: The Age of Reason," *Scholastic Parents*, April 12, 2019. https://www.scholastic.com/parents/family-life/social-emotional-learning/development-milestones/age-reason.html. See Theodore Shapiro and Richard Perry, "Latency Revisited: The Age of Seven, Plus or Minus One," *The Psychoanalytic Study of the Child* 31.1 (1976): 79–105.

65   Shapiro and Perry, "Latency Revisited."

66   Vance Havner, *The Best of Vance Havner*, 7th ed. (Grand Rapids: Baker, 1967), 25. Also see Havner, *Living in Kingdom Come* (Shoals, IN: Kingsley, 2017).

CHAPTER 27: I FOUND NEW LIFE AFTER THE DEATH OF MY SON

67   See Daniel Goleman, *Emotional Intelligence: Why It Can Matter More than IQ* (New York: Bantam Books, 1997), 44–45.

68   See Stephan R. Covey, *The Seven Habits of Highly Effective People: Restoring the Character Ethic* (New York: Simon & Schuster, 1989), 40–42.

69   For a detailed and varied discussion on the kingdom of God, see John Bright, *The Kingdom of God: The Biblical Concept and Its Meaning for the Church* (Nashville: Abingdon, 1981); George Eldon Ladd, *The Gospel of the Kingdom: Scriptural Studies in the Kingdom of God* (Grand Rapids: Eerdmans, 1959); Nicholas Perrin, *The Kingdom of God: A Biblical Theology* (Grand Rapids: Zondervan, 2019); and John Sanford, *The Kingdom Within: The Inner Meaning of Jesus' Sayings*, (San Francisco: HarperSanFrancisco, 1987).

CHAPTER 28: BUT THE PAIN DOESN'T GO AWAY

70   See Homer, *The Iliad and The Odyssey*, trans. Robert Fagles (New York: Barnes & Noble, 1970).

71   Jungian analyst Edward Edinger presents a detailed discussion of Jung's view that the mythological gods of ancient Greece (e.g., Zeus, Aphrodite, Apollo, Artemis, Athena) were archetypal expressions of the collective unconscious. He revisits all the major figures, myths, oracles, and legends of the ancient Greek religion, and he shows how these archetypal symbols are the mythic foundation of Western culture and are still relevant today. See Edward Edinger, *Eternal Drama: The Inner Meaning of Greek Mythology* (Boulder, CO: Shambhala, 2001). C. G. Jung, *Man and His Symbols* (New York: Bantam Books, 2023). In much the same way, Jungian analyst Marie-Louise von Franz describes the archetypal nature of the gods of ancient Greece by connecting them to modern-day experience. "Behind the chaotic white water of the external historical events our newspapers tell us about, there still flows a hidden stream of unconscious archetypal factors, which seemingly accidentally collide with one another, but in reality, may well be ruled by an unfathomable destiny, law, or meaning. This is portrayed with incomparable vividness, for example, in the *Iliad*, where on one level men contend with one another through brute force in war, while on another, in the Olympian beyond, the gods too—that is, the archetypal powers—are caught up in strife." See von Franz, *Archetypal Dimensions of the Psyche*, 264. Jung describes the relationship between the alchemical literature, his notion of archetypes, and the primordial images of Greek mythology in Jung, *Mysterium Coniunctionis*, 516 (§735).

72   See Hacking, *Representing and Intervening*, 23.

73   See Richard Dawkins, *The Selfish Gene* (New York: Oxford University Press, 1976), 201–15.

74   My statement that individual and collective psychological causation and sociocultural causation in third-level archetypal grievance stories can ultimately be reduced to physical causation and be explained as natural causes raises what philosophers call the mind-body problem. The mind-body problem focuses on the ways in which conscious thought in

the human mind and the physical workings of the brain and bodily sensory parts work together to create everyday human experience. For example, sad emotions (mental events) cause people to cry (bodily event). Therapeutic approaches that reshape our conscious mindset (cognitive behavioral theory and Luskin's model of forgiveness) can have significant impacts of bodily health; see Beck, *Cognitive Behavior Therapy*, and Luskin, *Forgive for Good*. In much the same way, changing our body chemistry, which in turn affects our brain, with drugs or alcohol changes the way we see ourselves, others, and the world around us in significant ways.

While unproblematic in everyday experience, understanding the causes and interactions between mind and body raises several thorny questions. For example, are the mind and the body separate entities or a single entity? How do the mind and body interact, and can the root cause of mental events be reduced to physical events (neurons) in the brain? Based on the definition of a biblical worldview in note 90, ancient Greek views of the gods and Jung's views of archetypes and the collective unconscious, are both reducible to natural causes that the God of the Bible created. More specifically, Jung's view continues the long historical view that was discussed by Aristotle and was popularized by the seventeenth-century philosopher Rene Descartes as related to dualism versus monism. Cartesian dualism maintains a sharp distinction between mind and matter, while monism claims that there is only one unifying reality of either matter (Hobbes) or essence (Leibniz and Berkeley). See Rene Descartes, *The Philosophical Writings of Descartes*, ed. John Cottingham, Robert Stoothoff, and Dugald Murdoch, 2 vols. (New York: Cambridge University Press, 2008); Thomas Hobbs, *Leviathan* (New York: Penguin, 2017); Gottfried Wilhelm Leibniz, *Discourse on Metaphysics and Other Essays*, 9th ed. (New York: Hackett, 1991); and George Berkeley, *Principles of Human Knowledge and Three Dialogues between Hylas and Philonous* (New York: Penguin, 1988).

In modern times, various forms of this discussion continue with Descartes's form of dualism being viewed as an innate way that humans see themselves, others, and the world around them (Bloom), as the interactive property dualism where mind has causal efficacy on the brain (Popper and Eccles), and a Hobbesian form of physicalism (Damasio, Churchland, and Dennett). See Paul Bloom, *Descartes' Baby: How the Science of Child Development Explains What Makes Us Human* (New York: Basic Books, 2004); Karl Popper and John Eccles, *The Self and Its Brain: An Argument for Interactionism* (Boston: Routledge & Kegan Paul, 1977); Antonio Damasio, *Looking for Spinoza: Joy, Sorrow, and the Feeling Brain* (New York: Harcourt, 2003); Paul Churchland, *Matter and Consciousness*, 3rd ed. (Boston: MIT Press, 2013); and Daniel Dennett, *Kinds of Minds: Toward an Understanding of Consciousness* (New York: Basic Books, 1997). From a theological perspective, Nancey Murphy holds to a physicalist view that does not diminish the ability of humans to relate to a Christian view of God, moral responsibility, and free will; see Nancey Murphy, *Bodies and Souls, or Spirited Bodies?* (New York: Cambridge University Press, 2006); and Nancey Murphy and Warren Brown, *Did My Neurons Make Me Do It?* (New York: Cambridge University Press, 2007).

Finally, the results of a fifteen-year interdisciplinary study involving scientists, scholars of religion, philosophers, and historians presents a rigorously researched study that argues that the prevailing scientific worldview (i.e., physicalism) is seriously incomplete, but in some key elements, it is incorrect; see Edward Kelly, Emily Williams Kelly, Adam Crabtree, Alan Gauld, Michael Grosso, and Bruce Greyson, eds., *Toward a Psychology for the Twenty-First Century*, (New York: Rowman & Littlefield, 2007); Edward Kelly, Adam Crabtree, and Paul Marshall, eds., *Beyond Physicalism: Toward Reconciliation of Science and Spirituality* (New York: Rowman & Littlefield, 2015); Edward Kelly and Paul Marshall, eds., *Consciousness Unbound: Liberating Mind from the Tyranny of Materialism* (New York: Rowman & Littlefield, 2021).

75 John Milton, *Paradise Lost*, 3rd ed. (Indianapolis: Hackett, 2005). God used two safeguards to ensure that our primordial parents (and humankind) would not permanently align with Satan as an unintended consequence of this original fourth-level grievance story. First, He put enmity between the serpent and his offspring, and the woman and her Descendant (a prophetic reference to Christ) who would prevail over Satan by the resurrection from the dead (Genesis 3:15). Second, He shut them out of the garden lest they eat of the tree of life and be alienated from God for eternity (Genesis 3:22-24). Other than John 3:16, these may be some of the most crucial verses in the Bible.

76 See Andrew Delbanco, *The Death of Satan: How Americans Have Lost the Sense of Evil* (New York: Farrar, Straus & Giroux, 1995), 9.

77 See Timothy Keller, *Walking with God through Pain and Suffering* (New York: Penguin, 2013), 113–14.

78 See C. S. Lewis, *The Problem of Pain* (New York: Macmillan, 1973), 81.

79 See Nicholson, *Shadowlands*, 87.

CHAPTER 29: ASSUMING EVERYTHING WOULD WORK OUT

80 See Drug Enforcement Agency Intelligence Report, *Fentanyl Flow to the United States*.

81 See Jung, *Memories, Dreams, Reflections*, 11ff.

82 Jung, *Memories, Dreams, Reflections*.

83 Jung, *Structure and Dynamics*, 237–97 (§§443–569), and C. G. Jung, *Children's Dreams: Notes from the Seminar Given in 1936–1940* (Princeton: Princeton University Press, 2008), 1–31.

84 I still use the same eight guiding principles to interpret dreams today. *First*, dreams must be benchmarked against a historical-grammatical view of the word of God in the Bible, especially the empirical reality of the three consequences of sin. *Second*, dreams don't have to be "understood" to transform. *Third*, dreams don't speak "English" and need to be interpreted (translated). *Fourth*, the primary focus of our dreams is intrapsychic, that is, *they* describe what's going on in our heads (our log in Matthew 7:1–5), *not* the heads of others or in the world (i.e., the personal or collective speck in others)—they reveal *our* inner response to people and the world. *Fifth*, dreams tell us the unvarnished truth about who we are. *Sixth*, dreams say what they mean, and they mean what they say.

Seventh, dreams and their primary meaning belong to the dreamer alone. *Eighth*, the Self is the creator and orchestrator of our dreams and the forces that shape and define our life. The eight guiding principles help structure dream work as an open-ended, dialectic process that allows the unconscious to communicate its objective, compensatory, or complementary message from the Inner Labyrinth to our conscious waking selves. The guiding principles can be used to do individual dream work, with or without a Jungian analyst as a guide.

 They can also be used when doing group dream work with the three stages of the Ullman Method of Group Dream Analysis, where the group process is moderated by a trained facilitator. In the *first* stage, the dreamer reads or tells their dream while group members write it down or read along. Then, the group members are free to ask clarifying questions about the dream content. When the questioning is complete, the facilitator begins stage *two* by inviting group members to share their reflections on the dream by beginning with the phrase "If this were my dream, I would feel," followed by comments on the images, metaphors, symbols, and narrative content of the dream as if the dream were theirs. The preamble acknowledges the fact that only the dreamer can say with any certainty what their dream really means (i.e., the seventh guiding principle). While members of the group share their reflections on the dream, the dreamer listens and takes notes. This allows group members to offer a wide variety of interpretations for the dreamer to ponder in search of deeper levels of hidden meaning beyond what they see in their dream. In the *third* stage, the dreamer "takes the dream back" from the group and shares any insights or "aha" experiences that emerged in consciousness as a result of the group's input. The dreamer also rereads the dream scene by scene, stopping to add additional insights that may have emerged. The session ends with the dreamer making closing comments about the dream and thanking the group for its input. When the dream group meets again, the facilitator gives the dreamer from the previous session an opportunity to share any additional insights they'd gotten about the dream since the previous meeting. For a more detailed description of the three stages, see Montague Ullman, *Appreciating Dreams* (Old Chelsea Station, NY: Cosimo Books, 2006); and Montague Ullman and Nan Zimmerman, *Working with Dreams* (Oxford: Routledge, 2017). For a Jungian approach to working with dream groups, see Tess Castleman, *Threads, Knots, Tapestries: How a Tribal Connection is Revealed through Dreams and Synchronicities* (Einsiedeln: Daimon Verlag, 2018); and Tess Castleman, *Sacred Dream Circles: A Guide to Facilitating Jungian Dream Groups* (Einsiedeln: Daimon Verlag, 2009). One of the most interesting examples of the inner healing and transforming power of the dream work are the dream groups Taylor led with hardened criminals inside San Quentin Prison; see Taylor, *Wisdom of Your Dreams*, 125–36.

85 For a discussion on various views on the doctrine of Scripture, see John Frame, *The Doctrine of the Word of God* (Philipsburg, NJ: P&R, 2010); N. T. Wright, *Scripture and the Authority of God: How to Read the Bible Today* (New York: HarperCollins, 2005); and N. T. Wright, *Surprised by Scripture: Engaging Contemporary Issues* (New York: Harper One,

2014). Also see, William Sanford Lasor, David Allan Hubbard, and Frederic William Bush, *Old Testament Survey: The Message, Form, and Background of the Old Testament*, 2nd ed. (Grand Rapids: Eerdmans, 1996); Robert Gromacki, *New Testament Survey* (Grand Rapids: Baker, 1974); Alfred Edersheim, *The Life and Times of Jesus the Messiah: Complete and Unabridged in One Volume* (Peabody, MA: Hendrickson, 1993); and Walter Kaiser and Moisés Silva, *Introduction to Biblical Hermeneutics: The Search for Meaning*, rev. ed. (Grand Rapids: Zondervan, 2007).

86   My definition of a biblical worldview is the belief that the deep underlying *causes* of what exists in the universe, and what's right and wrong with the world, are defined by the events described in the first three chapters of Genesis. Holding a biblical worldview provides a biblical foundation upon which to build a Christian understanding of the human psyche and its role in our personal and collective human relationships and in our relationship with the God, who created the universe. This underlying assumption is important because, as G. K. Chesterton argues, "The world does explain itself," and our assumption that God was the ultimate cause of the universe has enormous end-effects on how we live our lives. See G. K. Chesterton, *Orthodoxy: The Classic Account of a Remarkable Christian Experience* (Wheaton, IL: Shaw, 1994), 65.

More specifically, all theories, models, and explanations about life and what "causes" things are like lenses through which we view the empirical reality of day-to-day life. So, it's important to note that scientific, Jungian, New Age, political, and other religious worldviews (including Christianity) are explanatory, interpretive *overlays* on what the empirical reality of history and everyday life *mean* that we must choose between. This is important to remember when talking to non-Christians, because there are a lot of other ways to piece together a "worldview" that contains good components, powerful explanations, folk wisdom, and truth elements that have been tested over the years, sometimes with good explanatory success. So, the first guiding principle for interpreting dreams assumes that we consciously *choose* a biblical worldview above others, and then we use it as a benchmark against which all other human knowledge and endeavors are judged. For example, the three consequences of sin are an *empirical* reality that is experienced by Christians and non-Christians alike, but seeing those end-effects through the lens of a biblical worldview means the explanation of the root causes of our alienation from ourselves, our alienation from others, and our alienation from God are found in the events described in the first three chapters of Genesis.

The key indicator that a worldview *is not* biblical is that it attributes the underlying "cause" of what's wrong with this world to one or more "created" things that are *causal factors* rather than the root cause. By definition, a root cause is defined as the cause(s) that when removed eliminates the effect. Eliminating causal factors may mitigate the effect, but it does not go away. A created "thing" is anything God has caused to exist as part of the universe. Given the distinction between Jung's inside-out, subjective perspective of the God image (*Imago Dei*) and my own outside-in, objective perspective of God speaking the universe into existence in the Big Bang, Jung believed that the psyche (i.e., the Self) was eternal and not created by God. To reiterate Jung's view of the afterlife, he says, "Whether I believe in personal survival after death or not, I could not say that I believe in it, since I have not the gift of belief. I only can say whether I know something or not. I do know that the psyche possesses certain qualities transcending the confinement in time and space. . . . the psyche is capable of functioning unhampered by the categories of time and space. Ergo it is in itself an equally transcendental being and therefore relatively non-spatial and 'eternal.'" See Jung, "Letter to H. J. Barrett," 333.

87   The historical-grammatical method is a Christian hermeneutical method that has two main goals. The *first goal* is to discover the biblical authors' intended meaning by reconstructing the historical context in which the author wrote and understanding the clear grammatical meaning of the words and syntax used. The *second* goal is to create a "hermeneutical arch" that applies the meaning of the text within the writer's historical context to the challenges and issues that Christians face today along their journey of faith. The historical-grammatical method affirms the divine authority of the Bible, where the words of human authors are the verbally inspired Word of God that is without error *in the original writings*. The words in italics are key, because they are a statement of faith about documents we no longer possess. As biblical scholar F. F. Bruce explains:

> The books of the Bible were first written many centuries ago—the latest of them over eighteen centuries ago and they have been copied and recopied many times since then. They were, first written in Hebrew, Aramaic, or Greek, and the vast majority of people who read them today read them in translations. But neither the copyists nor translators are infallible and the cautionary phrase, 'as originally given', is inserted . . . to indicate that allowance must be made for errors in transmission and translation. With errors in translation, we are not concerned in this article. But it is the inevitability of errors in the process of copying and recopying documents that makes the science of textual criticism necessary. This science endeavors as far as possible to establish the exact wording that was used in the original document, in the original writer's autograph.

Quote from F. F. Bruce, "Textual Criticism," *The Christian Graduate* 6.4 (1953): 135. Bruce points out that the preface to the 1884 Revised Version of the Old Testament states that the earliest Hebrew manuscript that was known was from AD 916. There were translations of the Hebrew Scriptures, such as Jerome's Latin Vulgate, that dated from AD 400, and the Greek Septuagint dates even earlier from the third and second centuries BC. The archeological discovery of the Dead Sea Scrolls in 1946 included around nine hundred fragmentary scrolls in Hebrew and Aramaic dating from the third century BC to the first century AD. Carbon-14 dating has shown they are the oldest surviving Hebrew manuscripts of entire books later included in the biblical canon, along with extrabiblical and deuterocanonical manuscripts that preserve evidence of the diversity of religious thought in late Second Temple Judaism. For example, the Dead Sea Scroll manuscript for the book Jeremiah was likely one third shorter than the version of Jeremiah in the Masoretic text (following the Septuagint), but despite some discrepancies, is a remarkable consistency.

Bruce also notes an independent check on the first five books of the content of the Hebrew Bible in comparison with the text of the Samaritan Pentateuch, which traditionally has been dated from the fourth century BC. Bruce goes on to say, "The study of the early textual families has carried our researches back to the middle of the second century. Can we push them still further back, into the first century itself? Nearly seventy years ago D. Warfield said: 'The autographic text of the New Testament is distinctly within the reach of criticism in so immensely the greater part of the volume that we cannot despair of restoring to ourselves and the Church of God, His Book, word for word, as He gave it by inspiration to men' (*Textual Criticism of the New Testament*, p. 15). With the wealth of additional knowledge that has come to light since then, we need not be less hopeful today." Bruce made that comment about Warfield and his prognosis for the field of textual criticism over seventy years ago, and much progress has been made since then; see Benjamin B. Warfield, *The Theological Education: An Introduction to the Textual Criticism of the New Testament* (South Yarra: Leopold, 2016).

There have been a number of subsequent archeological discoveries of texts that have helped biblical scholars reconstruct earlier versions of the New Testament text. Bruce Metzger's commentary describes the details of how textual criticism works on the Greek text of the New Testament in Bruce Metzger, *A Textual Commentary on the Greek New Testament*, 2nd ed. (Peabody, MA: Hendrickson, 2005). Metzger tells us, "One of the chief purposes of the commentary is to set forth the reasons that led the Committee, or a majority of the members of the Committee, to adopt certain variant readings for inclusion in the text and to relegate certain other readings to the apparatus. On the basis of a record of the voting of the Committee, as well as, for most sessions, more or less full notes of the discussions that preceded the voting, the present writer has sought to frame and express concisely (a) the main problem, or problems involved in each set of variants and (b) the Committee's evaluation and resolution of those problems." For other resources on textual criticism and related topics, see G. K. Beale, *The Erosion of Inerrancy in Evangelicalism: Responding to New Challenges to Biblical Authority* (Wheaton, IL: Crossway, 2008); F. F. Bruce, *The History of the Bible in English*, 3rd ed. (New York: Oxford University Press, 1978); F. F. Bruce, *The New Testament Documents: Are They Reliable?* (Grand Rapids: Eerdmans, 2003); and F. F. Bruce, *Israel and the Nations: The History of Israel from the Exodus to the Fall of the Second Temple* (Downers Grove, IL: InterVarsity Academic, 1998).

From a Jungian perspective, the issues related to biblical inerrancy and textual criticism happen exclusively along the Outer Labyrinth of daily life (*chronos*) and the destiny that biblical scholars have created with their conscious choices. But in addition to the way God spoke in the Scriptures through the words of the original human authors, He has also acted with sovereignty along the Inner Labyrinth (*kairos*) to preserve the true meaning of the biblical text through the conscious and unconscious (intended and unintended) beliefs, strategies, mindsets, and actions of those who have worked with thousands of manuscripts over the centuries.

88 As I've described in note 2, the first two consequences of sin help to define the structure and dynamics of the conscious and unconscious dimensions of the human psyche (i.e., the Outer and Inner Labyrinths) at both the personal and collective levels, what Jung called the Spirit of the Times (everything that is conscious) and the Spirit of the Depths (everything that is unconscious). See Jung, *Red Book*, 229ff. So, prior to the fall of humans described in Genesis 3, the psyche (i.e., the Self) was a single unified whole that was in complete and full communion with the God of the universe. The radical severing between the conscious and unconscious mind (i.e., the structure of the psyche that Jung described) and the inner directionality and intentionality of the Self in the individuation process is a direct result of the first two consequences of sin, with the ultimate root cause of the first two consequences being the third consequence—alienation from God. For a discussion of all three consequences of sin from a biblical worldview, see Timothy Keller, *Every Good Endeavor: Connecting Your Work to God's Work* (New York: Dutton, 2012), 156–65.

89 Over seventy passages in the Bible refer to dreams and visions. Sam Martyn references Morton Kelsey on the importance of dreams to the cultural world of the New Testament, which is reflected in the fact that there were twelve Greek words available to refer to them. See Sam Martyn, "The Role of Pre-Conversion Dreams and Visions in Islamic Contexts: An Examination of the Evidence," *Southeastern Theological Review* 9.2 (2018): 55–74; Kelsey, *God, Dreams, and Revelation*, 81–87. Martyn also points out that dreams and visions appear in the post-resurrection church world in Acts with the ministries of Stephen, Paul, Ananias, Cornelius, and Peter (Acts 7:56; 9:4–6, 10–16; 10:3–6, 10–16; 12:7; 16:9; 18:9; 22:17; 23:11; 27:23–24). He goes on to say, "This is not to suggest that in the age of a closed canon, dreams and visions function similarly to the way they functioned in biblical times. The New Testament offers clear warnings about such visions (e.g., Galatians 1:8). Still, a wholly negative attitude that dismisses any role for dreams outright is clearly inconsonant with scripture" (60).

Morton Kelsey shows that for the first millennium of the church, almost all of the apostolic fathers expressed a positive attitude toward the role that postcanonical dreams played in the Christian life (e.g., Justin, Origen, Tertullian, Cyprian, Athanasius, Basil, Gregory of Nyssa, Gregory of Nazianzus, Chrysostom, Ambrose, Augustine, and Jerome). See Kelsey, *God, Dreams, and Revelation*, 99–167. Kelsey argues that the shift away from the importance of dreams began with the rediscovery of Aristotle's writings and the theology of Thomas Aquinas. Aquinas was pulled between Aristotle's naturalistic view of dreams and the church's positive teaching on dreams, and he subsequently ignored this key element of the Christian life (152–58). See also Steven Kruger, *Dreaming in the Middle Ages* (New York: Cambridge University Press, 1992); and Morton Kelsey, *Adventure Inward* (Minneapolis: Fortress, 1980). As a result, Kelsey writes, "In Western Christian society today there is no group, practically no voice at all, that would encourage people to understand their dreams as a source of religious insight into life. Instead, most twentieth-century Christians simply assume that the ideas of finding religious meaning or reality in dreams is a proven fallacy that went out with the Dark Ages, and they see no need to think about it again" (*God, Dreams, and Revelation*, 17).

In contradistinction, dreams continued to play a key role in Islam; see Martyn, "Pre-Conversion Dreams and Visions"; Bill Musk, "Dreams and the Ordinary Muslim," *Missiology: An International Review* 16.2 (1988): 163–72; Kelly Bulkeley, ed., *Dreaming in Christianity and Islam: Culture, Conflict, and Creativity* (New Brunswick: Rutgers University Press, 2009); Iain Edgar, *The Dream in Islam: From Qur'anic Tradition to Jihadist Inspiration* (New York: Berghahn Books, 2011); Kelly Bulkeley, *Big Dreams: The Science of Dreaming and the Origins of Religion* (New York: Oxford University Press, 2016); John Sanford, *Dreams and Healing: A Succinct and Lively Interpretation of Dreams* (New York: Paulist, 1978).

90   This first guiding principle is also what distinguishes the biblical approach to interpreting dreams presented here from other religions that have strong dream traditions, such as the Islam, where the teachings of the Qur'an and the hadiths are viewed as the ultimate authority by which every realm of human knowledge and endeavor should be judged. Islam identifies three types of dreams: true dreams, false dreams, and meaningless dreams, and only true dreams can be interpreted. Islamic dream expert Iain Edgar says, "In Islam, officially only a prophet—preferably Muhammed—is thought able to precisely interpret a dream, especially a true dream (*al-ruya*). Therefore, most of the lore of dream interpretation in Islam is based on the teachings of the Qur'an and the hadiths. . . . The first principle of dream interpretation is that it is permissible for others besides the Prophet to interpret dreams. However, when others interpret dreams, such as shaykhs, they run the risk of disagreeing among themselves. . . . Therefore, the fourth principle of dream interpretation states that the interpretations of ordinary humans, i.e., in contradistinction to prophets, are no more than educated guesses, based on knowledge of the symbols." See Edgar, *Dream in Islam*, 32. Edgar's research shows that in daily life, many people do interpret dreams, but they use dream dictionaries that categorize and classify interpretations of many dream symbols based on the Qur'an and the hadiths. So, unlike the traditional one-on-one Jungian approach to dream work, Montague Ullman's method of group dream work, and even the biblical approach to individuation and dream work described in this memoir, the process of Islamic dream interpretation is much more structured, scripturally based, and directive toward the dreamer. As Edgar puts it: "Islamic dream interpreters tend to tell the believer what the dream means based on their understanding of the Qur'an and the hadiths, which are perceived to contain all that humans need to know to live well" (16).

This approach is very different than the seventh guiding principle for interpreting dreams presented here, which states that the meaning of dreams belongs to the dreamer alone (i.e., only the dreamer can know what a dream means with any level of certainty). For more discussion on the Islamic method of dream work and the history of dream methodologies, see Iain R. Edgar, *Guide to Imagework* (London: Routledge, 2004); Bulkeley, *Dreaming in Christianity and Islam*; Bulkeley, *Big Dreams*; and Steven F. Kruger,

Dreaming in the Middle Ages, Cambridge Studies in Medieval Literature 14 (New York: Cambridge University Press, 2005).
91 See Jung, *Aion*, 70–71 (§126).
92 Neuroscience has shown that patterns of emotions are stored in the amygdala portion of the human brain prior to the neocortex being formed and prior to our ability to use of language. Because 55 percent of communication is visual, 38 percent is tone of voice, and only 7 percent is word choice, children receive 90 percent of emotional communication before being able to speak a single word. For a discussion on emotions and the amygdala, see Goleman, *Emotional Intelligence*, 14ff.; Joseph Ledoux, *The Emotional Brain: The Mysterious Underpinnings of Emotional Life* (New York: Simon & Schuster, 1998); and Joseph Ledoux, *Synaptic Self: How Our Brains Become Who We Are* (New York: Viking, 2002).

In addition, the language of emotions seen in facial expressions and body language tends to be universal. What varies from culture to culture are the cultural rules for expressing them. See Nico Frijda, *The Laws of Emotion* (Mahwah, NJ: Erlbaum Associates, 2007), 185–87; Richard Lazarus, *Emotion and Adaptation* (New York: Oxford University Press, 1991), 68–75; Robert Plutchik, *The Psychology and Biology of Emotions* (New York: HarperCollins, 1994), 54–61; Robin Dunbar, *The Human Story: A New History of Mankind's Evolution* (London: Faber & Faber, 2004), 130–32; Robin Dunbar, *Grooming, Gossip, and the Evolution of Language*, (London: Faber & Faber, 1996), 136–38; and Paul Ekman, "What We Become Emotional About," in *Feelings and Emotions: The Amsterdam Symposium*, ed. Anthony Manstead, Nico Frijda, and Agneta Fischer (New York: Cambridge University Press, 2004), 119–35. On the one hand, the nonverbal aboriginal language of dreams is present in our day-to-day conscious life, but we're largely unaware of it. We see this when a person tells us a dream and the unconscious creates an image of *their* dream in *our* minds. On the other hand, some people like Carl Rogers have experienced the fact that "what is most personal is most universal" in his therapeutic work with clients, as well as colleagues and other relationships. See Rogers, *On Becoming a Person*, 26.
93 This guideline is very different than the approach taken in the Islamic dream interpretation. Iain Edgar describes what Jung would call the Spirit of the Depths (i.e., everything that is unconscious) and the Spirit of the Times (i.e., everything that is conscious) like this: "As in all dream cultures, jihadists both dream and interpret their dreams within their own culturally specific world view, in this case that of Islam, according to which this material world is not our final destination, but rather a series of lessons and tests and a preparation for the hereafter and the time of judgement at death." See Edgar, *Dream in Islam*, 65. This doctrine is similar to the Christian doctrine that Jesus taught in John 14:2–6: "'In My Father's house are many rooms; if that were not so, I would have told you, because I am going there to prepare a place for you. And if I go and prepare a place for you, I am coming again and will take you to Myself, so that where I am, there you also will be. And you know the way where I am going.' Thomas said to Him, 'Lord, we do not know where You are going; how do we know the way?' Jesus

said to him, 'I am the way, and the truth, and the life; no one comes to the Father except through Me.'" Edgar goes to describe the ways in which the real world and the world of the afterlife intersect in night dreams and daytime visons. As such, Edgar states, "Islamic dream interpretation is much more scripturally based and therefore more directive towards the dreamer. Also, the manifest content of the dream often leads to very straightforward and literal interpretation" (33).

94 Rather than seeing the images, symbols, and narratives in dreams as patterns of inner psychological transformation, as the fourth guiding principle does, the Islamic tradition of dream interpretation often sees them as messages to be acted on. Iain Edgar states, "In regard to the dreamer's actions in real life, the fourth principle of Islamic dream interpretation states that the dreamer is permitted to carry out in real life what he has seen as good in the dream." See Edgar, *Dream in Islam*, 33. For example, Edgar says, "I also read a report that Mullah Omar, the Taliban leader, had founded the Taliban following a commandment from a sacred figure in a night dream." Edgar references an interview that he did with the very well-respected Muslim Pakistani BBC journalist who was virtually the only foreign journalist who had access to Mullah Omar before the events of 9/11. Based on the interview Edgar states, "This interview confirms the centrality of the inspirational role that Mullah Omar's reported dreams, whatever their actual veracity, had and possibly have today on Taliban leaders and foot soldiers" (4). And again, Edgar reports that "A companion of the Prophet, Abdulla b. Zayd, dreamed the *Adhan*, the five-time-daily Islamic call to prayer, at a time when the Prophet Muhammed and his followers were seeking a way of defining their new faith in contradistinction to the calling horn of the Jews and the bell of the Christians" (115). The Islamic method's focus on acting out the content in dreams is also very different than the fifth guiding principle that states that dreams tell the unvarnished truth about who the dreamer really is.

95 But at the same time, there's more to it than this, which Jung describes in Jung, *Children's Dreams*, 4–6.

96 What is important to note here is that there are dreams that anticipate future psychical aspects of personality along the Inner Labyrinth (*kairos*), but they don't predict future events in space-time along the Outer Labyrinth (*chronos*). Jung addresses this in Jung, *Children's Dreams*, 18ff. There are also dreams that actually do have precognitive elements, where they seem to predict events along the Outer Labyrinth events, but on Jung's view, both of these can be verified only by hindsight. Jung called dreams like this and waking life experiences, like my sharing my journey of faith in 2010, synchronicities. Iain Edgar's research has identified similar instances in Islamic dreams. For example, Edgar states that "Following the 9/11 attack in New York, many newspapers reported a transcript of a video in which bin Laden refers to the anticipatory dreams of some of his followers. While these followers apparently did not know of the planned attacks, bin Laden is concerned with the fact that 'the secret [of the attacks] would be revealed if everyone starts seeing it in their dreams.' Early in the video bin Laden says: 'Abu'l Hassan al Masri told me a year ago: "I saw in a dream; we were playing a soccer game against the

Americans. When our team showed up in the field, they were all pilots!" He [Al Masri] didn't know anything about the operation until he heard it on the radio. He said the game went on and we defeated them. That was a good omen for us.' The use of the term omen indicates a belief that dreams are a potential source of divination, especially for pious and spiritually oriented Muslims." See Edgar, *Dream in Islam*, 66–67. Edgar has identified other examples of dreams that predict the future, at least some of which are shared in the Qur'an and the Bible. For example, "The Joeseph sura in the Qur'an (12:6) makes this especially clear as Joeseph, through his interpretation of the dream of seven fat and thin cows of the Egyptian pharaoh, enables the pharaoh to plan ahead for a succession of bad harvests. . . . Muhammed dreams before the battle of Badr that the enemy forces are smaller than they actually are, so giving him and his army confidence in victory (Qur'an 8:43)" (66). On reflection, I'm left with the same lingering questions that I had about Thomas's dreams that I describe in Part 3 of this memoir. Are these dreams third-level archetypal grievance stories that emerged from the collective unconscious of the psyche, where the dreamers are like individual aspen trees that are all connected the same root system of the collective unconscious? Or are they fourth-level biblical grievance stories where spiritual forces are engaged in a collective proxy war, with dreamers acting out these inner images, symbols, and forces in space-time?

97   The fact that humans are "spiritual" beings is evidenced by a *vacuum*, something that's *missing* in life, eternally *dead* because we are alienated from God's eternal life (*aiōnios*), even though we may be alive in the biological (*bios*) and psychological (*psychē*) senses and may even experience a sense of meaning, significance, and life at its best (*zoē*). The fact that humans are spiritual beings is experienced not as definable attributes of the *presence* of spirit, like it is often portrayed, but rather by its *absence*—by the God-shaped vacuum that only God can fill. This important distinction helps to tease apart the ways in which Jung conflated the psychological (i.e., the first three grievance story levels) and spiritual dimensions of humans (i.e., a fourth-level grievance story), resulting in an overall ontology that claimed that the Self, the psyche, was eternal. So, Christians and non-Christians experience the "spiritual" as something that's *missing* in life, something that's really *gone wrong* with the world, not as something "we are." Jungians believe the lifelong process of individuation will fill this vacuum, when in reality it only addresses the first two consequences of sin—alienation from ourselves and others. Only a biblical approach to individuation addresses all three consequences, including our alienation from God through faith in the saving power of Jesus's life, death, and resurrection from the dead.

98   See John White, *The Fight: A Practical Handbook of Christian Living* (Downers Grove, IL: InterVarsity, 2008), 13–15.

99   White, *Practical Handbook of Christian Living*, 16.

100   In medieval alchemy, the Latin word *negredo* was the first step on the journey to the philosopher's stone, where the alchemical ingredients had to be cleaned and cooked into a black matter—a state of psychological being that Jungians call confronting the dark

side within, the shadow, or the experience of the dark night of the soul. Jung's insights about the relationship of alchemy and the individuation process describe four phases in this process. In the first phase, the person must confront and become painfully aware of the dark shadow elements of themselves that reside in the unconscious and must be brought into conscious awareness. The process transforms the darkness of *negredo* into the second phase (Latin: *albedo* or whiteness). Jung related the *albedo* part of the individuation process as one in which the previously unconscious, contrasexual images of the Anima and Animus provide insight into our darker shadow elements, and ego's perceived dominance over the personality, and psychological "light" begins to shine in the psyche. In the third phase described by the Latin *citrinitas* (yellowness), a person experienced the dawning of the metaphorical solar light inherent in one's being, so the reflective "lunar light or soul" was no longer needed. The Latin word for the final phase is *rubedo* (redness) where this psyche has once again been transformed metaphorically to be the overall goal of the both the alchemical process and the individuation process, symbolized by gold and the philosopher's stone (see my dream about the stone in note 27). For a detailed description of Jung's research on alchemy, see Jung, *Psychology and Alchemy*.

101 See Jung, *Children's Dreams*, 4–6.

102 What I had not yet experienced and recognized back then was that the unusual, obsessive, recurrent, and highly emotional nature of the dark and destructive images, symbols, and narratives in Thomas's dreams indicated they were not "individual" in the sense that they could not be derived entirely from personal experience. Nor could they be understood entirely in terms of what I would come to call a third-level archetypal grievance story (see chapter 28). Jung describes a case study at the archetypal level where a psychiatrist brought him a handwritten booklet that he'd received as a Christmas present from his ten-year-old daughter. It contained a series of dreams she'd had when she was eight years old. They were childlike images, but at the same time they contained dark, destructive symbols and images that were archetypal, with each dream starting with the words "Once upon a time." See C. G. Jung, *The Symbolic Life*, vol. 18 of *The Collected Works of C. G. Jung*, trans. R. F. C. Hull, 2nd ed. (Princeton: Princeton University Press, 1989), 229ff. (§§525ff.). Jung goes on to explain, "They are what Freud called 'archaic remnants'—thought forms whose presence cannot be explained by anything in the individual's own life, but seem to be aboriginal, innate, and inherited patterns of the human mind" (227 [§521]). The dark and destructive images and symbols that emerged from Thomas's unconscious were a combination of personal and collective archetypal images. But when viewed from a biblical worldview and biblical approach to individuation, these dark and destructive images also revealed what I would come to call a fourth-level biblical grievance story (see chapter 28). They revealed the spiritual warfare between God, the creator of the universe, and Satan, the rebel celestial being, who is the ruler of this world (John 12:31), and who will ultimately be defeated by God at the end of chronological time.

103 See G. K. Beale with David Campbell, *Revelation: A Shorter Commentary* (Grand Rapids: Eerdmans, 2015) and G. K. Beale, *The Book of Revelation*, New International

FINDING NEW LIFE AFTER THE DEATH OF MY SON

Greek New Testament Commentary (Grand Rapids: Eerdmans, 1999).
104 Polanyi argued that we can know more than we can tell. Not only can't we articulate things we know tacitly, but he also claimed that ultimately all knowledge was rooted in tacit knowledge. See Michael Polanyi, *The Tacit Dimension*, rev. ed. (Chicago: University of Chicago Press, 2009); and Michael Polanyi, *Personal Knowledge: Towards a Post-Critical Philosophy*, (Chicago: University of Chicago Press, 2015).

CHAPTER 30: THE PROXY WAR
105 See Jung, *Children's Dreams*, 2.
106 Jung, *Children's Dreams*, 28.
107 See Dawkins, *Selfish Gene*, 203ff.
108 See Mark Bodnarczuk, *The Breckenridge Enneagram: A Guide to Personal and Professional Growth*, (Breckenridge, CO: Breckenridge, 2009), 208.

CHAPTER 31: THE ORANGE HIPPIE VAN
109 See Sigmund Freud, *Introductory Lectures on Psychoanalysis, 1915–17* (New York: Norton, 1990).
110 See Greg Laurie and Ellen Vaughn, *Jesus Revolution* (Grand Rapids: Baker, 2018); and Lonnie Frisbee, *The Jesus Revolution* (Santa Monica, CA: Freedom, 2017).
111 See Peck, *People of the Lie*, 37.

CHAPTER 32: DIGGING DEEPER
112 Kessler, *Finding Meaning*, 49.
113 Kessler, *Finding Meaning*, 49–50.
114 For me, this second question was one of the most important, and difficult, in my quest to come to terms with Thomas's death. Having a firsthand *yada* experience of complexes and archetypes was necessary, but not sufficient, to determining this. More specifically, the first consequence of sin (i.e., alienation from ourselves) leads us to believe that we're just one person. But the truth is that we live in the three-pound universe between our ears. Yet, it's amazing how little most people know about themselves because of our natural tendency to experience ourselves as a single unified whole. Most of us have simply adopted the Cartesian intuition "I'm in here and the world's out there,"; see Rene Descartes, *The Philosophical Writings of Descartes*, trans. John Cottingham, Robert Stoothoff, and Dugald Murdoch (New York: Cambridge University Press, 2008), 2:16–23. The *I* who is in here is the person who has opinions, beliefs, favorite foods, and the strategies and knowledge for getting through life. It is this *I* who has had all our experiences in life, the "self" (small *s*) or *me*, who *creates* his or her own destiny along the Outer Labyrinth with my choices.

But if we hold to a single, unified sense of our personality, how can we explain the experience of saying we are going to do one thing but end up doing the exact opposite, even though "we" didn't want to (see Romans 7:7–25)? How can we explain the fact that we can't change our emotions because so often they have us, rather than us having them? How can we explain making a commitment to a person, project, or activity, and then our psychological energy goes south and something inside us refuses to keep the commitment? How do we explain the experience of "fringe consciousness" and creativity where ideas, insights, and creative solutions seem to come out of nowhere? How do we explain the objective independence of our sense of *calling* and destiny, if we insist on holding on to a unified sense of personality?

For the last forty years, I've known (in the *yada* sense) that the human personality is not a single unified entity. Rather, it is an interrelated system of competing and conflicting elements along the Inner and Outer Labyrinths that must be organized, harmonized, and unified into one integrated whole by what Jung called the Self. I first experienced the objective experience of *archetypes* and the Self in 1985 in the stone dream that I mentioned in note 27. My first experience with the objective nature of *complexes* came with the following dream I had in January of 1996:

In a previous dream, or an earlier part of this dream, I already knew about the Inner People in my company. They've been there all along, but I was just finding out about them. As the dream begins, I'm looking down a well, and the Inner People are looking back at me, deep and seemingly bottomless water below them. There were women and men in the company, like they were part of the mission statement—like they had roles to play. When I awoke, I was not afraid of anything. It's almost like it was inner confirmation of the inner company model I've been using to understand what I'm experiencing in daily life.

The symbol of the well in the dream was like the Ego-Self Axis that I've described earlier in the book, with the "me" in the dream being analogous to my conscious waking self, the people looking back up at me from down inside the well being analogous to the objective Inner People (what Jung called complexes), and the deep and seemingly bottomless water below them being the Self.

Back in 2003, I used a two-part thought experiment to describe my experience of these dreams in Bodnarczuk, *Diving In*, 82–87, and with an organizational development application in Bodnarczuk, *Island of Excellence*, 146–60 in 2004. I'll do the thought experiment again here in this note to demonstrate. In the *first* part of the thought experiment, imagine you are the president of a small company. As president, you have bottom-line responsibility for the company and can issue policies and procedures for how you want the company run, but you don't have direct control over the emotions, desires, and wills of the people in your company. These people are *objective* and independent of you. In addition, your employees are *real* in the sense that they make a physical difference to the company and what they do determines whether you fail or succeed as a business.

In the *second* part of the thought experiment, turn your introspective eye within. So, your conscious self (small *s*) is the president of the company and corporate facility that exists along the Outer Labyrinth of the destiny you create with your *choices*. What's done with that facility is what you do with your life. Now, imagine you have people in an "inner company" who occupy that facility, and although you want to run your life a certain way, you don't have direct control over the emotions, desires, and wills of these Inner People. They have their own little personalities, values, goals, and philosophy of life, and some of them are diametrically opposed to yours as president. You want to slow down and work fewer hours; they want to drive on. You say you love your wife and family, but they want to leave. You say you need to stay on a budget, but they go out and buy a new car. What is most problematic about these Inner People is they are every bit as objective and independent of you as the people in an actual company. They exist independently of you. This is not just like having different "sides" to a unified personality. The Inner People are like many different subpersonalities all within the multiplicity of your personality. Having a multiplicity of different personalities in each of us is a normal, psychologically healthy phenomenon that we all experience to one degree or another. If we were "abnormal" psychologically, we would have these different personalities within us and would move from one to the other and not be aware of it. Such people are often diagnosed as having something like a multiple personality disorder; see Ian Hacking, *Rewriting the Soul: Multiple Personality and the Science of Memory* (Princeton: Princeton University Press, 1995).

Consciousness about the presence and activities of the Inner People is the difference between being normal or abnormal psychologically. To put it another way, your Inner People exist in a virtual state, and they become real only when they take over your facility, because only then can they make a physical difference. You say you're going to be nice to your employees, and one of the Inner People grabs hold of the "microphone"—your vocal cords—and hammers them verbally, and you don't even realize it until after the fact. Or one of the Inner People takes over your facility and grabs your credit cards and goes shopping when you just swore that you would stop spending. When the Inner People have charge of your facility, they can control the way you talk, what you do, how you feel, where you go, and how long you stay. What they do when they have control of the facility can vitally affect the course of your life. The Inner People can make or break you, just like employees can make or break the president of a real company.

Most of the Inner People are psychologically and socially underdeveloped because they have been locked away in the unconscious and have not been given much facility time. The Inner People are like a child who has been locked in a closet for the first part of his or her life, and when they get control of your facility, it's like finally breaking out of this inner prison. Imagine that some of the Inner People routinely confront you (as president) and force you to give up control of the facility, which is essentially to force you to give up control of your life. You are aware of these challenges to your authority, and you have to deal with them all the time. Some of the Inner People are overt about their activities, while others exist only on the fringe of your consciousness. Sometimes, you as president have tried to be open to the desires of the Inner People. But then they demand things that change or disrupt your life, so you shut them down with a brutal, survival-type response. They simply retaliate and try more covert tactics to take charge of the facility—and the battle rages on for a lifetime.

MARK BODNARCZUK

All of your life, you have had to manage and control the duplicities and opposing forces of this group of inner insurgents and prevent them from ruining your life. You probably have succeeded at this fairly well, but it has cost you an enormous amount of psychological energy, energy you've squandered on damping down the inter-office politics of this ragtag group of people who live within you. The most radical implication of the Inner People model is that the turbulent emotions associated with this inner conflict belong to the Inner People but we experience them *as our own* emotions, not theirs, because we all live in the same body and because most of us have a unified view of the personality. So, who else's emotions could they be? Maintaining a unified view of our personality requires us to *fabricate* reasons why we have so much inner conflict. For example, if you're an easygoing person and one of the Inner People grabs the "microphone" and gets up in someone's face, maintaining a unified view of personality forces you to fabricate explanations for your behavior: "I must be under stress. Maybe I'm depressed. I must be having a midlife crisis. I must not have gotten a good night's sleep. You must have set me off. I must be grumpy because I'm hungry. I must be feeling insecure." We fabricate the most fantastic stories—anything to preserve the myth that we are a single, unified self.

What I'm calling the Inner People in my thought experiment, Jung called complexes—the psychological entities that populate the personal unconscious, with each complex having an archetype (that populates the collective unconscious) at its center. Jung coined the term "complex" and developed his theory of complexes early in his career while conducting word association experiments at the Burgholzli Psychiatric Hospital at the University of Zurich between 1900 and 1908. For Jung, complexes are emotionally charged feeling-toned clusters of unconscious feelings, beliefs, and ideas. He wrote:

[A complex] is the image of a certain psychic situation which is strongly accentuated emotionally and is, moreover, incompatible with the habitual attitude of consciousness. This image has a powerful inner coherence, it has its own wholeness and, in addition, a relatively high degree of autonomy, so that it is subject to the control of the conscious mind to only a limited extent, and therefore behaves like an animated foreign body in the sphere of consciousness. The complex can usually be suppressed with effort of will, but not argued out of existence, and at the first suitable opportunity it reappears in all its original strength. . . . But even the soberest formulation of the phenomenology of complexes cannot get around the impressive fact of their autonomy, and the deeper one penetrates into their nature—I might almost say into their biology—the more clearly do they reveal their character as *splinter psyches*.

See Jung, *Structure and Dynamics of the Psyche*, 96–97 (§§201 and 203). As Jungian analyst John Beebe points out, Harry Stack Sullivan used the words *parataxic distortions*, rather than complexes, to describe an unconscious obsessional appraisal and selection process that carves out a tiny portion of the totality of events that happen in the world, imposes meaning and intentionality on it, and subsequently moves us into action; see John Beebe's online discussion at the Myth Salon at https://www.youtube.com/watch?v=m-YA3DL1lvs; and Harry Stack Sullivan, Helen Perry, Mary Gawel, and

Martha Gibbon, eds., *The Collected Works of Harry Stack Sullivan* (New York: Norton, 1964), 2:30–31 and 40–41. I discuss the ways in which this complex-like unconscious obsessional appraisal and selection process is a key to the formation of personality type, and a mechanism for deep personal change, in Bodnarczuk, *Breckenridge Enneagram*, 19–23 and 288–93.

115 Jung, *Children's Dreams*, 1.
116 Jung, *Children's Dreams*, 3.
117 Barbara Hannah, *Encounters with the Soul: Active Imagination as Developed by C. G. Jung* (Ashville, NC: Chiron, 2015), 1. See also Joan Chodorow, ed., *Encountering Jung: Jung on Active Imagination* (Princeton: Princeton University Press, 1997).
118 It's important to note that I had an expert-level competency in designing, administering, and interpreting psychometrically validated assessment tools that measured Jungian type and Enneagram type. I was certified in the Meyers-Briggs Type Indicator, and the Majors PTI that measured Jungian type, and I was certified in the Enneagram by Don Riso and Russ Hudson. I also designed psychometrically validated assessment tools with high reliability and validity, like the Breckenridge Institute Type indicator (BTI), that measured Enneagram type.
119 Jung, *Children's Dreams*, 20.
120 See C. S. Lewis, "The Screwtape Letters," in *The Complete C. S. Lewis Signature Classics* (New York: HarperOne, 2002), 125.
121 Singer, *Boundaries of the Soul*, 215.
122 Lewis, "Screwtape Letters," 127–28.
123 See Keller, *Walking with God*, 132–33.
124 See https://www.neverthirsty.org/bible-qa/qa-archives/question/has-god-determined-how-many-days-every-person-will-live/.
125 See White, *Practical Handbook of Christian Living*, 94.
126 Keller, *Walking with God*, 152.
127 See John Hartley, *The Book of Job*, New International Commentary on the Old Testament (Grand Rapids: Eerdmans, 1988).
128 See Keller, *Walking with God*, 153.
129 Keller, *Walking with God*, 155.
130 See Anaïs Nin, "Seduction of the Minotaur," in *Cities of the Interior* (Athens, OH: Swallow, 1980), 463–589.
131 See Ernst Becker, *The Denial of Death* (New York: Free Press, 1973).
132 Keller, *Walking with God*, 2.
133 Covey, *Seven Habits*, 235ff.
134 Jung, *Children's Dreams*, 4.

CHAPTER 34: THE JOURNEY HOME
135 See Elisabeth Kubler-Ross, *On Death and Dying: What the Dying Have to Teach Doctors, Nurses, Clergy and Their Own Families* (New York: Scribner, 2019), and Kessler,

Finding Meaning. Lois Tonkin's notion of growing around grief is a different way of thinking about our lives after someone has died. It enables us to see a future that contains meaning and significance without disowning or pushing away our grief. Tonkin says, "Grief is a journey—a journey without an end. You just have to keep moving forward and take the person that's passed away along with you." See Lois Tonkin, "Growing around Grief: Another Way of Looking at Grief and Recovery," *Bereavement Care* 15.1 (1996): 10. J. William Worden suggests that there are specific "tasks" of grief that we must perform. Task 1 is to accept the reality of the loss. Task 2 is to process the pain of grief. Task 3 is to adjust to the world without the deceased. Task 4 is to find a way to remember the deceased while embarking on the rest of one's journey through life. See J. William Worden, *Grief Counseling and Grief Therapy: A Handbook for the Mental Health Practitioner*, 5th ed. (New York: Springer, 2018), 39–53. For another Jungian perspective of grief and the individuation process, see Susan Olson, *Images of the Dead in Grief Dreams: A Jungian View of Morning*, 2nd ed. (New York: Routledge, 2021).

136 The images and symbols in this dream I had on May 12, 2021, just ten days after finding Thomas dead in his room, helped me understand that Thomas's death initiated the next phase or project in the lifelong process of biblical individuation:

There was a project that I was supposed to work on, and I had previously been really involved in the activities associated with this project, but for some reason it had been a long time since I actually worked on it, so I had to refamiliarize myself with what it was about and get back into actually doing it and being involved in it. There was a woman who I was going to work with on this, and she was going to provide me with help and support. She was going to be like my partner in both the refamiliarizing process and then in actually doing and running the project. All this I knew prior to the beginning of the dream.

As the dream opens, I'm trying to contact this woman to get together with her and go over what had to be done. We were going to meet at someone's house to do some initial work, and I was going to meet her and then go to this place with her. I deeply appreciated her, and her willingness to help me, and I felt a deep bond and sense of common purpose and affection between her and me in the sense that we had a common goal, a common fate, and a common destiny in life. We met and then we were walking toward the place where we would work on the project.

The scene changes and we're at some type of hotel-restaurant type place, which was near where we were supposed to go to work on the project. I wanted to get something to eat before we started working. She didn't want to eat, but she said she'd wait for me while I ate. Apparently, there were other people at this place whom she knew, and she was going to see them and talk with them while I ate. I ordered my food and while I was waiting for it to arrive, I decided to walk through the very large restaurant area that had a high ceiling and was open windowed. I saw many people I knew, and the project was somehow related to what our church did but not directly related.

When I got back to the restaurant, my food was there, and so was the woman I came with. I pulled out a white three-ring binder that contained the material we were going to use to refamiliarize ourselves with the project. The woman began looking through what was in the folder, things I had not seen or worked with for a long time. It was like when I write a book. I get really involved with intense focus, time, energy, discipline, and creative power to get it done at the time. And when I return to it a year or two later, it's not like I'd forgotten what I had done, but I have to *reconnect* to it and turn my attention back to the material, ideas, purpose, meaning, and details of the process. When this happens, I almost always have a much deeper understanding of the meaning and implications of the material, and my connection to it is always at a higher, deeper, wider, more mature, and more insightful level because the unconscious has continued to work on the project, even though my conscious mind has been elsewhere doing other things for a long time. The dream ends with me and the woman sitting there looking through the material as a preliminary step to getting refamiliarized with the project.

This dream shows how the Anima was providing me with inner resources and support to help me continue down the lifelong path (project) of individuation within the historical context of the death of my son, just ten days after his death. As I mention in this chapter, one of the lessons I learned from processing the deep, painful grief from my son's death is that, while traumatic and previously unimaginable, surviving Thomas's death and finding new life have become woven into the fabric of my lifelong process of individuation.

137 See James Davies, *The Importance of Suffering: The Value and Meaning of Emotional Discontent* (New York: Routledge, 2012), 130–33.
138 See Robert Emmons, *The Psychology of Ultimate Concern: Motivation and Spirituality in Personality* (New York: Guilford, 1999); and Robert Emmons, "Personal Goals, Life Meaning, and Virtue," in *Flourishing: Positive Psychology and the Life Well Lived*, ed. Corey L. M. Keyes and Jonathan Haidt (Washington, DC: American Psychological Association, 2003), 105–28.
139 See Jonathan Haidt, *The Happiness Hypothesis: Finding Modern Truth in Ancient Wisdom* (New York: Basic Books, 2006), 135–41.
140 Haidt, *Happiness Hypothesis*, 141.
141 See Paul Brand and Philip Yancey, *The Gift of Pain: Why We Hurt and What We Can Do About It* (Grand Rapids: Zondervan, 1997).
142 This quote is taken from the back cover of Brand and Yancey, *Gift of Pain*.
143 Keller, *Walking with God*, 190. He cites biblical support for this view from James 1:2–4, 12; Hebrews 12:1–17; Romans 8:18–30; 2 Corinthians 1:3–12; 4:7–5:5; 11:24–12:10, as well as the entire book of 1 Peter.
144 Keller, *Walking with God*, 117.
145 See Brand and Yancey, *Gift of Pain*.

Printed in the USA
CPSIA information can be obtained
at www.ICGtesting.com
LVHW012049170924
791340LV00002B/3/J